Smokin' Valves:
A Headbanger's Guide To
900 NWOBHM
Records

Martin Popoff

Bedford, England

First published in Canada, 2013
Wymer Publishing
Bedford, England www.wymerpublishing.co.uk
Tel: 01234 326691
Wymer Publishing is a trading name of Wymer (UK) Ltd

Copyright © 2018 Martin Popoff/ Wymer Publishing.
This edition published 2019.

ISBN 978-1-912782-10-9

The Author hereby asserts his rights to be identified
as the author of this work in accordance with sections
77 to 78 of the Copyright, Designs & Patents Act 1988.

All rights reserved. No part of this publication may be
reproduced or transmitted in any form or by any means,
electronic or mechanical, including photocopying, or any
information storage and retrieval system, without written
permission from the publisher.

This publication is sold subject to the condition that it shall not,
by way of trade or otherwise, be lent, re-sold, hired out or
otherwise circulated without the publisher's prior consent in any
form of binding or cover other than that in which it is published
and without a similar condition including this condition
being imposed on the subsequent purchaser.

Every effort has been made to trace the copyright holders of the
photographs in this book but some were unreachable. We would
be grateful if the photographers concerned would contact us.

Printed and bound by
CMP, Dorset, England

A catalogue record for this book is available from the British Library.

Typesetting, layout and design by Eduardo Rodriguez.
Cover photographs © Martin Popoff

Table Of Contents

Table Of Contents	
A,	8
B	16
C	27
D	36
E	51
F	55
G	61
H	78
IJK	89
L	99
M	105
NO	122
PQ	129
R	138
S	148
T	178
UV	195
WXYZ	209
Appendix 1: Blood & Thunder: LPs Ranked 8, 9 Or 10	224
Appendix 2: One Helluva Night: Singles & EPs Ranked 8, 9 Or 10	226
Design Credit & About The Author	230
A Ye Olde Metal "Discography"	231

Martin Popoff – A Complete Bibliography

Smokin' Valves: A Headbanger's Guide To 900 NWOBHM Records (2014)

The Art Of Metal (2013; co-editorship with Malcolm Dome)

Metallica: The Complete Illustrated History (2013)

2 Minutes To Midnight: An Iron Maiden Day-By-Day (2013)

Ye Olde Metal: 1979 (2013)

Rush: The Illustrated History (2013)

Scorpions: Top Of The Bill (2013)

Epic Ted Nugent (2012)

Fade To Black: Hard Rock Cover Art Of The Vinyl Age (2012)

It's Getting Dangerous: Thin Lizzy 81-12 (2012)

We Will Be Strong: Thin Lizzy 76-81 (2012)

Fighting My Way Back: Thin Lizzy 69-76 (2011)

The Deep Purple Royal Family: Chain Of Events '80 – '11 (2011)

The Deep Purple Royal Family: Chain Of Events Through '79 (2011)

Black Sabbath FAQ (2011)

The Collector's Guide To Heavy Metal: Volume 4: The '00s (2011; co-authored with David Perri)

Goldmine Standard Catalog Of American Records 1948 – 1991, 7th Edition (2010)

Goldmine Record Album Price Guide, 6th Edition (2009)

Goldmine 45 RPM Price Guide, 7th Edition (2009)

A Castle Full Of Rascals: Deep Purple '83 – '09 (2009)

Worlds Away: Voivod And The Art Of Michel Langevin (2009)

Ye Olde Metal: 1978 (2009)

Gettin' Tighter: Deep Purple '68 – '76 (2008)

All Access: The Art Of The Backstage Pass (2008)

Ye Olde Metal: 1977 (2008)

Ye Olde Metal: 1976 (2008)

Judas Priest: Heavy Metal Painkillers (2007)

Ye Olde Metal: 1973 To 1975 (2007)

The Collector's Guide To Heavy Metal: Volume 3: The Nineties (2007)

Ye Olde Metal: 1968 To 1972 (2007)

Run For Cover: The Art Of Derek Riggs (2006)

Black Sabbath: Doom Let Loose (2006)

Dio: Light Beyond The Black (2006)

The Collector's Guide To Heavy Metal: Volume 2: The Eighties (2005)

Rainbow: English Castle Magic (2005)

UFO: Shoot Out The Lights (2005)

The New Wave Of British Heavy Metal Singles (2005)

Blue Öyster Cult: Secrets Revealed! (2004)

Contents Under Pressure: 30 Years Of Rush At Home & Away (2004)

The Top 500 Heavy Metal Albums Of All Time (2004)

The Collector's Guide To Heavy Metal: Volume 1: The Seventies (2003)

The Top 500 Heavy Metal Songs Of All Time (2003)

Southern Rock Review (2001)

Heavy Metal: 20th Century Rock And Roll (2000)

The Goldmine Price Guide To Heavy Metal Records (2000)

The Collector's Guide To Heavy Metal (1997)

Riff Kills Man! 25 Years Of Recorded Hard Rock & Heavy Metal (1993)

See martinpopoff.com for complete details and ordering information.

Introduction

Hey hey headbangers, I'll keep this short, just like the reign of the mighty mite that was the New Wave Of British Heavy Metal.

There were a couple of main motivations for this book. Number one, I had done a previous book called **The New Wave Of British Heavy Metal Singles** which is long out of print, and decided finally to accede to the metal minions' demands upon me to release the hounds of that material yet again.

But, to make the idea more complete, I've also gathered up all of the NWOBHM album reviews I'd written for the two relevant **The Collector's Guide To Heavy Metal** books, namely the '70s one and the '80s one. I get immense satisfaction of seeing this material in one place, resulting in a complete reviews book-type presentation of the genre, movement, moment in metal time, whatever ya wanna call it. The writing embedded within these reviews... man, well, these have been overhauled and tweaked over the years since their original penning, many as far back as my first book and go at these from 1993, and that process continues. Still, the perceptive amongst ye might notice a different rhythm and style and everything from both the singles chatter (and that book had a different tone all over again), and from my modern review writing. There's good and bad in that, but mostly, I guess, let's leave it at a demonstration of my ability to let the inexperienced angry young metalhead revisit you, beer in hand, dodgy writing abilities all too exposed—I mean, I stand by what I'm trying to get across, but I quite often find myself cringing at the way I said it.

Having gotten that out of the way, there's lots in here new to munch on whether you have one of the above books or the other, or, not so likely, both. And the reason for this is two-fold: one, a deep edit and rewrite of many of these reviews has occurred and two, much more of the material that wasn't so much reviewed but merely documented in the singles book (it was also a price guide, and yeah, didn't actually review every single), has now been heard and properly reviewed. There are some little fresh appointments as well, such as the providing of catalogue numbers now for all the LPs, which I don't do in the **Collector's Guide** series. What else? Well, different, higher quality graphics, mainly more LPs than would have been featured in the '80s book.

Couple other points on format and formality. I've tried, when possible, to place LP reviews in chronological order within the arc of 45 releases. When I had no clue and decided to decline to guess, I placed the LP at the top of a given year. As well, LPs, being the bigger, bolder statement times nine or ten over a 7", myself and my eminently skilled designer Eduardo Rodriguez decided to give them a bolder text treatment to emphasize their comparative importance. Of note, I haven't been that vigilant about including 12" versions of singles, although I've tried to grab EPs of original material. This is an area where a few things might have fallen between the cracks, given that the two main sources were my book on singles and my book on albums.

Another thing, to reiterate, I dropped the price guide conceit of the original singles books, mainly because it conflated the purpose, or new purpose, namely adding to my reviews book canon. Plus prices have changed so much with the internet and with CD issues, youtube, downloading, right now is not a good time to call any price one might attach to these items as particularly stable. Long story and don't want to go into it further. Believe me, I did the Goldmine price guides for a few years and the debates on value are endless. Bonus on the flip-flop though, whereas the book called **The New Wave Of British Heavy Metal Singles** gave "market values," like I say, I didn't rank the music. Here, that is done, jes' like all my books.

Uh, not like any of you who have read this far are at all in doubt, but what was the New Wave Of British Heavy Metal? To keep it dead simple and simplified (because I feel the explanation outs itself through the reviews), it's the explosion of heavy metal from mostly young upstart bands all over the UK, the critical mass of which gave metal good exposure and some level of respectability in the early '80s, its unsung effect, being the sparking off of metal in the US, beginning in LA, to the point where metal thrived in America for the entire rest of the decade.

Point of process re: the years of the NWOBHM, I've left the opening point vague, allowing for the rock-scrabble story of a few singles and albums ramping up through '77 and '78 with the real show hittin' the road in '79. The end date of the genre, or more concretely, this book? I've picked 1984, and thus have included all releases from that year and none after. Some may even argue that it was, for all intents and purposes, that the NWOBHM was a dim light bulb of itself by the end of '83, but I think that's selling it short. Another point: to keep things tight here, no dinosaur bands with the rare, rare exception, like Budgie—I can't think of a single pack of old-timers who felt more like NWOBHMers, for better or worse, between those years. But yeah, no Priest, UFO, Ozzy Osbourne Band (makes more sense than you might think), AC/DC, Heep, Sabbath with Ronnie. There's Gillan but no Whitesnake. There's Wild Horses but no Thin Lizzy. It's actually a quite compelling intellectual exercise to talk about certain bands and their relationship to the NWOBHM (think about Riot, Y&T, Sammy Hagar, Manowar, Rose Tattoo and even Ted Nugent!), but that's beyond the scope of this handy handbook.

So yeah, that's it, I suppose. To reiterate, I felt that to do the genre proper justice, one couldn't review just singles or just LPs. That always kinda bothered me about the singles book. So despite the fact that there really were so many bands that issued just singles, to tell the whole story, I figured I'd have to package the entire recorded history, or as much of it that I'm aware of anyway. So there ya go, here ya go, read on, look, learn, listen…

Martin Popoff
martinp@inforamp.net
www.martinpopoff.com

Ace Lane - See You In Heaven
(Expulsion '83, EXIT 3)

Playing rhythmic, barsy, bluesy, US-styled AOR in the midst of the NWOBHM, Ace Lane were an anomaly, creating one indie full-length and that's it. Vocalist Mick Clarke plied his pipes for similarly frustratingly dated act Gaskin, here sounding a little like Diamond Head's Sean Harris, or Michael Lee Smith from Starz on songs that frankly, went to that band as well, stiff, groove-sucking drumming included, same '70s-based riffing that had nothing to do with the Maiden-mania enveloping the home nation at the time. Barely a 6, but I gave it to 'em for a certain duck-out-of-water clarity and charm.
Rating 6

After Dark - Evil Woman
(After Dark '81, AD001)

Evil Woman sits curiously in that Demon, Shiva, White Spirit range, pomping with those throaty vocals and a soft disco pump buttressed with Hammond and sobbing twin leads. Definitely takes you to that stormy British crust zone. The much better b-sides were the retro, spiffy, speedy (save for the mellow break) and quite professional *Johnny*, plus *Lucy*, a dark semi-ballad that also gets sort of funky with both Hammond and cowbell. Note: a-side was featured on the **NWOBHM Vol. 4** boot as well as the ten track **Masked By Midnight** rarities CD from '95, issued on Germany's Brainstorm Division/Semaphore label, which revives the shelved, self-financed '84 album.
Rating 7

After Dark - Deathbringer
(Lazer '83, PROMO1)

Deathbringer sounds a bit like a trashcan take on Budgie's *In For The Kill*, emphasis on garbage, production being the biggest problem. B-side *Call Of The Wild* is a surprising ballad that goes to places Skynyrd or Bad Company might go, until the chorus reminds one of Blaze-era Maiden! But again the production drags it into the cheap bins. Note: apparently there were some test pressings without printed sleeves as well as the main release, a picture disc, put out as a teaser for the band's finished full-length album which died when the idea of the label was kiboshed. Post all of this, the band continued to tour, most notably with Y&T, but also with Gillan, Samson and Trust before calling it quits after amassing additional material for a second album.
Rating 6

After Hours – All Over Town
(JSG '80, JSG-102)
After Hours were a female-fronted band comparable but scrappier than Girlschool or Rock Goddess. B-side: *Suspicious* is less the rocker than the combative *All Over Town*.
Rating 5

Airrace - Shaft Of Light
(Atlantic '84, 790219)
Well, alright, this wasn't as bad as Virginia Wolf. In fact it's pretty good in a naive AOR sort of way, guitarist about town Laurie Mansworth working with Max Bacon-ish crooner Keith Murrell and producer Beau Hill in creation of a well-written pomp rock semi-gem, much more American-slanted than NWOBHM. Of course, years later now, this is known more as Jason Bonham's first recording band, but it is Murrell coupled with the enthusiastic melody of the thing that modestly stood out. One lone record was generated, then the band dissolved, Murrell moving on to the Mama's Boys.
Rating 6

Alaska – Heart Of The Storm
(Music For Nations '84, MFN23)
Old '70s rock geezers desperately tried to play catch-up with America's post-NWOBHM rock explosion, often coagulating into roughshod pop bands like this (usually named after a place). Alaska definitely got some hype and released a bunch of 12" singles around that hype, but the albums were horrid, **Heart Of The Storm** combining clean vocals, keyboards, uptempo pop patterns and the juiced, gritty but sparing retro-based guitar work of Bernie Marsden (Whitesnake, Babe Ruth, Wild Turkey) into something akin to bad Nightwing or reasonably pedigreed Shy.
Rating 4

Amazon – Hypnotising You
(Megamusic '81)
Amazon had the distinction of a tall female vocalist in Lori Chacko, who two years later, tried to revive the band with new players, thenceforth moving to the US to pursue acting. *Hypnotising You* is somewhat American-sounding barroom

metal with a screechy synth line. B-side, *Fallen Angel*, is less successful, crossing Pat Benatar with Saga-like pomp and pert keyboard-percolated post-punk – very Canadian An extremely rare single with a picture sleeve featuring Chacko herself.
Rating   3

Angel Street – Midnight Man
(Motor '79, MTR 003)

This single was released without a picture sleeve but with wicked graphics, featuring a head cut open with gears in it, and on blue vinyl. B-side *Running Away* is more of a retro rocker, not so much of a NWOBHM "missing link,", nor is the a-side, which is a thumping sort of American heartland rocker, evoking thoughts of Nutz turning into Rage. Dave "Bucket" Colwell ended up with Samson and Adrian Smith's ASaP before landing the on tour forever Bad Company gig. Note: I've not heard it, but there's also the non-ps *Done It Again* (Ellie Jay '79, EJSP 9290), the a-side being a Dave Page original.
Rating   5

Angel Witch - Angel Witch
(Bronze '80, BRON532)

Angel Witch is the New Wave Of British Heavy Metal's black metal feast of near mythic proportions, renowned, for all time, in discerning metal circles as the underground/underworld benchmark opus of that magical early '80s movement. Fiercely dark, messed-up and rumbling, full of weighty riffs worthy of vintage Sabbath, **Angel Witch** is a riveting and rarified blast through evil metal landscapes. Everything works in concert towards killer accomplishment here... the hurt, bleating vocals of mastermind Kevin Heybourne, the crunch recording with just the right amount of noisy uncontrolled edge, and above all, the hellishly superior song craft, which regularly lowers the boom outta nowhere with inspired British metal deviance. There's a feeling of singular pride here, of an album created wholly without influences, as if the band knew damn well they were blowing anything heretofore known off the metal map. **Angel Witch** would ultimately reign as the first panoramic black metal statement of the modern era, with its mix of gothic melody, sinister surprise, and scorching dense riffery killing Venom and pre-empting Mercyful Fate on such molten monoliths as *Atlantis*, *Confused*, and *Angel Of Death*, each establishing this band as genuinely scary, as genuinely isolated and elevated from the fun-loving metal community propping the bar. Unfortunately, this would be the only Angel Witch album of deep importance, as internal strife and critical derision at the band's apparently sloppy live shows would flame the band's self-doubts, causing line-up changes and subsequent loss of chemistry. After a low-key break-up in '81, the band resurfaced in an altered and less focused state for the ponderous **Screamin' n' Bleedin'**. Luckily, there are some rare, debut-era tracks floating around on various 45s, EPs and CD reissues, most notably *Flight 19*, *Hades Paradise*, *Loser*, *Suffer* and *Dr. Phibes* being exceedingly worth whatever collectibles price you might pay. Trivia note: *Confused* has been covered by both Onslaught (12") and Trouble (boot only).
Rating   10

Angel Witch - Sweet Danger
(EMI '80, EMI5064)
Both are storming debut-era tracks, first single melodic speedster *Sweet Danger* and the non-LP *Flight Nineteen* are classics of the early NWOBHM. *Flight Nineteen* is actually the stronger composition, rumbling through rain-swelled thunder, a dark and delicious melody supporting a lyric recounting an in-flight alien encounter and subsequent disappearance. *Hades Paradise* was added to the 12" release (12EMI5064), but both fared poor commercially, as did the entire catalogue. On the standard brown, red and black EMI label. Produced by Chris Rogers.
Rating   9

Angel Witch - Loser
(Bronze '81, BRO121)
A creepy tarot card peers out from this cool stand-alone Angel Witch piece, cool because it's the only post-debut LP material that is properly new and still linked to the hallowed golden years versus the dodgy later albums, starting with '85's **Screamin' n' Bleedin'**. But it's a bit of a letdown, reminding me of compressed NWOBHM Budgie. *Loser* is emotional and dark enough but it's a bit of an unpowerful slog. *Suffer* is just hyper and panicked, a punked-out boogie riff which collapses into an oddly-toned verse riff which I guess on the positive, recalls *Flight Nineteen*. The best riffs are saved for the pregnant pause-ridden instrumental *Dr. Phibes*, a foreboding Sabbathy spread that manages to struggle above this EP's shoddy recording. Rare band shot on the back of the band standing in front of a bus. Green Bronze label. Produced by Martin Smith, as were the *Angel Witch* tracks.
Rating   8

Angel Witch - Angel Witch
(Bronze '80, BRO108)
No big deal, simply two debut album tracks (b/w *Gorgon*), middling ones at that, save for the anthemic, turbo-grooved chorus of *Angel Witch* (here offered in slightly altered version to the LP recording). Further negative: same devil line drawing as the *Sweet Danger* 7" and 12", although this one's black and yellow, while *Sweet Danger* is black and white. Green Bronze label.
Rating   8

Anthem - England
(Anthem '81, EJSP9576)
Here's a plain-janer mystery piece, technically a double a-sider with *England* being a patience-trying prog rock power ballad with a few way-loud twin leads, while side two contains the stilted stripper gallop of *Some Like It Hot* (think April Wine's *Roller*) and a second track called *Do You Mind If We Butt In?*, which is actually a speedster with some authority, and a biting solo-driven passage near the end which reminds one of the traditional but fresh prowess of a Paul Samson crossed with brisk AC/DC. Issued in both black and brown sleeves.
Rating   7

Apocalypse - Stormchild
(Gate '82, SGR0001)

A-side is available on the **NWOBHM Vol. 8** boot, and is a creepy, old-style rocker with the sorriest of drum sounds. But there's a dark chill there, sort of a cross between the Trespass track of the same name, Witchfynde and bad punk production values. Quite the bass line though, again, the way they used to make 'em. B-side *Chosen Few* could loosely be called a dark power ballad, laughable drumming and silly stop/starts come inevitable wind-up, plus vocals like a young Lemmy, included free of charge. Note, as proof of the strength of the band, there are some pretty crazy non-issued Apocalypse tracks floating around, notably *Midnight Train* and *Night Stalker*.

Rating 6

Aragorn - Black Ice
(Neat '81, NEAT07)

Awesome, bruising carnal NWOBHMers Aragorn should have gone places with this Kraken/Angel Witch-like single, both *Black Ice* and b-side *Noonday* storming along with a punk edge adding inventive guitar breaks and a vocal performance from Chris Dunne that is almost glam. This single was recorded (at Impulse) as a three-piece with the band soon to expand to a five-piece. *Noonday* also showed up on Neat's **Lead Weight** compilation from '81 and both tracks are featured on **The Neat Singles Collection Volume One**. Two years and a spiffier new demo later, the band was no more.

Rating 9

Arc - Tribute (To Mike Hailwood)
(Orcrist '80, ORC1)

This dodgy debut for Midlands band Arc was a double a-side featuring the above-titled motorcycle racer (a solid enough NWOBHM anthem of the lower rungs) ode plus the curiously slight and trotting *For My Next Kick*. Much improved come single #2.

Rating 5

Arc - War Of The Ring
(Slipped Disc '81, SD001)

Arc, on this their second single, play a grimly underground '70s-style NWOBHM, sounding like a roughshod pre-clue Manowar crossed with Bang. The a-side is much more vigorous than the b-side *Ice Cream Theme* (better than its title!) which is a proper all-in song despite the curious title, but a bit more relaxed with soaring vocals from John Whitbread (there's also a Whitbread on guitar and one on drums). Note: a-side subtitled: Dedicated To The Inspirational Works Of J.R.R. Tolkein.

Rating 8

A.R.C. Rock Band – Home Made Wine
(Rock '79)
Recording for the same label as Slender Thread (and no other), this band (also known as Arc, but not the same as the band above) made this roughshod single (pretty much punk, with a bit of a boogie) and nothing else, b-side to the affair being clunky, bluesy quasi-ballad *The Chase*, which despite its mellow meander, plays more by NWOBHM rules than the boozy title track.
Rating 6

Argus – Holocaust
(ABS '84, SRT4KS258)
This five-piece was rather at the eccentric neo-prog end of the NWOBHM (and late as well), demonstrating on *Holocaust* a Demon meets Witchfynde meets b-grade Diamond Head sound that might have competed in 1981 but is considerably below grade this late in the game. B-side is called *The Widow*.
Rating 5

Atlantis Rising – Tightrope
(CMI '83, CAM700)
Similar to Saracen or proggy Demon, this London act could have wobbled into the neo-prog blip led by Marillion but alas fizzled. B-side is called *Reverie: A Vision*.
Rating 5

A-II-Z - The Witch Of Berkeley
(Polydor '80, 2383587)
Similar to Witchfynde in that they were at least superficially black metal originals who had no idea what they were doing, A-II-Z also showed major promise like that band... but not here. Instead, this eccentric debut is a live recording of what is basically a bar band no doubt playing quite casually in a bar, and not at all in keeping with the sick black metal packaging of the project. Hell, I even got a sew-on patch with purchase, meaning that somebody thought highly of this act with the finicky name. Anyways, the aforementioned promise A-II-Z exuded actually projected out from the band's professional, tuneful but heavy 45s and EPs, most notably the *No Fun After Midnight* EP, comprising three tidy rockers which resemble Diamond Head's early rockers, plus *Ringside Seat* (a b-side to Russ Ballard's grandly pop-directed *I'm The One Who Loves You*, the single featuring future AC/DC drummer Simon Wright), that kicks with a nice boogie groove and capable recording. Why this album exists is anyone's guess, but I for one would have loved to have gotten a proper and properly considered studio release after another 18 months of incubation.
Rating 4

A-II-Z - No Fun After Midnight
(Polydor '81, POSP243)
The a-side is a tidy little modulating rocker strangely in the vein of *Ringside Seat*, or a slowed down, almost timid *No Class* come chorus time, until those Sweet harmonies kick in. Well, well. Live version can be found as the first track on the band's one and only LP, the oddly live and blasphemously-sleeved **The Witch Of Berkeley**. B-side is *Treason*, a gritty, riff-

mad rocker not without charm, mixing melody in the verse with pure evil heavy metal come chorus time. 12" version (POSPX243) is red vinyl and adds *Valhalla Force*, a weirdly sour melodic rocker that evokes images of Tokyo Blade.
Rating 8

A-II-Z - I'm The One Who Loves You
(Polydor '81, POSP314)
Since their only album was live and scrappy, the singles (plus one red vinyl 12") are the real A-II-Z gems. This one's an oddly commercial Russ Ballard cover and is a muscular popster in the *Winning/I Surrender/Since You Been Gone* vein. *Ringside Seat* is a quick, energetic boogie riffster that points to a cool direction the band could have taken had they lasted. Nice sleeve too, demonstrating that these guys could have been big way off the evilmetal track they followed with that frightening album cover. Drumming by AC/DC's Simon Wright (previously with Tora Tora), production from Andy Scott, guest keys from late Sweet addition Gary Moberley.
Rating 7

Aurora - I'll Be Your Fantasy
(Diamond Dog '82, RAM9)
Aurora features A-II-Z vocalist Dave Owens, post implosion of the promising pop metallers. B-side *If I Really Knew Her* is a fairly charming and melodic pop metaller, sorta like a filler track from Thin Lizzy's **Chinatown**. A-side made it to the third volume of '92's NWOBHM boot series, and is an electrified party rocker with an innovative melody, great guitar sound and lots of star power.

Wicked looking centrepiece, and all told, very promising, punchy band, from the drumming right up through the twin leads to the Lynott/Sykes-like vocals of Owens.
Rating 8

Avalanche - The Preacher
(Childers '80, AVA-1)
A rare, non-picture sleeve release (but with a wicked skull on the label), this one's b-side is called *Mean Lady*; the band squarely heavy enough to be intentionally NWOBHM at this early juncture.
Rating 6

Avenger - Too Wild To Tame
(Neat '83, NEAT31)
The only single from these rough pubby mid-thrashers. B-side *On The Rocks* (a scruffy, brisk and somewhat convincing bit of mischief) is from their first of two albums **Blood Sports**, with the a-side on neither. Note: also contributed non-LP track *Hot 'n' Heavy Express* to the four track **One Take No Dubs** EP put out by Neat in '82. There were actually *Too*

Wild To Tame t-shirts available, offered on a flyer along with the single, which is a rumbling committed metal rocker built around a riff vaguely reminiscent of AC/DC's *Riff Raff*.
Rating 7

NWOBHM vocals of Neil Grafton. B-side *Messiah* is a bit of a prog rocker laced with synths and White Spirited keyboards. Great chorus and vocals once again and a killer traditional axe solo after a nice acoustic break, followed later by a Maiden-ish twin lead. Both tracks over four and a half minutes, both recorded at Neat's Impulse Studios in Newcastle. Note the clueless long-haired '70s post-hippie band shot on the back. *Messiah* showed up on the **Lead Weight** compilation, with the band's only other output being *Flame Burns On* (a tight, wicked rocker) on Neat's **All Hell Let Loose** and **60 Minutes Plus** comps.
Rating 8

Avenger - Blood Sports
(Neat '84, 1018)

Hapless British meatpackers Avenger paced the headbanging waiting room, doomed to a life of loitering with this painfully recorded but typical dumkopf crank from Neat. Sorta like bad Satan, Tysondog, Warfare, or demo-grade Tank, **Blood Sports** is one grimefest of long forgotten metal ideas recorded fast, loose, and mission-bent, but so hopelessly below the poverty line, it rarely rises above eight to ten beer terrain, save for *Matriarch*, which is a clanked, hollowed-out cover of the obscure Montrose track. Still, with the passage of time, one can embark upon the intellectual exercise of ripping this apart, locating and appreciating many of the riffs, despite the hurried fashion in which they are dismissed and dispensed.
Rating 4

Axis - Lady
(Metal Minded '80, IS/AX/1047)

Not without ideas, this five-piece kick off with a gritty, hard AOR number driven by a melodic riff featuring the quintessential

B

Backlash – Off With His Head
(Gargoyle '80, GRGL 777)
Cool little EP, comprising *Captain Pratt* and *Jackass* on side one and *Chess Game* and *Battle* on side two, on this non-PS record featuring reflex blue label with silver print. But it's questionable how NWOBHM this is, given its range from new wave through hard rock (side one, essentially) through prog.
Rating   5

Badge - Silver Woman
(Metal Minded '81, MM2)
Recording for the same simple red and white label as Axis (a short-lived subsidiary of Neat), and similarly recording at Impulse, Badge cranked out this single and nothing else. *Silver Woman* is a passionate, simple, little guy makes big riff rocker striving towards a hard AOR direction, while b-side *Something I've Lost* is a bit of a hapless power ballad, found all the parts, down the dark *Remember Tomorrow* corridor, somewhat achieving that drained pint, rained-out NWOBHM melancholy. Bassist Mike Cooper would move on to Blade Runner.
Rating   5

Bashful Alley - Running Blind
(Ellie Jay '82, BA001)
The title track manages to convince you that the guy's "tired of running blind" and that's half the battle right there. Basically an endearing enough mid-metal rocker so suited to the NWBOHM tag. B-side *My, My, My* bulks up a bit, darker melody, urgent gallop and a nice emotional break come chorus time, eventually followed with a long mellow jam and a return to theme. Both are ingratiating, likeable tracks. The band's only output outside of a three track demo the previous year. Black ink on yellow paper, butt-ugly two-tone brown label, or black and white label, both Ellie Jay command top dollar, with Graffiti issue attracting slightly less. Lasted another couple of years, while adding a guitarist, before petering out.
Rating   7

Battleaxe - Burn This Town
(Guardian '82, GRC132)
These guys actually cranked two albums that got a bit o' reach into North America. The sound however, was always pedestrian NWOBHM, unhewn, biker-ish, more of a Mausoleum act in spirit. *Burn This Town* is a crappy double bass barrage, an early one granted, just not any good. B-side *Battleaxe* was a little more locked-down, good guitar sound, tight punk drumming but still inferior in the writing department. Vaguely mainland European sound to this, down the path of early Sinner. Both tracks showed up on the Roadrunner debut of the following year, although re-recorded. Both were also on the legendary **Roxcalibur** compilation, but then the band saw the light, leaving Guardian for the much bigger Music For Nations.
Rating   6

Battleaxe - Burn This Town
(Music For Nations '82, MFN8)
British dirt bike rock goes down the drain on this early headbanging error, a fringe NWOBHM dweller seemingly built to cash in before talent is in place and the guys had any hope of executing their barking dog anthems with any sort of discipline. Bad mix to boot, as if anybody would care enough to dress this up with love. Alas however, through some sort of grim work ethic felt on the farm, **Burn This Town** has actually aged well, now sounding like a pleasant antique curio vaguely participatory in the alternative history of "true metal."
Rating 5

Battleaxe - Power From The Universe
(Roadrunner '83, MFN25)
Improvement abounds, with amusing, so-metal, vaguely Swedish cover art and cleaner production, while a menacing first track (*Chopper Attack*) leads the charge, much of the rest a mite laid back in comparison. Only of consequence if Battleaxe was one of your particular personal badges of honour back amongst the flood of similar unremarkable releases (many of which were my badges of honour for no good reason). This didn't amount to much for anybody I knew, but y'know, hearing it again decades later, the record's Krokus-like competence and faceless, timeless production values help it stand up better than similar low-key releases from the latter half of the decade.
Rating 6

Berlin Ritz – Crazy Nights
(Big Muff '80, BM001)
Pre-NWOBHM but heavy enough in (rickety) sound, this non-picture sleeve piece contained a b-side called *You're Where I Belong*.
Rating 4

Big Daisy - Fever
(Ellie Jay '80)
A-side *Fever* is a dark but punchy rocker with a mellow verse, too many drum fills, and Triumph-like plot twists turning the thing sort of dynamic and patience-testing at once. B-side *Footprints On The Water* is yet another ponderous power ballad with metal break. Features the high yelp of Mervyn Spence (again, think Geddy crossed with Rik) who later went on to Trapeze and Wishbone Ash (the ruff one: **Raw To The Bone**), both for short spells. Humourous cartoony fat lady picture sleeve. Subsequently, the band changed their name to Jury and popped a track onto

Ebony's **Metallic Storm** compilation.
Rating 6

Bitches Sin - Always Ready (For Love)
(Neat '81, NEAT09)
Most copies on black vinyl, with a few on yellow. A convincing, powerful, modern metal sound; neither of these tracks would feature on the classic Heavy Metal Records debut, **Predator**, after a Neat comp track called *Down The Road*, then a Heavy Metal comp. track called *Strangers On The Shore*. In any event, the a-side sports a deft arrangement that features dual speeds, a melodic chorus and an engaging, interesting verse riff. B-side *Sign Of The Times* is a speedy rocker without much of a riff (think *Motorcycle Man*), but nonetheless a full-on commitment to metal, most prevalently felt during the gnarly axe solo.
Rating 7

Bitches Sin - Predator
(Heavy Metal '82, HMRLP4)
Way too early NWOBHM that lurched forth lost within bad riffs, no focus, lack of tightness and poor mix values. Great breakthrough cover graphics but that's about it. File with Silverwing, Praying Mantis, Black Rose, and Wolf as third string originals flirting with simple American values, yet lacking the production acumen to make it seamless and airtight. Many CD reissue convolutions ensued which granted, belie the album's legendary status, which I bestow as well grudgingly, the grudge coming from the fact that the cover art far outclassed the scowling machine shop rock enclosed.
Rating 5

Black Axe - Highway Rider
(Metal '80, MELT1)
This high quality single gallops to a nice riff with clean high vocals and choice guitar stabs that keep it street. B-side *Red Lights* is a quicker, punkier track seething with energy and hot-stepping vocals harassed by a twin guitar attack and spit-shuffle drumming. Note: the single was well-regarded, the band getting signed to Chrysalis, changing their name to Wolf and somehow becoming unhinged, unproduced and incompetent, a bit of a dog's breakfast of a retrospective album showing up on Mausoleum called **Edge Of The World**, which actually included these two tracks. Note: Black Axe, along with Xero pulled up the rear on the otherwise mid-tier **The Friday Rock Shows** compilation.
Rating 6

Black Riders – Chosen Few
(G.I. '84, GILP-555)
A bit of a weird one here (and possibly an '85 release), Black Riders hailing from The Isle Of Man and turning in what would be a straight-faced, unremarkable, light in the loafers NWOBHM record, but for those utterly preposterous keyboards floating over many of the tracks. Now you'd have to call it very crudely rendered pomp, although half the album is fully metallic, another quarter melodic rock, and another quarter haplessly balladic. I suspect the piano man owned the equipment truck.
Rating   4

Black Rose - No Point Runnin'
(AJS/Tees-beat '82, TB5)
A-side on this first output for the band is the goes-nowhere ham-fister from the debut, b-side being non-LPer *Sucker For Your Love* which is a much-preferred fast hardball with some bracing twin lead work. Note, besides the LPs and singles, there's also a vicious little compactor called *Ridin' Higher* on the coveted **Roxcalibur** compilation, which also features this single's a-side as the lead track, a song that actually was made into a low budget video for the band, resulting in a bit of a career, including touring with the likes of Vardis and Raven.
Rating   7

Black Rose - Boys Will Be Boys
(Bullet '84, BULP3)
One of the late NWOBHM releases which took to a direction of chunky hard rock in hopes of Def Leppard-type financials. Unfortunately, the mix was muddy and yellow, slowing down the fairly amateurish and unwieldy tunes, offering the most base of melodies and the most cliché of lyrical blueprints. A band caught between time's mixed metaphor headlights, Black Rose I suspect would have acted much more NWOBHM in '81, but at this point, you can hear that they're being affected by the likes of yer Y&T, Quiet Riot and Motley.
Rating   5

Black Rose - Boys Will Be Boys
(Bullet '84, BOL9)
Maybe third in line after Def Leppard and Heavy Pettin', Black Rose had the stadium riffs but never got the producer nor the studio time they needed to break radio big. The a-side is the hard AOR title track from the first of two albums. B-side *Liar* is actually way better, a proud riff rocker like top flight **High 'n' Dry**-era Leps. But again it's undermined by scrappiness and a straining quality in Steve Bardsley's

vocals. Simple black and red cover art and label. Some came with a patch, that briefly in fashion blip of a swell freebie designed for the demonstration of one's allegiances, like the punk button, like the ballpoint pen jean-jacket illustration from a wistful tyme previous to both.
Rating   7

Blade Runner - Hunted
(Ebony '84, EBON 21)
These British lads about town were an idiosyncratic late NWOBHM entry that had much in common with medium sellers at the time such as Grim Reaper and Chateaux. Although their songs lacked the emotional impact of their comparatives, financial rogue Darryl Johnston provides the crazy, sunburned, kitchen mix, and Steve MacKay (McKay on the follow-up) adds those cool British bleatings until a punted headbang is at hand.
Rating   7

Blade Runner - Back Street Lady
(Ebony '84, EBON 26)
Both the a-side and the b-side *Too Far, Too Late* were from the excellent **Hunted** album, which displayed a band who sounded like a more commercial version of Savage, basically excellent hooks but a very heavy guitar and drum sound. The a-side is the album opener and thus fires along at a more carnal pace while *Back Street Lady* is a dour, melodic commercial "evil woman" type number. Both are more than serviceable NWOBHM from late in the game when competence was expected.
Rating   7

Blazer Blazer – Cecil B. Devine
(Logo '79, GO362)
These guys are pre-Maiden in a slight way, having barely contained Nicko McBrain and, in a later incarnation as Broadway Brats, Adrian Smith. The b-sides are *Warsaw*, a technical and punchy rocker with a melodic pre-chorus and a Thin Lizzy-like chorus proper, and *Six O'Clock In The Morning*, a track that also leans toward Lizzy, but down a buoyant pop punk road more akin to Lynott's various solo soul-searchings. Almost too poppy to be included, Blazer Blazer get in because of the connections plus the fact that none other than Tom Allom produced the thing. Plus *Cecil B. Devine* is a competent knock-off of (Killer?) Queen with nice McCartney-ish vocals, interesting, clean guitar tones balanced against a solid glam punch.
Rating   6

Bleak House - Rainbow Warrior
(Buzzard '80, BUZZ1)
These guys only cranked one single and one four track before calling it an obscure day. *Rainbow Warrior* is a pretty lame

power ballad which explodes into majestic but still lame metal, the lame coming from the tuneless, toneless vocals. Of course, there's the sped-up break 2/3 through with a silly bass/guitar duet before the final collapse to close out this uh, masterpiece. *Inquisition* (I've also seen it erroneously as *Isandiwana*, which is also one of the tracks here, spelled differently – long story) is surprisingly less esoteric, more or less a straight-faced NWOBHM rocker with a vicious, proud, almost visionary riff and guitar sound which lapses into a pedestrian melodic verse. Not bad, on the balance. An elder act, with bassist Gez Turner actually first showing up on classic '69 psych rarity **Pussy Plays** by Pussy.
Rating 5

Bleak House - Lions In Winter
(Buzzard '82, BUZZ2)
Four tracks of er, bleak but characteristic early NWOBHM, *Chase The Wind* being an impassioned melodic rocker, second a-side *No Reply* being a morose power ballad with a fast break. First track on the b-side, *Down To Zero*, is vaguely punky with a sour chorus melody (think Witchfynde crossed with Axis or Aragorn), another game attempt at bald-face NWOBHM with vocals that drag down the general mid-metal enthusiasm of it all. Second b, *Flight Of The Salamander (Pt. 1)*, is a snobby instrumental that sounds like Rush in the garage keeping warm with oven mitts. But all told, given that this thing is four tracks, a mood is set, chilled and lingered for the duration.
Rating 5

Blitzkrieg - Buried Alive
(Neat '81, NEAT10)
Recorded at Neat's Impulse Studios at the capable hands of label engineer Mickey Sweeney, **Buried Alive** is one of the cornerstone singles of the NWOBHM, given the future Metallica cover of the b-side, and the general star quality of the thing, something that seeps through like a ghostly chill, rather than hitting happy like the champagne of Leppard. The a-side is a seething, energetic melodic bit of hard metal, uncompromising but gracefully laced with a hook, sorta like Tygers crossed with Savage, mission-bent vocal courtesy of Brian Ross, who replaced original vocalist Sarah, Ross subsequently moving on to Avenger then Satan. The b-side *Blitzkrieg* is a classic grinding, almost post-NWOBHM riff (apparently conceived as an update on Focus' *Hocus Pocus*), well-appointed, Metallica's version not being all that much of an advancement or overhaul, although Blitzkrieg's suffers a bit from a cheap drum sound. The band's only output, outside of cassette demos and a track called *Inferno* to Neat's **Lead Weight** compilation in '81. Nine records/CDs would emerge sporadically to date throughout the balance of the '80s, '90s and '00s with various line-ps, but this single is the only true NWOBHM piece to see official release. It is by far the most collectible item from the Neat stable.
Rating 8

Bollweevil - Rock Solid
(Ellie Jay '81, EJSP 9716)
Soiled metal from the music down to the garish and ghoulish black and white sleeve, *Rock Solid* is only a recently discovered

single. The a-side is a mid-paced bit of rollick 'n' roll somewhat cheapened by a clean guitar lick recurring above the chunder. B-side *Sands Of Time* is over five seemingly endless minutes of Dark Star-vibed fantasy metal, main fantasy being that the band's drummer could play.
Rating 5

band with many later albums and singles. Barely into the NWOBHM, this is their first product and only piece that qualifies, next single being from '85. B-side: *Crying In The Rain*. Spot the obligatory Japanese rising sun shirt.
Rating 5

Boulevard - Dawn Raid
(Boulevard '81, VARD1)
This pre-Multi Storey band from Bristol started out quite grimly and atmospherically ensconced in the NWOBHM, *Dawn Raid* being the rocker here, *Take It Or Leave It* shooting unsuccessfully for epic ballad status, unsuccessful for three or four reasons, biggest being the tuneless, toneless vocals of Geoff Ford. A bash band with unattainable melodic aspirations. Both tracks are the same recordings as can be found on the band's cassette demo.
Rating 4

Bronz - Taken By Storm
(Bronze '84, BRON547)
File with Shy and Chrome Molly as commercial, key-laced Brit pop metal with generically perfect high register vocals. Probably the most annoying of the three but still heavier than you might think. Unless you're a historian of British melodic hard rock, there's no point in searching this one out. Lone cool decision: a cover of New England's *Don't Ever Wanna Lose Ya*.
Rating 4

Bronz – Send Down An Angel
(Bronze '84, BRO178)
Definitely down the major label AOR path rather than grubby NWOBHM, Bronz nevertheless were part of the circuit. This track also kicks off the band's lone album, **Taken By Storm**, and is squarely stadium rock in the vein of Journey, Magnum, Kansas or Saga. B-side *Tiger* is a heavier number but still over-produced and stiff. Of note, vocalist for Bronz was Max Bacon of GTR and Phenomena fame. *Send Down An Angel* was also issued as a 7" in the states, with *The Cold Truth* as the b-side, both from the remixed (for the US) version of the album. This latter track was as shamelessly radio-directed as the marquee track. Ultimately, Def Leppard

Briar - Rainbow (To The Skies)
(Happy Face '83, MM142)
This is really more of a sour English hair

would be the only UK act to ever make waves with poppy AOR. Brits just weren't accepted in this field.
Rating 8

Brooklyn – I Wanna Be A Detective
(Rondelet '80, ROUND3)
Quite pop for this punk label gone metal (Gaskin, Witchfynde) so we won't take up too much of your time, Brooklyn turning in for their a-side a tight yet layered synth rock, included here more because of the evil label connection. Still, b-side *Two Wheels* is a little more blue collar rockier with nice twin leads and vocal harmonies as bonus, both of which can be heard on the archival footage of the guys playin' 'er live on **Look Hear!**.
Rating 5

Brooklyn – You Never Know What You'll Find
(Rondelet '81, ABOUT3)
Often misconstrued as NWOBHM, given that their label was Rondelet and that they're dopey looking longhairs reminiscent of early Quartz, Brooklyn are in fact a glammy, poppy, new wavey, discoey band of wayward conundrums, included here because about a third to two-fifths of the album is slightly guitar-oxygenated like fey Teaze or demure Angel. So call them dancing around a hard rock topic, but closer to that vile form known as pomp rock (or power pop) than anything NWOBHM.
Rating 3

Brooklyn – Hollywood
(Rondelet '81, ROUND6)
B-side is called *Late Again*, and y'know, another comparative here is late period British glam, sorta that shift toward yer City Boy, Nutz, Mr. Big area.
Rating 5

Budgie - Power Supply
(Active/RCA '80, ACTLP1)
Well it's nothing new for great artists to go unloved. Budgie weren't the first, and they won't be the last. Thin Lizzy, Gamma, Badlands, King's X, Love/Hate and Last Crack have all seen commercial injustice despite critical raves, which just kills me, really. Anyways, back to the first creaks and feedbacks of the New Wave Of British Heavy Metal, on which Budgie would bandwagon—there's no other word for it. But count me along for the ride, when the bandwagon is metal, and the jumpers are Budgie, who through convoluted and involuntary means, are one of British metal's originators, inspirations and catalysts. Significantly, key Shelly sidekick and apparent co-author for life Tony Bourge is gone. Enter new, evidently headbanging axeman John Thomas, who cranks a convincing metallic din throughout this squarely heavy metal feast. No longer Budgie the unfathomable, this is Budgie as trench warfare rawk dudes, raw, blunted and hooked to one unrelenting supply of street-heated horsepower. Simply an accomplished, nostalgic and starkly

traditional heavy metal record, **Power Supply** bears no relation to what fluttered before, or indeed what comes after, offering a couple like AC/DC, one like AC/DC's best imitators, one **Nightflight**-style ballad, and some fierce unkempt pig iron in *Hellbender*, *Heavy Revolution* and smokin' combat classic *Secrets In My Head*, one bad mutha of a track which, plopped there, could have sent **In For The Kill** through the floorboards. A sell-out through and through, **Power Supply** sadly marked the demise of something special and timeless, replacing it with something simply really cool and entertaining. But with an air of luck to it, there was a grudging acceptance on the part of the (thirsty) fans - in one sense, this is what we punters bitch and moan for all the time, asking a metallic "what if?" from random rockers like Queen and Quo and Deep Purple and Nazareth. Well Budgie gave us The Heavy Metal Record we secretly wanted from them, and one can't help but feel some sort of loss, the loopy, fecund eccentricity of the guys gone. Like I say, we asked for it. The record's CD reissue contains the long-lost **If Swallowed, Do Not Induce Vomiting** EP.
Rating 9

Budgie - Crime Against The World
(Active/RCA '80, BUDGE2)
Always stingy with the rarities, Budgie go with a couple of tracks from their guns-blazing NWOBHM masterpiece **Power Supply**, *Crime Against The World* being one of the weaker numbers, a pandering AC/DC-ish radio ploy, while b-side *Hellbender* is a thick, metal-scraping, boot-stomping classic. Note: seven studio albums and five singles before this one for these Welsh weirdos, but of course, we're only going with material from their opportunistic (but I ain't complaining!) street metal years.
Rating 7

Budgie - If Swallowed, Do Not Induce Vomiting
(Active/RCA '80, BUDG1)
Roughly a $30 item in its virgin state, this four track EP catches up on a few tracks from the band's headbangin' **Power Supply** days, good solid hard rockers, but nuthin' special. The tracks enclosed — *Wildfire*, *High School Girls*, *Panzer Division Destroyed*, and *Lies Of Jim (The E-Type Lover)* — round the low income NWOBHM bases competently and with typical Budgie confidence. But no doubt, the right tracks made it to **Power Supply** proper.
Rating 5

Budgie - Nightflight
(RCA '81, RCALP6003)
As if the metallic panic had worn off, Budgie settles into a similar yet more relaxed take on **Power Supply**'s gritty basics. Infused with melody and simple charm, **Nightflight** makes its way down cobblestoned streets like the work of a hundred-year-old bar band, plainly telling the truth and laying it down with nary an ear-splitting crack despite the full metal jacket recording and overall look to the thing. Call it an experimental, pop version of **Power**

Supply, **Nightflight** offers a mix of metal, power balladry, light-headed hard rockers and atmospheric loudness, brash but not written so, in a sort of nonchalant display of working class integrity. I appreciate the album, always have, despite the sonic pull back on the ol' throttle, although this is still Budgie reveling in common man antics, well below the creative mania of **Impeckable** and back, yet still full of sturdy songcraft, although lush or bizarre wouldn't enter into the vocabulary here. Faves include opening track *I Turned To Stone* (spiritual descendant of *Riding My Nightmare*), soft rocker and minor UK hit *Apparatus*, and heaviest blockhead on the block, *She Used Me Up*. Brutish, almost dull but oddly heroic, **Nightflight** is, in ways, for Budgie fans only, its regression to a raw delivery of seemingly inconsequential song ideas not an approach that outsiders would have any patience for. Thereby, being a fan, I'm eminently ready year after year, to give it a wistful ol' spin or two.
Rating   8

Budgie - I Turned To Stone
(RCA '81, BUDGE4)
This elegant, successful doom ballad from **Nightflight** is backed with an instrumental version of the same, a cool tune for this sort of treatment, given its melancholy arrangement. Also comes in an orange vinyl version.
Rating   7

Budgie - Keeping A Rendezvous
(RCA '81, BUDGE3)
Bit of a limp dishrag after the distorted droolery of **Power Supply**, **Nightflight** yielded a couple half-hearted singles. *Keeping A Rendezvous* is a happy pop rocker buckling under the weight of a late Angel Witch-style recording, while b-side *Apparatus* (also an album track) is a hard-edged ballad with the same problem. Also released as a picture disc 7" with the same catalogue #.
Rating   6

Budgie - Deliver Us From Evil
(RCA '82, RCALP6054)
I knew little of Budgie's whereabouts past this elegant panorama of tried and true rock styles, for in truth, they sort of faded away, only to emerge as a fairly unambitious bar band years later, granted recording, although with compromised lineups. The first with no form of budgie on the cover, **Deliver Us From Evil** marked a new phase for the band, the guys rocking supra-intelligently, royally, and fairly metallic, the versatile array of axe work alloyed with arresting, seamless pop magic. Eminently

British, and layered with the multi-dimensional wisdom of experience, **Deliver Us From Evil** tells ten well-thought out stories, from opening harmonic pop rocker *Bored With Russia* to the heartfelt *Give Me The Truth*, through galloping NWOBHM rocker *Hold On To Love*. Simply a great hard rock record tempered with traditional classic nuance, technical creativity, and an overwhelming attentiveness to quality, this has always been an engaging journey, the band spiraling through dynamic after dynamic like a charmed BÖC or Thin Lizzy, enigmatic in its universal and generalist "rock" approach, not to mention the band's urge to entertain on its own intelligent terms. Unlike any other Budgie record (which is?), **Deliver Us From Evil** took the band into potential accessibility, where previously, records were either decipherable but too raw, or technical but bizarre. I dunno, I just remember playing it incessantly, the album somehow wrapping in a big bow all that Budgie had sampled, their graphic experience at working the fringes of the rock game becoming fittingly subjugated to a bold strength of song, track after classy track.
Rating 9

Budgie - Bored With Russia
(RCA '82, 271)
Final single for this great band was the infectious bouncy (dated) pop culture jam of *Bored With Russia*, backed with *Don't Cry*, **Deliver Us From Evil**'s heaviest track, a true NWOBHM offering from this (let's face it) bandwagoner of a legend. Also came in picture disc format (RCAP271).
Rating 8

Buffalo - Battle Torn Heroes
(Heavy Metal '80, HEAVY3)
Two singles and that's it for this Manchester hopeful, Buffalo also getting out on the tour trail with both Gillan and Motörhead. A-side *Battle Torn Heroes* (which previously showed up on the seminal **New Electric Warriors** compilation) fits into the adapted boogie category, that heavy Quo space into which so many NWOBHMers wandered. B-side *Women Of The Night* is somewhat in the same zone, although leaning more toward AC/DC-style biker rock (*Bad Boy Boogie?*) with a pint-swilling verve, or conversely, stomping like old Ted Nugent, admirable spirits lifted by the give 'er hell vocals of John Ralphs.
Rating 7

Buffalo - Mean Machine
(Heavy Metal '82, HEAVY15)
"I'm a mean machine, but I keep my motor clean!" bellows Mick Bailey (in his best Sean Harris cry) on this solid mid-rift NWOBHM single, the a-side going for those melancholy poverty melodies, while the b, *The Rumour* rocks a little harder, all in all a little cleaner and tentative compared to the earlier single. Garish red white and blue sleeve art, with a simpler blue and white label. Gary Taylor (ex-Streetfighter) onto Tank. Note: one other track called *Cold As Night*, on Heavy Metal's **Heavy Metal Heroes** sampler from '81.
Rating 7

C

Camargue – Howl Of The Pack
(Clubland '83, SJP 848)
Extremely rare, cool vintage red and black Clubland label, with some copies in b+w band shot picture sleeve, some not. A-side is a rocker; b-side *Someone Just Like You*, a ballad. Trivia note: the band had to change their name from Savage due to the other fine fellows, lasting as Camargue until '86.
Rating   5

Centurion – Two Wheels
(SRT '82, 0001)
Centurion's rough 'n' tumble non-picture sleeve single (but with cool homegrown winged raptor label) featured the gangland rock of the a-side plus a b-side called *Bitch*, which was even less NWOBHM (basically loud, guitary retro rock), than the title track. There's also a mis-press, where the label mistakenly says Nikki. Currently worth a good $50, this beauty is.
Rating   7

Chainsaw – Police And Politicians
(Square '80, SQSP2)
From Coventry. Scharnhorst, Mainline, Withered Man and Bitches Sin related. Neither track is on the band's **Massacre** EP (Thunderbolt '84). Also contributed *Devil's Daughter* (also from the EP) to an '84 Thunderbolt sampler. Raging biker cover art. And the music? Well, both tracks are heavy enough, crisped at the edges by punk, pop and pub rock, with *Hole In The Road* at least moving briskly, with a ripping axe solo to boot. The a-side is quite annoying though, with hollering vocals and political lyrics that are repetitive and haranguing.
Rating   6

Chainsaw – Massacre
(Thunderbolt '84, THBE 1006)
Weird kiddie-coloured cover art, but at least there's a chainsaw, and then inside, look for four unshaven tracks of dumpy, rusty, beastly biker metal. First up there's *Devil's Daughter*, followed by the equally caterwauled *Battle Axe* bar metal of *Ballad Of Mean Street*. *Rock 'n' Roll Gambler* sounds like a cross between Rose Tattoo and Ted Nugent, while closer *Accident Victim* goes for hair metal melody soured by Maiden and The Clash, in other words very British and... what, is that a saxophone? In any event, as would be expected, the sum total of this is more unified and codified toward metal than the unsure first single.
Rating   6

Chainsaw – Lonely Without You
(Pot Belly '80, EJSP9462)
Different band from Coventry act above. B-side: *On The Highway*. More a holdover from mid-'70s pub rock than truly NWOBHM.
Rating   5

Chainsaw – Long Legged Woman
(GMC '84, CS001)
This is the same Yorkshire-based band that released *Lonely Without You*. B-side: *Midnight Blue*, with both tracks including saxophones as part of the confused mix. Both Chainsaw singles were non-picture sleeve.
Rating 4

Challenger – So Sure Of Yourself
(CMC '81, C.M. 0001)
Another Yorkshire band here, Challenger writing themselves a NWOBHM gallop in *So Sure Of Yourself* but then starving it of instrumentation, the track's weak keys providing as much as the even weaker guitars and vocals. The band sounding similarly out of step on b-side Out To Kill, on this rare, b+w 45 of little consequence.
Rating 3

Chariot - The Warrior
(Shades '84)
The Warrior is basically a blunt, ham-fisted traditional chugorama, sporting a Motörheaded no-frills bell-ring, albeit with less zip and less personality. English biker metal that only rarely rises above yer Battle Axe, Dark Heart or Mausoleum porridge bowl of low expectations, which ain't necessarily a bad thing if a good out-of-fashion headbang is the call. Something proud about it, though. High points: *Evil Eye* and *Vigilante*. Note: also released on France's Axe Killer Records as **The Warriors**.
Rating 6

Charlie 'Ungry – House On Chester Road
(SRT '80, CU 001/S80CUS694)
Weird one here, definitely on the borderline side, Charlie 'Ungry rocking out like a cross between Cheap Trick, Slade and punk with what is likely an accidental collision with a handful of NWOBHM tenets. It's quite good, but fairly off-base, *Preacher* even sounding like '60s psych. Best of the bunch is *Who's My Killer*, which sounds like Ethel The Frog meets The Who, while the title track is almost pure pop (save for the moderately molten guitar solo), the whole conundrum propped by quality vocals. Very basic picture sleeve.
Rating 4

Chase – Evensong
(Corduroy Mouse Wax Co. '83, WAX 1002)
West Midlands band Chase eventually coughed up a drummer to a '90s lineup of Diamond Head, but back in the wooly days, he played for this heavy enough semi-NWOBHM act of prog persuasion, there being more than a little Rush to the band's somewhat accomplished and epic sound, a mélange that included early use of guitar synth. B-Side is called *Evermore Pt. 2*, which continues in a style the band's label compared to Zeppelin, Genesis and the aforementioned Rush.
Rating 6

Chaser - Raiders
(Chaser '84, SRT4KS 304)
Not to be confused with Scotland's Chasar (an actual album from them, but it's from '85 — past our cut-off), this was a late NWOBHM entry out of Ipswich, England with one single to their name, qualified to

be here but for their sunken old isolated sound. Both tracks (b-side being the more raucous, guitar-molten gallop of *Final Stand*) are probably better than average NWOBHM (save for the bland vocal work of Steve Baker), but you can't allow them too much credit, given the band's 1981-82 sound on what is a 1984 release. Non-picture sleeve, but fetching guitar-as-weapon label art.
Rating   7

Chateaux - Young Blood
(Ebony '82, EBON 9)
B-side is *Fight To The Last* and it is indeed a battle, the band building an urgent rocker with flair, drama, and that ridiculously amped guitar sound that would become the Ebony trademark. Both tracks are pre-first LP and neither were on any album. *Young Blood* also showed up on Ebony's **Metal Maniaxe** sampler from the same year, and is an awesome mellow then heavy-hitting rocker, searing sound, killer vocals and uncommonly good drumming for NWOBHM music. A classic, from one of the genre's best, Chateaux creating three albums of urgent, claustrophobic UK mad metal.
Rating   8

Chateaux - Chained And Desperate
(Ebony '83, EBON 13)
This raw and violent record embodied all the magic and steely-eyed determination of the exploding British metal movement in the early '80s. Dense and rumbling, **Chained And Desperate** cuts a rough 'n' tumble, street-ready path of destruction, laid waste by one of Darryl Johnston's acidic trademark Ebony recordings, resulting in a record so depressingly European and so darkly arresting that it stands as one of the grimly emotional, metal-committed greats of the NWOBHM. Aside from the guttural attack of the mix, **Chained And Desperate** claims further frenzied highs due to the appearance of labelmate Steve Grimmett of Grim Reaper on vocals, and some razor-sharp, metal-on-metal guitar histrionics from Tim Broughton. Riding the same mysterious mood as Reaper's first, plus the debuts from Diamond Head, Savage, and Witchfinder General, **Chained And Desperate** combines integrity, songcraft and pig iron in a way rarely seen outside the confines of these early Brit masters. A swirling cauldron of glorious noise.
Rating   9

Chateaux - Fire Power
(Ebony '84, EBON 18)
The gloomy Gus's from Gloucestershire are back and sounding addled and rattled. Producer Darryl Johnston delves deeper into his Ebony mindspace and pulls out an even thicker, more eclectic sound which nevertheless still makes the blood boil profusely, striking at the heart of electricity gone awry at the back of a previously much quieter pub that never knew what hit them. But the songwriting focus is lost, the singular garage din of the debut heaving forth to both

OTT excursions and flirtation with AOR rock structures. Skull-flattening classics such as *Eyes Of Stone, Hero* and *White Steel* make up for some of the less polished, less thought-through stuff, namely the meandering *Run In The Night* and the confusing *Roller Coaster*. Still, this is a searing, filthy record sonically speaking, featuring excellent vocal work by new Grimmett sound-alike Krys Mason. Excusing the bone thrown to the mainstream, **Fire Power** nonetheless rocks hurried and unhewn, Chateaux still burning with an intensity that melts lipsticked poseurs in their platform-booted tracks. To offer a little completism for ya, the band cranked one more heat-treated full length, namely **Highly Strung**, but its '85 release date puts 'er past our disciplined NWOBHM cleave of midnight the previous year.
Rating 8

Cheeky – Don't Mess Me Around
(Woodbine St. '80, WSR005)
A-side rocks properly and within the rules, sorta like a yobbish, half-speed punk version of *Breadfan* but b-side *Get Outa My 'Ouse* is a wholly inappropriate joke tune, I'd say a cross between Quo, UK Subs and Ian Dury. Both feature horrid, powerless recordings. Non-picture sleeve. Add it up, and the cues for inclusion here are quite minimal.
Rating 2

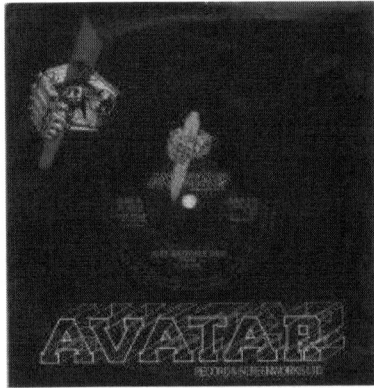

Chevy – Too Much Loving
(Avatar '80, AAA 104)
A-side is from well-received self-titled LP (also known as **The Taker**), issued in both the UK and Germany, on Bellaphon. Picture washed-up, poppy, post-Paul Rodgers Bad Company crossed with bad production from the Free days and yer close. B-side *See The Light* is non-LP, and reminds me very much of poppy Axe (granted from the **Nemesis** era), right down to the Bobby Barth vocal. As with the guys from Quartz, Bleak House and even Saxon, that the band's roots reach well back into the '70s, under names such as Cupid's Inspiration and 4-Wheel Drive. There was also a picture sleeve issue of this in Germany, also on the band's label there, Bellaphon.
Rating 5

Chevy – The Taker
(Avatar '81, AAA 107)
B-side: *Life On The Run* is non-LP. The a-side is from the LP, and is a sour sort of pop rocker with punchy arrangements and a vocal that goes all histrionic like Meatloaf. Sleeve art reproduces the effective LP art. Note: there's also a Spanish Avatar issue (cat. # 0226501)
Rating 5

Chevy – Just Another Day
(Avatar '81, AAA 114)
The a-side is a non-LP Russ Ballard composition, put forth for your perusal and hopeful purchase in the fine tradition of Samson, AIIZ and Rainbow, all coverers of Russ. It's a perfect fit for Chevy, as it would be for Foreigner or Heep circa **Abominog**, them guys also covering Ballard in hopes of a hit. *Just Another Day* would also be covered by Briar and Verity, that band's Rod Argent having played with Ballard in Argent. The b-side is from the LP, *Rock On* sounding like The Allmans crossed with Thin Lizzy in barroom blues mode. Not entirely disagreeable. Note I: most famous song remains *Chevy*, found on the band's lone LP as well as **Metal For Muthas Volume II**. Note II: there's another Chevy with a single called *Out On The Street* on Champ from 1979. Issued in black, evil-looking, but quite plain, generic Avatar sleeve.
Rating 5

China Doll – Oysters And Wine
(Wessex '80, WEX 273)
Nice picture sleeve rarity and adequately heavy too, with the a-side galloping moderately, adding a dark chord sequence,

all told, very NWOBHM if a bit timid with its tooling. B-side *Past Tense* begins with a ponderous, hilariously Rush-derived mellow passage before turning into a punky verse with added Rush chordings.
Rating   7

Chinatown - Short And Sweet
(Airship '81, AP138)
This single is cool because it's the only studio work released by the band (see review of album, which was live), the a-side being a metal/hard rock blend with a nice melody, professional guitar textures, and frankly, not the greatest recording. The live version kills this one dead. B-side *How Many Times* kicks off with a Diamond Head-worthy guitar signature and then lapses into a slightly pomp verse that reminds me of Wildfire. The cool thing is that the band write like veterans from the '70s trying to participate in the NWOBHM, something which usually resulted in explosive albums from tired guys. Both compositions are included in the live set that makes up the album. Nice sleeve to this single, which turns out to be quite similar to that of a certain Thin Lizzy album cover.
Rating   8

Chinatown - Play It To Death
(Airship '81)
On the strength of 4000 sales for their *Short And Sweet/How Many Times* single, this popular UK NWOBHM act decided to do the Stampede/AIIZ/Vardis thing and make their first album a live one. People kind of cared, due to the commercial nature of their metal (think Shy, UFO, Fastway, Schenker solo, Tokyo Blade), and the weird, high, borderline annoying vocals of Steve Pragnell. The cocky **Play It To Death** aspires to stadium rock heights, offering a versatile bunch of generalist "classic" tracks which could have made the radio, but given the wobbly, crackly, barely acceptable performances and sonics of the record, there wasn't much point. Highly collectible for years, Vinyl Tap reissued the album on CD, adding the single plus two non-LP live tracks recorded at Reading for the **Reading Rocks** album from '82. Most of the band members moved on to small-to-mid-size metal acts.
Rating   7

Chinawite - Blood On The Streets
(Future Earth '83, FER014)
Sheffield's Chinawite were one of those fence-straddling acts, *Blood On The Streets* focusing on the mean side of party metal but coming off plodding instead, while *Ready To Satisfy* goes straight for party metal, sorta like mod Kiss or even hard southern rock when the '70s bands converted to commercial metal. Note: both tracks are most readily available on Mausoleum's **Metal Prisoners** compilation. Neither track showed up on the band's lone LP **Run For Cover**, also on Belgium's maligned metal label Mausoleum.
Rating   6

Chinawite - Run For Cover
(Mausoleum '84, Skull 8351)

The front cover reeks of a Savage or Battleaxe album or something equally metal-mad, but the band looks like university students. And it sucks because Brits, with very few exceptions, have no idea how to execute a set of melodic hard rock. Hazardously fragile vox, pointless keyboard washes and thumpy production finish it off, the drum sound aspiring to Def Leppard circa **Pyromania** but arriving at Shy crossed with Wrathchild due to lack of both dosh and a clue.

Rating 5

Clientelle - Can't Forget
(Quest '79, BRS003)

B-side *Skyflyer* (both tracks hail from the band's lone LP – see review) is much more of a modern NWOBHM standard than the a-side, which is a bit of a dark new wave-inflected rocker with clean guitar but a chorus that is a bit more power chorded. But yeah, *Skyflier* is like one of those slow Saxon gallops (good Hawkwindy chorus), even if the power, once again, is a little diminished. The track, and the band's status albeit, is saved by a clear high Brit rock vocal. Rare, desired, but housed in a not so exciting picture sleeve featuring grainy b+w shots of the band members. Officially called a "Double "A" Side Single." The value of the single, and of the album, has been somewhat diminished by the recent CD reissue of the full album with bonus tracks.

Rating 6

Clientelle - Destination Unknown
(Banana '81)

Unremarkable that this pubby, questionably heavy metal UK act pooped out an indie single—that seemed to be the tradition in those days—but Clientelle were one of the rare NWOBHM bands to follow with an indie full-length, making both pieces highly collectible. The sound of the band, however, leaned to a number of rocks, including Bad Co., glam, pub rock, new wave, light Spider (or Vardis and Marseille), mid-rift Slade, intimate, cheap, but charming, at least at the vocal end of things. One gets a sense that left for another 18 months to incubate, **Clientelle** would have turned in a squarely NWOBHM record, but given its vintage, it's unsurprising that 80% of these ideas are anchored in the '70s.

Rating 5

Cloven Hoof - The Opening Ritual
(Elemental Music '82, E.M. 001)

The Opening Ritual 12" comprises three tracks that would not be repeated on the

band's debut album, plus an early version of *The Gates Of Gehenna*. All told, there's more magic here given the vintage as well as the attack, Cloven Hoof exuding the promise of Satan and Trespass and Maiden, even if still, they attempt too much within the confines of each track. Faves would be, at one extreme, the speedy blitz of *Stormrider*, and at the other, the epic Heavy Load of *Starship Sentinel*, while *Back In The USA* is a rough 'n' tumble meat and potatoes party rocker not without charm and *The Gates Of Gehenna* is pure Maiden mania, again, quite the proposal for its day, really.
Rating   8

Cloven Hoof - Cloven Hoof
(Neat '84, 1013)
Cloven Hoof's late LP recalls early Angel Witch and early Iron Maiden plus the Viking-inspired Swedish wave just around the corner, but the goods scamper and flip-flop around too much amongst the record's epic-based six tracks, lacking the power, conciseness and ideas to fry leather, especially up into '84 when all of this should have been worked out. Some sinister enough Euro-riffing here coupled with a substantially wicked and convincing black metal/Viking/action hero image make for a minor tragedy that the metal wasn't all that toothsome and muscle-bound on a sustained basis to match the theatrics, or, for that matter, to match the raw power of the debut and semi-legendary EP. Produced with complementary edginess by Keith Nichol, although this is not one of his best knob jobs. Alas, yet another band who messed up on the timing, arriving right on cue in '82, but out the door by '84.
Rating   6

Cobra - Lookin' For A Lady
(Rip Off '78, RIPOFF3)
This Belfast band broke more than a few of the NWOBHM rules, not altogether shaking the memory of pub rock's heyday, not surprising, given its age. The a-side is actually closer to wobbly Spider than pub or punk though, even if the looseness and crusty mix are pretty direly DIY. B-side *Graveyard Boogie* is a bit better, stomping along to some nice guitar tones, understated twin leads, doomy melodies and thunderclap sound effects. Both tracks showed up on the **Belfast Rocks** comp the following year. Creepy, quintessentially NWOBHM cover illustration.
Rating   5

Jess Cox - Third Step
(Neat '83, 1010)
Jess (and that gangland punter caw of his) was a big part of kicking off the NWOBHM through his work on the classic debut from Tygers Of Pan Tang. But once ousted, he found it necessary to make a keyboard-washed, pop-filled, ballad-marred AOR record. Lacking a singing voice, or, obviously a production budget, this was exactly the opposite move a guy like this should have made (see **Di'anno** by Paul Di'anno!). Rightly trounced in the press, **Third Step** never got to first base, and Jess found himself running Neat Records, not singing for it.
Rating   2

Jess Cox - Bridges
(Neat '83, NEAT26)
Tygers Of Pan Tang singer gone commercial solo. Later ran Neat Metal, still later sold to Sanctuary with Jess moving on with his Edgy imprint. B-side *Check It Out* is a lackadaisical AC/DC-esque rocker that comes off like middle America's The Godz meets Holocaust. *Bridges* is from the lone album two years later, and is a clunky thunky powerless "evil woman" song, vaguely sparse and new wavey, none to enjoyable. Artsy bridge illustration is this one's only distinction.
Rating   2

Jess Cox - One In A Million
(Neat '84, NEAT35)
It was always inexplicable why Jess took his gutter rock voice into the realm of poppy AOR. Bad fit to be sure. Here's the evidence, *One In A Million* pounding along to uptown drums and east of the city vocals. A dreadful collision. B-side *Bad Time Girl* sounds like clumsy April Wine in party mode. Note: besides the **Third Step** LP (from which the a-side hails) Jess also had the track *Devil's Triangle* show up on the second **Heavy Metal Heroes** compilation.
Rating   2

Crucifixion - The Fox
(Miramar '80, MIR4)
The Fox also shows up on Neat's **All Hell Let Loose** and **60 Minutes Plus** compilations, albeit re-recorded. Both tracks are quintessential rough 'n' ready NWOBHM, *The Fox* stomping along barsy and boozy but electric chugged convincingly down a metal path, the growling vocals of Glyn Morgan ice scrapings on the cake. B-side *Death*

Sentence is like molten garage rock, again alcoholic and chaotic, hot, sweaty and endearingly stupid. Non-picture sleeve.
Rating   7

Crucifixion - Take It Or Leave It
(Neat '82, NEAT19)
Howling wolf metal a-side here, Crucifixion proving themselves to be one of the most alert and edgy of NWOBHM acts. Driving riff, growling vocals, dirty-ass mix. Place gingerly near the top of this often embarrassing, somewhat arbitrarily fenced genre. B-side *On The Run* is urgent, punky, melodic but raw, like fast Holocaust – quintessential NWOBWM all the way. Killer sleeve to this single, the band's signature grim reaper caught in pensive, card-dealing pose.
Rating   9

Crucifixion - Green Eyes
(Neat '84, NEAT37)
Quite collectible this Essex act, Crucifixion bashing out a couple singles

and this three track 12" EP before slinking off to hell. The sound is vintage NWOBHM, like vintage '81, somewhere between Ethel The Frog, Witchfynde, Holocaust and Jaguar, Crucifixion offering *Moon Rising* and the title track, two in-character scary tunes (to biker soundtracks), plus one unfathomable drooler about getting caught with *Jailbait*. God, I must say I miss this kind of plain ol' punter singing.
Rating   7

Cryer - The Visionary
(Happy Face '80, MM124)
This quite decent piece (also known as **The Single**; b-side *Hesitate*) was recorded for the label made famous by its Diamond Head connection. The Birmingham-based Cryer was known for its theatrical club shows, as well as its touring with Gillan and the fact that they were a six-piece. The band recorded an album which was subsequently shelved, only to come out as **Set Me Free** under the band name Force – *Hesitate* can be heard there. There are also Dexy's Midnight Runners and Starfighters connections. Look for copies with the original form included, printed up for a contest in which punters were to try name the title track, hence the original title **The Single**. But yes, *The Visionary* is a huge, swelling, passionate slow rocker with lots of layers and powerful vocals, somewhat of a power ballad, with the emphasis on surging power, while *Hesitate*, unfortunately, is more of a conventional ballad, dark enough and again well-appointed and vocalized, but tinkled with piano and not all that heavy.
Rating   7

Crys – Lan Yn Y Gogledd
(Click '80, GMW2001)
Obviously one of our few Welsh entries, neither of these two pretty NWOBHM-attuned single tracks showed up on either of the band's two LPs. B-side: *Cadw Symud*.
Rating   5

Crys – Rhyfelwr
(Sain '81, 1216M)
Hollering in Welsh surely couldn't have done much for this band's prospects, which is a shame, given the convincing NWOBHM rollick and gallop to the band's songs, not to mention solid, full-range, if workmanlike production values. Highlight would be the title track (a.k.a. Warrior), which is buoyed by cool chord sequences and a groove beyond the band's years.
Rating   6

Crys – Tymor Yr Heliwr
(Sain '82, 1242M)
The bullethole through glass cover (not to mention the punk type) is a bit of a bust compared to the first record's magic and dramatic warrior illustration, but the punchy barroom NWOBHM continues, with the Welsh singing, albeit, starting to wear on me now like Russian. Interesting band though, one that attends to details like guitar textures, harmonies, and a sixth sense for chops and tightness, so it seems. Title translates to Season Of The Hunter.
Rating   5

Cynic – Suicide
(Cynic Productions '83, CYN1)
A-side is a more than competent power ballad while b-side: *No Time At All* is even closer to a full-on NWOBHM sound. Not to be confused with the pioneering American prog metal monsters.
Rating   6

D

Paul Dale Band – Alright On The Night
(KA '81, KA6)
Singer Paul Dale (ex-Marseille) cobbled together this AOR-ish band for one single and that's it, b-side being the heavier *Hold On*, the single creeping out in both black and clear vinyl editions, colour live shot picture sleeve included.
Rating   4

Damascus – Open Your Eyes
(Damascus '84)
Damascus was a Merseyside band, recording in Liverpool this four tracker consisting of *Something On My Mind*, *Cold Horizon*, *Midnight Train* and the title track. The EP came with two slightly different sleeves and with a paper insert and the sound was frankly quite amateurish at this late stage in the game, sounding like wobbly '81 NWOBHM, rumbling, frantic, not great vocals, gritty guitars and bass that stuck out above the bashed drums. Still, it's squarely heavy, and thus unarguably belonging unlike aged offerings along the same Ethel The Frog line.
Rating   4

Dark Heart – Shadows In The Night
(Roadrunner '84, RR9849)
Powerless pre-school gothic metal, short-sticked by a tone-deaf vocalist and to many clean guitar tones, Dark Heart was one of those talentless signings from the major flood of NWOBHM bands, plucked seemingly from nowhere when anybody with a stained Motörhead shirt could scrounge up a record contract. Aimless, silly and slapped together, which gives it a certain charm, its fey musicality beating out handily, say, any number of thrash or death acts, because despite the poverty metal surroundings, there's melody and adherence to certain values from the '70s. Frustrating like Demon, or Holocaust in transition toward Hologram.
Rating   5

Dark Star – Lady Of Mars
(Avatar '80, AAA 105)
Title track is from the classic and faithfully NWOBHM LP, *Lady Of Mars* being one of the genre's cornerstones, landing with a gallop and thump between Maiden and Trespass, melodicized with Viking flair. B-side is the non-LP *Rock 'n' Romancin'* on the standard UK single version, which also came in a plain Avatar label sleeve. This track is prime Dark Star, built on a bouncy gallop but blessed with twin leads, vocal harmonies and a pint-swilling boogie spirit. Odd single variants exist, including Spanish picture sleeve version (cat. # 0229702; basically reproduces the album art) with a different b-side (*Louisa*), and an Italian Avatar issue with a garish live shot sleeve. But the main cool item is the first version of the single on the band's own Steel Strike. Apparently only sleeves and labels were made before the money disappeared. Yet somehow, a few were cobbled together for a single which includes *Renegade* and the official Avatar single's two tracks. Of note, there was also a Spanish band illustration picture sleeve issue of a *Kaptain Amerika* single in '82, backed with *Louisa*. A reformed, but sadly lacking version for the band came back for '87's crappy **Real To Reel** album.
Rating   8

Dark Star – Dark Star
(Avatar '81, AALP 5003)

One of the more promising NWOBHM bands soon to be crashed on the rocks of obscurity, Dark Star had an accomplished sort of '70s/Maiden-ish sound, replete with the usual stylistic eccentricities that resulted in a record of fragmented ideas (see Gaskin, Witchfynde, Demon), despite occasional diamonds of carnal knowledge. *Lady Of Mars* and *Lady Love* reign smoothly galloping and gothic (like Trespass, Diamond Head and bits of Saxon; Darkstar and Trespass were highlights on the second **Metal For Muthas** comp.), but most else oscillated between patchy and amusing, not without a dated, pubby, earthy US rock charm rifling its way through the attic. Still, **Dark Star** was stronger than most of the scant few full-length platters at this early juncture in the heavy revolution, and really, it is its anchoring in the '70s, coupled with this new heavy metal enthusiasm of a widening '80s, that inspires. '93 Pony Canyon reissue includes six bonus tracks.
Rating   7

Dawn Trader - Dawn Trader
(AFE '80, DT1)

Pressed in a quantity of 1,000, this '70s rock-influenced EP included *Dawn Trader, No One Gonna Better Me, Orphan, You On My Mind*. The four-tracker was housed in a fairly drab red sleeve. Back in '84 with a heavier compilation track, but that's it.
Rating   6

Dawnwatcher – Spellbound
(Dawnwatcher '80, DWS001)

Non-picture sleeve but wicked Egypto label art; b-side *Hall Of Mirrors* actually sounds like heavy Stranglers until it hits an elliptical chord pattern that sends it modestly triumphant. This elaborate Bradford act was known for their old-school keyboards and synths, but the layering is deft and judicious, with *Spellbound* in particular impressing with a mesmerizing intro piece, followed by recurring twists and turns and an insistent, thumping drive throughout.
Rating   7

Dawnwatcher – Backlash
(Dawnwatcher '82, DWS002)

Picture sleeve which reinforces the band's pyramid theme from the debut single. The a-side is quite the enigma, imposing chords stacked against disconcerting Farfisa organ-type sounds set against a structure that is forceful, doomy and proggy at once (nice Iommi-type axe solo too). B-side *Salvador's Dream* is more like mellow Uriah Heep crossed with proggy psych. Of course, inevitably, the beat picks up, but without impressive riffing and attendant drama. Cool Iommi-like solo yet again though. Note: the band's only output besides these two singles was the ponderous, proggy but moderately professional *Firing On All Eight* on the **New Electric Warriors** comp.
Rating   7

Dealer - Better Things To Do
(Windrush '84, WR1030)

Preceding their Ebony-issued **First Strike** album by three years, this one and

only single portrays a knack for melodic Angel Witch-type melodies, which is also reinforced by the screechy metal-on-metal recording values. Both tracks lock step to the same stiff beat, the a-side being saved by a sick Witchfinder General-type twin lead, while the b-side *Suspected Foul Play* takes full advantage of Trev Short's clear Santers-style delivery. Neither track, unsurprisingly, would show up on the first and last album for the band.
Rating   7

Dedringer - Sunday Drivers
(Dindisc '80, DIN10)
B-side: *We Don't Mind* is from neither album. *Maxine* and the a-side however, are from the first album (different recording for *Sunday Drivers*), *Maxine* being a long melodic mid-paced rocker with an interesting chordal structure, while *Sunday Drivers* heavies it up a bit, pushing the band into more standard NWOBHM riffery, before lapsing back into a comfortable pub boogie zone. Cool band, accomplished, well-reasoned but perhaps a bit misnomered, much like Brit kin Rage. And it's kinda cool that *We Don't Mind* is the dark horse winner on this thing, rocking and rollicking and hooking the listener like A-II-Z's *Ringside Seat*.
Rating   6

Dedringer - Maxine
(Dindisc '80, DIN11)
B-side: *Innocent Til Proven Guilty* is offered live, thumping along like Whitesnake or heavy Foreigner, charming, really. Sticker says "Dedringer Double Pack 4 New Tracks 2 Singles For The Price Of One". Last two of the four are *Took A Long Time* and *We Don't Mind*, with the latter being a different version from that of the *Sunday Drivers* single. Nothing from the first album or indeed the second (**Second Arising**), after a break-up and reformation with a couple new members.
Rating   6

Dedringer - Direct Line
(Dindisc '81, DID7)
Had all-or-nothing expectations for this early Brit rocker that for one reason or another, escaped our grasp in the heady days of the steel revolt. No overt loss however, as Dedringer turned out to be an anemic but grudgingly acceptable rock machine, sorta like Rage (UK) or heavy Bad Company and then Thunder, simple-minded with simple concerns, more like pumped-up generalist rock than any sort of assimilator of newly dusted metal precepts. Ineffectual and common with its botched use of occasionally fine blues riffs, **Direct Line** ends life as a memorial to non-threatening pub rock, absorbing all the non-achieving affectations of those who slogged the wee stages before them. But call me a sucker for punishment, or a sympathizer for the underdog, I like it.
Rating   6

Dedringer - Direct Line
(Dindisc '81, DIN12)
The a-side is the ambitious opener to the album of the same name, combining AC/

DC and Rose Tattoo with Starfighters and Spider, iced by vocal harmonies that aspire to the Leps. B-side *She's Not Ready*, also from the album, is more of a compressed boogie with NWOBHM postures, using that specific *Tush* upgrade many bush leaguers from the genre seem to address.
Rating   7

Dedringer - Hot Lady
(Neatc '82, NEAT18)

An increasingly cool band with a nice balance between old boogie traditional and new rock punch, Dedringer chime in with two between-album non-album tracks, *Hot Lady* being a campy yet heavy enough party rocker with fat chords, rhythms and vocals, strafed by some carnal guitar work. B-side *Hot Licks And Rock 'n' Roll* is quite simply a gorgeous, almost beatific boogie. Both tracks are available on **The Neat Singles Collection Volume One**.
Rating   8

Dedringer - Second Arising
(Neat '83, 1009)

Dedringer seemed more determined to bang thy head second time around, conjuring images of bigger beat merchants like AC/DC, Quiet Riot and Dokken, while remaining dogged by their amateur grassroots grit which is more a workable accessory this time around, given the new muscle. In fact, the band had split after a car accident screwed up both of the guitar guys, only to reform, with the enclosed re-think. But the textbook bluesy rock 'n' rollsy influences are still erratically embedded, making this another "old time" record, firmly dated, unaware and garagey, an amusing, almost low-brow album accessible and timeless enough to be worth a spin every once in a classic rock while.
Rating   7

Def Leppard - The Def Leppard E.P.
(Bludgeon Riffola '79, SRTS78CUS232)

I'm only listing the pre-**Pyromania** Leps singles here (but I'll review the LP) as these are the singles truly considered to be NWOBHM artifacts, the band getting famous and less NWOBHM by the time their third album gashed a big wound in the genre. This one, also called The **Getcha Rocks Off** EP, is the grail, the initial music from the band, self-produced in November '78 and pressed under their own imprint at 1000 copies and then repressed once more for a second run (MSB001). Apparently only the first 150 have lyrics and picture sleeve. Anyway, these are cool scrappy versions of two tracks that would make it to the debut (*(Getcha) Rocks Off* rocking hard as the second a-side and *Overture* as the lone b), plus a bit of an underachiever called *Ride Into The Sun* (first a-side) heavy enough but uncommitted and aimless. This featured the band's second drummer Frank Noon, after Tony Kenning had quit the band, and vocalist Joe Elliott nicknamed as "Zeff". Doing fabulously, the EP would see two more reissues in late '79, one again as a three track and one as a two track. Prime copy has red label. Counterfeits exist.
Rating   8

Def Leppard - Wasted
(Vertigo '79, 6059247)

B-side to this is *Hello America*, both tracks competent, ready for prime time debut album compositions, both provided as early, raw versions produced by Nick Tauber and the band. Competently recorded, the performances are only a shade rough, the main difference being the considerably less metallic, less fuzzed-out guitar sound, particularly on *Hello America*, which also deletes the intro vocal harmonies. Perfectly serviceable and way above garage.

Rating 8

Def Leppard - On Through The Night
(Vertigo '80, 9102040)

The Leps were destined for fame, sounding like stadium rockers right outta the gates (not counting the raw 'n' rockscrabble **Rocks Off** EP), and rapidly getting adequate airplay and media buzz for their efforts. The band's premiere was one of the most polished and savvy of the NWOBHM brigade, descending from really out of nowhere with the class and skill of the old guard firmly in grasp, even out-stripping Maiden in its evocation of the sense of British high-mindedness earned by acts like Thin Lizzy, UFO, even Queen and Mott The Hoople, who were both heroes of the boys. Ergo, **On Through The Night** is blessed with a good Tom Allom recording (more the work of focus than good luck), universal rock 'n' roll anthems, and a uniform heaviness which courted the American way with just the right amount of self-promotion. All in all, given the tattered NWOBHM singles washing ashore, the record was a welcome breath of fresh air, an accessible and bright-shining gem plunked down in an atmosphere both sides of the Atlantic that was getting thrashy, fast, gothic, imitative or simply kinda rushed and punky. Unfortunately, Def Leppard would turn out to be one of the most pathetic sell-outs in the history of the world Part I, throwing into high relief the strengths of the debut plus follow-up **High 'n' Dry** until all us clucksters have beaten the concept to death, nattering on about Def Leppard's betrayal of metal like old ladies.

Rating 8

Def Leppard - Hello America
(Vertigo '80, LEPP1)

The a-side to this one is the album version of the band's great calling card, their prophetic anthem that proved the band was onto bigger and better stacks of cash. The b-side is the gem. *Good Morning Freedom* is an amazing, equally authoritative track, powered quickly with a sublime, almost southern rock melody, combining boogie-based NWOBHM with American stadium rock sounds of the '70s (think **California Jam**); total critical mass, star power, guitars textured to the future... it's a wonder why this track never saw greater exposure. Also an Italian issue (Vertigo 6059253) which is exceedingly rare and worth well over $100, the Japanese issue (Nippon Phonogram SFL-2485) worth maybe half that.

Rating 9

Def Leppard - Rock Brigade
(Vertigo '80, 76064)

Two album tracks here, both emitting stacks of star power, good mainstream rock with melodies and might. B-side is *When The Walls Come Tumblin' Down*, the single released three months after the debut album.

Rating 8

Def Leppard – High 'n' Dry
(Vertigo '81, 6359045)

In which the Leps continue to demonstrate their knack for catchy tunes that rage like the fine work of the English hot shots they are, primed for the road, beach and bonfire alike. **High 'n' Dry** began to reveal a penchant for space and dynamics along with a fondness for AC/DC percussive patterns amidst an ever-clarifying anthemic disposition that was simultaneously first class and so adolescent. Indeed, producer Mutt Lange had just come off of **Back In Black**, bringing with him those tappable rhythms as well as a daunting work ethic that reportedly almost killed the guys. In any event, the result was a record stacked with sturdy riffs, swooping dynamics and no lack of bravado. I mean, *Another Hit And Run*, *Let It Go*, *You Got Me Runnin'* and, most headbangingly, speedster *No No No* were on my teen playlist for months, the album as a whole quickly becoming this loud, proud, bubbling-under entity amongst anybody in high school known to tip a few brown bottles. So yeah, ultimately, **High 'n' Dry** felt like the exciting, enthusiastic work of blue collar rock fans on a mission to better themselves, and there's nothing wrong with that.
Rating   9

Def Leppard - Let It Go
(Vertigo '81, LEPP2)

Was **High 'n' Dry** the Leps' best album? Many think so, me included, although Joe Elliott dismisses it (and its fans) now as so much crap. Stellar rock anthem in the a-side, straddling AC/DC to a riffier form of stadium rock. B-side is the moody and aggressive instrumental *Switch 625*.
Rating   9

Def Leppard - Bringin' On The Heartache
(Vertigo '82, LEPP3)

A-side is a remix of the band's last good ballad while the b-side is the prophetic and harmful non-LP mid-rocker *Me And My Wine*, the single released six months after the second album. We're stopping here with the 45s, given that the next single is spiritually and intellectually distant from the NWOBHM, that being *Photograph* from **Pyromania**.
Rating   6

Def Leppard - Pyromania
(PolyGram '83, VERS2)

Superstardom arrives, and so begins what will turn out to be an unstoppable physical and creative degeneration. Musically, **Pyromania** marks a direct evolution from its stirring predecessor, however Mutt Lange's much bally-hooed production is sabotaged (in my opinion) by a disheartening over-electrolysis of the drum sound and an unwarranted, un-rock 'n' roll, painstaking approach to detail that strips what is actually a fairly heavy album of its sweat and grit. Look hard, and you'll find some more than acceptable weekend rock anthems here, as well as the preceding album's emphasis on big beat and mega-huge atmosphere, but Elliott's vocals sound strained and distantly mixed as if drowning and drowned by design. Harmonies are mechanical and mercilessly layered (I think the appropriate word is *phony*), and the overall sound is just too calculated and larger than life to rock, let alone breathe. Of

course, millions of fans might disagree (the record was officially seven times platinum by '88, certified ten times platinum in '04), but to me this marked the beginning of the odious decline to the abysmal muzak wretch that is **Hysteria**. However, you'll find no argument with glorious explosions like *Stagefright* and *Die Hard The Hunter*, both in possession of a sort of regal triumph, while even *Rock Rock ('Til You Drop)*, *Billy's Got A Gun* and *Foolin'* pulse with a sense of post-NWOBHM pride that makes you sorta meekly think perhaps it's a good idea to apply a little bit of a budget to the making of records.
Rating 7

Demolition – Hooker Hater
(Demolition Rock '81, ZELSPS296)
A-side *Hooker Hater* is one of those grim working class numbers like meat and potatoes debut-era Tygers or worse, Battleaxe. *Axeman* is similarly appointed but perhaps a bit more modern, the track helped by lots of creamy bass and a brisk groove. No second-guessing here: Demolition were solidly NWOBHM, and early into the game too. Stark, austere b+w cover art.
Rating 8

Demon - Liar
(Clay '80, CLAY4)
Demon, like Witchfynde, made little sense as a NWOBHM act, yet all those ghoulish graphics and eerily happy occult lyrics put them there but fast, despite pop, and later prog, predilection. In any event, the band's first single is this rough, hapless, endearing track, in different version to the album, this one being more intimate with a dirtier guitar sound. B-side is non-LPer *Wild Woman*, a surprising boogie woogie bar number imbued with a modicum of metal discipline. Two nice touches: red vinyl and the wild 'n' evil pre-logo, er, logo.
Rating 7

Demon - Night Of The Demon
(Carrere '81, CAL126)
These anonymous NWOBHM liggers from Staffordshire made a couple of amateurish but spirited melodic metal albums, thence switching to amateurish but spirited "thinking man's" hard rock albums, two or three of which I unfortunately own. **Night Of The Demon** is the gung-ho debut, basic, barroom black metal that betrays a band that has no idea what it takes to be rock stars, thus managing to sound cavernously depressed, doomed to stay underground and soaked to the skin like most early English nowhere-man metal-makers. Funny but so misguided it's sick, I recall **Night Of The Demon** sorta giving us the heebie jeebies at the time, for exactly that reason, this incongruous situation of a band writing a sort of dated, foreign pop metal and then singing evil stuff o'er top of it.
Rating 7

Demon- Ride The Wind
(Carrere '81, CAR185)
Graphically, this one more or less reproduces the front cover of the album. B-side is the non-LP *On The Road*, an extremely personable pop boogie road tale, closer to biker rock than it is the scourge of Beelzebub. And come to think of it, LP track *Ride The Wind* fits that description perfectly as well.
Rating   7

Demon - One Helluva Night
(Carrere '82, CAR226)
These are both album tracks (b/w *Into The Nightmare*: check out the snaky twin leads), but they are beauties, both capturing the steely grit metal that results when a band is quite sure they want to steer clear of metal clichés, or perhaps have no idea how to play to them in the first place. So what results is a curious mix of pop, '70s rock, the new metal and flirtatious occultism. File of course with Witchfynde, but even fuzzy propositions like Nightwing and Magnum. Note: *One Helluva Night* is one of the band's heaviest tracks ever, and arguably their very best riff. Cool ghoul sleeve. Also available as a picture disc 7", same cat. #.
Rating   8

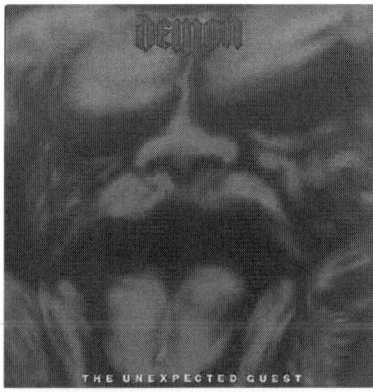

Demon - The Unexpected Guest
(Carrere '82, CAL129)
The Unexpected Guest is Demon's second sacrifice to the Gods of the Delete Bin, a record that is more of the same rudimentary black metal, with only tolerable production and only tolerable musicianship and vocals. But believe it or not it is genuinely scary and even a bit catchy due to its numbskullian insistence on providing hooks while serving your severed head to Satan in a gym bag. Guitarist and writer Malcolm Spooner, an asthmatic, is since deceased from pneumonia, to which he succumbed December '84 just prior to the release of the next record.
Rating   8

Demon - Have We Been Here Before?
(Carrere '82, CAR249)
The a-side goes way within the band's curious poppiness, placing a mysterious tale of reincarnation on a tune best suited to Pat Benatar, or at most Krokus. Strange, but strangely arresting. B-side *Victim Of Fortune* (both are album tracks, but presented here with different recordings), same thing; coulda been a Krokus or Mellenhead song if it wasn't for the sorry production or Dave Hill's histrionic whiskey vocals. Like *Ride The Wind*, this one merely mimics the source album's cover art.
Rating   6

Demon – The Plague
(Clay '83, CLAYLP6)
And so begins the weird career turn, Demon becoming an incongruous pomp band, keyboards now prominent despite the sound-scarring vocals of Dave Hill and the brash production values obscuring each subtlety. Lyrically and visually, Demon have dropped the dark stuff but unbeknownst to them, gotten darker with this uneasy, pan-world surreal bit they had saddling them

sadly now. If there's a human connectivity attempted here, it's failed badly, Demon sounding a million miles away and lonely in that place, Magnum passing by occasionally with a laconic wave, Marillion laughing from their career trajectory.
Rating   5

Demon - The Plague
(Clay '83, 25)
More deliberately addressing their prog streak, this lengthy title track from Demon's third album (different recording though) introduces keyboards in a big way, along with breaks, sweet melodies, with the same tough production and vocals. Strangely depressing (uh, must be the title). B-side *The Only Sane Man* is a theatrical piano ballad that must have been chosen in hopes of some sort of accidental *Beth* situation (i.e. radio starts playing the b-side). We're cutting it off here, due to the next single being late and even less NWOBHM, *Wonderland* (b/w *Blackheath*) being launched as a pre-release single to **British Standard Approved** over a year past this single, and a good five months prior to that album.
Rating   9

Demon Pact - Eaten Alive
(Slime '81, PACT1)
That's the spirit, Bromley, Kent's Demon Pact donning the leathers and choking the NWOBHM with their own brand of industrial wasteland atmosphere. Never mind that vocalist Donald Meckliffe sounds like a snotty punk rocker, 'cos the band has found a couple of good, grimly fiendish riffs to wrap around *Eaten Alive* and b-side *Raiders* ("You're one of the raiders. So am I!"). Note: only other output was the track *Escape* (a typically soiled AC/DC/Jess-era Tygers rocker for the band) on the stratospherically expensive **Kent Rocks** compilation. Cool red and silver record label.
Rating   8

Denigh - No Way
(Ace '80, ACE16)
This perennial back-up band from Kent was in operation for five years, cranking only this game and gamey Jaguar/Tysondog type single, *No Way* being one of those chaotic bush league rock rides, while b-side *Running* is more of a melodic mid-metal thumper with decent twin leads, vocal melodies and a raucous traditional guitar solo that makes me think of Ross The Boss or Andy McCoy. Look for the odd guitar surges which sound like electric waves crashing the shores of some dreary English b-city. Rumour has it much more output languishes, and indeed, the band at one time would burn you a CDR with 12 tracks spanning their career if you ask them nicely. Never issued with a picture sleeve. OK, update on that CDR talk from five years back: the good folks at Iron Pages have now issued the archival stuff on an 11 track CD called **Fire In The Sky**.
Rating   7

Desolation Angels - Valhalla
(Thames '83, AM266)
Valhalla's this band's only single, but then again, there's the incredibly desirable self-titled LP from '86, from which this song hails, albeit in a different version. But the track at hand is an odd mix of mournful and regular working class metal, grim like menacing Saxon perhaps, with a blustery twin guitar crunch. Goes on forever, as many of their tracks are wont to do. B-side is the non-LP *Bodecia*, a pedestrian evil woman track, but heavy enough. So yeah, quite a dark, distinctive, drawn-out style from these guys. Like Crucifixion and Grim Reaper, Desolation Angels have consistently promoted the grim reaper in their visuals.
Rating   9

Desperate Oates – Burning Alive
(Heavy Mental '82, no cat#)
A Lincolnshire power trio with nicknames playing unapologetic boogie metal, unsurprising, given that the leader of the band was a Vardis fan and roadie. B-sides were called *Why You Do It* and *Boogie Toon*.
Rating 4

Destroyer - Evil Place
(Clean Kill/Clubland '81, SJP829)
Another one of those nowhere bands with one single and that's it, London's Destroyer rocked hard and well-heeled, save for the slight new wave snarl in vocalist Rob Osborn. *Evil Place* actually has groove and more than acceptable production values, while b-side *Stand And Deliver* contains a visceral and textured double time, double bass chorus. Something that was definitely worth developing. Ghoulish and foolish skull label art.
Rating 8

Diamond Head - Shoot Out The Lights
(Happy Face '80, MMDH120)
The inaugural single for Diamond Head is of course rare, but the track *Shoot Out The Lights* has shown up on a good half dozen reissues and compilations, albeit not in this early boogie groove version. It's an odd underachiever built on a hard rocky, arguably AC/DC-ish riff, a typical b-side for this band with lots of album tracks that should have been b-sides. *Helpless* is of course the actual b-side, although it is the fraught riff racer from the debut album, here in its original tentative garage rock form, as is this early version of the a-side. Note: this white label single was mainly sold at gigs and through ads in hallowed UK rock paper Sounds.
Rating 7

Diamond Head - Sweet & Innocent
(Media '80, SCREEN1)
Single #2 was *Sweet & Innocent*, produced by Robin George (clunkier than the album version), a typical mid-paced rocker clinging to a surprisingly naff riff with cool harmonies come chorus time. Non-LPer *Streets Of Gold* was a sinister early rocker with some zip built into its Purple/Priest inspired riff, perhaps one of the band's best early non-LP tracks. Cool pre-logo sleeve.
Rating 7

Diamond Head - Lightning To The Nations
(Happy Face '80, MMDHLP1015)
Diamond Head was eminently worthy of the critical praise and legendary status heaped upon their unsuspecting shoulders, yet it's hard to articulate what lent the band's case such immediate psychological impact. This debut (originally self-financed on the band's own Happy Face label, with each copy signed by the band) crashed headlong into the NWOBHM, offering little in the way of agility or readily identifiable personal traits throughout its hypnotic, dark and messed-up tour, except perhaps the expressive, vocal presence of Sean Harris and the sturdy, earthy quality of Brian Tatler's riffs. The product of four years as a band, **Lightning To The Nations** embodies a foreboding bellwether sound doomed to abject failure, as if the band were

creating a confused monster in a dark void, picking up none of the good or bad habits of the then-exploding metal scene in Britain. **Lightning** was to become the band's most squarely metallic effort, with long ugly songs rumbling on like massive thundering jam sessions nobody knew how to stop. In some ways, it's a decidedly unprofessional debut; in others, it's a serious, soul-destroying effort of dark alchemical art, all the more twisted due to its accidental, imploding, doomy and doomed nature.
Rating 9

Diamond Head - Waited Too Long
(DHM '81, DHM004)
Kinda cool that neither of these were LP tracks, and major cool that *Play It Loud*, despite its cheese title is a sharp rocker, an improvement on the *It's Electric* premise with a dark little break, lustful enough drive and impassioned vocals from Sean Harris. *Waited Too Long* is a perky popster, the band no doubt trawling for a hit. Nice harmonies come chorus time, and in general, quite a nice attempt at the genre.
Rating 8

Diamond Head - Four Cuts
(MCA '82, DHM101)
This EP is comprised of er, four cuts, *Call Me* being the dark, elegant and insidious album track from **Borrowed Time**, another stab at pop metal, second a-side being *Trick Or Treat*, a rousing rumbler built on a vaguely '50s-ish convention but metalized with the band's usual lethargic drum and guitar sound. Pure accidental NWOBHM magic. The b-side sports a couple more non-LP tracks, *Dead Reckoning*, which is a debut-style dark horse rocker, and *Shoot Out The Lights* which we've talked about above. Note I: label is the band's proper modern logo in the band's purple. Cool live shot of the band on the back sleeve. Note II: Also released in 12" format with inferior artwork (DHMT101). Note III: there was also a US 7" release of *Call Me* with *Lightning To The Nations* as its b-side (52161).
Rating 8

Diamond Head - Borrowed Time
(MCA '82, DH1001)
Borrowed Time was supposed to put Diamond Head over the top, but one listen and it's obvious why most of the record-buying public just didn't get it at all. **Borrowed Time** clunks slowly, defiantly anti-social and depressing in its defeatist, lifeless approach to musicianship and song construction, as if the band were issuing some sort of timid protest at being heralded as the new Zeppelin. Still the album absolutely hypnotizes me, evoking through willful stupidity, the dark undercurrents only hinted at on the debut's angst-ridden rockers. **Borrowed Time** comes across as a sorrowful blues record caught in the downward vortex of some sort of unknowable black metal, the product of a band glumly self-destructing in full knowledge of the consequences. Of the seven included tracks, two are re-carves of classics from the debut, leaving only five new, unsure, and sickly cuts to carry the heavy load. All in all, it was obvious why this was a commercial disaster, but looking at it abstractly and perhaps from an obtuseness that only a metalhead could conjure, **Borrowed Time** becomes a beautiful, rainy expression of doomy Sabbatherian sadness, an evaluation that may be quite off the mark, yet proof of the adage that one's interpretation of art may be as valid as the artist's intentions themselves. First issue was swanky gatefold with poster.
Rating 8

Diamond Head - In The Heat Of The Night
(MCA '82 DHM102)
Here we find the sweeping album track from **Borrowed Time** backed with a carnal live rendition of *Play It Loud*. Note: there's also a 12" version of this (DHMT102) and a limited edition double 7" with gatefold that adds a 14-minute Tommy Vance interview with Sean Harris and Colin Kimberly, plus *Sweet And Innocent* live (cat.# for the second 7" is MSAM23). The gatefold sports the British tour dates and a brief band history written by Sean. Cute lavender logo labels.
Rating   7

Diamond Head - Canterbury
(MCA '83)
This ponderous but interesting re-wiring of the Diamond Head persona provides the band's third shift of philosophy in three albums, conjuring a mix of styles, including more acoustic guitar, more complexity, more self-importance, and heaps more production. **Canterbury** (originally titled Night Of The Swords), is more the product of the Diamond Head known as tireless Rush fans who could spend seemingly endless hours in soundchecks pouring over **2112** (true story). All this fussy, baroque readjustment makes for a record that is still an eerie Diamond Head experience, dark and sparse, while the variety of styles almost contemptuously attempted makes it also the most listenable and provocative. Career-wise however, **Canterbury** became the road to nowhere, as no one but the band itself seemed to buy the line that Diamond Head would save the world from fake or base rock 'n' roll. By '85 the original band had dissolved (very close to having finished a fourth record called **Flight East**), a victim of internal ego struggles and external management rip-offs, never really getting the chance to define its sound and reach its potential.
Rating   7

Diamond Head - Makin' Music
(MCA '83, DHM103)
This one, released August of '83, showed up in 7" and 12" versions (DHMT103) with a nice, clear, long interview with Andy Peebles as a b-side. *Makin' Music* is another one of the band's understated, stiff rockers full of space and restraint, a type of hard rock that second-guesses someone's idea of a hit during this confusing metallic time.
Rating   7

Diamond Head - Out Of Phase
(MCA '83, DHM104)
Diamond Head go all experimental on these two **Canterbury** tracks, *Out Of Phase* being a jump popster, innovative but daringly happy, while *The Kingmaker* points to the band's "new Zeppelin" direction, all fussy, over-arranged and under-recorded, blocky and choppy like all of the band's output. Note: 12" version (DHMT104) drops *The Kingmaker* and adds a rip and tear nine minute live at Reading '82 version of *Sucking My Love*, which is in fact the a-side, which means you may as well call it a different product, despite similarities including the same

cover art. 7" version also came in picture disc format (DHMP104).
Rating   6

Di'Anno – Di'Anno
(Heavy Metal '84, WKFMLP1)
Never one to pass up a paycheck, our favourite ex-Maiden yobbo Paul Di'Anno forsakes his punk roots back beyond his semi-compromise into metal, and makes an AOR record, one that he now laughs about good-naturedly, with a roll of the eyes and probably a wink and a lie or two. For British AOR it actually wasn't that bad (better 'n Alaska, geez), punchy, hummable, not terribly recorded, immediate and tasty like fast food. And if you're up for these sorts of futile pastimes, this is actually one of the places where you can hear some of the best pure singing from the loveable book-collecting thug.
Rating   5

Di'Anno – Heartuser
(FM Revolver '84, VHF1)
Here's ol' Paul trying his hand at AOR, even farther from his punk roots than Maiden was (note: different version form album). Happily, there was only one record under this moniker and philosophy. *Heartuser* finds the man downright behaved over a standard pre-hair plodder while b-side *Road Rat* rocked a little bolder and dare I say progressive, uptempo if not a mite too sprightly, once again Paul sounding nothing like the leonine roaring Paul we all love. Note: King Records in Japan also released a *Flaming Hearts/Don't Let Me Be Misunderstood* single the same year.
Rating   5

Dragonfly – E.P.
(Dragonfly '80, DF001)
This eminently collectible EP contains four tracks which demonstrate versatility, square NWOBHM values and some degree of brains. Opener *Silent Nights* is a Satan/Wildfire-style medium to brisk rocker, full-on NWOBHM, mildly OTT (if one can still use that term 25 years past expiry!). *Mercy* follows up in that charming low budget junk style, sort of faltering, stiff, but raised by some nice guitar licks and a dual twin lead. *Spacebound* kicks off with more twin lead, although, unsurprisingly, it's a spacey power ballad, menaced by turgid chords. Finally, *Disappear From View* closes the show with a speed metal flourish, cheap, endearing but sincerely new metal rockin'.
Rating   8

Dragonslayer - I Want Your Life
(Cavalier '83, CAV017)
Dragonslayer (initially Slayer, even up to the point where they had to sticker over their single!) can only claim this three track 7" to their name, on top of a few sampler/comp.

appearances. Totally swilling pints with the best of the middle tier, the band had a bombastic show for a band on their budget and climbed their way through the underground. *I Want Your Life* is an ambitious obtuse riffster with a whiff of funk, while *Satan Is Free* is a no-nonsense machine gun chugger like a million other worthy NWOBHM classics. Closing out, we've got a horrendous lead-weight ballad called *Broken Hearts* which manages to expose all of the band's faults, all minor but there nonetheless, having to do mostly with recording, drumming and vocals.
Rating   8

Dragster - Ambitions
(Heavy Metal '81, HEAVY4)
One of three Heavy Metal Records singles that deliberately go for cheapness, this one's got the one colour indie look with bonus Japanese writing (although they're all stamped prominently "Made In England"). In case you're wondering, that's a skull fitted with handlebars. Into the music, and Dragster's *Ambitions* was a hapless, awkward, three-legged brown rocker with vocals mixed so far back it sounds like a mistake. B-side *Won't Bring You Back* is obviously from the same sessions and is a meandering pointless power ballad with a salvageable riff and of course, a moderately blustery metal break. Can be found with both blue and brown labels. Only other output was S&M track *Do It* on the **Heavy Metal Heroes** compilation. Both of these also showed up on the 1996 British Steel **Heavy Metal Records Singles Collection Vol.1**.
Rating   4

Driveshaft - Heartbreaker
(Undercover '82, D.C. 003)
Middlingly heavy one here (er, they might be Irish; if so, I'm breaking an inclusion rule here—sorry). *Heartbreaker* cooks along with solid NWOBHM values, despite a vaguely retro Canadian hard rockiness. B-side is even more of a glam boogie number called *Now That It's Over*, its 1973-ness revolving around Mott, Quo, Slade, Kiss and Humble Pie.
Rating   7

Driveshaft - Live Cutz
(Revolving '84, REV 004)
No surprise that by '84 Driveshaft had heavied up their sound, issuing this mildly amusing 12", consisting of *Let It Rock*, *Stepping Stone* and *Take A Chance On Me*, each of which feature the uncommonly strong vocals of Gerry Lane (think Teaze's Brian Danter) and an overall sound that touches on the blues tinge of Samson, especially *Take A Chance On Me*, which is a rote heavy stripper blues.
Rating   7

Dutchess - Your Love
(Blitzkrieg Waxworks '81, EJSP 9580)
A-side *Your Love* is a competent enough power ballad with two metal breakdowns, good vocalist, tasty soloing, modulation, a relaxed groove all around. B-side *Dead And Gone* is a proudly rockin' affair that reminds me of prime Samson crossed with shoot 'em up Ted Nugent. Some of Dutchess moved on to Bombay and the hideous Rio. Non-picture sleeve but with ominous yet indie silver on black label. Label places this skilled and heavy artifact in early '81, February to be exact.
Rating   8

Dumpy's Rusty Nuts – Just For Kicks
(Cool King '82, CK006)
Graham "Dumpy" Dunnell's first single, after a transition from the bluesy Dirt Band. True to form garage rock with strong biker clichés. B-side is called *Ride With Me*. Killer cover art featuring a bunch of bikers all lined up and a big incredulous Dumpy projected onto a building.
Rating   7

Dumpy's Rusty Bolts - Dumpy's 2nd Single
(Coolking '82, CK008)
Biker dude and ex-Rivvits guy Dumpy actually started this thing as Dumpy's Rusty Nuts, but changed it to get more airplay. The sound remained the same however, a blue collar barroom boogie sound that is prevalent on both included tracks *Boxhill Or Bust!* and *It's Got To Be The Blues*, both sounding like mid-swill Quo with happy singalong choruses. Both would later show up live on the band's debut album. Single comes with a low budget "bikers patch."
Rating   7

with likeminded originals like *Boxhill Or Bust!* (amusing all-regions intro) and the Vardis redux of I'm A Hog For You Baby. Still, there's electricity and power in the performance and the mix and a good time is had by all. Plus it vibes like Edgar Broughton Band at Greasy Truckers.
Rating   6

Dumpy – Rock The Nation E.P.
(Landslide '84)
Changing names again to the ill-advised Dumpy, this spot of product is comprised of the title track, *Nothing To Lose* and *Hot Lover*, highlight being *Hot Lover* with its Spinal Tap stomp refreshingly away from boogie.
Rating   6

Dumpy's Rusty Nuts – Somewhere In England
(Landslide '84, LDLP 101)
This double live LP was reissued in '86 on Gas Music, but both versions are rare on the ground. The lineup at this point is Dumpy, bassist Kerry Langford and none other than Tank's Mark Brabbs on drums, a configuration of the band that would last a good three years. Pretty, ahem, patchy set though, with the likes of *Tush*, Wild Thing and *Route 66* rubbing epaulets

Eazie Ryder – Motorbikin'
(Graduate '78, GRAD1)
Early entry here, but then again, there's a hint of the new metal to come from this Midlands no man's lander, especially with the likes of Vardis, Spider and Dumpy's Rusty Nuts populating a vibrant boogie corner of the genre a couple years hence. Then there's the motorcycle on the cover. Vocalist Geoff Bate would resurface for Quartz's brooding **Against All Odds** album from '83. A-side is a Chris Spedding cover, also recorded by Rogue Male. All told, it's a tough enough riffster with an uneasy Johnny Thunders vibe to it. B-side is called *City Lights*.
Rating 6

EF Band – Another Day Gone
(ROK '79, ROK XI/ROK XII)
Swedish-UK transplant EF Band's first product (or E.F. Band, formally speaking here) is this split with power popsters Syncromesh, with the EF band contribution being a dated, boogie-based hard rocker like a mild an' rootsy Ted Nugent/Blackfoot/Moxy song better left back at the bars.
Rating 4

EF Band – Self Made Suicide
(Redball '80, RR026)
Kick-ass rocker *Self Made Suicide* once more finds EF Band riffing on Thunderbird like Ted Nugent, although now we're moving on up into the metal of *Stormtroopin'*. B-side *Sister Syne* begins with a stomp and a slide, thenceforth collapsing into a trashy BTO-type thing with stacked power chords but not much imagination save for the much heavier chorus and the aggressive drums throughout. Squarely metal, and a big part of why these guys are considered the top honourary NWOBHM band among baby acts.
Rating 8

EF Band – Devil's Eye
(Redball '80)
By this point EF band were playing live with the likes of Angel Witch and on the verge of getting tapped to appear on the first **Metal For Muthas**, solid, smart compositions like this a-side and its instrumental b-side *Comprende* helping build a buzz. Reissued once the band signed to Mercury.
Rating 7

EF Band – Night Angel
(Aerco '80, E.F. 1)
Two tracks here that were first suggested for ROK (who did indeed issue b-side *Another Day Gone* for the above split), and now getting their due through a licensing arrangement, no doubt to the rising status of the band in the underground. In any event, those Ted Nugent riffs are still attendant, only this time there's a strange proggy texture to the band's approach. Note: label says '79, but that's likely just a reference to the ROK connection, given that the front of the sleeve sez "As featured on the EMI "Metal For Muthas" album."
Rating 7

EF Band – The Last Laugh Is On You
(Mercury '81, 6362 076)
Sweden's EF Band (named for the last initials of the two founding members, if you care) got their first break as an inclusion on early, legendary compilation **Metal For Muthas**, the band having set up shop in the UK to participate in the exploding metal scene, two indie singles on Redball

garnering buzz. But before that, two of the three dudes had a one record prog band called Epizootic, which is where they must have gathered the chops to put together such an accomplished first full-length. Forsooth, **The Last Laugh Is On You** is one of the unsung records of the movement, modern at times, at others hearkening back to complex '70s rock maneuvers, even a bit of a Krautrock vibe, but at the harder boogie and Purple-derived end of it. In fact, the band ended up touring Europe as support to Rainbow, further testimony to a deserved upward swing.
Rating   7

EF Band - Deep Cut
(Ewita '83, LSPLP103)

The EF Band's second was a near classic chunk of rock royalty from the very origins of the NWOBHM, even if the band were always only, by origin, a satellite member. Smart, well-recorded retro-metal with just that touch of fragility that results in spontaneity, nicely low-budget sounding and experimental in scope, **Deep Cut** kicks off with its best foot forward in *Love Is A Game*, a galloping romp that recalls both early Quartz an' golden-era Samson. From hereon in, we get touches of pop, blues, and in the best cases, melodic hard rock, all delivered with rumbling, scrappy edge and disdain for posturing, set spinning beneath the fine, Sean Harris-style pipes of new vocalist, Englishman John Ridge (Ridge was to leave shortly, after dates with Saxon). One of those independent works that sounds like British rock vets slamming their way through a friendly, relaxed jam session just for the fun of it; ergo, eminently nostalgic and playable.
Rating   9

Emerson - Something Special
(Neat '83, NEAT34)

Here's one of those anonymous bands Neat was trying to propose as a viable pop metal option. To their credit, Neat was quick to realize the importance of hair bands, but neither their studio nor their acts were equipped to handle the sheen required to rival the Americans, not to mention England's own Def Leppard. As a result, *Something Special* is a sturdy enough Santers song with a brashness too stark for general consumption. *Stars On Hollywood* is better, especially with that cool Lizzy-like solo. Label features a crude drawing of Marilyn Monroe.
Rating   8

Energy - Energised
(Bips '80, Beck 927)

Tracks are *No-Go*, *Don't Show Your Face*, *Spoilt Child* and *Lovely Lady* with the sound from this Northamptonshire band early on being a little retro, pre-NWOBHM.
Rating   4

Energy - E.P. II
(GRN '81, GRN1)

Tracks are *Conquer The World*, *Make It* and *Law Breaker*. Red label with wicked, jagged band logo. Heavier, more modern

sound, with highlight being *Conquer The World*, a languid and proggy epic with a very "wet" recording. Closing off, *Make It* is a little funky, with a tasty Robin Trower-styled riff, while *Lawbreaker* offers yet another style, a bit of a heavy metal Knack or Cheap Trick directive. Nice versatility, all told.
Rating 7

Energy – Nowhere To Hide
(Aros '83, Aros11233)
B-side is called *Fight For Your Freedom*, which is a pretty darn impressive speed metaller that resurfaced on the **NWOBHM Vol. 5** bootleg CD, Energy coming across as melodic, fast, slightly chopsy, like an unrealized Satan, even if the a-side goes kinda sour with an excess of commercial melody, verging on the post-punk. Hilarious label art, with a vocalist giving 'er the heavy metal fist. Manufactured in France. After this, two more singles were unleashed (but after our cut-off date of '85), '85's *Too Good To Lose* and '86's *Radio Radio*, both on Aros Records.
Rating 8

E.S.P. – Another Way
(Gargoyle '81, GRGL783)
B-side is called *The Poem*, and is a bit of spoken word silliness, although the a-side is a solid rocker. Non-picture sleeve.
Rating 6

Ethel The Frog – Eleanor Rigby
(Best '78, SRTS/FMR014)
This fringe NWOBHM act seemed to have a distinctly bed-headed British disposition, their lone LP capturing the early darkness that was the new sound. The first version of the band's Beatles-penned single is backed with *Whatever Happened To Love*, also on the lone album, but there re-recorded. The b-side is an urgent, punky riff rocker with a whiff of the ol' Hawkwind. Non-picture sleeve.
Rating 6

Ethel The Frog - Ethel The Frog
(EMI '80, EMC3329)
Ethel The Frog sat right in the punted thick of the first wave of NWOBHM bands, yet suffered from a lack of press, due no doubt in part to their confusing moniker (not to be confused with bathwater popsters Toad The Wet Sprocket). It all added to the mystery of this uncommunicative debut, which is essentially a well-recorded album of barroom boogie mixed with dense, traditional, and usually depressing British metal directives, rising to the challenge with more energetic numbers such as *Apple Of Your Eye* and classy rocker *Fight Back* which scored a minor hit for the band, also appearing on genre kick-off compilation **Metal For Muthas**. Strange record, one which mixes elements of Quo, old heavy Zep, maybe early Moxy (!), old Deep Purple, and other things old, bass-driven, laid-back and stodgy. It's an album I respect but rarely play due to its ability to depress me every time. But what an album cover, so seductive in both collectible and metal ways.
Rating 7

Ethel The Frog - Eleanor Rigby
(EMI '80, 5041)
This single culls two tracks from the album, actually two of the best, a-side being their chugging rendition of the lonely Beatles classic with *Fight Back* being their marquee hit, all glide, drive and groove, melody and swagger. Heavy and classy stuff, better for the fact that the band somehow didn't get it, somehow sounded outside of time. Two singles and one album, that's it, with *Fight Back* propping up the duds on the landmark first **Metal For Muthas**. Note: a few of these were picture sleeve (reproducing the elegant cover art) but most weren't.
Rating   6

Everyone Else - Schooldays
(Woodbine St. '79, WSR001)
The tracks on this Midlands band's lone release are the title track, *Brainwashed*, *Don't Call Us* and *Out Of My Mind*. Unsurprisingly, given its date and budget, the sound is punky, rudimentary pre-NWOBHM only. Issued in picture sleeve.
Rating   3

Explorer - Exploding
(Dids '84, RSR006)
Formed by two Chinatown guys, Explorer played a similar commercial NWOBHM style, angling toward Wildfire, Shy, Stampede, Nightwing, but quite relentlessly guitary, although of a sort of chimy neo-prog Saga variety. Still, it's a pretty heavy collection of eight tracks, a bit anemic of recording, but mostly brisk and rocking all the same. After becoming Exxplorer for a brief spell, the band split, two of the gents moving on to form After Dark.
Rating   6

Expozer - Exposed At Last
(Hit Hard '80, HARD1)
Single was called **Exposed At Last**, but the a-side is *Rock Japan* (Tommy Vance-endorsed), a groovy, chummy chunk of modest Krokus boogie with a strange mellow break, backed with *On My Knees* which is a heavier, rowdier blast of biker metal blessed with a simple but effective riff. The a-side can also be found on the **Heavy Metal Heroes** comp from '81, reissued with the second volume on one CD by British Steel in '97. Issued in picture sleeve.
Rating   7

Expozer - Exposed At Last
(Hit Hard '80, HARD1)
Oddly, there is a much rarer four track version of the **Exposed At Last** single, with an additional two songs not even named, but essentially more aggressive, meat-and-potatoes metal of a barroom nature, notwithstanding the twin leads. This was not issued in picture sleeve and may not have even been sold commercially at all.
Rating   7

Ezy Meat - Not For Wimps
(Electric Storm/S.R.S. '84, ES001)
Ezy Meat were an Irish act that unfortunately didn't get product out until '84, when the band's three and a half year old batch of songs had already been rendered past due date. Still, despite the sorta '81 vibe of these songs, there's a gritty biker vibe that props them up, welling up from the very electric guitar tones and the ragged Jess Cox-like vocals. Highlights might be *Freedom Seeker* and more so *Vampire Lady*, which leans Dark Star and Maiden of gallop, with much of the rest evoking the boozy pint-swill of Dumpy's Rusty Nuts.
Rating   6

F

Factory – You Are The Music... We Are Just The Band
(Future Earth '82, FER011)
The a-side is a wildly inappropriate cover of the funky Trapeze track, very non-NWOBHM, badly played produced and especially sung. B-side *The History Of The Turkey* shows how and why a track like the a-side gets chosen, proving equally eccentric, sort of a pop metaller with a nice twin lead riff and new wavey chords come verse time. Both are featured on Mausoleum's **Metal Prisoners** sampler, as Mausoleum had a deal that saw them issue selected Future Earth product. Toneless vocals on both though. Silver die-cut sleeve. Future Earth also issued singles by Limelight and Chinawite.
Rating   6

False Idols – Ten Seconds To Midnight
(Caveman '81)
With False Idols being a bit to the punk side, the sea is also muddied by the fact that there was an even more punky band of the same name plying their trade around England at pretty much the same time. B-side is called *American Nightmare*.
Rating   4

Fastway – Easy Livin'
(CBS '83, A3196)
Almost too bold, America-ready, Def Leppard-proud and plain happy to be considered NWOBHM, Fastway was of course the post-Motörhead assemblage put together by Fast Eddie and Pete Way (you will notice he is already gone), featuring new wonder shrieker Dave King and old Humble Pie drummer Jerry Shirley. This single features two shoot 'em up album tracks (b-side being stripper gallop number *Say What You Will*, also a hit single), released a month before the launch of the fairly successful debut. It comes housed in a six panel poster sleeve with shots of the three guys, Pete Way, or any form of bassist for that matter, being conspicuously absent (apparently bass on the album was played by the now deceased Mickey Feat). 12" version (A133196) includes non-LPer *Far Far From Home*.
Rating   10

Fastway – Fastway
(Columbia '83, 25359)
A classic and accomplished debut, featuring 19-year-old wonder throat from Ireland Dave King, whose most bodacious shriek resembles that of early Plant, while stylistically blazing a trail that has soaked up more than a few ideas from the adjacent and recent rising of metal. Legendary ex-UFO souse Pete Way was of course supposed to be on board (hence, Fastway), but the guy up and left the band shortly after conception for an ill-fated liaison with Ozzy, who sacked the man after one tour. Nonetheless, Fastway wrote and red-line recorded a consistently smokin' album of traditional metal, traditional less in a British or European sense, more in the spirit of heady American highs, like updated and inspired Ted Nugent or Aerosmith—weighty, proud, rumbling yet clean. Other elements flirting the edges included adapted, Led Zeppelin-twisted blues (plus attendant Bonham drum sound), as heard on minor hit *Say What You Will*, plus traces of Sabbath in brooding duo *Heft!* and *We Become One*, a song of rock 'n' roll bravado if there ever was one. Throughout each rich metal hybrid, the delivery is kept spontaneous and warm, somewhat hard rock versus actual metal, with missionary,

starry-eyed focus that is singular and intense. Right out of the blocks, Fastway makes its shrill presence known, with a lusty debut that was a timeless slice of intrusive guitar machinery on par with the hallowed reputations of its many influences, first record loud 'n' proud in the spirit of Montrose and Van Halen. Close to gold in the US, fueled and fired by tour dates third on the bill to Saxon and Iron Maiden.
Rating 10

Fastway - We Become One
(CBS '83, A3480)
This heaving and doomy Sabbatherian classic is presented along with with the non-LP *Crazy Dream*, a menacing mid-paced rocker, albeit with a bit of a lackluster riff. US version (04112) is backed with non-LP *Back In The Game*, which is very similar to *Say What You Will*, actually, but without the confident star power. UK 12" version (TA3480) includes this track as well.
Rating 8

Fastway - All Fired Up
(CBS '84, 25958)
All Fired Up's title track revs up the old Harley where the debut left off, slamming into gear as King calls all headbangers to gather 'round and raise eyebrows and pints to the stadium rock potential of his bad-ass band. Unfortunately it's all downhill from there, **All Fired Up** committing all sorts of gaffs, including too much boring, blues-based material such as *Telephone*, *Non-Stop Love* and *Hurtin' Me*, amidst too many sleepy, failed hard rock riffs, most notably lead single *Tell Me* (basically an inferior copy of *Say What You Will*), and the painful, almost Scottish-sounding boogie(?) of *Station*, which goes for a time signature-challenged Zeppelin, ending up with a jig instead. Additionally, there are traces of insipid balladry, pointing to a discernible element of commercial panic. The recording and delivery swagger much like the debut – no beef there – so it all comes down around the sweet and sour songs, as if the first two albums were recorded in one session and somebody said "Keep this half, throw the rest out," the discards becoming **All Fired Up**. But hey, it's Fastway and there are other salvageables, f'rinstance the metallic *If You Could See* and a Zep-quality bloozer called *Misunderstood* propping the record at least to the point that it deserves to hang with the debut, rather than the ensuing rest of the increasingly crappy catalogue.
Rating 6

Fastway – All Fired Up
(CBS '84, A4503)
The a-side is hands-down the best, most NWOBHM track on the band's disappointing second album of the same name. B-side *Hurtin' Me* is also from the album, and is a raw, ponderous, wholly unattractive slow blues that is way more Great White than it is Zeppelin. Non-picture sleeve. As well, *All Fired Up* was released as a 12". Note: we're mercifully cutting it off for ol' Eddie right there, as the band would tank badly after the first two albums (not to mention the fact that we get past our cut-off date).
Rating 6

Firebird – Change
(Rat '80, CUS576)
Keyboardy white metal (Christian) band produced by Ian Gillan at his own Kingsway studio. B-side is called *Nightride*. Apparently only 50 pressed. Issued in picture sleeve. Quite hilarious actually, *Change* pulsating to full-on church organ and the most amusing vocal

mumble, before picking up a head of sticky, claustrophobic steam, church organ dreadfully intact. *Nightride* features more of the same Sunday morning keyboard work, over a poppy ballad that might have been salvaged into something useful at the hands of another band, preferably a new wave one from Manchester. It too has a fast bit, which I suppose is why anybody at all calls this NWOBHM.
Rating   4

Fireclown – Invasion
(Fireclown '83, FC1001)
Manchester's Fireclown created a glorious din, the a-side of their 10" single howling into play with a guitar solo before the song begins proper, *Invasion* sounding like smart Holocaust. Unfortunately b-side *Poor Man* is a dark NWOBHM power ballad, funereal, stormy, five minutes long and longing, definitely anticlimactic after the self-assured rumble of the a-side.
Rating   7

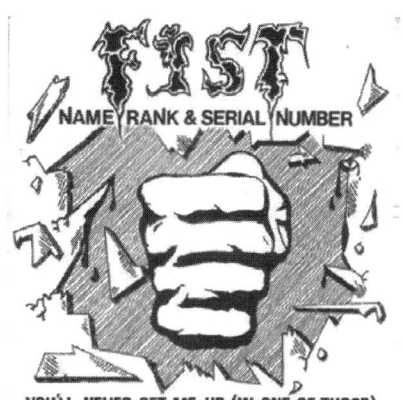

Fist - Name, Rank And Serial Number
(Neat '80, NEAT04)
Fist's first single found the band chomping right into the M in NWOBHM, rocking hard and early if not a tad punkified, especially the wayward but lustified vocals of Keith Satchfield, eventually replaced by Glenn Coates. B-side *You'll Never Get Me Up (In One Of Those)* is also from the first LP and is a high alcohol content OTT'er, kinda like Tank but so Fist because of those vocals. Produced by Mickey Sweeney at Impulse, this one gives you a forlorn band photo on the back, as well as the lyric to the a-side. Both tracks were revived for **The Neat Single Collection Volume One**, 42 tracks and two CDs of crash bang wallop, with **Volume Two** adding another 39!. Note: issued by Neat in April of 1980 (some with small poster; different recording to album versions) and then in June by MCA as MCA615.
Rating   7

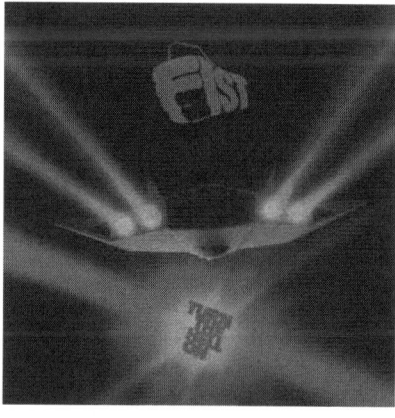

Fist - Turn The Hell On
(MCA '80, MCF3082)
Fist's debut album (not to be confused with the Canadian fist, renamed Myofist for the US) rocked with an attitude and pride that put most of these fighting tunes over the top in the spirit of boastfully delivered rough 'n' roll, if not in terms of originality or recording finesse. Not as life-sustaining as the follow-up, **Turn The Hell On** nevertheless sports some choice no-frills hard rock such as lead track *Hole In The Wall Gang* and minor hit in Britain, *Forever Amber*. Fist was another example of the fact that among the amateur metal that polluted the early '80s, the British stuff held up much better over time versus the stroke-inducing, faddish stateside product. Don't know why, but I think it's got something to do with the fact that there was simply less of it, and that the Brits were slower to leap all over the sword and sorcery, violence and leather clichés that ruined so much Shrapnel and Metal Blade flak. In any event, Fist evokes rockin' out in the basement, offering something personable and pintable and charming in these times of complete metal profusion.
Rating   7

Fist - Forever Amber
(MCA '80, 640)

This was Fist's most successful a-side, a friendly rocker that combines boogie, meat-and-potatoes rock, AOR and a nice pint-sipping chorus. B-side *Brain Damage* (a non-LPer that showed up on the **Brute Force** comp.) is another matter. One of the band's heaviest tracks, this one sounds like friggin' Race Against Time's *Bedtime* crossed with Mercyful Fate, vocalist Keith Satchfield soiling the tune real metal-like with his gutter-sniped vocals.
Rating 9

Fist - Collision Course
(MCA '81, 663)

A-side *Collision Course* is track #3 on the band's debut album, and is an attempt to take things up and over the pubs a bit, being a ponderous ballad with greater than average electric sizzle and a nice UFO-ish guitar break. But with this album's raw and ear-splitting recording, it comes off sounding like Shiva or Demon. Non-LP b-side *Law Of The Jungle* rips along tidily, not without bits of humour, once more, proving that this was a band distinguished by exuberant vocal stylings.
Rating 7

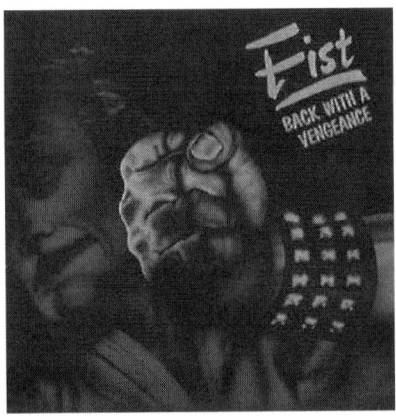

Fist - Back With A Vengeance
(Neat '82, 1003)

Britain's answer to metal's foremost concert gesture was an original NWOBHM gutter rock combo that combined low-budget punkiness with traditional '70s metal songcraft and edgy growling vocals from leader Keith Satchfield. **Back With A Vengeance** is a fairly solid bump and grinder, holding up like an early Samson record with hooks. Fave raves include the title track, *The Feeling's Right* and *All I Can Do*, dirty-faced pressure cookers that reveal a band that wants to kick ass but don't have enough leg room. Although **Back With A Vengeance** rolls loose and lo-fi, it's barroom, paid-our-dues integrity lends it ambiance, possessive of a sound steeped from endless tours of boozy dark dungeons and occasional moments of glory, such as those culled from a memorable jaunt with the mighty UFO. As a final impression for ya, methinks both of these albums stand the test of time, their modest songs coming off charmed, due to an odd smallness, an intimacy, a palpable lack of airs. End result is I feel invited to play them somewhat regularly, in place of albums of similar vintage that possess an air of menace.
Rating 8

Fist - The Wanderer
(Neat '82, NEAT21)

Aah yes, *The Wanderer*, annoying, cloying drinking cover song, best suited to English audiences, here Fist semi-metalizing it, even if you can't remove the glitter. Producer Keith Nichol has gotten a good crunchy sound out of Neat's Impulse Studios though, something which he's put to good use on chummy mid-rocker *Too Hot* from the band's second and last album **Back With A Vengeance**, also featuring second vocalist Glenn Coates. Black, white and red Neat label.
Rating 6

Force – Set Me Free
(Heavy Metal '84, HMRLP16)

Ha! OK, Force's lone LP sports a cover way thrashier than this book, a sound considerably lighter, and a record label this is this book personified. In any event, yeah, Birmingham's Cryer had busted up, becoming Force, who emerged with a full LP of tracks that fit somewhere between Grand Prix, Praying Mantis, Airrace, Nightwing, Shy, Saga and, come the pomp metal of *Footsteps*, the Diamond Head of **Canterbury** (quite a cool track, ths one). The mandate in general is pert, perky, keyboard-splayed 'n' played AOR of an anchored English sensibility, with clean vocals, vocal harmonies, and skilled neo-prog playing. And then there's that album cover, sorta **Blackout** in a light socket.
Rating   5

Founded – Looking For Love
(Heroes '82, ER-02)

B-side *Run To Hell* is pure, brisk, boozy NWOBHM but the a-side is an anti-climactic let-down, a dreadful, perky pop song with off-key vocals. Hard to believe it's the work of the same band, as even the production and the vocals sound different. Hilariously rudimentary label art with a big ear and band name in lurid red gothic type.
Rating   5

Frenzy – This Is The Last Time
(Frenzy '81, FRENZY1)

Previously the pan-rock Anniversary, Frenzy eventually looked around and saw the metal future, even if their take on it would be fairly sweet and melodic. A-side can be heard on the seventh volume of the NWOBHM boot series. Borderline as a NWOBHM band, Frenzy are a little more rock 'n' rollsy with a new wave edge. But that doesn't stop them from loading this song up with effects, twin leads and a heap of melody. OK, I guess it fits 'cos there's a little boogie woogie in there too, and a pretty vicious verse riff. Nice chorus-in-the-round also, helped by the fact that these guys can sing. B-side *Gypsy Dancer* is totally weak garage pop, with pert rhythms, wandered, detached vocals, but quite hilariously along the lines of other evil woman metal songs melodically speaking – I can even hear Sabbath in there, possibly er, *Gypsy*. Non-picture sleeve with very plain white label art; pressed in France.
Rating   6

Frenzy – Blackburn Rovers
(Frenzy '81, FRENZY2)

An anthem to the band's favourite football team, *Blackburn Rovers* is a joke of a Gary Glitter-ish pop rocker with a cheesy lyric that is quite hard to believe. B-side is more of the same with *Up The Rovers* – I mean, it's virtually the same song, save for the extra synth riff, and the fact that there are none of the ludicrous verses. The odd man out; non-picture sleeve, although the label art depicts a big soccer ball.
Rating   2

Frenzy – Without You
(Frenzy '81, FRENZY3)

The a-side is a fairly annoying cross between upbeat glam, bubblegum and new wave, only heavy through "power" chords and a fey attempt at twin leads. B-side is called *Thanx For Nothing.*, and is an improvement, although heavy new wave would still be the best description, those light in the loafers vocals keeping this philosophically away from NWOBHM territory, despite a slight gallop late in the ordeal. Non-picture sleeve with lurid red "slasher" logo label art on yellow background. Pressed in France.
Rating   3

Friends – Night Walker
(Rock Shop '83, RSR 002)
B-side is called *Wasted Time* and is squarely NWOBHM with the a-side being a bit more ponderous, a sort of ballad with a rocky chorus, the band as a whole noted for the Robert Plant-like vocals of Mark Russell (this is a stretch, lemme tell ya, as is calling this band NWOBHM). Another track called *Pyramid Blue* is featured on a rare regional comp. called **Spit 'n' Finish**.
Rating   5

Fury – River Deep Mountain High
(Anchor '83, JET7035)
Recording for Anchor (a Jet subsidiary), Fury worked up this rock-able chestnut (made famous by Ike and Tina Turner, covered by The Four Tops, The Animals, even Deep Purple), plus a keyboardy b-side called *Helpless*, to no commercial avail. The band actually once got to back up AC/DC. Mark and Steve Owers would eventually wind up in Steve Grimmett's AOR project Lionsheart.
Rating   5

Fugitive – Need My Freedom
(Fugitive '81, FMR050)
The a-side can be heard on the **NWOBHM Vol. 7** boot, and is a menacing blue collar rocker with a stomping bass line and surprise fast bit come chorus time. B-side, *Don't Tell Me I'm Crazy*, begins rote biker metal and then descends into vicious riffing that could have come from Angel Witch on a dull Sunday. Singing takes a while to arrive and there's a fast break late in the sequence, so all told, one might call this a compressed epic. Fact is, this is a band wholly cognizant of the metal revolution and fully prepared to take up arms.
Rating   8

Full Moon – Stand Up
(SRT '79, SRTS79/CUS279)
B-side is called *Fly Away* and both tracks are squarely early NWOBHM-directed, although the b-side is a power ballad. Picture sleeve's got a butt on it, hence the band name!
Rating   6

G

Garbo – The Dancing Strange
(Rarn '82, RARN201)

A scattered, barely qualifiable three track EP by a band best known for being post-Janine (also post-Janine are Deep Machine and Bordello). Tracks are *Dancing Strange*, *Why Don't You Call Me?* and *Everyday Hallucinations*.
Rating   3

Gaskin – End Of The World
(Rondelet '81, ABOUT4)

Hapless NWOBHMetallers who weren't in the least ready to record, Gaskin added cheap production, amateurish execution and barwipe song skills, making this clunky oldster dull and forgettable, except for the surprise gatefold sleeve, lead track *Sweet Dream Maker*, the dark Legend-like *Despiser* and the carnal title track. To be fair, Paul Gaskin was aspiring to a bit of epic madness with Gaskin, especially with this first album. Unfortunately, everything seems rushed, raw and like I say, unready, as well as handcuffed by '70s clichés from o'er in America. But man, there's added mystique to any NWOBHM record that seems steeped in the '70s, and this one's got that indeed.
Rating   6

Gaskin – I'm No Fool
(Rondelet '81, ROUND7)

The a-side (from the debut LP) reminds me of the no-nonsense plod of Buffalo's *Woman Of The Night*, although it carouses like old Motörhead, all except for those oddly calm pop vocals. But b-side *Sweet Dream Maker* is a decidedly heavy tune for the band, wedged right in the thick of the NWOBHM sound, built around a committed riff somewhere between Quartz and Tygers. Explosive mix, all the more convincing due to the crashing, trashing performances. On Rondelet's cool red, white and blue label, this single's tracks feature different recordings from the album.
Rating   7

Gaskin - No Way Out
(Rondelet '82, ABOUT8)

Almost cavalier improvement, but **No Way Out** still suffers from mediocre songcraft, treble-weak production, and strained, unexpressive vocals. Heavy and well-paced for early metal but still no big whoop. Exceptions: kick ass rockers, *High Crime Zone* and the roaring riff-from-hell-bound title track, which recalls the desperate black wind of labelmates Witchfynde. Note: '96 British Steel/Metal Collectors series CD reissue contains both this one and **End Of The World** on one disc, three years after Japan released them separately.
Rating   7

Gaskin - Mony, Mony
(Rondelet '82, ROUND21)

Yes, that *Mony, Mony*, same one covered by Billy Idol, horrid song, awful performance, equally bad recording. B-side *Queen Of Flames* was on Gaskin's barely solid second and last album **No Way Out**, and is a cloddish riff rocker like b-level Tygers, something you could envision as a **Crazy Nights** throwaway (look for the lame Lizzy solo 2/3 through). The cover art of this single simply reproduces the cover of **No Way Out** in purple tint. Pretty pointless single all 'round.
Rating   5

Geddes Axe - Return Of The Gods
(A.C.S. '81, A.C.S.1)

Achieving far beyond their talents, Geddes Axe were a bit of a bash 'um like heavy Demon with a hint of Shiva amongst a white trash dose of Vardis. Attaching to some major tours (Def Leppard and Saxon), and rising to #1 on the Sounds charts, Geddes Axe hatched only the two singles and the all-new three track 12" **Escape From New York**. *Return Of The Gods* features the mid-melodic metal of the title track (the grand entrance would cause Rush comparisons forever) plus a couple more vaguely Tygers-inflected numbers on the b called *Wildfire* and *Aftermath*. One of the plainest picture sleeves you're likely to see.
Rating   6

Geddes Axe - Sharpen Your Wits
(Steel City '82, AXE1)

On the back we get this explanation of the band moniker: "During the years 1921/1922, Eric Geddes passed an act in parliament cutting all teachers (sic) salaries. This cut was termed the Geddes Axe." And in the grooves we get more of the same scampering Vardis-like pub metal for both the a and the b, *Rock And Roll Is The Way*, both tracks finding that sweet spot between hard-assed Quo boogie and metal riffery that many from the mid-pack exploited.
Rating   7

Geddes Axe - Escape From New York
(Bullet '83, BOLT4)

Funny how these bands from Europe have a big fear on for New York (see Arrow). Well, hapless NWOBHM bashers Geddes Axe do a kind of Cloven Hoof with it, then try overt commercial ploys within *The Day The Wells Ran Dry* (the day this was released, actually), and a spooky power

ballad called *Six-Six-Six*, a Maiden-derived tune that would be prog metal if the band could play. Quite collectible nonetheless, 'cos this was one of the underclass giving it a go.
Rating   6

Gemage – The Story So Far
(Gemage '80, BGA1)
B-side is called *Bring Me Death* and alas it's way to the poppy new wave end of things, and – you can tell – no lean toward wanting to be NWOBHM, whatever that is, sez one B.Gemage, writer of these pleasant enough pop songs. Non-picture sleeve, and in fact, hand-drawn label type 'n' logo.
Rating   4

Genghis Khan – Double Dealin
(Genghis Khan '83, GK 1,2)
Genghis Khan began as Killer and then, of course, became NWOBHM luminaries Tokyo Blade (see entries). Before that solid career took hold however, the band released this double single in picture sleeve with four tracks: *If Heaven Is Hell*, *Highway Passion*, *Midnight Rendezvous* and *Mean Streak*. The material was that of a band damn near ready for prime time, engagingly evoking a cross between the commercial (hard Def Leppard and Heavy Pettin', with all the fast, heavy rules of NWOBHM staples like Tygers, Maiden and Satan. *Midnight Rendezvous* crunched with authority and then breaks into a well-fitting commercial chorus. *Mean Streak* is quick and professional. *If Heaven Is Hell* is a bit more Maiden-like, iced with Angel Witch-styled melodies. And finally, *Highway Passion* is another infectious fastbacker, capping a quartet of songs that demonstrate all the positives of the new metal explosion. The EP was essentially withdrawn when a name change was forced upon the band, then they pasted over the labels of the remaining vinyl, printed new Tokyo Blade sleeves and sold what was left of the two records separately. One change in the guitar slot later (enter John Wiggins), and the band would adopt the new name, and eventually reissue this material. Post-note: pirate/boot "test pressing" versions also sleazily exist.
Rating   9

G-Force - G-Force
(Jet '80, JETLP229)
Gary Moore's brief foray into a full-on band concept G-Force smokes and slides with more boozy desperation than the guy's other cold, ill-fitting records, although the usual bookish metal riffs aren't all that prevalent, leaving way for a comfortable, no pretensions pop lilt, completely at odds with the record's hot sweaty delivery. I mean *She's Got You* is club rockin' warfare, with a closing solo that is wonky, one of Moore's most liberated and free, aided and abetted by an extremely fuzzy Chris Tsangarides guitar mix, the man obviously turning it way up every time Moore blazes into his weapon. Weird record but oddly one of the most engaging and cohesive of the catalogue, having none of that doomed stadium posturing which I'm afraid the

Moore concept has never been able to live up to. It's no surprise really, given the man's secret dislike for metal through all those difficult yet semi-lucrative years leading up to his big blues breakthrough in the early '90s. Note, given that G-Force is a tangential piece of the NWOBHM puzzle (both by sound and personnel), I'm not going to bore you with singles.
Rating 7

The Game, a funky rocker that highlights Gillan's cool partnership with keyboardist Colin Towns, who essentially writes all the music for the album. Yikes. Yet somehow the dastardly joy of living that rakes and rifles through **Mr. Universe** is not here; I mean, the half that is common to that record sings and singes, but the half that is more rock generalist without a mission, not so much.
Rating 8

Gillan – Gillan
(Eastworld '78, EWS81120)
Commonly referred to as "the Japanese album," **Gillan** is a record that is roughly half of **Mr. Universe** in preview, with tracks from (future semi-release) **For Gillan Fan Only** as adjunct. I guess it's the true debut and actually, everybody forgets about this thing, given that it only came out in Japan. The album is one of those thick, rock-solid Japanese gatefolds with shots of Gillan looking like Kurtz more than Jesus Christ Superstar. The music is a veritable joy though, with many of **Mr. Universe**'s best tracks like *Fighting Man, Secret Of The Dance, Message In A Bottle* and *Dead Of Night* banging away tightly like the semi-slack work of drunk punks right here. Not on that album are the grand and swaggering *I'm Your Man*, the r+b-ish *Not Weird Enough, Bringing Joanna Back*, which is too Ian Gillan Band for my liking, and *Abbey Of Thelema*, a happy, nice tune with an evil title. Closing it out is *Back In*

Gillan - Mr. Universe
(Acrobat '79, ACRO3)
Mr. Universe is an accomplished display of '70s metal styles which manages to sound innovative due to superior, heaven-sent songcraft and grating but extensive keyboard embellishments. Frightful speed rockers like *Secret Of The Dance, Roller*, and *Message In A Bottle* strike at the heart of (new) youth, while powerful and driven mid-pace classics like the head-throbbing *Dead Of Night* and the ambitious title track (the first of three sky-high, philosophical, sociological, state-of-the-nation addresses from the man's catalogue) offer reduced velocities but no less creative intensity. The only weak partners on the whole thing would be out-of-place lunkhead rocker *Vengeance* and the upside-down comatose blues of *Puget Sound*, each subtly charming in their own ways but ne'er too regal like the rest of the punk-shocked pageant. Down the sound tunnel, **Mr. Universe** features

Gillan's typical low-budget-on-purpose production values—loose, noisy, and somewhat low on treble—yet strangely, this is no hindrance to listenability, all that bleeding between instruments making sense with all that scraping from same. Verdict: excellent traditional metal reminiscent of Gillan's work with Purple at its most focused, a masterpiece of spontaneous, artfully controlled scatter-brained genius, a record welcoming a legend back to the smoking and drinking hard-working basics of heavy metal. And yeah, it's quite possibly the first NWOBHM album ever, if you overlook the time and place from whence this ragtag army assembled. OK, OK, maybe first NWOBHM album is **Motörhead**, and if you don't cop to the first one, then more likely you'll affirm and confirm **Overkill**, which precedes **Mr. Universe** by six months, as well as Saxon's debut by two months.
Rating   10

Gillan - Sleeping On The Job
(Virgin '80, VS355)
A case could be made for a couple of earlier Gillan pieces to be called the Purple singer's first NWOBHM offerings, but I'm going to go with this tight, sturdy two-fister, both tracks shaking the cobwebs of both the man's classic rock and fusion years completely. *Sleeping On The Job* comes from the third Gillan album **Glory Road**, and is a sly disciplined update on Deep Purple's most modern songs. Non-LP b-side *Higher And Higher* is even slicker, finding a keyboard guitar cooperation that will never be more purposeful in Gillan's very classy catalogue than right here.
Rating   10

Gillan - Glory Road
(Virgin '80, V2171)
Gillan's follow-up to the confident and combative **Mr. Universe** contains a similar mix of AOR-ish hard rock, fast, mid-pace and slowpoke metal, and more than a touch of distressed greaser blues. So although **Glory Road** is a rock-solid, axe-laden pub-terrorizing grinder, soaking up quickly the good habits from the exploding metal scene in the UK, two blues-by-the-book slowpokes, *If You Believe Me* and *Time And Again*, coupled with the snail-paced trudge metal of *Nervous*, make it less a percentage winner than **Mr. Universe**, which, if you can believe it (I bloody can't), I've started Rating as one of my favourite albums of all time. And yes, **Glory Road** is nipping at its heels, still deserving of high marks due to the dazzling quality of the two perkiest numbers, *Unchain Your Brain* and *Running, White Face, City Boy*, while *On The Rocks*, the record's atmospheric, key-swirled epic, becomes soul sister to *Mr. Universe* and **Double Trouble**'s *Born To Kill*, the three working a tri-partite concept that eloquently explains Ian's peculiar, blithely disgusted outlook on life. All in all, distinctive and thoughtful keyboard metal replete with Ian Gillan's strange and gnarled lyrical style, **Glory Road** offers state-of-the-art Brit metal that is just a

touch too obscure and willfully opaque to be considered mainstream, exposing the offbeat humour Gillan always felt to be an integral part of his crazy, hard-drinking life.
Rating   9

Gillan - For Gillan Fans Only
(Virgin '80, VJD32)
This non-official studio album "for no money" and "for Gillan fans only" (an adjunct to purchase) comes in plain white cardboard with a hole for the label like a disco 12", sporting four serious Gillan tunes plus assorted sound effects, spoken comments, instrumentals, lounge act blues, and general joking around. Two of the four real tunes, *Higher And Higher* and *Your Mother Was Right*, were excellent heavy b-sides. A full-length album, but basically just a fun one-off. Van Halen made a record like this, only they sold it as their next new album, calling it **Diver Down**, I believe.
Rating   6

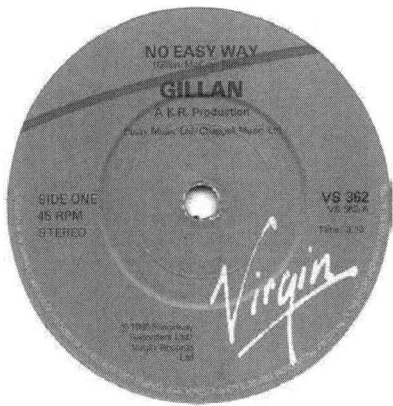

Gillan - No Easy Way
(Virgin '80, VS362)
No Easy Way is one of **Glory Road**'s hands extended to the singles market, commercial, immediate, hooky and a bit naff. More casual is the first non-LP b-side *Handles On Her Hips*, which is one of the band's boogie/metal hybrids, distinguished by those odd new wavey keyboards, and the fact that it's scarcely two minutes long. Second b-side *I Might As Well Go Home (Mystic)* is also just over two minutes long,

hence the offering of two b's. It's also very casual, very dirty, rocking smartly with a cheeky Gillan lyric. One of the gems. The worst Gillan single artwork.
Rating   7

Gillan - Trouble
(Virgiin '80, VS377)
Merely another novelty ploy to feed England's frenzied singles mentality, *Trouble* is a brief 2:39 of old chooglin' Lieber/Stoller boogie sent through the trademark Gillan grinder. B-side *Your Sister's On My List* is a snappy metal funkster built upon a choppy keyboard/guitar unison riff. The second single ("free" or whatever with the first half) are live versions of *Mr. Universe*, *Vengeance* and *Smoke On The Water*. Presented in a thin paper gatefold with live shots of Ian on the front and back, band shot in the gate.
Rating   6

Gillan - Mutually Assured Destruction
(Virgin '81, VSK103)
The big plus here is the packaging, *M.A.D.* coming housed in a slightly oversize booklet sleeve that is a saddle-stitched 16 pager with colour band shots and "A One Act Play by Ian Gillan" called *Ivan And Reg (The Last Two Men On Earth)* which is essentially a debate about nuclear war, tying in with the lyrics to the a-side, which are provided. The b-side is a rough, somewhat unfinished and rudimentary fast track called *The Maelstrom*, a bit like *Bite The Bullet* but not as interesting.
Rating   7

Gillan - New Orleans
(Virgin '81, VS406)
Here's an old boogie cover done up Gillan-style, great yelps, heavy riffing by Bernie Torme, backed with a thick blues metal thing called *Take A Hold Of Yourself* that could have easily come off of **Machine Head**. Not one of my fave Gillan b-sides, it's an original that barely sounds like one, very much making a nice pairing with *New Orleans*.
Rating 6

Gillan - Future Shock
(Virgin '81, VK2196)
Something about this confident yet thorny third Gillan spread sounds detached, subdued, offputtingly British, especially side two, which somehow reminds me of the wasteland encountered exactly halfway through Nazareth's **Hair Of The Dog**. Again the composition is similar to the first two of Ian's shock-rocking blaze kings, **Future Shock** offering manic, almost punky speed metal, mid-paced rockers, and hard, bitter blues interlaced with moody mellow fare. And almost all of **Future Shock** is finely-wrought, experimental, aristocratic rock down hard-ish pathways, but there really aren't too many truly insistent and persistent numbers (save for the driving and philosophical title track, a cruiser eminently worthy of Purple), to match the three or four flagship tracks consistently studding Gillan's other fine works. So yes, solid, but a notch below the inspired songcraft elsewhere in the catalogue. The first 60,000 British copies came with an elegant 16 page booklet saddle-stitched into the gatefold featuring great shots of the band, historical snapshots, full lyrics, and three additional paintings similar in theme to the cover art. And if that ain't enough, the CD reissue contains no less than ten extra tracks, known b-sides and other oddities, including classic branding irons like *One For The Road* and *Higher And Higher*, plus funkier, bloozy bangers like *Your Sister's On My List*, *Handles On Her Hips* and *Bad News*, among other less-polished off tossers, all of this existing because the band had their own studio and drank like fish. Of note, **Future Shock** is Ian Gillan's favourite Gillan record, and also of note, increasingly when I'm asked, I can't think of any goddamn reason not to call Gillan my favourite band of all time, quickly offering Max Webster in the same vein, both making six records (depending how you count; anyway it's enough to call a goodly amount) that are *all* arguably worthy of my Top 50 or 75 or thereabouts.
Rating 9

Gillan - No Laughing In Heaven
(Virgin '81, VS425)
A true EP for our man Ian, this one features **Future Shock**'s comedy moment, *No Laughing In Heaven*, a stomping blues metal (think DLR's *Yankee Rose*) that is blasphemous but all in fun, Ian playing the parts of both gatekeeper and gatecrasher. Second a-side *One For The Road* is arguably Gillan's best non-LP track, a stirring keyboard swirled double-time smasher that collapses into a dramatic chorus that is doomy and hooky at the same time. Brilliant. The b-side keeps the festivities moving with the band's tossed-off speed metal new wave version of '50s chestnut *Lucille*. Brief, briefly funny. The last b-side *Bad News* is a weird one, a kind of jangly blues metal piece that is all texture and morose melody punctuated by Gillan screeching and a chorus that at least shines a little light. All in all, four tracks going four distinct places from a band always going places, no matter

the consequence. Cool Steven O'Leary illustration on front, band photo on back.
Rating 7

Gillan - Double Trouble
(Virgin '81, VGD3506)
Double Trouble's a studio record and a live record, the live one being less than useless, for the same reasons the first two Deep Purple live offerings were so boring they could even bore boredom (despite **Made In Japan**'s unwarranted reputation...zzz). I'm not sure I've even played it right through once, given its six murky tracks, two covers, no neck-snappers. The studio LP however is classic Gillan, maybe the band's masterpiece, full of strange but intelligent keyboard-laced fringe metal, encrusted with a loose, driving, somewhat awkward and weighty recording. The metallicuts, most notably *I'll Rip Your Spine Out*, *Sunbeam*, and the killer-riffed *Life Goes On* are powerful and ambitious, novel in construct and drunk with the band's fragile yet explosive and aggressive chemistry; and *Born To Kill* is simply the band's proudest lofty epic, espousing a somewhat brutish and inescapable philosophy for a doomed mankind. Poking around in its ribs, **Double Trouble** is yet another inspired but stylistically perplexing Gillan gem where arrangement and songcraft, rather than anyone's particular musical skills, stand out. Because indeed none really do, rendering Gillan albums creations from a vacuum, where none of the individual players seem to draw on any technical influences from the outside world, where their skills, or at least the execution of the parts perked and picked, seem hurried, roughshod and all about the ball of energy that results Who-like. Nonetheless, despite this or because of this, what you end up with is riveting and fresh and spontaneous hard rock, sort of like Deep Purple boozing and blowing without discussing of ramification.
Rating 10

Gillan - Nightmare
(Virgin '81, VS441)
A-side is the blustery melodic rocker from the **Double Trouble** double album, yet another track that would be AOR in less meatheaded hands, here the band turning in a pounding headache of a performance on a song nearly too delicate to handle the beating. B-side is a fierce and forward live at Reading rendition of *Bite The Bullet*, slightly extended, very much a class bit of arranging.
Rating 8

Gillan - Restless
(Virgin '82, VS465)
Here's one of the enigmatic pieces from a very enigmatic album, **Double Trouble**. *Restless* is sorta heavy, sorta pop, oddly melodic, and as per the band's other AOR-type tracks, pounded home with no truck to delicacy. B-side is an oddly laid-back live version of sweeping epic *On The Rocks* recorded at the venerable Reading festival August '81. Note also comes in picture disc format (VSY465).
Rating 8

Gillan - Magic
(Virgin '82, V2238)

Gillan's last-before-hiatus is also Gillan's heaviest, most complex, and maybe the band's brightest in terms of human connectivity. **Magic** is full up with Gillan's usual obscure but dazzling arrangements, overt keyboards, unique metal made all the more assertive by Ian Gillan's vocal and lyrical charm. Gillan, the band thrived on breaking all the house rules, gracing us with intelligent metal that was never cliché; approximating an experimental, yet punky version of reunion-era Deep Purple, complete with surprise mood and tempo shifts throughout. Highlights here include speed rocker *What's The Matter*, the Sabbath/blues hybrid of *Bluesy Blue Sea* and ponderous, pessimistic yet melodic ballad *Living A Lie*. We also get a metalized version of Stevie Wonder's *Living For The City*, where the subtleties of Wonder's keyboard jazzisms have been miraculously retained. Gillan was one of the classiest of exploratory chapters in early '80s metal, a collection of divergent and often bickering talents, their friction and intensity fuelling fine rock, mirroring in this modern day and way, the constant wars that marked Ian's all too few glory years with Purple in the '70s. And now nearly 30 moons later, after the soul-searching, often playful, sometimes disastrous material that comprised **Accidentally On Purpose**, **Naked Thunder** and **Toolbox**, Ian has logged a total of seven further studio albums with the Purps, most of them among my favourite of that catalogue or any other for that matter.
Rating 10

Gillan - Living For The City
(Virgin '82, VS519)

Easily making it their own, Gillan pile up their gritty guitars and cheesy keyboards on an old Stevie Wonder classic, pounding it out in their eccentric metal way. A success all around. Non-LP b-side *Breaking Chains* sounds very much like an old Deep Purple boogie, except for those key-prominent arrangements. The breaks are nice, featuring a Sykes-like solo from future Maiden guy Janick Gers. Not the best Gillan b, but less casual than some. Note: also available in picture disc form (VSY519) with *Purple Sky*, a quick-stepping melodic rocker, as the b-side in place of *Breaking Chains*.
Rating 7

Gillan - Long Gone
(Virgin '82, VS537)

One of the poppier songs from **Magic**, *Long Gone* would be called AOR, given a better producer. All in all it's pretty annoying, especially come chorus time. Love the soft pulsing ending though, 'cos you know *Driving Me Wild* is just around the corner. Non-LP b-side *Fiji* is a moody mid-tempo half-measure popster with no power chords except for a brief part of the chorus and the interesting slog of a break. Gillan's second best graphic presentation: die-cut gatefold with "show your hand" swing piece. Note: here's our cut-off point for Gillan as a NWOBHMer, his next single being six years hence in early '88 with Gillan/Glover's poptastic *She Took My Breath Away* and later in the year with the trendy studio sheen of *South Africa*, once again as solo artist.
Rating 6

Girl - My Number
(Jet '79, 159)

Arriving at Don Arden and Jet Records through the party circuit, Girl's first output was this single, *My Number* showing up on both sides, released in a 7" clear vinyl version (black vinyl demo versions exist as well). It's a heavy, moody number with nice textures, and alas, shows up on the

Sheer Greed debut three months hence, that record being closer to the oblique Americanized end of the new hard rock, somewhat along the lines of Def Leppard but even poppier.
Rating   6

Girl - Sheer Greed
(Jet '80, 224)
Girl was a band ahead of its time, a UK precursor to the rafts of mischievous glam metal that were blowing into L.A. bars (sorry, clubs) every day from America's heartland from roughly '82 through '90 when it became obvious it was down to fumes. **Sheer Greed** turned out to be a solid and well-paced hard rock record, not outstanding, yet a pleasing listen throughout, sporting a cover of Kiss' *Do You Love Me* and a general display of stripped, hard-edged AOR that at times borders on the temptress danger of fringe Hanoi Rocks. Although **Sheer Greed** feels more like a business venture, it succeeds by avoiding the play-by-numbers safety of later, modern-day Girls, who unfortunately had to play the game with increasing rigidity, the intense levels of micro-categorization eventually imploding the genre. First recording band for a press-maligned Phil Lewis, before his bitter forsaking of ol' Blighty in favour of LA (Guns).
Rating   7

Girl - "The Single"
(Jet '80, 169)
Comprised of two tracks from the solid **Sheer Greed** debut, *Do You Love Me* is the Kiss klassic from **Destroyer** handled with more Sweet groove than Kiss, the track being instrumental in the band getting added to Kiss' UK tour. B-side *Strawberries* is an eccentric art glam new waver that works with early metal's obsession with all things Japanese. It's a bit cliché, but nevertheless adds an extra dimension to the band's complicated persona, one mirrored in a handful of ways by the equally perplexing Marseille.
Rating   7

Girl - Hollywood Tease
(Jet '80, 176)
A-side is a great choice for a single, less eclectic than the album as a whole, powerful with a sense of purpose, here provided in remix format. On the b-side, Girl join the cover sweepstakes, turning in a really powerful, well-juiced but tidy rendition of the Kinks classic, *You Really Got Me*, as well as adding the perennial *My Number*. Note: Japanese version exists with *My Number* as the b. Some copies with free full colour poster.
Rating   6

Girl - Wasted Youth
(CBS '81, 238)
Scrappier and punkier than the slightly corporate debut, with increasingly desperate songs and a honed sense of survival, **Wasted Youth** marked a shift from the Poison penthouse to the GN'R bunker, gritty, stark production and exposed architecture to match. However, Girl's only lasting contributions would be guitarist Phil Collen to Def Leppard and Phil Lewis to LA Guns, as the rumoured lack of direction (made all the more obvious at the band's confused live gigs), sabotaged the band's potential shot at success.
Rating   7

Girl - Love Is A Game
(Jet '80, 191)
A-side finds Girl once more going to the covers trough, dredging Russ Ballard's

Love Is A Game, stiff but passionate under certain light, and repetitive enough to be construed as catchy. Girl's version is trashy, much like the whole second album. *Little Miss Ann* is simply an add-on from the debut album. Released on white vinyl only, as a 7" as well as a 10" (10191) with some including a free patch. Japanese issue exists as well (of note, there's a Japan-only issue of *Heartbreak America* from the same year).
Rating 7

Girl - Old Dogs
(Jet '81, 7009)
The a-side to this one just proves how confused about their identity this band was, *Old Dogs* being a sort of unplugged rocker, a convincing enough mid tempo blues that forgets that this band was supposed to be either glam or heavy or both. *Passing Clouds* is from the band's debut, and oddly enough is an appropriate pairing with the a, sounding like a replay of The Clash's *Police And Thieves* ploy, Girl dropping a reggae tune in the middle of something decidedly not. Plus the band kinda blow it, playing it hi-fi and stiff from a percussion standpoint.
Rating 6

Girl - Thru The Twilight
(Jet '81, 7014)
Both tracks are from the ill-fated and ill-fitting second album **Wasted Youth**, which Phil Collen (shortly leaving for Def Leppard) has called a disaster due to personnel problems, management problems, label problems and musical chairs with respect to studios. You can hear it in the hurried brashness of both the audio and the performances here, *Thru The Twilight* being a clumsy attempt at mean metal, *McKitty's Back* being an artsy, ambitious AOR rocker with four parts that do not belong in the same room. Strange record and strange band all around. Also comes in picture disc form (JETP7014).
Rating 6

Girlschool - Take It All Away
(City '79, NIK6)
This is Girlschool's first output, recorded two years after the band's inception, cut in just four hours. *Take It All Away* is a sort of behaved, boogie/hard rock hybrid, and eventually gets cleaned up for inclusion on the first LP. *It Could Be Better* is like new wavey punk with a Stones jones, harkening back to the band's cover days. It's funny how early on, these gals were closer to The Runaways than the later biker rock would let on. City was a UK label (basically a one man show, Phil Scott putting it together to work with the UK Subs), but manufactured in France. Pressed on black vinyl and on red vinyl, as is the Irish Mulligan pressing, which lacks a picture sleeve. City issue also has two different sleeves. The red vinyl version uses the pink, black and white live shot with a cool silver label dropping out the text to the red vinyl. The black vinyl version features an orange, black and white sleeve with a metallic green label that drops out the text to the black vinyl. It also uses four separate band shots. Both are made in France. Next up came support from (and for) Motörhead who collared the gals for their **Overkill** tour, and the rest, for about three years anyway, was loud proud history. Pressed in pretty high quantities.
Rating 6

Girlschool - Demolition
(Bronze '80, BRON525)
Loud and ringing garage metal marks this UK debut by Britain's female scuz rock survivors. Sticking closely to a sustained Motörhead stomp, Girlschool dish up a spirited performance, especially drummer Denise Dufort, who dominates the mix with trashcan resolve. Oddly, the most urgent record of the bunch, featuring logical Lemmy-like extensions such as *Not For Sale* (rightfully re-cut for **Hit And Run**), *Breakdown*, and *Midnight Ride*. First and last of the band's classy cover graphics. The Bronze deal came about after Motörhead took a fancy to the gals, dragging them along on their legendary **Overkill** tour.
Rating 6

Girlschool - Emergency
(Bronze '80, BRO89)
A-side *Emergency*, from the debut LP, is a trashy baby doll punk metal-like piece of chainmail featuring the familiar refrain "999 emergency," soon to be more familiar

when Motörhead would send it up on the **St. Valentine's Day Massacre** spit-swap EP. B-side *Furniture Fire* is a non-LPer built like grade-A Runaways, buttressed by an enjoyable guitar twang and rapid-fire melody switchbacks, demonstrating thoughtful, competent construction early in this new metal game.
Rating   8

Girlschool - Nothing To Lose
(Bronze '80, BRO95)
Built around the same punk rock boot stomp as most of their most memorable songs, *Nothing To Lose* is an LP track that is worthy enough as a novelty single, more or less redeemed by drums and production thereof. B-side *Baby Doll* is also from **Demolition** and is on the glam side for these spirited NWOBHM females. One of the band's unraveled tracks.
Rating   7

Girlschool - Race With The Devil
(Bronze '80, BRO100)
The a-side is less devilish a song than its title, even if it's got that little Fast Eddie lick that sears deep into the mind. B-side *Take It All Away*, like the a-side, is also from the LP. It is, of course, a bulked version of the band's original calling card. Hit #49 in the UK charts.
Rating   7

Girlschool - Yeah Right
(Bronze '80, BRO110)
Well on the rise at this point, Girlschool didn't help matters with this awkward single that sounds like mid-grade Damned. Turned out to be one of the band's lowest charting early singles. B-side *The Hunter*, also from the **Hit And Run** LP, was a much more confident and metallic track, thumping along in that Motörhead zone, good mix, sexy vocals, even a crunchy train-like axe solo and a nice build to the finish.
Rating   6

Girlschool - Hit & Run
(Bronze '80, BRO118)
The a-side ties a done-me-wrong emotion to the band's usual numbskull bash. No big deal and an LP track to boot. But b-side *Tonight* is a vicious delicious fast rocker with a bloodthirsty riff built for prowling and brawling. 10" version adds the band's pulse-void version of *Tush*. #32 in the UK charts.
Rating   8

Girlschool - C'mon Let's Go
(Bronze '81, BRO126)
Yet another LP track single from the successful **Hit And Run** LP, albeit in different version. Note the Damned-derived intro again, after which the song rumbles off into the thin zone, still, actually reminiscent of The Damned. One of the band's more alcoholic numbers anyhoo, winning through verve. I mean, you really wanna go with them. Live non-LPer *Tonight* rocks with might, great recording, even more of a drinking anthem than the a-side. One of the band's heaviest tracks and a bit reminiscent of *Bomber*. A live take on *Demolition Boys* is added for the 10" version. #42 in the UK charts. Japanese Victor issue uses *Kick It Down* as the b; Spanish Bronze issue uses *Hit And Run*.
Rating   8

Girlschool - C'mon Let's Go
(Bronze '81, BRO126)
Yet another LP track single from the successful **Hit And Run** LP, albeit in different version. Note the Damned-derived intro again, after which the song rumbles off into the thin zone, still, actually reminiscent of The Damned. One of the band's more alcoholic numbers anyhoo, winning through verve. I mean, you really wanna go with them. Live non-LPer *Tonight* rocks with might, great recording, even more of a drinking anthem than the a-side. One of the band's heaviest tracks and a bit reminiscent of *Bomber*. A live take on *Demolition Boys* is added for the 10" version. #42 in the UK charts. Japanese Victor issue uses *Kick It Down* as the b; Spanish Bronze issue uses *Hit And Run*.
Rating   8

Girlschool - Don't Call It Love
(Bronze '81, BRO144)
Girlschool collared Nigel Gray to produce the band's next album **Screaming Blue**

Murder, Gray stiffening the band and getting them to tone down the screechy biker fare. This lead single demonstrates the results, fans welcoming the upswing in professionalism but lamenting the loss of life. *Wildlife* contains the same sort of stilted delivery, even if compositionally it harkened back to the old Fast Eddie influence. 12" version adds tense non-LP chugger *Don't Stop*. Also issued in red vinyl. As well, there's a Japanese Victor issue, with different cover art.
Rating   7

Girlschool - Screaming Blue Murder
(Bronze '82, BRON541)
The biker metal of the debut caves way to a cleaner, commercial sound and no idea how to use it. Similar to skeletal Saxon, or low-grade Tank (at least with the title track), **Screaming Blue Murder** collapses into naff experiments with economical new wave structures in marked contrast to the band's previous walls of metal, in an effort to clean it up so we all can hear screechless. Very British and well recorded (at the hands of Nigel Gray, producer of The Police), but it's still chicks doing metal, which... welll, we can debate that for hours, but perhaps we shouldn't. Features *It Turns Your Head Around*, an awesome *Killed By Death*-style greaseball, plus an unlistenable cover of *Tush*, sabotaged by an odd hiccup beat. Hit #27 on the UK charts and went gold in Canada.
Rating   5

Girlschool - Play Dirty
(Bronze '83, BRON548)
With the writing on the wall, Kim and the gang go somewhere new, arriving at this over-produced pop metal ploy, packed and frozen with tons of stiff Rick Allen-style drum patterns, which here, due to volume, drag all toons caught in its vortex down to a dull stomp. Still, there is some pleasant experimentation, traces of cleverness, and a welcome taming of the band's usual yelp into studied harmonies. But the general drift is into jack-off studio rock, glammed self-consciously by Slade's Noddy Holder and Jimmy Lea at the production helm. Featured singles this time: a stiff cover of T. Rex's *20th Century Boy* and a sappy gloss popper written by the Slade boys called *Burning In The Heat*. One of the band's own favourite albums from the catalogue.
Rating   5

Girlschool - 1-2-3-4 Rock 'n Roll
(Bronze '83, BRO169)
Lead novelty cover was pretty much done against the girls' wishes, needing Gerry Bron and his engineers to complete the tracks in the studio. It's yer basic hokey but spirited hockey barn anthem in the spirit of Sweet and Gary Glitter. Elsewhere we get the band's three-legged version of *Tush* (don't get fancy; just rock), the flogged-to-death *Don't Call It Love* (different from LP recording), and *Emergency*. Also available in 12" format (BROX169).
Rating   4

Girlschool - 20th Century Boy
(Bronze '83, BRO171)
Noddy Holder and Jimmy Lea of Slade came in to produce the band's **Play Dirty** album, bringing up the glam tendencies and underscoring the direction with another cheap novelty cover, T. Rex's *20th Century Boy*, here dealt a heavy hand foiled with those sweet but nasty vocals. B-side *Breaking All The Rules* (also from the album) is a fairly raucous piece that sounds like Kiss doing *Ballroom Blitz*. 12" (BROX171) adds *I Like It Like That* which is more like Kiss doing Kiss. Exactly like that actually.
Rating 6

Girlschool - Burning In The Heat
(Bronze '84, BRO176)
Containing melodies completely foreign to the band, *Burning In The Heat* was actually written by **Play Dirty**'s producers, Noddy Holder and Jimmy Lea. It's the first flagrant pop ploy from the band single-wise and spelled the beginning of the end. B-side *Surrender* is also a mite too poppy, even if the band's ham-fisted drumming is still driving things into the ground. All in all quite sad, and those keyboards didn't help, even if looking back, this is from one of the band's favourite albums.
Rating 5

Glasgow - Stranded
(Neat '84, NEAT40)
Glasgow's Glasgow merely chipped the tail end of the NWOBHM with this single, moving on to two more, an album and another single which saw them commercializing their sound. But this first single for Neat is quite a grinding rocker, a little proggy, mysterious, and committed to metal, a true NWOBHM artifact. B-side is called *Heat Of The Night*, and this one is a blazing double-kick OTT rocker with a vicious *Breadfan*-ish riff. Yow. Neither made it to the band's '87 LP, **Zero Four One**. Picture sleeve, with Maiden-ish lettering.
Rating 8

Glasgow - Miles Better
(Clyde '84, CLY001)
After basically disowning their heavy and brutish debut single (the band had frazzled themselves, being in a car crash on the way to the studio), Glasgow reconvened for this three track 12" EP (*Under The Lights* b/w *Searching For Glory* and *After Midnight*), which saw the band transitioning to more of a tough AOR sound despite the all-metal pose for the band photo.
Rating 6

Goldsmith - Life Is Killing Me
(Bedlam '82, BLM001)
Guitarist/vocalist Pez Hodder is ex-Bitches Sin, and after aborted dalliances with Neat, financed their own hearty, true NWOBHM picture sleeve single. The band's *Give Me Your Love* track appears on **Neat's 60 Minutes Plus** cassette comp. Nice, Hellanbach-ish heft and fuzz to the fast-rockin' a-side, with major guitars and a vocal/lyric combo that makes one crack a smile while lifting a pint. B-side *Music Man* is a little funkier but still solidly heavy and woefully electrocuted, Holder telling the standard tale of living one's miserable life for metal.
Rating 7

Golgotha - Dangerous Games
(Golgotha '84, GOTH002)
This proggy, quirky, folky, non-picture sleeve EP (evil logo though) featured four tracks: *Dangerous Games*, *Old England's Dream*, *Air* (essentially a Bach melody turned into a minute-and-a-half instrumental, twin lead power ballad), and *The Great Divide*, only the latter reaching NWOBHM heights, the band at least rocking out for a whole song there, even

if the vocals are off-key. *Dangerous Games* starts upbeat, acoustic and folky, the band then introducing – quite inexplicably – smoking, choking power chords. *Old England's Dream* is moody, misty, mystical and acoustic right through. An even proggier full-length called **Unmaker Of Worlds** would emerge in '90, followed by **Symphony In Extremis** in '93.
Rating   7

Grand Prix - Grand Prix
(RCA '80, PL25321)
Hyped at the time, Grand Prix featured Dirty Tricks drummer Andy Bierne and Phil Lanzon, keyboardist for misunderstood soft rock crafters Sad Café. The sound was punchy, roughly recorded pomp with a touch of Styx but very much ahead of its time, hence the buzz about the boys. In fact, some of this is right at the edge of discovery with respect to two other solitudes as well, those of the NWOBHM and neo-prog. Bernie Shaw's vocals are a definite positive, his sunny style propelling these songs forthrightly towards a valid shot at US success. Instead, what the band got was a European tour with Manfred Mann.
Rating   6

Grand Prix - Thinking Of You
(RCA '80, RCA7)
Poppy, major label concern Grand Prix are most famous for eventually coughing up Phil Lanzon and western Canadian Bernie Shaw to Uriah Heep (Shaw first to Praying Mantis), along with second vocalist Robin McAuley to MSG. Originally named Paris, the band quickly made a name for themselves through a high billing at Reading (under Maiden and UFO), and through the UK's dearth of and subsequent thirst for glossy, Americanized keyboard pap. Debut single featured this album track, a poppy power chord rocker with little charm, and the non-LP *Feels Good*. Late October issue, coinciding with the release of the debut self-titled album. Note: there also exists a Japanese RCA issue of album track *Feel Like I Do* (*Waiting For An Alibi* meets Toto) with *Thinking Of You* as its b, which comes in white label promo form as well.
Rating   6

Grand Prix - Which Way Did The Wind Blow
(RCA '81, RCA18)
Issued three months after the debut album, the band's second single featured this album track (different version), once more using non-LPer *Feels Good* as a b-side. A-side is a grand, progressive power ballad glossed and drossed beyond good taste, but competitive enough for the times. Promo version as well (DJ10).
Rating   6

Grand Prix - There For No One To See
(RCA '82, RCALP6027)
Now with future MSGer Robin McAuley, formerly of Raw Deal, on board, Grand Prix continue with a new record of syrupy melodic hard rock awash in dated keyboards and too many ashamedly mellow bits. But dark Saga-like ballad *Keep On Believing* was a bit of a hit for the band, and indeed the guys got up to a UK tour with Sammy Hagar for the record, before getting unceremoniously dropped. I suppose there's no shortage of guitars though, and there's enough amusing low-'80s variety to keep one amused. But Greg Walsh produces again and gets it all wrong, quite surprising for a major label release.
Rating   5

Grand Prix - Keep On Believing
(RCA '82, RCA162)
Keep On Believing would, six months hence and in different version, feature on the band's second album **There For None To See**, which also significantly documents the adoption of Robin McAuley as vocalist. The song is a trendy and tribal move away from the hard rock of the time, basically an atmospheric romancer with a deft riff and overall, a Genesis-esque, GTR-like mood. B-side *Life On The Line* is non-LP. Also issued as picture disc.
Rating   6

Grand Prix - Give Me What's Mine
(Chrysalis '83, PRIX1)
Onto their new deal with Chrysalis, Grand Prix release this single one month in advance of their most widely celebrated album **Samurai**, a record distinguished by its classy samurai warrior artwork.

The track is pure Toto/Styx/Journey-inspired pomp rock blessed with some nice harmonies. The band subsequently, in early '83, latched onto Maiden's UK tour. B-side is the non-LP *One Five Jive*.
Rating 6

Grand Prix – Samurai
(Chrysalis '83, CHR1430)

Grand Prix's third and last is also by far the most readily available, **Samurai** seeing both Canadian and US issue. The band's sound at this juncture was standard mid-'80s pomp rock, but botched in the inimitable UK style. Also by this point, as discussed, Bernie Shaw (now longtime Heep vocalist), was gone, McAuley crooning along weakly in his place, as he did on the second album. Phil Lanzon would also end up in (a) Heep, but for the present, what he had on his hands was a record of big harmonies, sickly sweet melodies, and an over-extended drum mix, which tended to dominate and make the record stodgy. Reminds me a bit of Nightwing and also perhaps Magnum and Terraplane.
Rating 4

Grand Prix - Shout
(Chrysalis '83, PRIX2)

Grand Prix's last single featured this fairly heavy album track plus a live version of well-regarded Grand Prix chestnut, the punchy and neo-progressive *Keep On Believing* as the b-side, recorded at Reading, naturally. Quite annoying actually, *Shout* comes off as dull, thumping stadium rock with stiff production and bad lyrics, albeit a nice buoyant break segment. Issued in picture disc format (PRIXP2), as well as 12" (PRIXX2). 7" issue came with patch.
Rating 6

Grim Reaper - See You In Hell
(Ebony '83, EBON16)

A grand and impressive debut, **See You In Hell** exudes confidence and an uncanny talent for purity of metal essence, rocking roughshod and simplified, lacking the ego one expects to hear rampant on a debut album. Rich and full-up with integrity, this album features one in a long line of excellent Darryl Johnston/Ebony Records recordings, this particular one boomy and loose, perfect for the band's brand of tunnel-visioned chaos. Another shaft of brilliance is Steve Grimmett's voice, an expressive and chivalrous wail that leads the Reaper's rumbling and careening juggernaut with class, sincerity, and capable control. Hard to pin down the genius behind this album. It's a mix of the aforementioned heroic vocals, production and songcraft, but maybe most importantly, the absolutely focused delivery of these straight-forward and metallic yet richly melodic tunes, like a bus out of control, like Diamond Head, like a gauzy metal sinkhole. Classic, magical and timeless British metal rifled through with a mystique that did not go unnoticed by punters both sides of the Atlantic.
Rating 10

Grim Reaper - The Show Must Go On
(RCA '84, 13932)
Although there's a bewildering collection of flexi 7" and 12" promos that were produced for this near peerless NWOBHM giant, it looks like the only single proper was RCA's US issue of the band's worst track, melancholic, unimaginative, wholly unrepresentative power ballad *The Show Must Go On*. Indeed, this track featured on some of those aforementioned promos and flexis. B-side *Dead On Arrival* is closer to the **See You In Hell** album's rousing, enigmatic, magnet NWOBHM dementia, an effect achieved through Steve Grimmett's vocal prowess and production values that cut to the bone. To confuse matters, there seems to be a promo 7" of *The Show Must Go On* with a repeat of the track on side b, with the same catalogue number.
Rating   6

and Dolls punk, wrapped in biker-ish graphics (witness the band's "moons"), yet complex enough to pass as chaotic, histrionic metal. B-side *Every Mother's Son* is a little closer to hard rock, of a retro nature, but still rudimentary riff rock miles from Maiden-mania. Gatefold sleeve with nice Tank-like graphics. I dunno, the high value of this one, I assume, has more to do with the present elevated status of punk collectability than a lingering drift in NWOBHM prices.
Rating   6

Gypsy - We Came To Be Free
(Fairview '84, FMR 080)
Squarely characteristic, non-picture sleeve NWOBHMer, if on the melodic side, recorded at Fairview studios and privately pressed with groovy hand-drawn label art. B-side is called *Get It Right*.
Rating   8

Ground Attack - Red Lion
(G.A. Records '81, GAR001)
Red Lion is an odd sort of bashing Stooges

H

Hammerhead – Time Will Tell
(Linden Sounds '80, LS009)
The a-side is a lusty galloping rocker that would do Saxon or Dark Star proud, while b-side *Lonely Man* is a low-slung, rock the pocket mid-pacer with both heft and swagger. Note: **NWOBHM Vol. 6** bootleg contains another Hammerhead track called *Lochinvar*, a sloggy spooky screechy power ballad. Drab live shot picture sleeve; pressed in France. Cool band with hearty guitar tones to help walk the talk, in fact, memorable enough to warrant an '03 reissue of this thing, also as a 7", in a run of 250 blue vinyl copies, along with an EP and full-length CD compilation called **Will To Survive**.
Rating 7

Handsome Beasts - All Riot Now
(Heavy Metal '80, HEAVY1)
The Wolverhampton-based Handsome Beasts actually caused the famed Heavy Metal Records into being, manager of the band Paul Birch forming the label around his biker-rocking act. So HEAVY1 gets to be this single, a sort of Saxon-goofed, post-'70s stomper, with the b-side being *The Mark Of The Beast*, an even worse track, sort of thinly power-chorded into pop and new wave, sort of like a really bad Samson b-side. Neither track hailed from the notorious **Beastiality** album.
Rating 5

Handsome Beasts - Breaker
(Heavy Metal '81, HEAVY2)
Vocalist Garry Dalloway and his extensive gut are back for single #2, *Breaker*, *Crazy* and *One In A Crowd* all hailing from the long player to be released a month later. The recording is much improved on this second output, although the tracks are still rudimentary and unimaginative. *Breaker* is fast and dull, *Crazy* is one of those boogies duct-taped to slightly smart NWOBHM riffery (sort of a variation on the band's biggest song *Sweeties*), and *One In A Crowd* is straight fish 'n' crisps biker metal set to a military snare beat. Yawners all, but personable like Dalloway's face and girth. Note: the single was sub-titled **Digital Spiral Groove EP** as it used a rarely seen gimmick where either b-side would play, depending on where the needle came down (Kiss and Monty Python have both used this).
Rating 6

Handsome Beasts - Beastiality
(Heavy Metal '82)
As discussed, previous to this scrappy, unsure and unfinished record were the singles, each better than the last, culminating in this record's marquee track *Sweeties*. All told, the Handsome Beasts sound was a hapless NWOBHM, rooted in bluesy, biker (Dumpy's Rusty Nuts) scruff from the UK '70s, plus bands like Nutz, Alex Harvey, Nazareth, Quo, then early Saxon and Motörhead. Bar-wipes to the max, the band's early-on full-length became more famous for the cover art: Dalloway in all his extended girth, hanging out in a pigpen with its rightful owner. Fine British Steel CD reissue from '96 also includes all of the singles tracks, a short bio, and pictures of the three semi-rare singles. A reunion album from '90 called **The Beast Within** failed to make any new waves (OBHM).
Rating 6

Handsome Beasts - Sweeties
(Heavy Metal '82, HEAVY11)
Here's the band's catchiest track, propped by a passionate vocal performance and

melody, a nice bridge between AC/DC-ish party metal, redneck rock and bands like Tygers. And speaking of AC/DC, non-LP b-side *You're On Your Own Now* sounds like one of that band's ballads (*Ride On?*), an unplugged slow cooker that might have worked with slicker production values. A worthy experiment in calming old-timer rock with an underground Hawkwinded vibe. Released months after the album, *Sweeties* would mark the end for the band until the half-hearted reunion album.
Rating   7

Harrier – Out On The Street
(Black Horse '83, HARR 1T)
OK, barely squeaking in as an entry due to lightness of being, this is a three track 12" EP from the dog days of the NWOBHM, the poppy Harrier having nothing new to offer to the dialogue, two of these being unremarkable but pert, energetic melodic rockers, the last, a standard dark power ballad of the genre, odd only in that the band drag it out to nearly ten minutes. Compare artwork with Schenker's **Thank You** series then quietly return, please.
Rating   2

Hazzard – Snake In The Grass
(Rammy '81, EJSP9600)
Cool riff to this one, sort of **Balls To The Wall** or commercial Priest or most pertinently *Wheels Of Steel*, Scotland's Hazzard driving forward with a tinge of the blues, good pocket despite the slightly naff production (except for that nifty phase shifter). B-side *Kicked To The Ground* continues the boozy scrum, Hazzard rocking like mid-quality Ted Nugent, a bit repetitive but intentionally and admirably heavy somewhat early in the cycle. Not to be confused of course with Hermann Frank's excellent band of the same name from a year or so later. Non-picture sleeve, featuring quite plain white label with red text.
Rating   7

The Headbangers – Status Rock
(Magnet '81, MAG206)
An offhanded project from producer Biddu, who enlisted Wildfire's Jeff Summers and vocalist Peter French (Atomic Rooster, Leafhound) to crank this out but fast. The b-side, *Headbang Boogie*, is an instrumental and the a-side is a Status Quo medley.
Rating   7

Heavy Pettin' – Roll The Dice
(Neat '81, NEAT17)
Other than their **Big Bang** LP in '89, this Neat single is this Glasgow band's only non-Polydor release. Blows my mind hearing Hamie and crew bashing through trashy, speedy and unimpressive non-LP a-side *Roll The Dice* (for Keith Nichol at Impulse) plus an early version of anthem *Love Times Love* (called *Love X Love* on the label), a track which is almost a honky tonk at this point, good groove, unassuming, I guess offering a hint at the band's semi-sterling future. This version is actually stiffer, more sluggish than the LP though, Hamie sounding quite odd to boot, kind of pinched, restrained and badly recorded.
Rating   5

Heavy Pettin' – Lettin' Loose
(Polydor '83, HEPLP1)
Highly touted as the next Def Leppard, Glasgow's Heavy Pettin' were an ass-kickin', pretty boy entry to the American hard rock fray, landing somewhere between **On Through The Night** and **High 'n' Dry**, all dueling axes, big grooves, gargantuan luv songs and overblown tramp vocals from our man Hamie. And on this debut (which came out with various song lists, cover arts, titles, etc.), it all works a well-oiled magic,

the band injecting into accessible anthems a loose, irreverent and urgent heavy metalness that the Leps never had. Choruses usually build to soaring harmony (see *In And Out Of Love*, *Love On The Run* and *Devil In Her Eyes*), the whole record maintaining a sense of excitement, hooks for miles, Heavy Pettin' plopped basically at the top of a second string heap, relegated there-so by the band's obvious derivation. Most importantly, **Heavy Pettin'** holds up a decade later, due to its missionary zeal for world domination, not to mention the fact that optimistic, hopeful melodic rock contains, at its kernel, a likeability that never goes out of style. Dry, oddly Zeppelin-like production from Queen's Brian May, and, like the knob-jobs of Zeppelin, this one sounded ill-advised at the time, but now somehow eccentric and worthy and timeless.
Rating 8

Heavy Pettin' - In And Out Of Love
(Polydor '83, HEP1)
Both the stirring, high 'n' dry a-side (presented here in different version) and the b-side *Love On The Run* are gorgeous examples of this band's raw texture, their dangerous Stones-edged tangy twang, their added personality upon the premise that is classic early Def Leppard. Lethal chorus to that b-track as well. Sheesh. Some with badge. 12" version also exists (HEPX1), which adds *Roll The Dice*. Released a month before the seminal Brian May-produced **Lettin' Loose** album (actually Brian May and Mack, hence the nihilistic trashiness).
Rating 9

Heavy Pettin' - Rock Me
(Polydor '83, HEP2)
The energetic, almost inspiring a-side is presented in a different version, while the b-side, *Shadows Of The Night*, is non-LP. 12" issue as well (HEPX2), which adds a second version of the a-side.
Rating 8

Heavy Pettin' - Love Times Love
(Polydor '83, HEP3)
B-side is the frantic and ballsy *Shout It Out* and both anthems are from the album. 12"

version (HEPX3) adds alternate version of impassioned speedster *Hell Is Beautiful*. Note: also shaped picture disc version, a heart pierced by a Flying V.
Rating 9

Hell - Save Us From Those Who Would Save Us
(Deadly Weapon '83, DWS666)
Vocalist and guitarist of this decidedly Satanic outfit was Dave Halliday, moved on from the excellent Race Against Time, while others are ex-Paralex and ex-Overdrive. The a-side is a truly ferocious metal highball with howling guitars, a stunning intro, manic dueling leads, and yelping vocals almost as extreme as Cirith Ungol. A roaring, dramatic metal classic that encompasses so much more than the mere NWOBHM. B-side of this double a-side is the instrumental *Death Squad*, once again, Hell proving their deft manipulation of a proliferation of pioneering metal ideas. Non-picture sleeve but oddly scary looking all the same.
Rating 9

Hellanbach - Out To Get You EP
(Guardian '80, GRHC56)
It probably did them way more good than harm, but journalists locked onto this band as some kind of cross between the NWOBHM and Van Halen, mostly because of vocalist Jimmy Brash's lazy, often spoken patter. Dave Patton's guitar work could be oddly casual and confident at the same time as well. In any event, the band's lone single (there were two albums), comprised the fast and melodic non-LP a-side, tuneful OTT'er *Let's Get This Show On The Road* (pretty much the same song as the a-side!), *Light Of The World* (a hair band rocker not without charm) and *Nobody's Fool* (the most Halen-esque of the bunch), with the latter two "re-worked" and included on the first and second LPs as melodic Eddie-styled riffster *Look At Me* and *Little Darlin'* respectively.
Rating 6

Hellanbach - Now Hear This
(Neat '83, 1006)
A cheap and rickety disdain for taking full advantage of the art of the LP chops this loose and charming act of duplication and derision at the knees. Comparisons with Van

Halen started making the rounds from press o'er to fanbase, and y'know, there's no such thing as bad publicity. Yet it's hard to take seriously, given the plentiful and slab-thick layers of talent found within the legitimate originals, and those wafer-thin within this mouse-like band of boastful British rogues. Still, gotta give 'em credit for raising ire. If they weren't worth getting upset over, then it wouldn't happen. Fact is, these guys had solid, workable ideas, and fact is, we'd really never get to hear those volatile plans for world domination fully matured.
Rating   5

Hellanbach - The Big H
(Neat '84, 1019)
Hellanbach were a slightly interesting UK band that always seemed to inspire hefty praise or equally intense ridicule at the time. As mentioned, the press considered them some sort of Van Halen rip-off for no good reason I could ascertain, except perhaps the big talk at the mic and traces of Eddie-like picking hither and thither. Believe it or not, given a massively beefed recording, **The Big H** might have been a pretty cool disc, given its fluid, eccentric axe-driven melodic hard rock vibe, not to mention a fragile chemistry, which again, points to Van Halen, one supposes. But alas, the mix is dreadfully scuzzy and thin, rendering the overall experience more like hemorrhoids. Contains a punky, no-results cover of Elton John anemic "Oh look how rock I am" hit *Saturday Night's Alright For Fighting*.
Rating   6

Hellrazer - The Devil's Got The Deeds To Rock 'n' Roll
(Alias Smith And Jones '81, S/81/CUS 1058)
B-side is called *Glam Girl*, and both tracks on this non-picture sleeve point to a fringe, new wavey, glam-directed entry at most. Later single, *Made Of Metal/Hooligan* (Speed Machine '87) is more of a link to the genre than the debut.
Rating   3

Heretic - Burnt At The Stake
(Thunderbolt '84, THBE1004)
Late for the NWOBHM (you always want to get that last witch burnt), Heretic also forgot to listen to the competition. And by '84, there was lots of it. Sure, the front cover of this four track EP (and come to think of it, the back too) was fully creepy, but the songs were no better than what Black Rose, Black Riders, Wild Horses or Handsome Beasts might muster between sandwiches down at the pub, Heretic turning up at the studio with boogie rock, glam, melodic hard rock, and only the vaguest, most abstract of heretical intentions.
Rating   4

Heritage - Strange Place To Be
(Rondelet '81, ROUND8)
Another promising act doomed to obscurity, Heritage put out this single followed by the **Remorse Code** full-length in '82. *Strange Place To Be*, (which shows up on **Remorse**

Code, in re-recorded form and in another key) is a cool mid-pacer with a connecting harmonized chorus and a nice restrained break filled with a bluesy solo. Non-LP b-side *Misunderstood* is a trashy dirt rocker with a biting vocal melody undermined by stiff drumming. Rearranged and re-recorded with an emphasis on the harmony guitars, this could have been a classic. Next stop for the Johnson Brothers was a stint with Gary Barden in Statetrooper.
Rating 8

Heritage - Remorse Code
(Rondelet '82, ABOUT12)
Known mainly for Gaskin and Witchfynde, Rondelet also had this one-record (and one single) band, Heritage possessing the songs to compete with Heavy Pettin' or Stampede, but production values that were thin and ultimately counter-productive. Indeed, the band tried their hand at both guitar harmonies circa Lizzy, and sparse, occasional vocal harmonies, while injecting curious pop melodies into most every track. Pity about that punky drum sound and the spontaneous performances, Heritage matching Shiva or Demon or Black Riders for lost potential. British Steel reissue from '96 adds the single version of *Strange Place To Be* along with that track's non-LP b-side *Misunderstood*, as discussed, one of the band's meaner, leaner fist rockers.
Rating 7

HGB – Chase The Night Away
(Backshop '81, BS001)
This melodic, poppy Scottish act (stands for Henry Gorman Band) had their single released in a professional-looking picture sleeve, b-side being *Keep Off The Grass*. Really pushing it calling this stuff NWOBHM, as the b-side is more like American heartland AOR from the late '70s, Eagles into John Cougar, *Chase The Night Away*, on the other hand, sounding like heavy Saga crossed with Moxy lite.
Rating 3

High Risk - Must Be Crazy
(Air Ship '81, AP 164)
This flamboyant, dramatic act (female back-up singers included) from Sussex featured a hard '70s sound on their lone EP, a three-tracker consisting of the title track, *I Go To Pieces* and *Rich Kid*.
Rating 4

High Treason - Saturday Night Special
(Burlington '80, BURLS001)
Major big dollars rarity here, and that's no surprise, for musically, you've got a fast, compressed, tiny NWOBHM crammed to the brim with characteristic ideas, twin leads, an early Samson exuberance and an almost punky beat. B-side *Waste My Love* is a little on the poppy and harmonized side however. Two more tracks were featured on a sampler called **The Quest Tapes** (Quest '82). Most copies are non-picture sleeve, with a handful out there featuring the handwritten/hangman's noose cover art.
Rating 8

Hoggs – See It Now
(Now '80, 2001)
Weird one here, *See It Now* thumping along to what is almost a disco beat, despite raw retro hard rock textures. Still, not a NWOBHM tenet observed, save perhaps for a certain vocal tone. B-side is called *Time On The Line* and it also certainly doesn't fit the bill, although as ballads go, it could hang as the wedding dance number on any given hard rock record, its melody vaguely recalling *Whiter Shade Of Pale*.
Rating 3

Holland - Early Warning
(Ebony '84, EBON 17)
This one stood above the fray, garnering patches of positive press for its savvy,

controlled, but looming chaos, as well as the Americanly competent vocals (from a guy named Doggy), which vaguely inflect towards Glenn Hughes. Closest approximation I can think of would be early Tokyo Blade, with an ever so slight shift towards boozy grime like Savage or Grim Reaper; appropriate given the label's trademark sound. Look for warm, blue collar barroom metal with nice, time-worn touches on such tracks as the melodic title cut, chomper *Do It*, the phase-shifted *Kicking Back*, and lead rouser *Shout It Out*, with the album as a whole harkening back to all that was honourable and universal about the NWOBHM. Trench rockin' with sensitive to quite strong, working class hooks, Holland became Hammer and released **Contract With Hell** for the same notorious label the following year, unfortunately late for pretty much anything metal-related in the UK.

Rating   7

Hollow Ground - Don't Chase The Dragon
(Guardian '80, GR/HGC57)

Hollow Ground came up with six tracks for the tiny, rare and revered Guardian Records label. Four showed up on the **Roksnax** compilation, two of which also showed up on this four track 7" EP, *Flying High* being an old school speed metaller which captures an Angel Witch vibe and *Rock On* which is a dull funk metal thing that feels claustrophobic, restrained and vaguely Zepp-ish with those high-pitched "Rock On"s. Closing out, *Warlord* reminds me of Jaguar's trashy *Dutch Connection*, while anti-drug track *Don't Chase The Dragon* is a mid-paced riffster with a sinister change of gears two-thirds the way through; well-written but tragically recorded, sorta like all that early Samson stuff. On Guardian's unassuming black ink on orange label. Note: only 500 pressed and almost all of them without a picture sleeve.

Rating   8

Holocaust - Heavy Metal Mania
(Phoenix '80, PSP1)

One of the hapless classics of the NWOBHM, *Heavy Metal Mania* is an anthem for the talentless downtrodden, but what an anthem it is, capturing gutter-rising metal bravado before Saxon will make the big bux from it. Non-LPer *Only As Young As You Feel* goes to the same credo-proud places, although with a less sinister riff, one you might hear all over AC/DC in the '90s, after Angus plundered southern rock for new redneck permutations. 12" version (12PSP1) adds *Love's Power*, yet another warm AC/DC-ish lolligag. The a-side is a different version from the one found on raging classic full-length **The Nightcomers**, this one featuring more of a dramatic, laid-back, milking-it vocal and a deeper, more relaxed groove overall.

Rating   9

Holocaust - Smokin' Valves
(Phoenix '80, PSP2)

Kick-out track to **The Nightcomers**, *Smokin' Valves* establishes the unique Holocaust mystique that some might get and others quickly forget. It's a loveable sound, simple, effective, the best they could do. B-side is the non-LP *Out My Book*, which almost gets to *Smokin' Valves* speeds, basically a fairly heavy b-side with the band's trademark essence of boogie without actually going there. 12" version (12PSP2) adds *Friend Or Foe*, which kicks in just a little more of that boogie power than usual, not to mention a really crooked out-of-tune chorus. Non-picture sleeve.

Rating   8

Holocaust - The Nightcomers
(Phoenix '81, PSPLP1)

And what better way to celebrate the New Wave Of British Heavy Metal than under the dumb decibels of hapless Edinburgh bashers Holocaust, perennial undermutt favourites of an exploding genre characterized by acts that in most cases could both play their instruments and sing, unlike the punks they derided as talentless. **The Nightcomers** is legendary more for what it can't do rather than what it can, kickin' ass on guts and patched jean jacket alone, as it variously rips, plods and slogs through a set of bar band compositions so perfectly attuned to the metal mentality as it exists after a dozen or so brown bottles deep into the night and two feet of snow, most of it in your sneakers (least that's how we best remember it). *Smokin Valves, Cryin Shame* and the definitive *Heavy Metal Mania*... what better soundtrack to impending hypothermia is there? So whence again, foist ye drafts on high for the geezers in the band, for **The Nightcomers** hath come and gone, leaving only a distant ringing memory of crashing cymbals in its polluted wake. CD reissue blows corn on packaging, but adds eight bonus tracks from three different 12" EPs, most of which lollygag about the place just like the composition of the official album, warm, boogie-southern, young at heart and filled with optimism's flame. Charmed, I'm sure. Note: as discussed, a few of the band's cooler non-LP tunes at the time came from the following: 1) the **Heavy Metal Mania** EP, which contained the AC/DC-paced title track plus two of the band's amusing hi skool-kool riff rockers, *Loves Power* and *Only As Young As You Feel*, the latter of which sums it all up with "I like bands like AC/DC, I like to headbash every night" (incidentally both embed super-creamy AC/DC riffs which could have been cornerstones for big Aussie hits); and 2) the **Coming Through** EP, noted below.
Rating   10

Holocaust - Live From The Raw Loud n' Live Tour
(Phoenix '81, PSP3)

Here's a nice four tracker that breaks down thusly: second a-side *No Nonsense* and second b *Forcedown Breakdown* are boozy fire-branded live tracks from the **Live (Hot Curry & Wine)** album. First b, *Death Or Glory* is the track from **The Nightcomers**, live, fast, dressed up and missionary, from the same gig that made up the live album (The Nite Club, Edinburgh, '81, admission: one and a half pounds). But the real gem is the first a-side, *Lovin Feelin Danger* deriving and driving again from the same innocent neo-metal gathering, but not showing up on said live album or any other by the band. And it's up there with the band's other hook metal classics, trampling the tried, true and simple until the slightly brainier chorus marauds like AC/DC might when metal-headed.
Rating   7

Holocaust - Coming Through
(Phoenix '82, PSP4)

All tracks on this 12-incher (also issued in Belgium on Lark, like my **Balls To The Wall** – yeah!), are non-LP, which contains the Tyger-tracked title track, Ramones romp *Don't Wanna Be (A Loser)* and thumping metal flop *Good Thing Going*. A bit too casual, even for these punks.
Rating   7

Holocaust - Live (hot curry and wine)
(Phoenix '83, PSPLP4)

The live document of the walking dead (or at least the beer-bonged asleep), **Live** was recorded way back in '81 in front of about

12 people, at least ten of which sounded like they were being burned at the stake across the country in Witchfinder General's neck of the wood. This record's major claim to fame is that Metallica lifted a tune from it, the previously unavailable *The Small Hours*, for Lars and Co.'s nifty covers EP. Other than its understandably low budget recording, there's much to like about this rock ride through hell town, most notably the fact that five of eight cuts are non-**Nightcomers** tracks, while wholly worthy of that classic of dumb Scottish metal hooliganism. Ergo **Live** kills scores of brain cells by example, Holocaust blowing its arsenal in a mid-paced mosh of morons, the Ramones of the NWOBHM going one extra by providing us modest anthems from deep in their rascally repertoire. Nobody said rock 'n' roll was pretty. Note I: the band had already dissolved when this record was released. Note II: there exist bootlegs of both the full concert video from this show, as well as the full concert CD (called **The Small Hours**), but despite this, the 2000 Neat reissue of the album only adds a couple of bonus tracks when there might have been half dozen or so.
Rating 7

Holocaust - No Mans Land
(Phoenix '84, PSPLP5)
Becoming one of the big disappointments of the NWOBHM, Holocaust proudly flew their tattered metal banner on high with **The Nightcomers**, a perfect tangle of wires for the times, only to degenerate into jokeweights with wimp rock project Hologram, and this present sordid mess that simply defies understanding, a record that sounds like it was recorded under the garage. Where to start? Anywhere and nowhere... which is where this awful one-take lives, the product of major depressed swilling no doubt, given the no-talent playing, out-of-tune vocal chores and fatalistically loaded attempts at song construction. If you're thinking, sure, no problem, that's why **The Nightcomers** was such a blast, forget it, this ain't even remotely in the same piss tank.
Rating 2

Hologram - Steal The Stars
(Phoenix '82, PSPLP2)
The metal thing wasn't working cabbage-wise, so Holocaust decided to pull a Tygers/Jaguar and "lighten" their name (geddit?), and chat up the gurls in the crowd, coming up with this vaguely intricate but ultimately ludicrous piece of garage pop. You can't cover up this band's metal drool, and the unfinished, unkempt, perfume-on-zit pop metal that weakly seeps from **Steal The Stars** would ultimately cause all two of this band's fans to bolt for scuzzier pastures. Note: Hologram was really only one original guy, and within a year, a new fantastic disaster of a Holocaust album was errantly brought to birth.
Rating 1

Horizon - Stage Struck
(SRT '81, 81432)
This brief non-picture sleever features the proggy *Remember The Bad Boys* as its b-side.
Rating 5

Horsepower - Outrageous!
(Square '82, SQS2)
Cozy and old school, *Outrageous* (no exclamation mark) lifts AC/DC's *Bad Boy Boogie* riff and sets it to a Stonesy swagger underneath vocals that sound like any number of hard but not heavy UK or US blues metal belters from the early '70s, recalling Dan McCafferty, Slade and Rod Stewart. B-side *Highway Robbery* goes for a thick Zeppelin soup that works through a raw but bassy mix and a sly, understated drum performance. Horsepower's only other claim to fame was the boisterous *You Give Me Candy* on the second **Metal For Muthas** compilation.
Rating 7

Influence – No Survivors
(Influence '83, INF 1)

If this was 1978, you'd call it punky, but up into '83, and given the obvious skill with which it's crafted, what we have is smart, stomping, gritty, non-obvious NWOBHM. O'er to the b-side, *Queen Of Madness* is more of a stacked power chord thing from the '70s, sorta like Kiss and BTO but heavier with an eccentric, growling vocal which you'd have to call amateurish. Issued in upscale picture sleeve, the back of which featured the lyrics.
Rating 8

Iona – Don't Cry For The Innocent
(Loco '82, 1003)

The work of a Welsh band that was previously called GBH, this one is considered a solid collectible for both authentic sound and rarity, with *Don't Cry For The Innocent* being a pulsating, solid enough pop metaller with a sort of Ethel The Frog-like passion, especially come chorus time. B-side *You Ain't No Lady* is almost like a heavier, faster version of the title track, Iona offering a double standard loose woman lyric, typical of the NWOBHM and perhaps much of metal in general.
Rating 6

Iron Maiden – The Soundhouse Tapes
(Rock Hard '79, ROK1)

Here's the grail of the NWOBHM singles, maybe not the most exciting of pieces anymore, due to its over-discussion, but definitely the watermark of the scene, DJ Neal Kaye signaling that something was up, and that here was a band and a sound that was about to take over. Maiden's first output consisted of these early, quite different versions of tracks we all know and love. The a-side, in the fine Black Sabbath tradition, is the band's and debut album's title track, here rendered slower and more about groove, which is strangely the same effect found within second b, *Prowler*, which lends it a little more meat. First b *Invasion* is the only track that wouldn't show on the band's debut over a year later, and here is provided in a hilarious stop/start, multi-speed version. Back cover features a testimonial from Kay plus ten small live shots. At least one bootleg exists (Hard Rock Music, HR09) which offers crappy black and white artwork, yellow vinyl, and *Iron Maiden* misnamed on the label as *Metal Maiden*. Anything more competent than that, of which copies have existed for years, you'd have to call pirate.
Rating 9

Iron Maiden – Running Free
(EMI '80, 5032)

Full-on Eddie artwork more or less distinguishes this as the first Maiden single proper, featuring the infectious rough-riding gallop of the debut album's *Running Free*, plus a non-LP b-side called *Burning Ambition* which is a surprisingly poppy affair with a silly lead lilt and a disturbing new wave disposition. The only convincing metal comes with the double time break which features a pre-Maiden traditional style solo followed by a brief Maiden trademark twinner.
Rating 8

Iron Maiden – Iron Maiden
(EMI '80, EMC3330)

The neon green spraypaint was on the wall for Iron Maiden to make a large metal dent with what amounts to the simplest of approaches. Maiden were one of the first NWOBHM bands to get their act together

enough to put out a decent album, after a good five years as the original princes of the poverty line, while simultaneously filling a theatrical void in music at a time more accustomed to punk nihilism, packing Eddie, their large green dude, and a recognizable logo ready for the marketing age. Maiden also had attitude, the punter work ethic, headbangin' along side and never above the growing legion of rivetheads worldwide, despite a tacit understanding reigned down from Steve that this was more like a progressive rock band gone very heavy and dark. Despite the many lineups through the latter '70s, by the time the full-length arrived, Maiden had it all together, locked-down, as underdogs with hugely upward momentum, well-regarded pub-crawlers who were fans first, respecting of their metal (and often classic rock) precursors, working with an obsessed enthusiasm for creation. **Iron Maiden** was a fitting debut, setting the mood for the historical, neon horror concept that mutates Eddie to this day. The record is decidedly gothic and ghoulish of vibe, based firmly in the horror metal camp through such Euro-tinged roustabouts as *Prowler*, *Phantom Of The Opera*, and *Charlotte The Harlot*, each emphasizing the album's hurried, energetic delivery, the record as a whole representing a souped-up although less ground-breaking version of then recent Priest or Rainbow, textured with a newer, more metalized version of harmony-based soloing made famous first by Wishbone Ash then Thin Lizzy. *Remember Tomorrow*, although a ballad and written to mourn the death of Paul Di'Anno's grandfather, also fits this hurry-up-and-wait vibe to the record, this idea that Maiden had something to prove and couldn't wait to get to the end of the record so they could start on the next one. The result was an admirable, if not musically earth-shattering first step that went a long way towards establishing a base on which to build the more than impressive Maiden empire. And even though I find minor fault with this album, mainly in its slightly anemic mix, the album nonetheless creates an atmosphere of excitement full up with NWOBHM hopes and aspirations, a secondary timeless vibe also resulting from the album's unmistakable evocations of classic Victorian gothic literatures. Note: In '95, Castle Communications reissued the entire catalogue up to **Fear Of The Dark**, as double picture disc CD sets, exhaustively and methodically providing Maiden's wealth of b-sides, rarities etc., on each second provided disc. Disc at hand, **Iron Maiden**, offered *Drifter* (live), silly 1980 pop metal rarity *Burning Ambition*, and a live Di'Anno-era take on *I've Got The Fire*, Montrose's best, blessed classic, even though it wasn't from the torrid reaches of the monumental debut.
Rating   9

Iron Maiden - Sanctuary
(EMI '80, 5065)

Three non-LP tracks for this one, *Sanctuary* (debuted on the legendary **Metal For Muthas** compilation, now available in many permutations and on many a' reissue), being the band's hooky heart-paced boogie number, surprisingly left off the first album. *Drifter* shows up pre-**Killers**, in live format, a little more personable and bar-wiped than the studio version, especially with that Police-like crowd participation section. *I've Got The Fire* is of course the Montrose number, killer live version, although not as good as their studio version with Bruce, which slays the original from '74 but quick.
Rating   9

Iron Maiden - Women In Uniform
(EMI '80, 5015)
Perhaps the first metal band to comb the catacombs for interesting covers, Maiden offers their second oddity of '80, a spirited smoke through Aussie band Skyhooks' *Women In Uniform*, which surprisingly isn't that much more metalized than the quite heavy original, Skyhooks going fairly Slade all over it. B-side is a heavy but frantic b-quality non-LPer called *Invasion*, too choppy and punked to really fit the band's blustery direction, especially come **Killers**. 12" version (12EMI5105) offers a live version of *Phantom Of The Opera*.
Rating 8

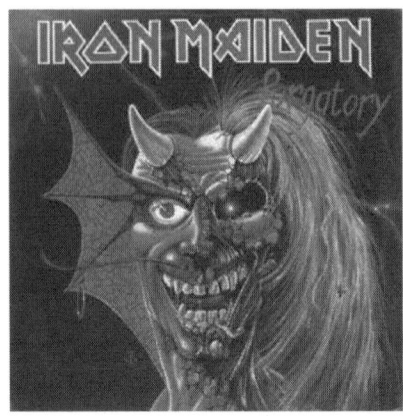

Iron Maiden - Purgatory
(EMI '80, 5184)
Once again, two album tracks, both from **Killers**, a-side being mysterious and debutish speed rocker *Purgatory*, b-side being prog metal instrumental *Ghengis Khan*.
Rating 8

Iron Maiden - Killers
(EMI '81, EMC3357)
Young punters went absolutely nutters when this ghoulish beast feast first hit the racks, and many still thinks it's Maiden's best record ever. I on the other hand marvel at the concept, the recording, the power and the energy, but find it a bit flawed in terms of consistency, a thought mirrored by some of the poo-pooing British press who found the album ponderous and slagged it accordingly. But hard denying the righteous ground-breaking metal enclosed, driving such anthemic classics as *Wrathchild*,

Iron Maiden - Twilight Zone
(EMI '80, 5145)
No big deal here, simply one of the worst tracks from **Killers** backed with *Wrathchild*, one of the best. Clear and red vinyl versions exist and are worth roughly double the black vinyl price.
Rating 8

Murders In The Rue Morgue, *Innocent Exile*, and the galloping proto-speed title track to new creative plateaus, each still maintaining the band's "antique" feel as they modestly riffed afresh. But, to look askance for a second, there is one instrumental and, yea and verily, *Twilight Zone* and *Drifter* somewhat suck. Still, these are minor drawbacks on an early NWOBHM cornerstone with so many innovative ideas, emotive riffs and confident technical touches. And **Killers** is worlds ahead of the band's debut in class and maturity, Maiden no longer being denied star status given this huge, exuberant leap into respectability, something which in fact drove Di'Anno out of the band, Paul finding himself ill at ease over the band's new attention to detail in concert, and with the hiring on of Martin Birch to produce. Still, this is the work of a speedy, rough, impatient version of Maiden, **Killers** offering all sorts of twists on gothic themes and other still fresh '70s traditions, while Di'Anno proves himself an enigmatic voice at the mic, refreshing in his thuggish stance and short hair amongst so many pencil-necked longhairs. So yes, **Killers** found Maiden poised nicely to take over the British metal throne so willingly vacated by Judas Priest, and in subsequent years, the band would prove more than worthy of the position as kings of the genre. That is, until Priest stormed the palace and raped its subjects wielding **Painkiller**, their awe-inspiring battle royal for the '90s, while Maiden would sit mired in complex impotence – just a snapshot of that particular point in time I thought I would bring up, y'understand? Castle reissue bonus tracks: catchy beefed-up Skyhooks number *Women In Uniform*, third-rate Maiden scamper camper *Invasion*, *Phantom* (live), and all of **Maiden Japan**.
Rating   9

Iron Maiden - Maiden Japan
(EMI '81, 5219)
Interesting piece here, this four tracker showing up in both 7" and 12" form, with slight differences (and additions) in various territories. **Maiden Japan** slices and dices sinister selections from **Iron Maiden** and **Killers**, serving as a decent swan song for founding (recording) vocalist Paul Di'Anno who would shortly hereafter be replaced by manic Samson troll, Bruce Dickinson. The tracks are culled from the band's Nagoya date, on the **Killers** tour, Maiden's first time in Japan, which was just one of 15 countries visited by the band on the jaunt. Total tracklisting comprises *Running Free* and *Remember Tomorrow* backed with *Killers* and *Innocent Exile*, all giving us the best slice of Di'Anno era live stuff we're likely ever going to see. Live the band really let their punky trashy side show, much of it due to Burr's drumming, some due to Di'Anno's rowdy fish 'n' chips rocker stage presence. A cool single, although the artwork is standard on all issues.
Rating   8

Iron Maiden - The Number Of The Beast
(EMI '82, EMC3400)
One might surmise that Maiden make or break on how convincingly the percussive attack carries the momentum. On **The Number Of The Beast**, Clive Burr's drumming and indeed the overall sound is loose, midrangy and clumsy, which tends to undermine the heaviness of songs like the pointless *Run To The Hills* (really guys, this one is so over-rated), *Gangland* (*Total Eclipse* shoulda made the record instead), and to some extent, the much feared but amusingly sing-songy title track. It's as if the tunes were too fast for a band scurrying along trying to keep up with faster, more

threatening metal from overseas, and thrashier vibes from the likes of Venom. However, the odd, open on-display recording lends a more successful chaos to more imposing tracks like *Invaders*, *The Prisoner*, and top fave and furious *Charlotte The Harlot* sequel *22, Acacia Avenue*. Strange that after the accomplished, sure-footed whomp of **Killers**, Maiden would make such a punk-drunk disc, one that has more in common with the debut's hurried tone, one that Paul should have sung and stung. In any event, **The Number Of The Beast** proved to be a flawed charmer as well as a lightning rod, as we soon witnessed the ludicrous scorn heaped upon Eddie's green-skinned shoulders by the religious right, who suddenly were seeing more metal than they could have imagined, given the rise of MTV. Bruce Dickinson puts in a maniacal performance as he convincing slides into the driver's seat as both vocal hellion and circus master (Note: Bruce was, of course, already a proven screamer – check out his awesome performance on Samson's fierce **Shock Tactics** as well as earlier, less impressive Samson rustbuckets). So yes, even though this album was undeniably and unfortunately taken to hellish heart by busloads of messed-up teenage Satanic dudes, those of us who kept it in perspective rocked to a celebratory, drinkin' at the pub, "Up The Hammers" sort of record, a spontaneous, compact, aggressive, merely mischievous batch of tunes exuding the freshness of a band on their way to bigger and better wallets through an over-profusion of youthful energy and Who-chaotic creativity. I mean, in retrospect, that's what this record is: a brighter, more comical record from the band, from the artwork right down to the subject matter, even if *Hallowed Be Thy Name* would rank as the band's best and most ambitious epic to date. And with respect to its franticness compared to **Killers**, well, Bruce knows about that too, intimating that the thing was put together on the fly, on dodgy technology that kept breaking down.

Castle reissue bonus tracks (not much of which to speak) include awesome Maiden original *Total Eclipse* and a live *Remember Tomorrow*. And one other thing, for those who bristle at my **8** Rating, I stand by it, for no other reason than that *Gangland*, *Run To The Hills* and yes, the main musical premise of that goofy title track, are all a bit suspect. Three duffers on an eight track record does not a **10** make, despite the simplifying revisionism that seems to drift toward this album being Maiden's essential platter.
Rating   **8**

Iron Maiden - Run To The Hills
(EMI '82, 5263)
Into their Bruce years, Maiden lead with this surprisingly crappy track (OK, maybe I'm alone on this), *Run To The Hills* being too topical, too choppy and wholly lacking in groove. B-side *Total Eclipse* is a great track, a meat and potatoes metal-muncher recorded as rock solid as the next album (and not this one), Bruce of the opinion it should have made it to **The Number Of The Beast** in place of *Gangland*. Also available in picture disc form (EMIP5263).
Rating   **6**

Iron Maiden - The Number Of The Beast
(EMI '82, 5287)
A-side is the melodically arcane title track, a bane to religious establishments around the world at the time. B-side is a live version of *Remember Tomorrow* which finds Bruce singing way lower than usual (remember Ozzy on the first Sabbath

album?), and a heavy part that is sped up so much, the thing sounds like a parody. Also available on red vinyl.
Rating 4

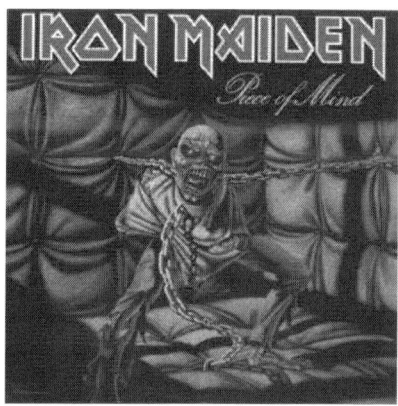

Iron Maiden - Piece Of Mind
(EMI '83, EMA800)

Eddie's pissed, and so we have it, Maiden's finest hour, a heaping slab of molten sullen gothic lead poisoning that wasted all pretenders with a single unstoppable offensive of doom. **Piece Of Mind** rages most heavily against pretty much anything out of the early '80s, due in no small part to two elements: Martin Birch's most purely punishing recording to date and beyond, and Nicko's most convincing kick-ass percussive performance ever stamped with the Maiden seal of approval. The two work a rhythmic whirlwind of fear, caging and expressing the core element of the Maiden persona for really the first time, forming a rock-solid backbone that carries some of the weightiest grooves forged in metallic fire (even Harris and his over-active bass find synergy; and then for once he's recorded properly). Bruce lays waste a healthy piece of his own mind, belting out truly interesting tales of deceit and intrigue over well-written riff-dependable backing tracks, notably the percussively complex *Where Eagles Dare*, the heads-down *Die With Your Boots On*, and Maiden catalogue centerpiece *The Trooper*, which features the single most remembered and celebrated Murray/Smith death-from-the-skies twin-lead riff from what is one long, and granted often insufferable catalogue.

Only the filler-ish *Quest For Fire* falls short, as the band otherwise has never sounded so steadfast, driven and focused towards war-torn battle, so at peace with their mission from 'Arry, so sonically idiosyncratic, so over-juiced with personal chemistry. **Piece Of Mind** becomes and then lives on to this day as the thickest, most uncompromised, most unified chapter in the often disjointed (to the point of laughable) Iron Maiden catalogue, garnering further distinction as one of the most oft-cited metal records that inspired and drove other musicians towards getting into the bars and kicking some Marshall ass. It is, in the final analysis, a stirring display of triumph for players and listeners alike, a record capturing a band's classic lineup at the height of its powers. Castle reissue bonus tracks: raging studio covers of Montrose's *I've Got The Fire* and Jethro Tull's *Cross Eyed Mary*, both rendered top-flight by a **Piece Of Mind**-inspired production vibe and intoxicating personal performances, most notable being that of Nicko, who manages to distinguish himself both as a persona and as a well-regarded trademark component of a top band's sound, roles usually not the domain of the drummer.
Rating 10

Iron Maiden - Flight Of Icarus
(EMI '83, 5378)

Here's one of the standout tracks from what is arguably Maiden's best album, *Flight Of Icarus* finally finding the band with a rhythm section, propelled by ol' Nicko, ex-Trust and Travers. B-side is the now newly fired band's version of Montrose's

I've Got The Fire, Bruce proving his mettle like we didn't already know he's the man. Also available in 12" (12EMI5378) and 12" picture disc (12EMIP5378) formats.
Rating 10

Iron Maiden - The Trooper
(EMI '83, 5397)

And here's arguably the best track from the proudest Maiden LP, *The Trooper* being a call to arms and then a quick storming of the Bastille, a trademark track with a scary Bruce-alone vocal signature. And speaking of the Air Raid Siren, Tull cover *Cross Eyed Mary* finds the man way up the register for a long, long time, the band making the song metal, Bruce making us uneasy that he's going to crack. Also issued as limited edition shaped picture disc.
Rating 10

Iron Maiden - Powerslave
(EMI '84, POWER1)

Powerslave is what **No Prayer For The Dying** attempts to be, a roughshod back to the roots record with fire. Lacking the cohesive creative brilliance and emotional focus of **Piece Of Mind**, **Powerslave** is nevertheless chock full of fierce British metal, recorded with considerably more spontaneous edge and danger than any previous Maiden slab (indeed, the band's quickest assembled record to date), as witnessed on no-frills classic *2 Minutes To Midnight*, one of the band's most passionate and powerful, yet least characteristic Maiden tracks ever, a song penned by Adrian Smith who will forever get tagged as the "rock 'n' roller" in the band because of it. Main shortcoming though, is that stylistically and lyrically, **Powerslave** is a chaotic disjointed ride through time and history and friggin' sport. Concepts are too cute and encapsulated, as we get a World War II story, a tune (or two – ha!) about dueling, and an all too simple and direct re-telling of *Rime Of The Ancient Mariner*, only *2 Minutes To Midnight* rising above trite, offering a poetic apocalyptic vision that exceeds the summarizing and pretentious story-telling slant of the rest of the album. Luckily, the screaming live-feel metal tends to deafen the conceptual shortness as rockers like *Aces High*, *Flash Of The Blade*, and the epic crunching title track kick with a conviction that matches at least the spark of **Piece Of Mind**, if not the professional execution. So even if one could argue that **Powerslave** is musically up to snuff, for the first time we witness an uneasy writer's block, as toys, trinkets, and novelty topicality crowd the foreground where amps once stood alone. Castle reissue bonus tracks (a classic batch), include two very good covers, *Rainbow's Gold* and *King Of Twilight*, a live tune, plus the covert recording of that hilarious, legendary backstage band dust-up, Nicko all upset over a roadie trying to get him a message during his drum solo. Absolutely eye-watering—don't miss it.
Rating 9

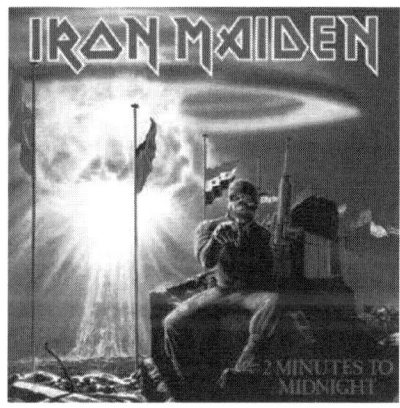

Iron Maiden - 2 Minutes To Midnight
(EMI '84, 5489)
This track really stood out as an oddity on **Powerslave**, sounding much more rock 'n' roll than most Maiden tracks, no hint of the gothic, medieval or fantasy, a riff closer to what one might have expected from Tygers Of Pan Tang. B-side was the Slesser/Mountain composition *Rainbow's Gold*, once more Maiden finding a little-known track and smothering it in all their unique flavours, Steve's bass, those twin leads, Nicko's uncanny grooves and Bruce's readily identifiable vocals making this a vaguely southern rocking metalfest worth sidling up to. Also released in 12" and 12" picture disc format with the aforementioned hilarious backstage Nicko tantrum hastily titled *Mission From 'Arry*, even more quickly made an underground classic.
Rating   10

Iron Maiden - Aces High
(EMI '84, 5502)
Like *The Trooper* before it, here's another one of the band's thrilling statements of intent, *Aces High* indeed, setting the bar at challenging altitudes for the rest of the set to come. *King Of Twilight* is another in a long tradition of covers, perhaps the first to be a bit pedestrian, and off-energy for a band hitting it so hard at this point in their career. Also released in 12" (12EMI5502) and 12" picture disc (12EMIP5502) formats, with the additional b-side *The Number Of The Beast* live.
Rating   8

J

Jaguar - Back Street Woman
(Heavy Metal '81, HEAVY10)
Even though this was a fabulously successful first kick for the band (selling 4000 copies in two months, November and December of '81), it is marred by the tuneless presence of original vocalist Bob Reiss who would be gone come LP time. Musically, it's a head of OTT steam, good guitar sound, solid riff, the product of a band going places, especially impressive given the fact that it was recorded and mixed in nine hours. B-side *Chasing The Dragon* sounds like clean Motörhead, or alternately, Vardis' *If I Were King*, all in all a bit colourless. Neither track made it to either of the band's two LPs. Recorded at Spaceward Studios in Cambridge, released on the black and navy Heavy Metal label.
Rating 6

Jaguar - Axe Crazy
(Neat '82, NEAT16)
After acquiring miles-better singer Paul Merrell, the band recorded this second fast and furious single for their new label Neat, *Axe Crazy* once more sounding like an amphetamine-amped Motörhead with clear, almost AOR-ish vocals, a mix that worked splendidly. *War Machine*, which dated back to the band's second demo in '80, is a dark *Remember Tomorrow*-style power ballad with full-on metal breaks. The single was a big seller for Neat, and got the band in the Kerrang! and Sounds charts. Both tracks are available on the '99 reissue of **Power Games**, as is compilation-only track *Dirty Tricks*. Neither *Axe Crazy* or *War Machine* made it to either of the band's two records at the time. Cool red, white and black Neat label.
Rating 8

Jaguar - Power Games
(Neat '83, 1007)
Simple British headbanging fare from a wildly grinding gang of restless punters, **Power Games** reconciles the guts of Motörhead and early Saxon with the compositional over-extension of Tokyo Blade, making Bristol's Jaguar one of the better pent-up, over-enthusiastic and impatient of NWOBHM powerplants, blasted with punky emotional drive and, as bonus, competent metal vocals from Paul Merrell, all delivered feet firmly planted knee-deep in reality's mundane, daily struggles. Highlights include *Ain't No Fantasy* and *Raw Deal*, both infectious and almost hummable. Note: reissued and remastered in December '97, with full lyrics, band bio and three bonus tracks, Neat proving themselves caring and capable when it comes to celebrating the high points of their past. Salute their efforts.
Rating 8

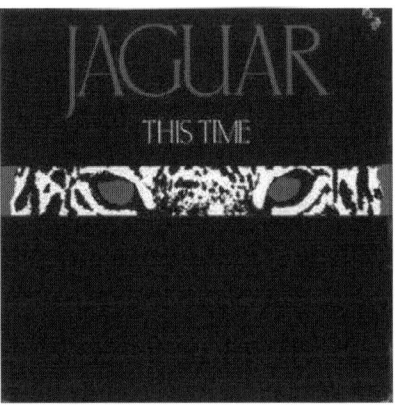

Jaguar - This Time
(Roadrunner '84, RR9851)
This Time amounts to a concerted ideological shift from the scruff rockin' punk metal of **Power Games** to what was hoped to be a cash-generating melodic hard rock sound – "Muppet metal" to "dance metal," in the band's own words. Well, the production is annoying enough, but a stodgy lack of buoyancy or groove keeps even the most earnest and hooky lite metal crooners on **This Time** sounding like nothing more than lazy, toned-down heavy metal. Contributing to the lack of sweetness in Jaguar's commercial ploy is the fact that

the drums are too damn loud, exuberant, and overwhelmingly steeped in the ways of metal. It's always been said that Brits can't do hard rock, and Jaguar perpetuates the long line of strained and ultimately unsuccessful forays into such American left coast tunefulness, even though this record could be construed as a kind of nostalgic blast for those with a greater interest in the NWOBHM. Considering **Power Games** and **This Time**, the steelier moments on the latter did indeed demonstrate a general maturing that could have raised Jaguar out of the bush leagues, given a shot of life from the former, and a re-think of the production. In any event, **This Time** does little but reflect the band's admitted widening tastes for acts like U2 and Big Country. And hey, scoring one for experience over youth, quite incredibly, Jaguar make better NWOBHM records now in the new century than they did back when.

Rating   6

Jameson Raid - Seven Days Of Splendour
(GBH '79, GBH001)

Formerly punk band Notre Dame, Jameson Raid made, raw, personable hook-laden NWOBHM, matching the heights of No Quarter in terms of potential. The title track (the first of two a-sides) is a well-written double time UFO abduction tale with a high twisty riff, featuring thespian vocals by Terry Dark. Second a-side *It's A Crime* is a galloping pure metal feast with a hint of Witchfinder General or Quartz buried in its depressive riff. B-side *Catcher In The Rye* further displays the band's depth, Jameson Raid going for the raw prog arrangements of a Demon or Shiva, both fresh and medieval at the same time. All in all, a masterful bit of songwriting throughout these three tracks. Pity, given a proper studio, these guys could have mattered. Packaging features a spoofed band history and the lyrics to all three tracks. The band were to appear as The Raid on the second **Metal For Muthas** compilation with the track *Hard Lines*. Available in white sleeve/black print and black sleeve/white print.

Rating   9

Jameson Raid - The Hypnotist
(Blackbird '80, BRAID001)

The a-side of this four-tracker is a vaguely unsatisfying and bluesy rocker with bad, un-rhyming lyrics. I dunno, it's heavy, but sort of browned-out. Things pick up with *The Raid*, the band coming up with a dramatic and proggy structure that is both urgent and novel. *Getting Hotter* continues to solidify the band's sense of NWOBHM purpose, with a gallop set to a siren, before going all Maiden on us. Finally, *Straight From The Butchers* crossed *La Grange* with the signature dank foxtrot of the form, capping off a competent, well-recorded, well-played picture sleeve single that holds together nicely. Note, a further track called *Hard Lines* would show up on the second **Metal For Muthas**, under band name The Raid.

Rating   8

Janine - Crazy On You
(Stiletto '81, SUSS152)

Active on the UK club circuit, and together (discontinuously) for three years, Janine only managed this 7", even as the b-side *Candy*,

with its *Waiting For An Alibi* intro, became a bit of an underground hit. Good poppy, almost glam vocals from Bo Hamilton on the a-side, which is a sweet sort of hair band song way before there was such a thing, or I guess, something akin to old Kiss or Starz. Cheap Anglo hair band cover art.
Rating 6

Jeddah – Eleanor Rigby
(Death '83, RIP 2001)
A-side was the Beatles track, also semi-famously covered by Ethel The Frog, Jeddah's version being chugging metal with inventive breaks but woefully without production values. B-side was the poppy but metallically galloping *Ghosts (Never Leave You Behind)*, which really aspired to something come chorus time. Packaged with humourous two-panel poster, a nice adjunct to the ominous and artless label art.
Rating 5

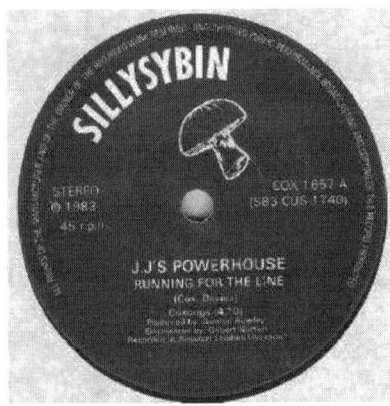

J.J.'s Powerhouse – Running For The Line
(Sillysbin '83, COX1657)
This one's produced (rather thinly) by Nightwing's Gordon Rowley, but it's a barnstormer of a speed metal track nonetheless, added feature being histrionic vocals. B-side *Blackrods* is also unquestionably heavy, a thundering, screeching, squealing anthem to the Hell's Angels chapter of the same name. A-side is available on the **NWOBHM Vol. 8** boot. First issue is actually a white label promo which prompted a full issue at 1000 copies. Label name derives from the magic mushroom, also pictured on the label art, lest there's any doubt.
Rating 8

Jodey – The Rocker
(Ellie Jay '79, EJSP 9242)
Jodey is pre-Chinatown, leaning toward tough glam, with *The Rocker* sounding like Bad Company meets Thin Lizzy's *Rosalie*, all fuzzed up with… actually, some place to go, given its thick, boozy quality, an effect bolstered by distorted synths. B-side *Frontman* takes us into Stranglers terrain, until the Saga-like chorus, noses wrinkling at the band's odd arrival at middling metal from arcane and obscure sourcing, extra spanner in the works being vocals that lean toward a Roger Daltrey dialect.
Rating 4

Jody St. – Fight Back
(indie '81)
This multi-racial band is known more for their legendary and rare self-titled album (bootlegged on CD) than the single, both of which were "issued" in a stark, plainly stamped cover. B-side is called *Granny Did It*, and is a sort of thumping American roots rock thing, like .38 Special meets power pop. Both tracks were from the album.
Rating 6

Alec Johnson Band – Busmans Holiday
(RFP '79, RFP 001)
Produced by Strife's Gordon Rowley, who snatched personnel from the band to form Nightwing, this would be borderline NWOBHM, closer to generic but hard-ish '70s rock, even if there's an intriguing almost krautrock vibe to *Busmans Holiday*, not to mention some tasty axe licks. B-side *My Lady* is the happier and humpier of the two, working its way through a number

of traditional riffs, buttressed by very distorted guitars and a powerful drum mix, as well as groovy, in-the-pocket drum performance. But yes, this one sounds very American and boogie-rocked, boozy and sun-dappled. Now where are my Hydra albums? Actually, frankly, this band reminds me of Budgie, and that's of course a good thing. Now all they needed was to get rid of the stupid name, which I guarantee you, held back whatever modest career momentum Mr. Johnson and his buddies had goin'.
Rating   8

Joker - Back On The Road
(Lost Moment '84, LM018)
Issued in ghoulish devil-grinning picture sleeve, this one hauls ass with a great guitar sound, raucous hoodlum vocal, squealing leads, and booming drums. B-side *Pusher* is more of the same, making this one of the more blustery, straight-lining and power packed pieces of indie 7" vinyl. Granted, quality was somewhat expected this far into the metal explosion.
Rating   8

Juno's Claw - Barbara
(MPA '79, EMP 081)
This solid non-picture sleever from up Manchester way featured the title track plus *Big City* and *The Master*, the latter being one of the better and more squarely modern and deliberate of NWOBHM grinders to hit the underground, and the heaviest of the three on offer. Highly recommended, with killer guitar sound and performance, kick-ass drumming and creepy, laconic vocals so deliciously perfect for early days NWOBHM.
Rating   7

K

Knock Up – Telling Lies
(Movie Music '82, MM002)
B-side of this Welsh an' wobbly, thinly produced piece is called *Need Your Love*. Non-picture sleeve, simple orange label with black text.
Rating 4

Karrier – I'm Back
(Unit '84, TRANS101)
Karrier were actually late to the game, hatching this single (12" version adds *Dreaming*), a full-length in '85 and a second single (*Poor Little Rich Girl/ Endless Shadow*) in '86. *I'm Back*, a true NWOBHMer in the post-Ted Nugent mold, is backed with the similarly speedy and riffy *Way Beyond The Night*, which is also the name of the album, also out on Unit. This latter track is actually quite sophisticated, urgently pop-tinged come verse time, metallic at the chorus… worthy of success down a commercial Grand Prix pathway.
Rating 8

Kick – Rough 'n' Smooth
(EMI '79, 2962)
The **Rough 'n' Smooth** EP contains "rough" tracks *Goggle Box (Whole Lot Better Than You)* and *The Writer*, and "smooth" track, a ballad, called *Wrong For You*. Cool to see that EMI, the most NWOBHM of majors, was actually in even earlier than we thought, this single preceding even the **Metal For Muthas** compilations.
Rating 6

Kraken – Fantasy Reality
(Knave '80, EJSP9370)
This Midlands-based incarnation of Kraken is one of three, the others being an English one and a legendary Canadian one with a full-length, very authentic NWOBHM-styled bootleg/pirate album to their name. Tracks on this lengthy, progressive-rocking, non-picture sleeve EP are the title track, *Deadmans Dreamland* and *Winged Bulls Of Ninevh*. *Fantasy Reality* is a driving metal rocker with a too-long intro section, technical riffs, but a general adherence to critical mass. Exotic, and tricky at times, it basically rocks briskly within the dark, underground spirit of the best NWOBHM, despite its near six minute length. *Deadman's Dreamland* admirably sticks to this fussy formula (and length, at over five minutes), being both swift and heavy, yet proggy, the overall effect actually helped by somewhat burying the anguished, Witchfinder General-like vocals of Andy Hopkins. Finally, *Winged Bulls Of Ninevh* blows the concept at the seams, being the longest, most Rush-like track of the three, quite insufferable really, given the sketchy production values of this intriguing, very collectible piece.
Rating 8

L

Lady Jane – In Concert: The Sheer Power Of Live Rock
(Schizoid '84)
A little late to the game (granted we're talking *early* '84), this one is nevertheless squarely within the style parameters. This picture sleeve EP (red, white and black motif – sleeve folds out to a small poster) comprised three tracks, namely *Out For The Count*, *For You Tonight* and *Whiskey And Leather*, rocking quite "pure metal," which is to be expected given its tail-end vintage.
Rating   8

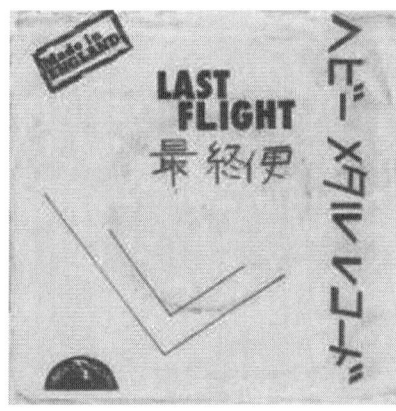

Last Flight - Dance To The Music
(Heavy Metal '81, HEAVY5)
The a-side is quite a fetching, majestic party rocker, lots of electricity, good vocals, evoking thoughts of Tokyo Blade or Heavy Pettin', sort of a Def Leppard in waiting, although the wait is still keepin' on. B-side *I'm Ready* is an oddly similar open architecture tune, once more pointing to a stadium rock star quality that could have been nurtured into fame with a good studio and producer. Vocalist Rob Hawthorn is ex-Strider, moving on after this band to Bernie Marsden's Alaska. *Dance To The Music* also showed up on Tommy Vance's **The Friday Rock Show** compilation in much rowdier live rendition. Three additional tracks were cut in demo form but nothing came of it, the band calling it quits by '84. A visual note: same cheap indie/Japanese writing design as singles for Dragster and Buffalo.
Rating   7

Lautrec – Mean Gasoline
(Street Tunes '80, STS001)
This incredibly rare single never made it past the white label promo stage. However, the a-side showed up on the **Steel Crazy** compilation while the b-side, *Shoot Out The Lights*, is available on the **NWOBHM Vol. 8** bootleg, and is a rollicking rocker with a dark Quartz touch, NWOBHM by all measures, softly graced by organ tones, but rough around the edges. I've also seen a listing for the single as *Mean Gasoline/Someone To Kill* – apparently *Someone to Kill* and *Shoot Out The Lights* are one and the same. Lautrec were lucky enough to tour with Saxon, also having backed up Def Leppard and Magnum. Both Reuben and Laurence Archer would move on to NWOBHM mid-marketers Stampede, with Laurence further distinguishing himself with a stint in Phil Lynott's Grand Slam and then UFO.
Rating   8

The Law – Be My Girl
(Smile '79, SR 011)
This retro-tinged, slightly biker-ish non-picture sleeve three-tracker, recorded at Smile Studios in Manchester, included the a-side plus *Dead City Kicks* and *I Just Want Your Body*. Of Welsh origin, and printed in a quantity of 500.
Rating   4

Leargo – The Artist
(Motor City Rhythm '79, DNS 87903)
It's got the look, it's an indie 45… where do we go from here? Well, Leargo (one of a surprise handful of Channel Islands NWOBHM-ish acts!) slide in under the gun due more to a neo-prog bent, playing those Byrds-like picked chords the way Alex Lifeson from Rush would during that band's golden era. It's the case on both of these songs – the a-side as well as b-side *Played Out Angels* – lending the band cohesion if nothing else. Nice melodies and smart use of synths complete the pleasant progressive pop daydream.
Rating   5

Legend - Hideaway
(Legend '81, LEG1)

The Kent (as opposed to the Jersey) Legend's only release is this gravely indie black and white-sleeved single which may as well have been called *Running Free/Remember Tomorrow*, given the competent stutter groove of a-side *Hideaway* (cool closing solo not to mention a solid harmony-laden pint-swilling chorus: in total, better than *Running Free*) and the dark balladry of b-side *Heaven Sent* (first five seconds sounds like Savatage's *Sirens*; the rest sounds like Byron-era Heep). Vocally, it's that signature NWOBHM sound somewhere in the Sean Harris zone. In '94, Vinyl Tap released a 13 track full-length called **A.D. 1980**, made up of the band's early demos with the conspicuous absence of *Hideaway*. Cheap sleeve yes, but it's cool to see a drummer, with his double bass kit, featured so prominently.
Rating   6

Legend - Legend
(Workshop '81, WR2007)

Jersey's version of Legend was one of the more adventurous and lesser-known of NWOBHM acts, adventurous because they felt like it, lesser-known because of their all 'round amateurishness, although Mike Lezala was an interesting and fully competent vocalist. The biggest culprit was the band's thin productions, these spare and sparse recordings (not to mention the talent of the band) not up to the standards of these ambitious, dark proggy metal compositions. But that doesn't mean the trip ain't a treat. You gotta put it in temporal and financial context, and then for real enjoyment, notch the clock back to about 1972. Then this rips, although even without the mind games, Legend had something going with their brave genre-straddling work ethic, sounding like Demon crossed with Saracen, Nightwing and Witchfynde, dripping with arty Anglo-isms and a sense of impending doom.
Rating   6

Legend - Death In The Nursery
(Workshop '82, WR3477)

Legend's second and last full-length is a long-lost, early NWOBHM squeaker along the lines of the lovably stunned Saracen, Samurai, Hollow Ground, Crucifixion, Holocaust, Gaskin or Paralex. Really sinister and soot-stained, approaching Angel Witch tone-wise for about six minutes total, but hilariously low budget and queer, almost like the band took more direction from Pentagram, High Tide, Blue Cheer and Bang than from Priest. Whether it's **Death In The Nursery** or the debut, Legend just had no idea, flapping in a garage-imprisoned Nightwing netherzone, and for that I salute them. I mean, the band's sound was always on the poppy, dopey side, unhewn, unfinished like the string of singles bands Legend never was able to properly rise above. Still, there was a certain rain rot to this band that imbued them with a foreboding, anti-social air, a mystique that crept and seeped through, much help to this record's malevolent yet enigmatic cover art.
Rating   7

Le Griffe - Fast Bikes
(Bullet '83, BOLT1)
Promising, and now collectible, three track debut by a fish 'n' chips Staffordshire unit with a French name. But I said promising, not fully arrived and looking for the backstage buffet tray, Le Griffe cranking competent Quo metal, close to the Gaskins of the world but pulsed with boogie on two of the three here (*Where Are You Now?* And the title track), but not *The Actor*, which isn't the Tygers hit of the same era, but a ponderous wrench-headed slow thing akin to Witchfynde in tone.
Rating 7

Le Griffe - You're Killing Me
(Bullet '84, BOLT7)
Also just an EP, this one features two versions of the solid, moody, metallic and gloriously olden title track, plus one of those dancy metal riff mistakes called *E.T.A.*. Showing much growth as a band, guitars have gotten meatier and more traditional in tandem with the warm production. Just try and figure out the cover's mammary situation.
Rating 8

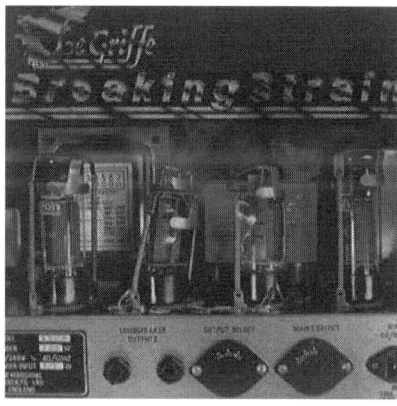

Le Griffe - Breaking Strain
(Bullet '84, BULP2)
Easily their best work, **Breaking Strain** (yet another EP) restores one's faith in the restorative nature of classic hard rock, from the power-packed album art, to the lyrics, through the stellar grey-shaded NWOBHM contained through its blustery five tracks. *You're Killing Me* of course rules, but the best is saved for *Silent Running*, while *Movin' On* is almost a pub rock epic. All told, a brilliant period timepiece aided by the early metal prowess of new guitarist Amos Sanfillipo. Basically the best half of the Dark Star album all in one, painfully too brief whistle stop.
Rating 9

Liaison – Play It With Passion
(Catweazle '82, CR001)
Liaison is on the melodic, proggy, acoustic side of the genre with dramatic, high, Saga-like vocals from Howard Rogers. Forsooth, they pretty much don't belong. The a-side is close to pure power pop, with pert rhythms and rainy guitars carrying the buoyant track. B-side *Caught In A Landslide* is even mellower, courting reggae and jazz and none of the tenets we hold dear with beer. This single was released with two different covers, one yellow, one grey. Later on, the band was courted by both Bronze and RCA, but neither deal materialized. Still later, the prog tendencies took over, as the band became to be more associated with that scene.
Rating 3

Liaison - Only Heaven Knows
(Liaison '84, LSN0020/SRT 4 KS050)
It would be a stretch even calling this a power ballad. It's more like that crappy Gary Moore hit, more of a blues ballad with a truly distracting high-pitched vocal and a drum performance too busy for such a drooper. B-side *Ease The Pain Away* leans us o'er to validation, but only a little. Liaison lasted until the summer of '85.
Rating   4

Lightning Raiders - Psychedelik Musik
(Arista '80, ARIST341)
This band included a number of traveled UK musicians, not to mention Sex Pistols connections, which makes sense given that *Psychedelik Music* sounds like a thin, reedy, underwhelming Sex Pistols anthem. Actually, this would have sounded awesome on the Pistols album, made by those guys, produced by that guy. B-side *Views* is both a little poppier and more metal, ergo, increasingly multi-dimensional, even containing additional textures, notably a nice twin lead. Interestingly, there was a "clean" version of this single for radio (non-picture sleeve) and the regular "adult" picture sleeve version for the general public.
Rating   6

Lightning Raiders - Criminal World
(Revenge '81, REVS200)
Criminal World perpetuates the band's poppy punk style, and is actually weaker than both tracks on the debut single. *Citizens*, however, is the heaviest of the lot, although still more of a metalized punk rocker than anything gloomy, doomy and Maiden-blueprinted. Stupid really, that these guys get considered NWOBHM at all, I suppose most of the qualification coming from the damn band name. Anyway, also licensed to Island for a 12" format issue in Europe, with different artwork. The band's last release would be a promo-only four track sampler EP.
Rating   6

Limelight - Metal Man
(Future Earth '80, FER006)
This long-suffering act got together way before the NWOBHM gave them new life. *Metal Man* was their marquee song and it was a deliberate enough speed rocker with nice albeit brief twin leads that were thoughtful and hooky. Sort of a proggier version of Witchfynde with a Laurence Archer-alike, whatever that means. B-side *Hold Me, Touch Me* sounds like barroom rock from rural Ontario circa '76 (picture Helix before their major label deal), slide guitar and funk lope included.
Rating   5

Limelight - Limelight
(Future Earth '80, FER008)
Limelight were a one record phenom who were a mite better than their lack of accolades would suggest, rattling along with a capable-for-'80 sound that was equal parts old Lizzy, old UFO, White Spirit, pop-inflected Maiden and eccentric prog. *Metal Man* and *Walk On Water* were kinda played and discussed in metal circles at the time, and the whole album works a respectable proto-

power metal mojo, lots of double leads, proficient vocals and general NWOBHM magic. Re-released with a different cover on Mausoleum as **Ashes To Ashes** in '84, and again as a Mausoleum Classix CD in '94.
Rating   6

Limelight - Ashes To Ashes
(Future Earth '82, FERO10)
Good solid NWOBHM that follows all the best rules of the form, *Ashes To Ashes* is like a cross between *Angel Witch* and *Lady Of Mars*, a happy melodic update on *Doctor, Doctor*, great White Spirit authority to the thing. B-side *Knife In Your Back* is a cool stomper with another White Spirit vibe, also sorta like heavy Magnum or Nightwing or Styx with a great lead harmony vocal. All in all, awesome mystique to these guys. Note: a-side shows up on the re-named (also as **Ashes To Ashes**) Mausoleum reissue of the band's album. The b-side is presented in a different version from the album. The album and the single shared the same live shot artwork, albeit with colour differentiation.
Rating   8

Lionheart - Hot Tonight
(Epic '84, EPC26214)
Not to be confused with Steve Grimmett's also post-NWOBHM Lionsheart, Lionheart were a pomp rock supergroup which at various times early on included, all on vocals, Jess Cox of Tygers, Reuben Archer of Stampede and finally John Farnham. Other alumni included Def Leppard's Frank Noon on drums, as well as Les Binks from Judas Priest and Clive Edwards from Wild Horses on the road in that role. Anyway, once the album finally happened, joining founders Dennis Stratton (ex-Iron Maiden) and Steve Mann (ex-Liar), was singer Chad Brown and bassist Rocky Newton, soon to see the wars with MSG. The album is a mess, yer basic and typically cloistered British AOR, big bad corporate production by Kevin Beamish, ill-advised Styx harmonies, songs that thump along with no clear purpose other than to suggest a stiff cardboard composite rendition of American bands doing the same thing better. Included for full facial cringe, a stodgy, stiff, clattery version of Gillan's (well, Colin Towns') *Nightmare*, which, played back-to-back with the original, demonstrates all that was wrong with big budget records in the '80s.
Rating   3

Lonely Hearts - F.M. Fantasy
(Tenacity '84, TR01)
This post-Panza Division act decided to try the melodic side of things as the tide shifted in '84, coming up with the boogie-rocking title track plus the heavier *Young Girl*. The 12" *Believe* EP was released (even more lightweight than the first single) in '86 before the band finally threw in the towel at the turn of the decade.
Rating   5

Lone Wolf - Leave Me Behind
(Guardian '82, GRC144)
Funny, many consider this single borderline NWOBHM, but the a-side is squarely AC/DC-ish in nature with a

hard-ass production sound and a gritty vocal. B-side is called *High Class Hooker*, and it's better than its title, starting with an epic Maiden/Savatage wail before it gets bluesy and Samson-like. Not issued with a picture sleeve, so just look for the gangly and garish orange Guardian label. Note, Lone Wolf were semi-famous due to Satan/Avenger/Blitzkrieg vocalist Brian Ross being part and parcel (and manager) of the band, come '84's *Nobody's Move* three track EP for Neat. However, the original version of *Leave It Behind* of which we speak, features a different guy.
Rating 5

Lone Wolf - Nobody's Move
(Neat '84, 44)
The fact that this three track scab features Satan's Brian Ross (wrapped in a python) and is early Neat with a quixotic indie-looking album cover does little to cheer up the sonically duff dross enclosed. There's little skill anywhere on these dour coal-mining metal mittens, the band sounding like label buds Crucifixion or a Tygers Of Pots 'n' Pan Tang in a freezing English rehearsal space in October.
Rating 4

Lone Wolf – Cash For Candy
(Wolf Music '80, 001)
The less famous of the two Lone Wolfs, these guys issued this white label two-tracker in a very low quantity, subsequently hand-numbering them. *Cash For Candy* is certainly a heavy enough track, but so unique in its rhythmic stutter and thespian vocal phrasings that it fits neither the NWOBHM style or anything particularly retro or American, save for the killer Brit metal break – a nice touch indeed. B-side

Pipeline Mary is an effortlessly likeable, guitar-drenched, melodic hard rocker that captures the excitement of the new metal without courting it unimaginatively or obediently. A fine, fine single both coming and going.
Rating 8

Lotus Cruise - Billy's Got A Gun
(Armbury '83, ARM603)
The a-side of this scarce non-picture sleever is a bit of lame weak hard rock that tries for the drama of its title but falls flat due to the calm skinny tie new wave vocals. B-side *Tonight* sits on much the same rudimentary framework although the riff is a bit more grey-skied and NWOBHM. Pitiful guitar work. Note: this pre-Cry band's only other output was a cassette-only album called **A Fistful Of Heartache**.
Rating 5

Lyadrive – Anytime
(Bridge '83, BR003)
Likely infected by the British press's preoccupation with American AOR, Lyadrive turn in a dumb riff rocker plagued with a pointless keyboard lilt, which turns into The Stranglers come break time. B-side *White Dress* is another thing, near mesmerizingly commercial and metallic at once, novel melodically and rhythmically, a near underground classic. Only other output released during the band's existence was the speedy and metal-committed *We've Got The Rock (You're Gonna Roll)* on Ebony's **Metal Warriors** sampler, and *Another Time, Another Place* on a compilation called **The Bridge Album**. Post-Tempest Drive.
Rating 6

Maineeaxe - Gonna Make You Rock
(Powerstation '84, OHM6)
The raucous hot-riffed a-side can be found on the band's bright, fetching, quick-rawkin' and commercially viable **Shout It Out** LP while b-side *Snatch* is a novel pastiche of excerpts from the album. Spanish version also exists, with different artwork, using *Are You Ready* for the flipside.
Rating 7

Maineeaxe - Shout It Out
(Powerstation '84, AMP3)
One of those weird situations where the debut exhibits more polish than the follow-up, **Shout It Out** straddles more conservative production values and indeed more conservative riffing, which is basic and uneventful yet still palatable. Vocals are flat although strangely arresting, and side two shows major slam. Trying too hard to express calm maturity, this band slotted into a commercial hair band look, but had songs too bold for that watery genre, especially the UK's sorry version of it. Trivia: Maineeaxe had roots in bands such as Trans-am, Flight and Syar.
Rating 7

Maineeaxe - The Game
(Powerstation '84, OHM8)
The Game is unfortunately a by-rote ballad, not up to the band's Mama's Boys-vibed happy metal standards, but nicely arranged all the same, brightly propped by clean production and strong vocals. By the way, Mama's Boys have been left out of the book a) 'cos their sound is a bit too clean and b) they're Irish, so strictly not NWOBHM! Anyhoo, *The Game* can be found on **Shout It Out**, while b-side *No Foolin'* is non-LP. The band would follow up with one more album, '85's **Going For Gold**, before calling it a day two years hence.
Rating 6

Mammath - Rock Me
(Neat '84, NEAT42)
Post-Chinatown and Stallion, and pre-Air-Raide, Preyer and Ashamata, the dudes in Mammath have pretty much earned their NWOBHM obscurity badges, although the band lasted for scarcely a year. But this single is competent enough, going for that big Neat sound that is written like stadium rock, recorded like yer bones are dragging the pavement. The drums boom, the vocals screech, the guitars paint-strip. It's metal alright, problem is, it's metal on metal. B-side is more of the rollicked same, *Rough 'n' Ready* sounding like the woeful Black Rose crossed with Quiet Riot.
Rating 6

Mantas - Winds Of Change
(Neat '84, 1042)
The ol' Venom rogue fancies a bit of a change evidently, assembling this prissy keyboard-tainted project to show his serious side. Despite the record's heart-palpitating pace, nothing's all that aggressive here, although martial artist Mantas absolutely shines on axe, surprising wholesale with licks, riffs and solo excursions that are variously exact and fluid, very often creative and enjoyable. The rest of the show's piffle though, flat-on-its-face pop metal with theatrically British vocals from one Pete Harrison, band on hi-tech overdrive, songs stuck in climate-controlled commercial comfort. Verdict: now two bands are a waste of this man's talents.
Rating 4

Marquis De Sade – Somewhere Up In The Mountains
(X-Pose '81, XP02)
The a-side is a ponderous, mostly light and proggy thing sliced by interesting synths and harrowing, thespian vocals, but b-side *Black Angel* churns like Angel Witch, resoundingly heavy and modern for '81, to be sure, great yelping vocalist to boot, nice keyboard touches to ice the cake. Indeed Pete Gordelier would hook up with Angel Witch's Kevin Heybourne for the excellent Blind Fury album and then stay on through crappy Angel Witch incarnations. Picture sleeve, with band photo insert.
Rating   7

Marseille – Red, White And Slightly Blue
(Mountain '78, TOPC5012)
Fitting nowhere in the history of metal, Liverpool's Marseille were a fully-actualized British hard rock act, stumbling out of the gates with this withdrawn album but then storming back quickly with a solid "debut." As explanation, copies of **Red, White And Slightly Blue** were given away to press as promos with copies of the self-titled. The story is unsurprisingly a little deeper than that, with **Red, White** being the *true* debut, meant for sale, scrapped but only after copies were pressed. Hence the giveaway status, although some were very likely sold in the shops as well. Listening to this album, it's understandable why the band was disappointed. The sound is thin, the performances rough, frantic and awkward, with an annoying French theme. But – perhaps the band's own fault – the style is a cross between hard rock, glam, punk and sassy new wave, perhaps like Girl crossed with Trust, Heavy Metal Kids, Little Bob Story and the novelty of old Sweet.
Rating   6

Marseille - The French Way
(Mountain '78, BON1)
A-side was from the withdrawn debut LP **Red White And Slightly Blue**, but in different version, while b-side *Cold Steel* is non-LP. *The French Way* is quite the humourous punk metal glam rocker about getting your sex life sorted out. *Cold Steel*, on the other hand, is similarly punky in the manner of The Vibrators and Eater, but clean enough to pass as Americanized hard rock, what with those harmonies countering a palpable sneer. Note: there's also a 12" version from a year earlier, with the song called *Do It The French Way*.
Rating   6

Marseille - Over And Over
(Mountain '78, BON2)
The a-side as well as the b-side *You're A Woman* hail from the second, or "proper" album, on which the band had found a cogent Def Leppard-proud, Girl-like sound and solid big budget production to boot, courtesy of Nazareth's Manny Charlton (Mountain waz Naz's label o'er in the UK). The band's bold logo signaled the move as well, Marseille canning the wobbly French image, which saw the withdrawn debut and the first single both adorned with the red, white and blue of the French flag. Still, *Over And Over* is a pretty poppy number, notwithstanding the strong two-part chorus. *You're A Woman* more than makes up for it with a tough yet still commercial riff over a stomping groove.
Rating   7

Marseille - Marseille
(Mountain '79, TOPS125)

Marseille pre-dated Def Leppard by a year with this smooth, professional modern metal meal, a little light on riffery compared to the grit dealers of the NWOBHM, but definitely no worse in many departments than the Leps' landmark debut. As explained above, this is the record the band quickly found they really wanted to make, the collection enclosed rocking very energetically with nods to American '70s rockers such as Riot, Ted Nugent, Starz or Legs Diamond, if a little towards the party zone songcraft-wise, adding a dose of Quo boogie to send these songs pistol-packin'. Definitely a little isolated and naive, but remarkably well put together and visionary of stadium rock postures to come, this thing sounded like the work or a whole different band versus the playfully sneering false start of a debut. Of note, Marseille were the proverbial and perennial back-up band to the stars, including Gillan, Priest, Wishbone Ash, Nazareth, Blackfoot, Whitesnake and UFO. After Mountain went bankrupt, the band went into a state of shocked suspension, re-emerging in '84 with the quite awful and unrepresentative **Touch The Night** release.
Rating   7

Marseille - Kiss Like Rock 'n' Roll
(Mountain '79, TOP39)

A-side is non-LP while *Can Can* reaches back to the confused first record. You can really hear the band's indecision with this one, *Kiss Like Rock 'n' Roll* sounding like uptempo Mott, stroked by Slade and pre-metal Sweet, while *Can Can* boogies moderately aggressively like Spider crossed with the pub rock of Heavy Metal Kids.
Rating   6

Marseille - Bring On The Dancin' Girls
(Mountain '79, TOP49)

Both the a-side and the b-side *Rock You Tonight* are LP tracks, but are presented here in different versions. Of the two, *Rock You Tonight* is the real gem, a party metal showstopper, if one ignores the similarities to the marquee Spinal Tap number. The a-side on the other hand, an acoustic-driven number with the band's requisite solid harmonies and a fussy arrangement. Sounds maudlin, like something Kiss might do.
Rating   8

Marseille - Kites
(Mountain '80, TOP51)

The a-side is a catchy, daring, proggy cover diversion for the band, successful in its Splti Enz-like novelty, while *Some Like It Hot* is standard speedy goodtime Van Halen-esque rock fare for the band, darn near the heaviest track on the album. A-side is non-LP, although the North American version of the album, did in fact carry the track.
Rating   7

Marseille - Touch The Night
(Ultra Noise '84, ULTRA3)

A polished and very promising second album dissipates into this awkward pop metal sellout, a record too wide open production-wise to have such skeletal and airy structures carry the weight. Marks a general English tendency to either bulk up on the metal or court the sickly sweet affections of the Americans. Here it's the latter, as Marseille and countless others fed off a Kerrang!-fueled appetite for weedy wimphem.
Rating   4

Marseille - Walking On A High Wire
(Ultra Noise '84, WALK1)

Barely a shell of who they were, a reformed Marseille fall into the trap of writing forced AOR. Both tracks (b-side is a gamey

Heavy Pettin'-styled fastback rocker called *Too Late*) are from the abysmal third and last LP **Touch The Night**, although the a-side, a stiff, turgid hair metal rocker, is a different version. Black plus limited edition silver vinyl.
Rating 4

Marz – Lady Of The Night
(Frozen Owl '80, SRR0023)
From the Grantham area, Marz had a semi-committed hard riff rock sound, quite commercial, melodic, recorded quite raw, but with good vocals, including solid harmonies. The stout-riffed but simple "evil woman" a-side is available on the **NWOBHM Vol. 8** bootleg. The b-sides were foreboding and typically lengthy ballad (turned hummable rocker) *Daydreamer* and *On The Road To Freedom*, an understated retro-styled rocker solid enough but a bit pubby. Memorable for the music as well as the alien-with-guitar cover art.
Rating 8

Masai – Stranger To Myself
(Turbo '82, TURB01)
Masai were Cagey Bee renamed (with one personnel change), and this single was actually accompanied by a full-length album called **Good Boys Never Grumble**. The poppy (yet somewhat AC/DC-ish of riff, come sturdy verse time) a-side is from that record while the rougher b-side *Lightning* is non-LP. The band was to morph once more into an even poppier outfit such as The Storm.
Rating 5

Mass – Rebel With A Cause
(SRT '82, SRTS82 CUS 1419)
The b-side on this flagrantly commercial non-picture sleeve single was called *Running From The Morning*. Later on, this rare six-man band dropped one member and changed their name to Chase.
Rating 6

Masterstroke – Prisoner Of Love
(DTS '82, DTS 043)
A-side to this non-picture sleever, *Prisoner Of Love*, is a strange NWOBHM/pop hybrid, sounding like Dire Straits with mournful Brit metal melodies and eerie guitar textures supporting the Angel Witch bleat of the vocals. Big, thick dirty recording as well, despite the metal-lite bounce to the thing. B-side *Burning Heart* seals the deal, stomping along 'neath hopelessly caustic guitars like early days Samson cavorting with Handsome Beasts at a cheap Chateaux.
Rating 7

Mayday - Day After Day
(Reddingtons Rare '80, DAN2)
Recording for a store/label renowned for releasing cool early Quartz product, Midlands band Mayday actually had this single produced by Mick Hopkins of that legendary, stellar band. It actually sounds – quite horrifically – like a Soft Cell or OMD song, perhaps crossed with the music for a feminine hygiene television ad. B-side is called *Love In The Spaceage*, and it's almost as bad, but more of a rock song I guess, if one can ignore the popcorn-popping synths. In here for the connections to the almighty Quartz, and that is emphatically all.
Rating 2

McCoy – Oh Well
(Legacy '83, LGY9)
John McCoy is the big, bald bassist in sunglasses known for his sojourn in both Samson and Gillan. Indeed, Paul Samson is credited as one of the guitarists, and Colin Towns is o'er from the drunken Gillan experience. The central piece of the guy's brief, unremarkable solo legacy is **Mini Album**. Central to that is a cover of Fleetwood Mac's *Oh Well*, which is the a-side of this single, but in different

version. Scrappy, spare, fast and lacking in every kind of depth, the treatment is very much in the crackly, roughshod style of both Samson and Gillan. B-side *Because You Lied* (also from the EP) is even more like Samson, down that band's spooky, pulsating ballad road, the track buttressed by a nice chorus harmony.
Rating   5

McCoy - Mini Album
(Legacy '83, LLM109)
It never ceases to amaze me how Gillan's particular circle of wizened veterans managed to sound like such talent show drop-outs when out on their own in search of a crust. McCoy's four-track EP comprises three very basic metallic originals, one mellow anesthetic, and a cover of Fleetwood Mac's awesome *Oh Well*, the inclusion of which was my sole reason for buying this way back in college days. Of course big John and his jam buddies blast through it without a second's plan, giving it a biker-ish speed metal spin, still leaving the only brilliant rendition that I can recall as one by The Rockets, which, granted, I've not heard in 20 years (of note, the EP version is different from that of the above discussed single).
Rating   3

McCoy – The Sound OF Thunder
(Legacy '84, LGY17)
The second and last single from McCoy is this biker-ish hard rocker, with an appropriately whiskey-soaked vocal from T. Bone Rees, whose voice bears a passing resemblance to that of Fin from Waysted. B-side, once again, is *Because You Lied*.
Rating   4

Meanstreak – Played It Right
(SRT '81, MS1)
Trashy production, poppy American hard rock sound, fey harmonies, and even some cowbell for this Brighton-based act, along with the requisite crack at Thin Lizzy harmonies. Quaint, and if a positive spin be put on it, sorta before their time, given that hair metal wasn't even a going concern yet. Tracks are *Played It Right*, the hectic and trainwrecked *You Took The Fire* and *I Know*, even more of a scurried, shuffling disaster. Barely belongs.
Rating   5

Megaton - Aluminum Lady
(Hot Metal Music '81, HMM69)
B-side is *Die Hard*, both tracks being convincing NWOBHM romps, the a-side telling the humorous and anachronistic tale of a violent evil (and very silver) woman in a curious French accent. But it pounds along nicely, quite riffy and molten for its age. *Die Hard* sounds too similar to its a-side, same goofy vocal (are these guys even English?), a bit of a Krokus vibe. Non-picture sleeve.
Rating   8

Mendes Prey - On To The Borderline
(Mendes Prey '82, AM076)
A-side *On To The Borderline* is a nice cross between melodic hard rock, chuggy NWOBHM and a strange Bad Company vibe what with those desperado lyrics. Solid enough production, a fey attempt at vocal harmonies and by track's end, an endearing melodic quality that is not hard on the ears. Mendes Prey featured ex-Vardis bassist Tony Boulton. B-side

Runnin' For You is a tough but dour professional boogie, more like a mid-speed metal gallop that reminds me a bit of Trespass; nice emotional build to the thing from a band proven to be fully ready for dotted line signing. Note: Mendes Prey had one more (post-NWOBHM) single, a cover of Demon's *Wonderland* in 1986, backed with *Can You Believe It* (Wag Records, WAG2), also available in 12" format (12WAG2). Only other output is the likeable enough mid-rocker *What The Hell's Going On?* from the second **Heavy Metal Heroes** compilation.
Rating 7

Metal Mirror - Rock An' Roll Ain't Never Gonna Leave Us
(M+M '80, MM001)

One single, plus a jammin' beer goggles boogie called *Hard Life* on the **Heavy Metal Heroes** comp., and that's all she wrote, although lead singer Cameron Vagges went on to two albums as a solo artist as Cameron Vegas, '90's **Life's A Bitch And Then You Die** and '93's **Live Rollin' In Greece**. The raw, groovy a-side almost convinces us that these guys could shot glass 'em like Savage, but b-side *English Booze* (called *Living On English Booze* on the label) sounds er, tipsy and ill-prepared, trying to be funky but merely stumbling about. Cool band forged in the drinking spirit of scroungy metal.
Rating 7

Midas – Can't Stop Loving You Now
(S-R-R '83, SRR 0008)

Ahem, pretty weak calling this tragically independent indie a NWOBHM artifact, what with the a-side's poppy chorus, drum performance that sounds like a cheap drum machine and pedal steel (like?) licks butted in for unintended comic effect. However, the b-side, *Power In The Sky* is a heavier affair. It's a promising track indeed, bleak, freshly arranged, essentially trundling metal set to a thumping, angular 4/4 stomp. Shortly thereafter the band would splinter, with vocalist Paul Taylor moving on to Elixir. Crudely drawn yet amusing sleeve, but the presentation is helped with a fold-out lyric sheet.
Rating 6

Millennium – Millennium
(Guardian '84, GRC2263)

One of the less talked-about NWOBHM acts with a full album to their name, Millennium's only other output was inclusion on Guardian's **Pure Overkill** comp. The sound, as with all Guardian output is rough 'n' tumble, gritty and dated, Millennium rocking considerably committed with a chug that sounds like pre-clue Krokus without the boogie. Simple, accessible pub metal, evenly acceptable, highly collectible, yet none too lovable, a bit like lower grade Dark Star.
Rating 6

Mithrandir – Magick
(New Leaf '82, SVC01)

Known for being one of the most amateurish, tuneless, toneless NWOBHM recordings ever released, **Magick** showcases *Eyes Of The Madman*, which proves emphatically that point, even if the song, in better hands (say Trespass, Dark Star or Maiden), might have been saved as a b-level galloper. *All The Time* really isn't that bad either, outside of the AM radio recording, while *Call Of The Wild* is an ambitious dark power ballad, successfully creepy like the best of NWOBHM crease-dwellers. Y'know, despite Graham Gargiulo's one-take imprecision, he's actually got a pretty cool high-register voice. Thus I defend Mithrandir! With a budget and some time, this ridiculed single could have been a contender.
Rating 6

Mithrandir – Dreamers Of Fortune
(New Leaf '82, SVC570)
A cool and characteristic crude drawing graces this second and mercifully last single for Mithrander. Our resident a-side begins with off-tune pixie tinkling and then becomes powerless pop prog, guitars turned off, listener subsequently so as well. B-side *After Tomorrow* is actually metal of a sort, in truth, a potentially good song recorded out back in the tool shed; heck, even those thin, reedy vocals are starting to sound obtusely useful.
Rating 6

Moby Dick – Nothing To Fear
(Ebony '82, EBON 5)
B-side of this non-picture sleever (yellow Ebony with trademark pentagram) is called *Can't Have My Body Tonight*. A-side can also be found on Ebony's **Metallic Storm** sampler for '82. Moby Dick featured Max Bacon of Nightwing, Bronz and GTR fame. Musically speaking, both tracks are raw, thumping, melodic mid-paced rockers so at odds with what one associates with Max Bacon, although amusingly, it's obvious he's the one with talent in this lackluster, rudimentary band.
Rating 6

Money – (Aren't We All) Searching
(Gull '78, GULS64)
Money are most known for their *Leo The Jester* track on the well-traveled **Metal Explosion** comp., plus the fact that they managed a full-length album, called **First Investment**, way back in '79. The record was produced by Chris Tsangarides, and was issued by Gull, early (and hotly scorned) label for Judas Priest, as well as for Nightwing. This a-side hails from that record, however b-side *Where Have All The Dancers Gone?* is non-LP. Note: there's also a Japanese picture sleeve version, with *Mari-Anna*, also from the album, as the b-side.
Rating 7

Money – First Investment
(Gull '79, GULP1031)
Not exactly NWOBHM or even proto, yet not 'cos of the usual "too light" grumble, **First Investment** is in fact thumping and guitary throughout, a bit like Stampede and Marseille crossed with Mott and mebbee Sweet. In other words, this is quite the rockin' act, spanning hard-tailed glam to things North American like Legs Diamond, Moxy and Teaze. The men of Money, however, rise above the weirdness and confusion through tasty performances of their difficult hybrids (see *Finale* – wow!), as well as the Chris Tsangarides inaugural production ever, the Tygers/Anvil/Lizzy master capturing the band grinding of groove, explosive of bottom end, warm, vibrant, and then not scrimping against the demands of vocal harmonies either, stacking bombastic cause of effect like Queen. Highly interesting act that should have gone places. Note: in '08, **First Investment** justifiably saw reissue by Derek Oliver and his classy retro Rock Candy label, tacking on *Where Have All The Dancers Gone?* as a bonus track.
Rating 8

Money – EP.
(Hobo '80, HOS 011)

Rarer (and heavier) than the Gull single and on average the expensive-sounding album, this indie picture sleeve EP featured *Fast World* and *Small Time Criminal* on the "Heads" side and the 9:12 *Another Case Of Suicide* on the "Tails." Chris Tsangarides, once again, turns the knobs, although he gets more of a scrappy Tygers vibe than the bulbous Queen sound proffered for the album. So yeah, *Fast World* is fast and squarely NWOBHM, *Small Time Criminal* is a little draggy, chuggy and barroom, while the epic side two-er is what's to be expected, a morose ballad of death, nonetheless propped by chilly atmospherics, glam dramatics and thoughtful guitar textures. Smart stuff.
Rating 8

Nicky Moore Band – Year Of The Lie
(Street Tunes '81, STS006)

Under this moniker, ex-Tiger singer Nicky Moore had supported his future employer Samson, which, one presumes, is where Paul caught wind of the big man with even bigger pipes. The band's first single included the a-side plus covers of Boston's *Smokin'* and Journey's *Walks Like A Lady* on the flip. Note: there was also an album called **Samson and Nicky Moore** (Street Tunes '83, STLP008).
Rating 6

Nicky Moore Band – The Other Side
(Street Tunes '82, STS008)

B-side is another Boston cover, this one being *Long Time*. Shortly after this, it was off to Samson, once Bruce had left the band for the Iron Maiden gig.
Rating 6

More – Warhead
(Atlantic '81, K50775)

More quietly and without warning fell out of the NWOBHM pack onto a major label, but alas to no avail, as for reasons unbeknownst to me, the record bombed, as did the gravity-defying follow-up. Both, at least on the merit of music alone, were well-paced, smoothly-assembled hard rock contenders. **Warhead** benefits from the ready-for-prime-time belt of soon-to-depart vocalist Paul Mario Day (Iron Maiden's first vocalist back in '76!), and the underwhelming but solid production of Henry (H-Bomb) Weck, who adds his southern Blackfoot-like flavour to this considerably riff-packed record. But no matter how academically proud **Warhead** stacks up, I never play it, due to a pervasive sense of restraint borne of a rhythm section and supporting mix that forces the songs to live on riff alone. Strange one to pin, but I immediately think early Armored Saint crossed with heavy Blackfoot or Boyzz, whatever that means. Definitely ahead of its time but sabotaged by a '70s tendency to remove the edges from metal. Note: North American version is different from the original UK, in areas of cover, song sequence, and one track, *Lord Of Twilight*, having been deleted.
Rating 6

More – We Are The Band
(Atlantic '81, K11561)

The a-side hails from the strangely lifeless debut album, **Warhead** being produced

by Al Nalli and Brownsville's Henry Weck to sound like Armored Saint crossed with heavy Blackfoot. Tame with a cheesy chorus. The b-side on the other hand is a masterpiece, a non-LPer called *Atomic Rock* which, even though it still sounds like heavy southern rock, injects a dose of Maiden and Angel Witch into those twisty leads, o'er which Paul Mario Day turns in an ankle-biter of a performance. Urgent stuff, if still a shade shy of the magic of **Blood & Thunder**. Also available in 12" version (K115611), free patch, oddly no extra track, same catalogue number. Dutch version also exists, with different cover art, as does an Italian issue, different cover art again.
Rating   7

More - Blood & Thunder
(Atlantic '82, SD19339)

Totally gutting a gutless lineup, Kenny Cox retains only ligger-look-alike Brian Day on bass while adding two exquisite talents in drummer A. J. Burton and vocalist Mick Stratton, whose pipes blow this record into a rare level of rock 'n' roll euphoria, Mick joining mid-production, rewriting all the lyrics, while Paul Mario Day jumped ship to Wildfire. And man, I ain't kidding ya, **Blood & Thunder** has no trouble carrying its own with the likes of Quartz' **Stand Up And Fight**, Diamond Head's **Lightning To The Nations** and Witchfinder General's **Friends Of Hell** as seminal wedges of the UK metal resurgence, while taking a decidedly more mainstream metal directive, featuring flashy, tuneful, polished and intelligent rockers of all speeds, gleaming with strong choruses racing in and out of tasteful riffs and lofty ambitions. When it blazes it blazes, exemplified by *Traitors Gate*, instrumental *The Eye* and the epic title track, and when it explores hard rock, it triumphs with elegance as on *I Just Can't Believe It* and *Rock And Roll*. And above all, it's just vintage metal to the bone, solid track after track, in the proudest of metal traditions, Kenny Cox proving his mercurial talent for synthesizing UFO, Priest and Purple with the barrage of recent talents competing alongside him, carving technical but effortlessly enjoyable anthems at will. Supreme metal magic in the making, More deserved to be rock royalty, having that star quality borne of being blessed with four distinct personalities whose talents can be attended to in isolation, yet who combine for such strong songs, versus so many acts that were off on flights of fancy. One of a hallowed few task forces to which this book is dedicated. And man, bloody Mick Stratton... why did this guy not end up a star?
Rating   10

More - Trickster
(Atlantic '82, K11744)

Way poppier than the magnificent **Blood & Thunder** as a whole, this hard rocker sounds more like Axe or early barsy non-LP Heavy Pettin', the label perhaps doing some mining for a hit. B-side *Hey Joe* (also non-LP), is the chestnut immortalized by Jimi Hendrix. But More does a bizarre, galloping, rocked-up version of it, trashy and raw in such temporal proximity to **Blood & Thunder**, which granted, boasted different production credits, this thing featuring George Nicholson, the album being splendidly self-produced. Strange single, perhaps signifying cracks in the band's resolve.
Rating   6

Moselle - Call Me
(SRT '83, SRTS 83 CUS1792)

A-side betrays a band not exactly thinking NWOBHM, but more American pomp rock. B-side was the heavier, quicker,

less poppy *Rock Anthem*. Moselle soon changed their name to General Wolf and re-sold the single under than name, the previously non-ps issue now slapped with cheap black and white photo-and-logo artwork.
Rating 4

Mother's Ruin - Streetlights
(Spectra '82, SPC6)
Both the a-side *Streetlights* and the b-side *Turn Another Corner* sound like big-chorded upbeat Sweet, solid, simple harmonies, nice mix, hooky but unremarkable, except for a nice harmony lead guitar break in the latter.
Rating 6

Mother's Ruin - Streetfighter
(Spectra '81, SPC1)
Borderline NWOBHMers Mother's Ruin actually managed an LP, from which neither of these tracks hail. The a-side rocks pretty insistently, buttressed by twin leads and a polite yet impermeable wall-of-guitars sound. A chorus made memorable by vocal harmonies and a subsequent eccentric break and spirited guitar solo lift the band a cut above. B-side, a ballad called *Leaving You*, is the typical five minutes of dreary weather NWOBHMers tinkle and tinker with when trying to write a slow dancer.
Rating 6

Mother's Ruin - Road To Ruin
(Spectra '82, SPA1)
Perhaps feeding off **Kerrang**'s love of what they called wimphem at the time (basically anything poptastic from Canada or the US), Mother's Ruin do a sort of New England/Touch bounce 'n' flounce, total soft metal, nonetheless with some nice Lizzy-ish guitar work and general good will toward all charts. Nice harmonies too, but just a little too light-footed to infiltrate the metal mainstream buzzing deafeningly at the time.
Rating 6

Mother's Ruin - Say It's Not True
(Spectra '82)
Both tracks hail from the light but tasteful **Road To Ruin** album, a record somewhat down the class path of Money and Stampede. The a-side is a thoughtful stab at a commercial ballad, drawing from the R&B end of Journey, perhaps. B-side *It's Illogical* is quite the mid-rock charmer, again the band's odd Thin Lizzy vibe coming to the fore, even if the end result is something one might image a shelved Lizzy track, a heavy Phil solo track or most sensibly, along the pedestrian lines of Grand Slam.
Rating 6

Motörhead - Leaving Here
(Stiff '77, BUY9)

Motörhead's first single was the only release without the band's patented arced logo, although it was more or less the same typeface. Curious choice going with a campy cover, *Leaving Here* being an old Holland/Dozier chestnut that is in fact, quite lame. *White Line Fever* is the opposite end of the spectrum, grinding, heavy, urgent, and right to the punted thick of the band's pre-Venom repulsion for repulsion's sake vibe.

Rating   5

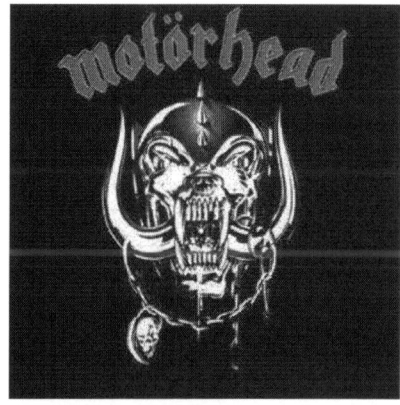

Motörhead - Motörhead
(Chiswick '77, WIK2)

Falling into a collapsed dogpile of a metal band so unkempt that it was the punks that thought they were the ones being serenaded, wizened rock pigs Fast Eddie Clarke, Philthy Animal Taylor and the warted wizard ("one of the good guys," he sez) Ian "Lemmy" Kilmister (ex-Hendrix roadie, ex-Hawkwind bass guy) converged upon a world unprepared for the brutish bashing to come. Motörhead were big, bad and loud, recorded rank and putrid as they slogged their way through shabby pounder after shabby pounder, here sent to make a single, the boys emerging from a night of speed a whole lot sweatier with a whole lot more. And **Motörhead**, the bonafide studio debut would stand, now years down the road, as the most viral, belligerent and hapless Motörhead record of them all, the band of brawling brothers creating a caterwauling yet unified, headache-inducing distorted drone through all eight scrapyard anthems enclosed. Ergo Motörhead were instantly recognizable as the first metal band who weren't trying to look good, play good or record good, which resulted in the ultimate deception (and warted reception) of the punks who were unwittingly embracing these most fossilized of hippies. Critics, who generally despised the tenets of metal were also sucked in, to this day, Motörhead's goodly name being tossed around by those scribes who yearn to show that they walk on the wild side. The record had tons of songs loaded for bear that would become live anthems, personal favourites being *Keep Us On The Road*, *Lost Johnny* and *The Watcher*, with the title track being a sorry tangle of wires you just gotta scoop up and take home. Above dissection or dissertation, **Motörhead** stands pretty much specifically as the key influence on those who would create purposefully polluted metal (next up, Venom), the band embodying faint (never!) echoes of the Stooges, but really occupying a space as the original grunge rockers, being the first who could actually play, but rather chose to stink up the place. A crass act all the way.

Rating   8

Motörhead - Motörhead
(Chiswick '77, S13)

A-side is of course the band's oddly melodic, purely punk title anthem, gurgling bass, hapless everything, gleefully under-achieving. B-side *City Kids* is a retread from Wallis' Pink Fairies days (**Kings Of Oblivion**, 1973), and is also discomfortingly melodic to the point of singsongy. Never thee mind though, coked up to Motörhead's grease levels, it succeeds. Also available on 12" and later opportunistically reissued in late '79 through Big Beat on coloured vinyl (NS13) and picture disc (NSP13), eventually joined by NS61 (see below).

Rating   6

Motörhead - Louie Louie
(Bronze '78, BRO60)

Yet another dil novelty cover from a band which nevertheless made their albums all business. *Louie Louie* is rendered close,

laid back and not all that serious, lending it a certain charm. *Tear Ya Down* is the ripping album track from **Overkill**, driven by that ubiquitous Philthy shuffle beat that unwittingly lets the guitars, bass and vocals define the word heaviness.
Rating 7

Motörhead - Overkill
(Bronze '79, BRO67)
Preceding the launch of the classic drastic fantastic album by a month, *Overkill* was one of the first double bass drum "OTT" metal classics to ever build a wall of sonics. Destined to become a Motörhead classic, it's actually pretty dull butted up against the band's '90s work. Just ask Lemmy. Non-LP b-side *Too Late, Too Late* remains one of the band's coolest non-LP tracks, built around a modern metal riff and classic Motörhead melodies come chorus time. A rare bit of discipline for the band. Also available in 12" format (12BRO67).
Rating 9

Motörhead - Overkill
(Bronze '79, BRON515)
With a raging front wrapper like this one, and with that masked mascot looking totally bitchin' in full four-colour flare, blue ink on schoolbook, or black felt pen on jean jacket, how can you lose? **Overkill** was ergo a growler of a record tattooed on our life in most of those formats during our dwindling high school days. The record was one obnoxious crank of a rocker, sticking its finger in the eye of punk and shaking up a bloated metal aristocracy with one vile mess of decibel lunacy. Lemmy in full flak throat leads the charge, croaking through such cat-swinging gems as *I'll Be Your Sister*, *Stay Clean*, and ultimately *No Class* with its slaughtering of *Tush*'s classic riff amidst WWII (the big one) axe solos from one pillaging Fast Eddie. The ultimate power trio, Motörhead as a recorded experience was pure unharnessed, unvarnished wattage. They were a band of unrelenting destruction, playing the role of rock soldier, the hapless underdog sent to the front with a jammed weapon. The rough surface of records like **Overkill** is actually borne of a love of many musics, the band then setting upon, with drunken double vision, a pogrom to gleefully and with good intention, stomp the blues, psychedelia, old Chuck Berry riffs (as Lemmy will tell you) and last week's punk rock under a tarnished metal hammer that always lives to swing another day. Thus **Overkill** became the band's first realized manifesto, a collection of barbs the band tears from its bleeding, weathered, unshowered flesh in unnecessary demonstration of a most deadly seriousness of intention.
Rating 9

Motörhead - No Class
(Bronze '79, BRO78)
This single was distinguished by the fact that it came in three different cover, one each featuring an individual band member on the front sleeve. *No Class* is of course the bikerized remake of ZZ Top's *Tush* (well, sort of), while non-LPer *Like A Nightmare* is either a psychedelic and modulating blues metal or just plain dull. Still, it invokes white line fever better than the track for which the phenom is named.
Rating 7

Motörhead - Bomber
(Bronze '79, BRON523)
And the mental harassment drags ever on, as Fast Eddie Clarke, Philthy Animal Taylor and "Lemme a fiver" explore the effects of further corrosion between conspiring aged hippies forced to battle alone a

world that is appreciative, in the main, of sensible music. **Overkill**, **Bomber**... what's the difference? Both records, and to a lesser extent, the malnourished debut, rocked proudly and loudly, the new, hastily assembled collection strafing the crowd with the likes of bitter classics *Poison* and *All The Aces*, plus the catchy, automotive speed-riffing of the title track. If anything, **Bomber** is even more shabby and imploded than its turf-busting predecessor, its patina downright diseased as Philthy buries every attempt at pattern under layers of crashing trash can lids and power shuffles nearly too fast for the creaking digits of his cranky cohorts. The end result, when those who can still hear look back and listen to these things, is a record that is considered the least classic of the first four. I mean, **Motörhead**, you feel sorry for, **Overkill** is the true debut, and **Ace Of Spades** is the unchallenged hit record. **Bomber**... call it the red-headed stepchild.

Rating 9

Motörhead - Bomber
(Bronze '79, BRO85)

Bomber is sort of a mix of *Overkill*'s brains and the wobbly legs of *Motörhead*, dim-wittedly moshing along on a melody that takes the tune to happy anthem status. Non-LPer *Over The Top* is almost a throwback to *On Parole*, a bit dated, debilitated and slack-jawed compared to much of what made it onto **Bomber**. Still, the atmosphere is rife with World War II aircraft. Also available on blue vinyl to match the blue vinyl version of the LP.

Rating 8

Motörhead - On Parole
(Liberty/United Artists '79, LBR1004)

Comprising mostly timid takes on greaseballers that would rage full fester on the **Motörhead** debut, **On Parole** is like a demo, b-side, barrel-scraping trip through the formative stages of a concept, Lemmy getting his first bitter taste of label skullduggery, UA sitting on their ass, doing nothing with their deal with the band until they went and made it elsewhere through hard work and determination. So yeah **On Parole** documents the band's first sessions after their name change from Bastard, different lineup, and different label, who like I say, didn't like what they heard, shelving the stuff until the band got famous enough to exploit. Kinda behaved and dopey and fraught with production inconsistencies, this pre-Philthy look back is a weak collection of calling cards indeed, what with *City Kids*, a low juice *Vibrator*, a totally bumbling version of Hawkwind classic *The Watcher* and a guitar-void *Lost Johnny* wandering about the acetate looking for amps that go to 11. Old chestnut *Leaving Here* is kinda funny though, totally punky and brainless like a good Motörhead b-side should be. Still, this is one mangy mutt even though it sounds like the guys were trying to record on their best behaviour.

Rating 7

Motörhead - 'The Golden Years' Live EP
(Bronze '80, BRO92)

Biting scrappy performances march headlong into a storm of nails and thumbtacks on this scourge of a four-fister. Even *Leaving Here* finds ways to rock, or more accurately punk, while *Stone Dead Forever*, *Dead Men Tell No Tales* and *Too Late, Too Late* are miserably wonderful, true chaotic rock both charred and lifted by awful AM radio sound. Also available in 12" format (12BRO92), which sounds a bit better.

Rating 8

Motörhead - Ace Of Spades
(Bronze '80, BRON531)

Man, it doesn't get any better than this. With a heads-down conviction fortified by frothing mugs of battery acid, Motörhead reach their peak, strangling the gullet of rock 'n' roll with this four alarm fire, their best collection of survival tales yet, packed full of buzzing bass, crazy old hippie guitar noises, and totally blitzed drumming, while Lemmy spits like nails his truth, the only truth, the hard truth. Heavy as hell throughout, **Ace Of Spades** is a raging demolition derby of tortuous battle-torn sounds, from the frantic opening title track through *Love Me Like A Reptile*, *Fast And Loose* and finally after one sledge of a hangover, *The Hammer*, closing the wound with as much terminal velocity as the opener. Ultimately **Ace Of Spades** buries once and for all any catatonic jamming qualities that occasionally frayed the edges of past tunes, the band intensifying into inhospitable terrains into the seediest of seething metals, wrestling 12 foot alligators with frenetic sheer force, all the while tightening up their three part disharmony o'er top a traditional Motör-masochist mix. Rumbling, corrosive machinery from the masters of formidable noise – I need gin.

Rating 10

Motörhead - Motörhead
(Big Beat '80, NS61)

Very cool piece this one, **Motörhead** (whatever, I'm just calling it that because that's all it's got on front, although some call it the **Beer Drinkers EP**) being extra tracks recorded during the debut album sessions, not the '76 **On Parole** sessions with Fritz Fryer, but the true self-titled debut, recorded by Speedy Keen at Escape Studios in Kent. So we've got four tracks in all, first a-side being the band's inferior cover of ZZ Top's hardball tumbler *Beer Drinkers And Hell Raisers*. Second a-side is a newer, faster, boogier, punkier version of *On Parole*, quite different from the original, sillier but perhaps more charming. First b-side is the band's grinding instrumental called *Instro*, followed by John Mayall's *I'm Your Witchdoctor*, revved and bikerized, expertly melodicized. So basically no album tracks, although all have popped up on various comps over the years. Note: same cover art as the *Motörhead/City Kids* single.

Rating 7

Motörhead - Ace Of Spades
(Bronze '80, BRO106)

Ace Of Spades finally gets this fast title track thing right, being the heaviest of the four so far, and the most influential. B-side *Dirty Love* is an under-rated high quality b-side from the band, driving with groove and soul and dare I say it, class performances, especially from Eddie. Vague similarity to the Zappa song too! Also available in 12" format (BROX106).

Rating 8

Motörheadgirlschool - St Valentines Day Massacre
(Bronze '81, BRO116)

This collaboration by Motörhead and their fairer drinking mates Girlschool yielded one of the catchiest songs either band ever wrote, a-side cover *Please Don't Touch* rollicking with spirited vocals, an unstoppable groove, and a verve that sounds like pure fun between the sexes. The b-side sports Girlschool's cover of *Bomber*: nicely strapped down musical track, horrible vocals. Second b features Motörhead with Denise Dufort on drums, race-stomping through Girlschool's totally Motörheaded *Emergency*. The key here was Vic Maile's production, everything rough but ready, hurtful guitars, buzzing bass, bashed drums all bent on near chaos. No drums from Philthy Animal, the Motor Rat credited only with Insults & Inspiration. Note that back sleeve has the two b-sides incorrectly reversed. Also available in 10" variety (BROX116).
Rating 8

Motörhead - No Sleep 'til Hammersmith
(Bronze '81, BRON535)

Power trio is the ultimate understatement here, as the three blighted ones—Lemmy in classic stance bellowing northward into a mic tilted down at eye level—belt out highlights from record I through IV, most letting fly with thrashy abandon, best being the oddly melodic *Bomber* and greatly improved closer *Motörhead*. After this record however, I don't know why I would ever go see this legendary band live again (easy mate, it's been many, many times), the word dynamics nowhere to be seen within 20 miles of the stage (audible radius). All told, **No Sleep** is only an adequately recorded testimony to a force with loads of no compromise integrity. Yet it is a record considered to be a live classic in many punter circles. Reality pie, anyone?
Rating   7

Motörhead - Motörhead
(Bronze '81, BRO124)

To celebrate the somewhat surprise phenom that was Motörhead's first ear-splitting live album, Bronze handed off this single of the band's signature track, absolutely fried, stomped and somehow living to fight another day. B-side is a live *Over The Top*, a track not on the LP, similarly broken for you the way all the band's songs are in front of a larger crowd. Also available as a picture disc (BROP124).
Rating 6

Motörhead - Iron Fist
(Mercury '82, BRNA539)

After punctuating massive English success with a "cheers, mates!" sort of live opus, Motörhead make perhaps an ill-timed trip back to the studio with this most thoughtful 'head case, a record which steps aside from the ever-intensifying head-exploding frenzy of the band's output thus far, with an ever so slight riff and dynamic upgrade, not to mention a barely detectable smoothing of production edges. Although there's better quality metal here, most notably *America*, the complex and meaty *(Don't Let 'Em) Grind Ya Down* and finally *(Don't Need) Religion*, a tune that demonstrates Lemmy's colourful and independent grasp of living, there's also a liberal dose of mindless headbanging, like *Speedfreak* and the frash-rehashing title track. It all makes for another good Motörhead whipping, if somewhat uneven, as half the record becomes the new anthems of the year, and half begin what will eventually comprise a sizeable scrap pile of filler based mostly on repetitive, progressively self-deprecating and comical reiterations of the Lemmy philosophy over punk-unquality speed riffs. Verdict: hazy memories of good loud mileage push this higher for me personally, than history—and Lemmy's own low opinion of it—would have it.
Rating   8

Motörhead - Iron Fist
(Bronze '82, BRO146)

Speedy title track as metaphor for rise and fall, *Iron Fist* finds Motörhead spinning their wheels for the first time, not adding to the frenzy, losing sales, although not tanking terribly. This last kick with Fast Eddie was actually a pretty solid album, although this particular tune was a bit dull and pointless. Non-LP b-side *Remember Me, I'm Gone* sounds like the same straight-line construct with a few chords switched around, once more, pointless but

pleasantly punky. Also available in red and blue vinyl versions. Unsurprisingly, the only single from the album.
Rating 7

Motörhead - Another Perfect Day
(Mercury '83, BRON546)
Sure Lizzy's "rock music" stringsmith Brian Robertson is the wrong shorts-wearing man for the job, but what results (in my very lonely opinion) is an interesting new lease on life for a concept that was beginning to wear through the scalp. What we get are fully melodious fragments of finesse woven throughout the usual celebration of noise, and a slightly more reverent attention to song, albeit still of crippled and scowling disposition. No question, Robbo causes no wholesale paradigm shift to the hot mess that is Motörhead, most likely dragged into playing as much like Eddie as possible, which may have been cause for his speedy exit. Anyhoo, **Another Perfect Day** versus **Iron Fist** manages to sound drunker and more mature at the same time. Faves would include the hot/cold lead single *I Got Mine* and the even more eccentric *Dancing On Your Grave*—both cantankerous grunge rockers with tasty Robbo fills from outta nowhere—plus total punk rave closer *Die You Bastard*, a tune pumped full of bullets but defiant of death. I dunno, somehow with this weird record, Motörhead seemed back to making a hell of a din, capturing the blinding ozone blur of past pub-rounders like **Ace Of Spades**, almost over-compensation for acquiring a guy that can play so dog-gone good.
Rating 9

Motörhead - I Got Mine
(Bronze '83, BRO165)
As touched upon, enter Thin Lizzy's Brian Robertson for a disastrous turn of personnel, and a record that is becoming many a Motörheadbanger's dark horse favourite. The pre-release single this time was a daring bit of melodic chording called *I Got Mine*, strapped to a somewhat tamed rhythm section. Great, almost southern rocking track, with a doomy turn come break time. Non-LP b-side *Turn You Round Again* finds Robbo subjugating his urges for a blast of Eddie, although his awesome melodic ideas can't help but leach through the peat. Killer Philthy Phil shuffle too, the man cooking the track to a steady boil. 12" version (BROX165) adds *Tales Of Glory*.
Rating 8

Motörhead - Shine
(Bronze '83, BRO167)
Two months after the release of **Another Perfect Day**, we get the second single, *Shine* being an instantly agreeable quickster with cool blues-based modulations, once again the band following Robbo into a world of barely detectable finesse. Again, the b-side is a non-LPer, an annoying, unpleasant, unproductive live version of *Hoochie Coochie Man*, the Motörhead equivalent of running out the clock. 12" version adds *(Don't Need) Religion*. Note: here's a good

point to cut the Motorcord in terms of calling the band NWOBHM, given their next album proper is three years hence with yet another line-up change.
Rating   7

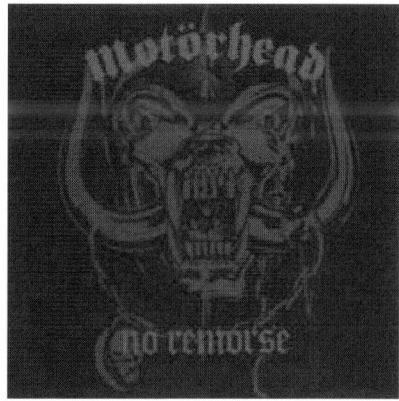

Motörhead - No Remorse
(Bronze '84, MOTOR1)

My kinda compilation, one with buying incentive even for actual fans, if you can believe it. **No Remorse** is a hits package that goes the extra mile, offering a detailed history of the band to date, amusing notes from Lemmy on each included cut, lyrics to everything, plus a beefy ten tracks previously unreleased on LP. Besides a bunch of classics, (too many pulled from **No Sleep**), there's three punky scroungers done with pint-swilling partners Girlschool, a couple of oldies, including an endearingly abrasive version of *Louie Louie*, some b-sides, best being marauding riffster *Too Late Too Late*, and four brand new hot rods - sustained wall of noise *Steal Your Face*, two OTT thrashers, and one of the grooviest survival tales of the band's vast and greasy repertoire, *Killed By Death*, an almost Stonesy low-slung distortion piece, the highlight of the whole damn record. A well-conceived, if not premature history of a legend, with lots to stimulate the pistons, **No Remorse** just may be flashy enough to fill your Motörhead fix more often than the official studio booty. Notable omission: the boozier of the two totally different *Under The Knife*'s.
Rating   7

Movie Stars - No Time To Kill
(Lancaster '82)

Nice melodic gallop to this one, *No Time To Kill* sounding like polite Dark Star, although b-side *Heroes* is not metal but the sort of fairly guitary ballad a neo-prog band might play, bold and memorable twin lead solo included. Cool Quartz and even Trespass vibe to these preppies from Buckinghamshire.
Rating   7

Mythra - Death And Destiny
(Guardian '79, GRMA16)

One of the NWOBHM's holy grails, Mythra were one of the purest acts from the movement, being a mean medium average of all the ideas that were soon to explode from, let's say, a composite of Fist, Tank, Holocaust, Angel Witch and the first half of the Tygers catalogue. This EP, originally on the orange Guardian label with no picture sleeve, comprised four tracks. The title track is a melodic mid-pacer, complete with those adolescent NWOBHM vocals we've all grown to love. *Killer* is a fast stiff one, prefaced by a *Breadfan*/Maiden/*Fire Down Under* type riff, which then evaporates into average punk metal. *Overlord* ain't much better. *U.F.O.* starts like *He's A Woman, She's A Man* and then alas, the band once more finds their inner Holocaust. The accessible pub rock face of the NWOBHM. Reissued in 1980 on Street Beat with a picture sleeve and one less track, in both 7" and 12" formats (both same cat. #, LAMP2).
Rating   10

N

National Gold – I Need Your Time
(K&M '81)
Fairly retro sound to these east Londoners; b-side is the heavier *I'm A Loner*.
Rating   4

Neon Spirit – Loser
(indie '82)
Amateurish, glam-ish Welsh item; b-side is called *Cruisin' Into The Unknown*.
Rating   4

The Next Band – Four By Three
(Gannet '78, CUS159)
Tracks included on this "ripped look" picture sleever are: *Close Encounters* (melodic, accessible speed metal), *Too Many Losers* (the heaviest and riffiest of the four), *Never On A Win* (energetic with a nice melody; cool, almost new wavey leads), and *Red Alert*, which is the duff track here, a sort of lackadaisical medium rock. Fairly heavy for its day, with a nice mix of styles. Frank Noon would be the drummer on Def Leppard's inaugural EP and then move on to a number of slots with luminaries gone solo. Rocky Newton would do time with Lionheart and MSG, with John Lockton end up with the ragged, ill-conceived Wild Horses.
Rating   5

Night Games – Searching For An Angel
(indie '84)
Solid melodic, commercial NWOBHM sorta down a Black Rose, Saracen, Heavy Pettin', late Neat Records direction, *Searching For An Angel* is the work of Welsh drummer Huw Williams and some buddies from Gwent. Solid sound here, with solid, high lead vocals, vocal harmonies, and tasteful lead work. No b-side to this white label promo only rarity.
Rating   7

Night Time Flyer – Out With A Vengeance
(Red Eye '80, EYE2)
This Welsh band was squarely NWOBHM and early, especially come sparse, raw, doomy, primal b-side *Heavy Metal Rules*, which says just that over and over again. Strange, pinched Kevin DuBrow-like vocals though, somewhat made up for by the band's Hellanbach-like exuberance and howling leads, most prevalent on the a-side. Sorta like a handicapped version of Quartz. Interesting and admirably thudding for 1980.
Rating   7

Nightwing - Something In The Air
(Ovation '80, 1757)
Ahead of their time in terms of scary album covers and even their thin attempts at metal, Nightwing (used to be Strife, putting out two records), perennial losers due to their own delusions of grandeur, get off to a pretty weak stride early on with this plain

jane record of bad Uriah Heep ideas, in an ill-fated and unprepared crusade towards mature and less technically adorned progressive rock. Softest offering from a band that rarely punted booty anyways.
Rating   3

Nightwing – Barrel Of Pain
(Ovation '80, OVS 1209)
As mentioned, Nightwing evolved around the proggy power trio Strife, quickly becoming more succinct and cleanly pomp rocking. This first single comes housed in a righteous NWOBHM sleeve and twins the wildly unexpected prog-poppy a-side (written by Graham Nash!) with a smooth and cruising Deep Purple-styled speed metaller simply called *Nightwing*, a track blessed with choice Hammond sounds from Nutz's Kenny Newton, hi-fidelity yet thin guitar sounds, and endearing if inaccurate vocals from hirsute leader Gordon Rowley.
Rating   7

Nightwing - Black Summer
(Gull '82, GULP1036)
For the only time in its near anonymous existence, Nightwing dish out a concentrated dose of their heavier Heep Purple visions, zippy but hokey melodic metal flying everywhere like picks at a guitar clinic, achieving Magnum filler on full throttle. As a self-produced effort, **Black Summer** ain't half bad, trodding forth with an incestuous sense of "hockey barn soundcheck" audio leakage, blending together the band's not so compatible mix of barroom mucking about with a predilection for expensive electronics. Only the eerie title track commands any sort of notice, evoking vintage Jon Lord grafted onto any number of third string NWOBHMetallers. The best record from Nightwing, but avoid nevertheless, despite there being no ballads.
Rating   6

Nightwing – Treading Water
(Gull '83, GULS 75)
Continuing to exasperate with their metal flirtations amongst pomp more akin to Grand Prix and Magnum, Nightwing return with more great metal man album covers (both songs here hail from the second album **Stand Up And Be Counted**) and songs that confuse. B-side to this is *Call Your Name*, a warm but muscular AOR number, albeit one with very fuzzy guitars and an odd Canadian melodic amiability. The a-side is a decent enough stab at a tough yet commercial riff—anthemic, with a menacing guitar undertone, solid chorus, dour and pulsating. Note, this single also came in limited 12" red vinyl edition (GULS7512; adding *Barrel Of Pain*) plus as a German 7" issue on Intercord (INT110135; some with sticker), and finally as a German 12" (INT125210).
Rating   6

Nightwing - My Kingdom Come
(Gull '84, GULP1040)

The flirtation with progressive rock continues and elevates on this dressing up of the eminently Anglo-Saxon Nightwing sound. Steve Hackett provides one song (*Cell 151* from his **Highly Strung** LP), some production and some axework, notorious egomaniac Max Bacon is in on yelpy vocals fresh from Bronz, and spaceman Roger Dean comes up with one of his classiest cover concepts yet. Musically things are quite busy and over-produced as one might expect, although ideas remain dumb as a wet bag of hammers. **My Kingdom Come** ultimately closes its existence with the band sleepwalking through various keyboard-laced pomp rock styles which betray a surprising continuance of arrested song skills, again like the worst of Heep from the unexplainable middle 2/3 of that band's career. Why must the pain continue?
Rating   5

Nightwing - Night Of Mystery
(Gull '84, GULS 77)

The a-side is the lush ballad from the equally lush full album (the band's third) **My Kingdom Come**, while the b-side, urgent, tough yet atmospheric pomp rocker *Dressed To Kill*, reaches back to **Stand Up And Be Counted**. **My Kingdom Come** featured new vocalist Max Bacon, soon of GTR, which included Steve Hackett among its ranks, who beforehand had contributed to the aforementioned elegant yet badly written Nightwing album. Also available in 12" version (GULS7712).
Rating   6

Nightwing - Strangers Are Welcome
(Gull '84, GULS 80)

Nightwing's last seven inch included the non-LP a-side plus *Games To Play*, a layered AOR ballad with a few nice melodic twists, from **Stand Up And Be Counted** in new version. Both tracks featured new Bacon-like singer Dave Evans, who can also be heard on this gatefold EP's two live tracks, both taken from the forthcoming **A Night Of Mystery Alive! Alive!**. *Cell 151* is the politely bombastic pop-progged Steve Hackett hit, a highlight of **My Kingdom Come**, while *The Devil Walks Behind You* is borderline brisk heavy metal, but still too much of a sweetly rendered alloy to convince the punters. A decisive step backwards in the artwork department.
Rating   6

No Faith - Double Trouble
(indie '81, NF001)

B-side on the only single from this Midlands band is called *Only The Good Die Young*. Only other output was a cover of Fleetwood Mac's *Oh Well* (also covered by McCoy) on the second **Heavy Metal Heroes** comp. Raucous live shot picture sleeve.
Rating   6

No Quarter - Survivors
(Reel '83)
Here's a lost NWOBHM outfit that should have been big news, No Quarter offering three tracks that sing wonderfully in three directions. First off, *Survivors* sounds like Sweet crossed with Teaze, solid, upbeat pop metal that oozes personality. Next, we get a bit o' daring in a Zep acoustic number (complete with chirping birds; all a bit silly really) called *Time And Space*. Side two contains the band's tour de force, *Racing For Home* containing twists at every turn, cool *Highway Star* arrangements, a great jam towards the end, once more, personality for miles, much credit to the bluesy vaguely Quartz-coloured growl of Snappi. High up the esteemed list of "black and white" NWOBHM EPs (see Holocaust, Quartz, Warrior, Paralex, Crucifixion, Witchfinder General, Angel Witch etc.), this one's actually wrapped in a big poster.
Rating   9

North Star - Too Many Chances
(Bridge '83)
Debuting with *It's Only Money* on the rare Bridge sampler **The Bridge Album**, North Star then recorded this heavier, more modern track, with *It's Only Money* on the reverse, to constitute this non-picture sleeve double a-sider.
Rating   5

No Sweat - Start All Over Again
(Rip Off '78)
No Sweat and Cobra were the two most notable borderline NWOBHM bands on the **Belfast Rocks** compilation (both tracks from this picture sleeve single can be found there). This AOR-ish a-side was paired with the more metallic *You Should Be Lucky* as its b-side.
Rating   5

Nuthin Fancy - Lookin' For A Good Time
(Dynamic Cat '81, DC1001)
Nuthin Fancy is the precursor to softish but successful NWOBHMers Terraplane, which in turn precedes blues metal behemoth Thunder. Post-Nuthin Fancy, Danny Bowes and Luke Morley moved on to Terraplane while Mac McKenzie and Chris Hussey veered o'er to Dumpy's Rusty Nuts. All told, this is a killer track with a buoyant, groovy beat and stylish Paul Rodgers-style vocals. B-side to this nut-and-wrench picture sleever is *Too Much Rock And Roll*, a speedy yet commercial rocker with tidy stops and starts and a cool swaggering melody. Great, success-ready stuff all around.
Rating   7

oi!" Finally, *What's The Cost* is the heaviest, most sophisticated track, while *Resurrection* is a boring slow instrumental turned boring fast instrumental.
Rating 5

100% Proof – 100% Proof
(Myrrh '81, MYR1107)
Weirdest thing on here is the somewhat creepy creeping boogie of *The Loner*, which is nonetheless a Handsome Beasts kind of charmer, on which the singer laments the choices Bon Scott made in life. More fun that **Power And The Glory** in the composite due to its naive old Krokus writing style, organic '70s sound and all 'round garage vibe. Plus that album cover crosses Gaskin's second with **Restless And Wild**.
Rating 6

Omen Searcher - Teacher Of Sin
(O.C.S. '82, 002)
Back of sleeve lists *Too Much* as the a-side with *Teacher Of Sin* as the b, but the label says otherwise. In any event, neither was rivaling Priest, Maiden or Sabbath in '82's metal charts. Nice guitar sound to the Derby four-piece though, even if *Teacher Of Sin* is a little punky, save for the killer solo to wind it up. *Too Much* is a frenetic NWOBHM OTTer, featuring an explosive though seamless rhythm section, plus once again, a frenzied and fuzzy guitar sound. Character. Pity this single is all they ever did.
Rating 8

100% Proof – New Way Of Livin'
(Smile '80, SR020)
This Manchester band was known both for its Christian rock leanings as well as its boogie metal sound. Tracks included are the title track, *Lookin' In*, *What's The Cost* and *Resurrection*. All four tracks are on neither the band's first or second full-length albums. *New Way Of Livin'* is quite accomplished, quite speedy and quit heavy boogie rock with an endearingly shiftless Tank vibe. *Lookin' In* is bouncy, poppy and new wavey, distinguished by the refrain "They're all on the outside, but God is looking in. Oi oi

100% Proof – Power And The Glory
(S.B. '83)
Ominous Blake-borne white metal cover to this Manchester oddity, 100% Proof being a squarely NWOBHM band with Christian leanings, a clunky drum sound, some interesting vocal harmonies but all told a fairly raw, gritty sound, sorta like the money ran out. I guess it's the modern turn at the drums that drags the record turgid and even biker-ish, even if the variety to the thing uplifts. Second and last from the band, who show a marked improvement from the debut, but nonetheless lost as this commercial style failed to catch on in the UK.
Rating 5

Ore - Your Time Will Come
(Bandit '82, BR003)

A solid, unapologetic NWOBHM hopeful, Ore kicks up considerable dust with this driving, muscular non-picture sleeve single, all corners of the game handled with acceptable aplomb. Love the way the a-side's excitement level builds and builds (does it get faster?), those nasty guitars matching pound for pound the song's rock-sturdy bass line. B-side *Yellow Fever* changes things up with more of a melodic and pubby sound, the track made successful again due to an abundance of electric excitement in the mix. Only notable career move amongst the guys: bassist Dave Boyce to Samson up into the revolving door years of the late '80s.
Rating 8

Original Sin – The Shadow
(indie '84)

Considerably heavy late-fer-dinner Liverpool act unfortunately hampered by a bad recording despite grim ideas like Grim Reaper. Both the a-side and trundling, rumbling b (or double-a, as it were) are fully committed to the metal cause, and presented as a 12-inch single with a simple but effective black and white picture sleeve. Support slots to Mama's Boys and Budgie didn't help bring the band to the prominence these dense rockers promised, although, granted, the sound is three years late.
Rating 8

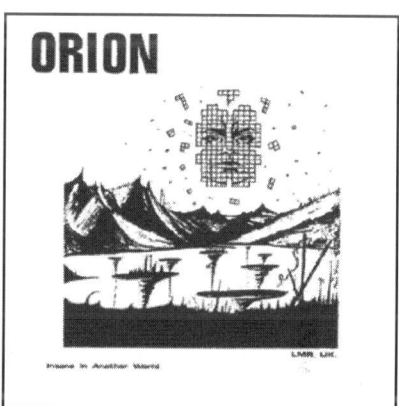

Orion - Insane In Another World
(Lost Moment '84, LM02)

Seems like a discard on first play, but then the band's eerie prog hook-worthiness kind of pulls you in. The a-side is a full surrender to oddity, sort of loitered until the clouds part and that chugging chorus kicks in, eventually laced with a gorgeous and succinct guitar solo featuring great tone. B-side *Storm* seems even less appealing until a similar wall of sound hits accompanied by nicely arranged but out-of-tune harmonies. Sort of melodic hard rock with a self-flagellating anti-commercial deathwish, Orion would have been a pleasure to hear given a full album of ideas. The brutal artwork here didn't help the cause.
Rating 7

Overdrive – On The Run
(Boring Grantham '81, BGR1)

Workable, functional NWOBHM for this early in the game, *On The Run* is a punky, shuffly track infused with the sounds of the street and the bikes therein enclosed. Nice mid-vocal like early Witchfynde. B-sides are called *Nightmare* and *Stonehenge*, both adding to the doomy Midlands vibe of the thing, *Nightmare* doing *Give 'Em Hell*, but on wobblier ground, while *Stonehenge* snorts, stomps and gallops like a black steed through misty cairn-notable moors. Album in '90 called **Dishonest Words**, none of these tracks included. Drummer Ian Padgett and singer Steve Farmer were also in one single band Marz. Cool military eagle cover art.
Rating   7

Oxym - Music Power
(Cargo '80, CRS003)

A-side *Music Power* is your typical low budget piece of turgid post-'70s spoo, the band obviously excited about the new metal wave, desperately looking for their own Maiden doom with this burgled update of Priest's *Beyond The Realms Of Death* riddled with a damp chill circa ELP or Moody Blues. B-side *Mind Keys* is quicker to the chase, opening with amusing evil axe noodling before a cowbell announces a plodding (though worth applauding) pure metal malevolence. Note: most known for their urgent *Hard Rain* track on the seminal **New Electric Warriors** compilation.
Rating   6

Overkill - Elemental
(Killer '81, EJSP9357)

Quite tolerable for its age, *Elemental* is an awkward but firmly heavy and pubby riff rocker with a few strange twists and a solid vocal. B-side to this non-picture sleever is *On My Own*, which underscores the band's predilection for convoluted, circular riffs over angular, Stranglers-like rhythms. An interesting two tracks of a kind. Note: also a track called *Out Of My Head* on the second **Heavy Metal Heroes** comp.
Rating   7

P

Pail Gap - Under The Sun
(Synister '82, SYN001)
Although quite collectible, this isolated piece suffers from dull riffs and slightly flat vocals, although the rhythm section and the recording pack a wallop. The a-side is like hard new wave or something, a bit too happy for metal, while the b-side, *The Knives Are Out* kicks off with Ian Ellis' own version of Eddie's *Eruption* before launching into a lifeless hanging chord track. Changes in the drum and vocal slots ensued but no other product ever came to pass. Non-picture sleeve; priced with insert.
Rating 5

Panza Division - We'll Rock The World
(Panza Trax '82, PTO1)
Beginning life as Rokka as far back as '78, Sheffield's Panza Division garnered some label interest due to some choice back-up slots during the heady days of the NWOBHM. The a-side of this shows their ace chemistry, sounding assured like a Heavy Pettin' or a Pretty Maids, blending nicely heaviness with hook. B-side *Standing On The Outside* is a little less remarkable, sounding like lame April Wine, especially with that Styx-like opening. The band's only other output was two tracks on the very expensive **Scene Of The Crime** compilation (*Blitz* and *The Day Delta 4 Played Mars*), before they eventually became Lonely Hearts (two indie singles), with their bassist off to join Witchfynde.
Rating 7

Paradyne - Take Your Time
(Airship '82)
This squarely heavy non-picture sleeve from Hampshire features two long tracks, the a-side plus *Down To Amsterdam* as its b, the better track with its grim, workmanlike melody and punk vocals. Shame about those matchbox drums though.
Rating 7

Paralex - White Lightning
(Reddingtons Rare '80, DAN4)
Another of the hallowed black and white NWOBHM EPs, this one's as good as any, giving up a few points for yobbish, barely in tune vocals, but getting them back for heads-down punk boogie metal mayhem, Paralex squeezing into that glowing space between Tank, Fist and Tygers. Produced by one Darryl Johnston, future of Ebony fame. Green vinyl and rare as hell. Full track listing: *Travelling Man*, *Black Widow* and *White Lightning*, and really I

guess technically an untitled EP. Attainable on CD in its entirety on British Steel's **N.W.O.B.H.M. Metal Rarities Vol. 2**.
Rating 8

Penetrations – Coming To You
(Kik '80)
B-side to this Scottish band's non-picture sleeve but quite properly NWOBHM single is the boogie rocking *Cheap Thrills*, but it's the a-side that is the knees-up rocker. Not to be confused with post-punkers Penetration.
Rating 7

Persian Risk – Calling For You
(SRT '81, CUS1146)
Persian Risk are known for having many recording band connections both before and after their unsuccessful run, most notable past member being Phil Campbell, present guitarist for Motörhead. Also, Jon Deverill puts in a pre-Tygers Of Pan Tang appearance on this single. A-side *Calling For You* is a happy hard AOR number with a lean into metal, but generally uncommitted either way. Some promise, technically proficient, tight, well-recorded but weakly written. B-side *Chase The Dragon* is more maliciously metal, the carnal riff somewhat undercut by an awkward and modest rhythm section performance. Note: neither track, nor either from the *Ridin' High* single, are on the High Vaultage CD reissue of **Rise Up**, which opts instead to include the three tracks that comprise the **Too Different** EP.
Rating 7

Persian Risk – Ridin' High
(Neat '83, NEAT24)
Perhaps marking the era of the band that contained the best chemistry, *Ridin' High* found the band full of back-up-able bravado, led by the strong pipes of Carl Sentance who moved onto a brief collaboration with Geezer Butler and then Tokyo Blade. Both the a-side and b-side *Hurt You* are heavy but pleasant and fully accomplished, due to Sentance's Diamond Head-like vocals and the musical arrangements around him. Note: catalogue in entirety (during the band's existence) includes these two singles, three sampler tracks (only one of which isn't on one of the band's own releases: *50,000 Stallions*, a visceral mid-riffster, on Neat's cassette-only **60 Minutes Plus** comp.), one three track 12" on Razor called **Too Different** (12RA3), and an LP in '86 on Razor called **Rise Up** (METALLP2).
Rating 8

Pet Hate – The Bride Wore Red
(Heavy Metal '84, HMRLP17)
Sort of out on their own in the early days of poverty metal, Pet Hate's sleazy street rock won some acclaim by avoiding the trappings and overall scurry of traditional shoot 'em up, leather and chains metal combos at the time. Their totally Hanoi Rocks feel showed promise, but never quite left the ground, due to a stiff, plodding song list, sabotaged by a blocky percussive performance over uni-speed marches, a situation that begins to sound nice and comfortable by side two's *The Party's Over* and a welcome cover of *Roll Away The Stone*, where Al does an

uncanny Ian Hunter. In fact, side two's kind of a groundbreaker, revealing a risky band not without cool ideas, off on Mars with an oxygenated flat right next door to McCoy and Monroe. Production's a bit crunchy, and Al's vocals are mixed too far back, but otherwise a fresh albeit grimly low income stance that could have bore fruit had it left metal even more boldly and confidently.
Rating   5

in Toronto) moving on to a poppy solo album that Kerrang! gave 3 1/2 K's.
Rating   4

Pheetus – Nomads
(RIC-RAC Productions '78, RRS002)
Early boogie metal, which is a valid stream of NWOBHM, led of course by Vardis and Spider. B-side is the comparatively ponderous *Blind Man*.
Rating   5

Pet Hate - Bad Publicity
(Heavy Metal '84, HMRLP23)
One of a scant few NWOBHM outfits that chased neither goth 'n' gloom nor prissy AOR, Pet Hate was after a stripped Kiss-type sound with shades of Hanoi Rocks, sort of a street scum version of plain guitar-driven rock, through this record and their more spontaneous predecessor, **The Bride Wore Red**. The proceeds don't really strike stride until the fourth toon, a laid-back cover of the Stones' *Street Fighting Man*. After that, the party begins to achieve that play-stupid-on-purpose nostalgia with Ace Frehley-drawled glamster *She's Got The Action*, the poppier *Stale Lipstick*, and the steely-eyed *Wreck The Radio*. **Bad Publicity** might have succeeded given a deeper, sludgier mix and more adventuresome, drunken performances from the individual dudes. But, the band would break up shortly after this second effort, lead guy, Alistair Terry (who once rented downstairs from me here

Phyne Thanquz – Into The Sun
(ERC '82)
As much a form of semi-accomplished punk as anything, *Into The Sun* at least rocks fast and hard, if one ignores the reedy keyboards. Its metal-ness is also helped by a classy, sparse guitar solo. B-side to this mysterious Scottish picture sleeve (Eddie-like skull included) is *Curse Of The Gods*, which reinforces a suspected garage punk ethic from the band. Cool song though, with aggressive drumming, slashing chords, and unfortunately that same perennial new wavey keyboard line. Note: name derived merely from "fine thank yous."
Rating   5

Praying Mantis - The Soundhouse Tapes Part 2
(Ripper '79, HAR5201)
These guys are important because of all the connections and confusion, their important **Time Tells No Lies** full-length from '81, their future as Stratus, and ultimately their reformation in '90, after which a flurry of Japanese releases ensued. This is obviously a follow-up of sorts to the mythical Maiden

piece, which was part 1. I wouldn't say you're looking at the same caliber of song here though, *Captured City* fussing around and not really getting anywhere, even while trying a number of things under a cloud of panic. B-side *Johnny Cool* is a similarly lackadaisical, white bread boogie rocking song, which tends to have me believe this band was seen as important because they weren't about splitting eardrums. 12" version (12HAR5201; no picture sleeve) adds *The Ripper*, which rips off *Sabbra Cadabra* and predicts the rise of Spider at the same time. All told, three tracks of hard rock silliness, if you ask me. Note *Captured City* can be found on the first **Metal For Muthas** and a live crack at *Johnny Cool* can be located on **Metal Explosion**.
Rating   5

Praying Mantis - Praying Mantis
(Gem '80, GEMS36)
This is a cool single first and foremost because of the Rodney Matthews fantasy artwork (on both cover and label), plus the fact that neither *Praying Mantis* or b-side *High Roller* showed up on the full-length. *Praying Mantis* is one of their typical half boogie, half Maiden, all NWOBHM harmony tracks. No bite, sort of like White Spirit but jovial enough. *High Roller* sounds like BTO or Krokus or Vardis with a chorus straight out of California country rock. Very strange but again, kinda warm all over in that confused scattershot methodology found within Demon, AIIZ and Witchfynde. Includes cheap tattoo thing.
Rating   6

only on the front cover. Marquee track is pop rocker *Cheated*, from the one and only NWOBHM album from the band, but here in different version. It's still quite a limp sound, although things are starting to gel and an identity is being forged. B-side *Thirty Pieces Of Silver* is non-LP, and is a considerably brisk and lively piece of work for the band, slamming with a metal enough verse and then injecting the harmonies come chorus time. Both live tracks originally hail from the lone LP, *Flirting With Suicide* being an example of the good, solid White Spirit-like songcraft that can emerge from this band, and *Panic In The Streets* being a fast, tough rocker that still manages the band's star vocal quality. Gatefold features live shots, back cover features a scientific explanation of the curious sexual dance found within the praying mantis species.
Rating   6

Praying Mantis - All Day And All Of The Night
(Arista '80, ARIST397)
Strange choice for a cover, although it seems the cross culture of it all is what has caused a bulging collection of novelty hits for NWOBHM bands. So in wade Praying Mantis, who keep this Kinks song rough, while changing around a couple of chords, not really making it their own, just someone else's. B-side *Beads Of Ebony* is also from the LP (although in different version), and is another vanilla-accessible hard rocker with the odd misplaced prog frill.
Rating   4

Praying Mantis - Cheated
(Arista '80, ARIST378)
This double 7" features more Rodney Matthews artwork, although this time

Praying Mantis - Time Tells No Lies
(Arista '81, SPART1153)
An early NWOBHM full-lengther from a band that was woefully unready for

primetime, **Time Tells No Lies** suffers from cheesy riffs, unraveled, addled constructions, vocal inadequacy, and middling fence-sitting between sweetened American hard rock and the new, snarly and grime-caked British metal. Contains a half decent cover of the Kinks' *All Day And All Of The Night* and little else that is of more than historical value. Later changed their name to Stratus and then all sorts of complications in the catalogue occurred before they came back to stay as Praying Mantis. Bisecting the life of this band: Clive Burr, Paul Di'Anno (this is also an incestuous story involving project band English Steel), Dennis Stratton and Bernie Shaw.
Rating 5

Praying Mantis - Turn The Tables
(Jet '82, 7026)
Here we've got the band's worst graphics, but best material, Canadian Bernie Shaw joining the ranks en route to his productive gig with Uriah Heep. The a-side is a pleasing, galloping pomp rocker with a forlorn melody, while the two b-sides continue the synergy between the band and Shaw. First b-side *Tell Me The Nightmares Wrong* (the back sleeve has the tracks reversed) is a stout-of-harmony popster a la Journey, Styx or Magnum, while instrumental *A Question Of Time* brings back the metal, going for a gothic, keyboard-ornate double bass drive. A significant piece in that it displays a transitional state for the band, one that never got to make a full-length album.
Rating 6

Predatur - Take A Walk
(Quicksilver '82, QUICK5)
B-side of this boogie rock seven incher *Seen You Here* is the faster and heavier of the two offerings, while the a-side is a shiftless but likeable enough mid-speed retro rocker similar to old Quo. Somewhat charming vocals from Baz Barry and amusingly fuzzy production values help spin the Spider web.
Rating 7

Prowler - Forgotten Angel
(Pirate '83, S226S8)
Sorta nobodies who are now quite collectible, Prowler cranked two singles and then eventually evolved into the quasi-hair Passion, releasing a single in 1990. The band's main forte was their sick Savage-style guitar sound, an attack for which the vocals and rhythm section lent little support. *Forgotten Angel* has a Helix *Rock You* type pound to it, and therefore a somewhat memorable chorus. The guitar solos rip like Grim Reaper. *Don't Let Go* is a quicker number, once more with loud, slightly off-time drums and vocals which are a little, er, rushed. But you can see why people care. Second and last single is from '85, so outside of our parameters. Briefly, it paired *Alcatraz* with *So Lonely*, and featured a new vocalist.
Rating 8

Pyramid - Star
(Scorpion '82, PYRA1)
The NWOBHM proper of the a-side gives way on side two to a power ballad called *Wasted Time*.
Rating 5

Q

Quartz - Quartz
(Jet '77, UAG30081)
A confounding outfit that gave us some of the most deadly metal of the NWOBHM, Quartz were always waiting in the wings, somewhat unhinged and unsure, this debut being no exception, representing a pastiche of eminently British rock stylings from Sabbath to Sweet through Supertramp, Heep and even Nightwing. **Deleted** (gutsy title, eh?) consequently makes for a mysterious, downward spiraling record, letting its treasures reflect available light only through a thin crack in the door. Soar-away track is undoubtedly *Mainline Riders*, which bridges Sabbath to Angel Witch in reverent fashion, a killer doom metal saga, brooding, suicidal and a fitting tribute to the record's surprise producer Tony Iommi. Elsewhere it's a swirling mass of styles, many of them acoustic-based, most infused with rich harmonies of both vocals and guitars. Cream of the remainder would be creepy black metalizer *Devil's Brew*, the similarly gloom-shrouded *Around And Around* and meathook rocker *Pleasure Seekers*. Hypnotic and serious, but also disorientingly varied, **Deleted** is a qualified underground gem, qualifier being your personal opinions on the above stated influences, and the confused sort of record that necessarily emerges. Mine came lovingly wrapped in a brown paper bag— no cardboard sleeve, just a brown paper bag, although there's also the regular, non-bag self-titled issue.

Rating   7

Quartz - Sugar Rain
(Jet '77, UP36290)
After three singles as Bandylegs, Quartz get their act together, offering on this single 3/4 of side one of their debut album. *Sugar Rain* is one of their pre-clue prog power ballads, something you might expect from Nightwing or Magnum. *Street Fighting Lady* is classic Quartz, half Sweet, half Angel Witch, all enigma. *Mainline Riders* is possibly the finest NWOBHM song ever, expert production and arrangement, borrowing the best from Sabbath with the band making it all their own. Note: this single was recalled before release. As well, *Sugar Rain* and *Street Fighting Lady* are alternate versions to what was on the squarely accomplished LP.

Rating   8

Quartz - Street Fighting Lady
(Jet '77, UP36317)
Here's the flouncy uptempo rocker from the LP as the a-side, with *Mainline Riders* as the b-side, the latter being perhaps the scariest NWOBHM composition of all time; basically the cancelled UP36290 with *Sugar Rain* deleted. Reissued in '80 as JET189, with a cool paper bag sleeve that

mimics the LP (essentially worth the same amount on the collectible market); demo edition of the '80 issue also exists.
Rating   8

Quartz - Nantucket Sleighride
(Reddingtons Rare '80, DAN1)
This extremely cool piece features an alternate version of the *Megalomania*-cal *Wildfire*, which quite possibly eclipses the LP version, catching a sly groove through the more eclectic drumming and purely cat-like arrangement. Awesome song, awesome band, incredibly professional for 1980. The a-side is a novelty cover of Mountain's whaling epic *Nantucket Sleighride*, Quartz taking it away from the Cream into the realm of Deep Purple or heavy Tull. Note that the ink illustration is a continuation of the style used on the gate and the booklet for Mountain's album of the same name. Released in a two different monochrome sleeves (black ink or red ink) on black, red, white or blue vinyl, with three possible label colourations: silver, brown or red. Back sleeve features live shots of the band plus the lyric to the a-side. Made in France, with the coloured vinyl versions being actual French issues.
Rating   9

Quartz - Live
(Reddington's Rare '80, REDD001)
Immensely talented losers Quartz always had a twisted way of doing business, releasing four records completely incompatible with each other during their short stint as seminal metal force, one being this useless, drink 'em, bash 'em live record as all-strategic Album II. Smooth move. The sorry stats: Seven cuts, three from the confusing **Deleted/Quartz** debut thing (including a hyper version of the suicidally depressive *Around & Around*), two awful covers, and two self-penned ditties, pedestrian metal boogie *Belinda*, and lone meal on the record, *Count Dracula*, an acceptable pummel, crossing Sabbath with Sweet due to Mike Taylor's highly expressive voice. Everybody sounds hammered, especially the guy at the soundboard, for this legendary performance at Digbeth Civic Hall.
Rating   4

Quartz - Satan's Serenade
(Logo '80, SFI549)
Showing their depth, Quartz offer two more solid non-LP tracks, both *Satan's Serenade* and *Bloody Fool* (comically about what happens when the lights get pulled at a show) being doomy rockers with just the right amount of NWOBHM confusion. *Satan's Serenade* is the prouder, more ambitious of the two, almost like a poor cousin to *Mainline Riders*. Note: the commercial release of this item is as 12" EP (GOT387) available in red and rarer blue vinyl. Third track on the 12" is the band's *Roll Over Beethoven* live, in remixed form. The only 7" release is as promo clear vinyl flexi-disc, which includes the two tracks discussed plus the accomplished and enigmatic *Count Dracula*.
Rating   8

Quartz - Stand Up And Fight
(MCA '80, MCF3080)

A work of uncommon distinction that continues to blow my mind to this day, **Stand Up And Fight** was probably the most sure-footed and metallically expressive of NWOBHM albums, stomping all comers... Maiden, Tygers, Leppard, you name it—it's just the best. Fat, drum-driven grooves, regal, intelligent riffs, bobbing bass lines, and swashbuckling vocals glide through a percolating, headphone-quality mix on a record that can do no wrong, save for one lurching, ill-fitting, inconsequential pop rocker. Possessing all the hellish doom tones of the most foreboding of early black metallurgists (basically Mercyful Fate—this is too hi-fidelity to compare with anything else) with few of the overt references and none of the crap musicianship, **Stand Up And Fight** was heady wizardry to our small gathering of ragged jean jackets, taking us to intense, personal metalhead frontiers like no other record from the era, its solidity coupled with its underground cache matching only More's **Blood & Thunder** and the self-titled from Angel Witch for full package bloodmanship. Favourites would include the evil, melodic *Stoking Up The Fires Of Hell*, the rattling *Questions*, and the widespread Sabbath ooze of closer *Wildfire*, which re-wires *Megalomania*'s central riff, an act of sabotage that I'm sure was exercised with deepest respect. Ultimately years later, **Stand Up And Fight** hasn't lost a shred of its largess, exalted for time everlasting by princely but haunting manipulation of hallowed heavy metal traditions learned at the hands of the greats, most pertinently Sabbath, who nicked keyboardist Geoff Nicholls for much future work. A fireball flung into the souls of a scattered few, **Stand Up And Fight** renders Quartz the peerless unsung of the UK metal pack.
Rating   10

Quartz - Stoking Up The Fires Of Hell
(MCA '80, 642)

A-side is the magnificent title track from the LP of course, while the b-side *Circles* is a quirky, professional prog-inflected metal rocker which apparently features Brian May production and Ozzy on background vocals.
Rating   10

Quartz - Stand Up And Fight
(MCA '81, 661)

This one's merely two post-LP release album tracks, both heavy metal thrillers from the NWOBHM's most well-crafted

album, b-side being *Charlie Snow*. Sleeve mimics the LP in a garish orange tint.
Rating   10

Quartz - Against All Odds
(Heavy Metal '83, HMRLP9)

Possessing a more poisonous sound (co-producer Robin George!) than masterpiece **Stand Up And Fight**, **Against All Odds** represents a band shrouded in misfortune. At least that's the way we saw it, what with grimier production values, new vocalist, new bassist, new smaller label, and a raft of paeans to pain that owe more to underground metal than the sky-straddling majesty of the band's crown jewel. Against All Odds aligned Quartz with a new, more desperate, more violent crowd, running neck and neck for the pulverization of our souls with the likes of Oz, Witchfynde, and Witchfinder General, not so overtly black metal, but just as weary and resigned to hell with the crippling depression of *Hard Road*, *Tell Me Why* and *Avalon*. As the madness intensifies, the band descends into the Sabbatherian squalor for *Buried Alive*, *Love 'Em & Run* and final twitch before twilight *(It's) Hell, Livin' Without You*. But this is no down-the-gullet metalfest, much of the record in possession of lonely melodic gothic tones, all the more creepy due to the cold and clanky recording. New vocalist Geoff Bate does the memory of Mike Taylor proud, steering the band through this hypnotic and tragic collection of variously accelerated dirges. Lifeless but beautiful. And as mentioned above, sort of band member keyboardist Geoff Nicholls is the same guy silently propping all sorts of Sabbath albums, hence a second connection after Iommi's benefactorship as producer on the debut. Mine's on blue vinyl, perhaps adding to the unreal, less than perfect feel of this record compared to its glory-bound predecessor.
Rating   9

Quartz - Tell Me Why
(Heavy Metal '83, HEAVY17)

Up into their sorrowful **Against All Odds** years, Heavy Metal releases the saddest, most effective song on the record *Tell Me Why* as the a-side (different version) with the non-LP *Streetwalker* as the b.
Rating   8

R

Radar - Leave Her Alone
(House Of Wax '83, WAX1)
On the strength of the a-side, Radar could be branded a musical new wave band with a few too many guitar notes. But the b-side (actually AA) *Reach For The Sky* firmly places this Leicester act with the NWOBHM punters, despite its vaguely hardcore scrappiness. Back cover proclaims that this to be "A Bagpipe Free Record." The band's only output.
Rating   5

Radium - Through The Smoke
(Isotope '81, ISO731)
There's a reason this sucker is so damn collectible, and that's its compressed, urgent, early NWOBHM sound, Radium dragging enough oddity from the '70s with them that when the '80s are confronted, a loud noise with lots of scatter is reported. There are three tracks on here, none of which are called **Through The Smoke**. First a-side is called *Angel Of Fear*, and is a heavenly clatter to be sure, tumbling loose-bolted underneath vocals from Healy that capture that agitated psychotic vibe that the first NWOBHMers were on about. Note the silly 'OK stop once, now twice, now three times now four times' thing, which the drummer screws up the second time through anyway. Second a-side is a dreary live ballad called *Dusty Road*, a fully electric but turned-down drooper that serves little purpose (like it's going to be a hit or something). B-side *Making Changes* is a daffy heavy metal instrumental (until the vocals kick in 3/4 through) that seems to be designed as a workout for drummer Tonka. Just hilarious. I mean, this is the sound of rare.
Rating   8

Rage - Money
(Carrere '80, CAR159)
Rage were a Dedringer-styled bluesy metal act remonikered from Nutz, an A&M act of flirtatious hard rock appeal semi-popular through the late '70s. The Humble Pie-eating principals are here, but significantly, keyboardist Kenny Newton was, at this point, tinkling for Nightwing. Both the a-side and its flip *Thank That Woman* hail from the band's first LP, although the latter is here in different version. Also released as a red vinyl 12" (CAR159CT).
Rating   6

Rage - Out Of Control
(Carrere '81, CAR159CT)
Hapless veterans of the Brit scene, Rage (Liverpool band; formerly known as Nutz) played a sort of retro-'70s, hard-hitting blues metal, with all the detrimental effects thereof, and few of the benefits. Like much English music, Rage move with an intensity-undermining simplicity that betrays naiveté as to present trends, many of which are potentially favourable additions to any band's repertoire. As a result, these guys have an old-fashioned, traditional approach, which evokes images of a heavier, more forward-massing Faces, Free or Bad Company. The nostalgia is comforting, but not mind-altering, although *Out Of Control* is a thrilling anthem with a surging, inspiring chorus, far and away the best seconds of a three record catalogue.
Rating   6

Rage - Out Of Control
(Carrere '81, CAR182)
Arguably the finest, most impassioned and most insistent anthem from the band's catalogue, *Out Of Control* (in different

version here) should have been a big hit with those big and ever-building chord patterns. 'Twas not to be. B-side *Double Dealer* (spelled *Deeler* on the label) is non-LP and is more of a true NWOBHM basher, recorded in a wind tunnel, running like a fat man until finish. The purging of all things Nutz is now complete. Also released as a yellow vinyl 12" as CAR182CT.
Rating   9

Rage - Bootliggers
(Carrere '81, CAR199)
The a-side is a new, scrappy live version of the old Krokus-like, quite riffy Nutz classic, while the b-side was the poppy yet moderately booming cover of Couchois' *Roll The Dice*, from the debut **Out Of Control** LP. Also released as limited edition picture disc (CAR199P).
Rating   7

Rage - Nice 'N' Dirty
(Carrere '82, CAL138)
With the same blooz-driven chunder as **Out Of Control**, only more blocky, modern, energetic, and commercially-directed, **Nice 'N' Dirty** leans heavily on the beer-stained bar, trumpeting the cause of party metal along the lines of AC/DC or Starfighters. However, Rage stumbles badly, almost apologetically resigned to failure, suffering terribly from an almost total void of songwriting skill. About as lowbrow and blue collar as humanly possible, this thing is unsurprisingly effortlessly edible, but dull, dull, dull. I mean, ultimately what you have are wizened vets who plod on in the mistaken belief that they are in possession of the personal arsenal necessary in bringing "timeless" charm to bare-bones past-glory rock, much like later down the pike, Thunder and The Quireboys.
Rating   4

Rage - Woman
(Carrere '82, CAR240)
Here's two album tracks from the band's second album, *Woman* rocking like heavy Foreigner or Loverboy, juiced with metal, dusted with the blues, recorded like a Panzer division. *Ready To Go* is the more metallic number, capturing a buzzing party vibe while it smacks you over the head, albeit in the band's uniquely radio-friendly manner.
Rating   6

Rage - Run For The Night
(Carrere '83, CAL149)
Now the idea is to gussy up the arrangements, add in a bunch of pop hooks and get professional. Of course, old dogs still do old tricks, so there's much retro-rocking between the electronic production accents and high harmonies. Oh they try, and then they give up, closing the album with a screechy, unproduced boogie rocker called *Rock Fever* which, three records too late, points to where the band might have bloomed, in a vase with Rose Tattoo and Krokus. A US jaunt backing up Meatloaf couldn't reverse the slide, the band splintering shortly thereafter.
Rating   4

Rage - Never Before
(Carrere '83, CAR291)
Into their screechy, hysterical commercial phase, Rage try something silly with *Never Before*, adding sax to an underachiever that sounds like a Bryan Adams boogie. B-side *Rock Fever* is more of an arena rock metal number, stomping along to drums that are way to mid-ranged and loud, likely an enjoyable enough '70s-style rocker with a more forgiving mix. Both tracks hail from the third and last album **Run For The Night**.
Rating   4

Rage - Cry From A Hill
(Carrere '84, CAR304)
Cry From A Hill is the lead-off track on the band's most flagrantly commercial album **Run For The Night**, and it's an epic of sorts, quite hi-tech and electronic, sweeping like Big Country or The Alarm, a definite and deliberate attempt to branch out from anything to do with pub rock. B-side *Ladykiller*, also an album track, is a typical Rage number, finding the sweet spot between pre-hair metal AOR and the band's patented no-frills power chord stomp. Note: *Never Before* was launched

to coincide with the album's release, and this single was put together well on six months after the fact.
Rating   5

Raven - Don't Need Your Money
(Neat '81, NEAT6)
Here's two very similar mighty mice on Raven's pre-logo first single, *Don't Need Your Money* being the a-side (different version from LP), backed with the title track to the second album **Wiped Out**, which strangely ends up being a non-LP track. Great riff and more importantly a rock solid recording, wrapped around a tricky pre-thrasher that manages to wedge in a little melody at the same time.
Rating   7

Raven - Rock Until You Drop
(Neat '81, 1001)
An instantly likeable band of hapless punters, Raven quickly left behind this cheaply assembled but feisty debut for the whiplash grandeur of **Wiped Out**. Still, **Rock Until You Drop** is a gutsy record full of valuable punk metal booty, artillery like *For The Future, Tyrant Of The Airwaves* (look for the mistake, no-explosions mix on the Italian Neat issue) and trench-wrestling opener *Hard Ride* (to be revisited on **Stay Hard**) which work wonders slotting Raven somewherz between the marauding riffs of debut-era Tygers Of Pan Tang and the gutter grind of Tank, sort of a compact car version of Saxon with better ideas. With personal charisma right outta the blocks, built of John Gallagher's extreme vocal yelpings and a riff-mad love of mayhem, Raven were a unique Newcastle Everyman sort of force, the quintessential NWOBHM power trio, the band working an endearing three-way creative bounty that emanated honesty and an enthusiasm to hit the stage blazing, whipping whatever size crowd that happens to show up into a headbanging feeding frenzy, all in sweaty attendance being denim-clad buddies out to lig a few pints. Still, if **Rock Until You Drop** is well-written and almost visionary in its speed and heaviness (just ask Metallica), it is also scurried, scampered and sabotaged on its way to the pressing plant (this was the first ever full-length fashioned by the boys from Neat), lack of coinage no doubt the culprit. Neat/Roadrunner CD reissue from the early '90s (and again in '99) adds three tracks: original hyper-tense versions of *Wiped Out, Crazy World* and *Inquisitor*, the latter provided in thick gluey demo tones for your archeological listening pleasure.
Rating   8

Raven - Hard Ride
(Neat '81, NEAT11)
Hard Ride was a great way to kick off Raven's first album. It's not too fast, it's got a boogie woogie hook and a slice of glam to 'er, despite being a fairly percussive nu metal, er, hard ride. Non-LP b-side *Crazy World* is a bit of a dog's breakfast, the band going to their challenging place but leaving logic somewhere back on paper.
Rating   8

Raven - Crash, Bang, Wallop
(Neat '82, NEAT15)
Another couple of solid non-LP tracks, Raven benefiting from Neat owning their own studio (Impulse Studios in Newcastle), the band basically dicking around when they felt like it. The title track is seminal early speed/OTT, while *Rock Hard* is a bit more pedestrian, back to the **Rock Until You Drop** sound. Non-picture sleeve and also expanded 12" version (NEAT1512) which adds *Run Them Down* and *Firepower*. Some added as bonus to copies of **Wiped Out**.
Rating   9

Raven - Wiped Out
(Neat '82, 1004)
With iron-clad resolve, one humble, no-frills rock 'n' roll power trio from jolly ol' cranks one of the most spectacular artifacts of the early NWOBHM, a record smeared with energy, chops, and loosely-harnessed anarchy, Wacko and the brothers Gallagher sending a thundering wake-up call to all thirsty metalheads who live to mosh in earnest. Massive improvements abound, as previous cracks in the sound are filled

in by low frequency throbs and a steely resolve to offer gravitas with speed, all points of the triangle, like The Who, like Cream, like Sabbath, hell-bent on being heard amongst the carnage. Despite a sense of aural inundation (John sez the wrong mix was used, resulting in low vocal levels), the layers heroically gel, fortifying another strong batch of speedy proto-OTT smokers. As a personal note, **Wiped Out** was repeatedly pasted to our circuits during the mid-'80s, becoming the record we proudly unleashed on unbelievers (usually snobby jazz guys) to represent the cutting edge of metal, a hard sell given Raven's crazed and almost haphazard approach and disdain for subtlety, the band's caffeine sharpness resulting in a record of punk-inspired high science, brilliance without pomp, hair-raising velocities without concern for safety harnesses. Personal anthems (near attack-inducing with coffee or gin) would include the brooding *Star War* and hostess with the mostest *Hold Back The Fire*, probably fave neuron-fryer of the whole Raven panorama, personally speaking, the focal point of the NWOBHM as I so lovingly embraced it. More than enough underdog amperage to rumble the bones of any unruly denim-clad hoodlum. This time 'round, the Neat/Roadrunner CD reissue adds another three tracks, the **Crash, Bang, Wallop** EP, comprising the title track, *Rock Hard* and *Run Them Down*, all loopy, nattery, hormonal and Raven-mad to the loving core.
Rating 10

Raven - Break The Chain
(Neat '83, NEAT28)
From the seminal **All For One** headpounder, *Break The Chain* is the perfect metaphor for the album as a whole, hook heaven, bottom end anchored to a beat stout of heart and all about metal celebration. B-side *The Ballad Of Marshall Stack* is almost as bloody good, captured during the same hallowed sessions, slow to the point of sticky, but saved by a great hard rock chorus and a smartly understated John Gallagher vocal. You know the band could do no wrong when even their b-sides were this worthy.
Rating 10

Raven - Break The Chain
(Neat '83, 2912)
Taking deep drags on the infinite wattage that enthroned **All For One,** Raven clash skulls with Udo Dirkschneider (one half of Double Trouble) to produce a ferocious, concise package of six tracks, flagshipped by the rowdy-beyond-words single *Break The Chain* and far and away the most manic, saber-toothed cover of *Born To Be Wild* ever commandeered... friggin' hilarious as Udo and John Gallagher trade belts and canine frothings above the heaviest version of this tired old '60s tune I've ever found. Elsewhere, one is slapped by four more non-LPers (until the CD reissues): *Wiped Out* is vintage **Wiped Out,** *Rock Hard* flounders, *Inquisitor* annihilates in this redone version, and to close out the invasion, *The Ballad Of Marshall Stack* stomps off with the prize, staging a thieving, thumping display of cinder block rock, one "ballad" that could easily sink criminally-altered torsos with anything on **All For One.**
Rating 10

Raven - Born To Be Wild
(Neat '83, NEAT29)
Officially billed as Raven + Udo, Udo of course being Accept's Udo Dirkschneider. Udo had actually left Accept and then quickly rejoined after **Restless And Wild,** although there were never any thoughts of him joining Raven. This was for a bit of fun, Raven always being a fan of the man and band, in fact using Michael Wagener as producer for **All For One** because of his work with Accept. The sleeve (front and back) shows the band goofing around in the studio. The music is prime non-LP magic, although these tracks have shown up repeatedly on reissues since. *Born To be Wild* is the Steppenwolf classic, and this is the best cover ever, period. *Inquisitor* is killer Raven OTT, well recorded, venomous. This single also came out on Neat as a picture disc 7" (same cat #). Note: this is our cut-off point for Raven, the next single for the band, *Pray For The Sun,* being in 1985 and uh, not worth talking about even if it was earlier.
Rating 8

Raven - All For One
(Neat '83, 1011)

The magnet opus, the big noise, the leadfoot, the stupenating, cannonating Classic. All superlatives converge on this Powerhouse of Metal, an orderly mass of truck-size power riffs laid down with bone-breaking precision, as Raven cements the brains of unbelievers with the pulverization production murdalization of Michael Wagener (Raven liked his work with Accept) and Double Trouble. Bass (courtesy Mark Gallagher) blobbed way up front, guitars stomping the world with inhuman chords, and Wacko pummeling cave walls miles below the substrata combine for a thick heaviness of groove rarely matched and arguably never exceeded, as blood can't help but synchronize with the tidal flow of riff and rhythm. Basically, this was a response to the merciless slagging **Wiped Out** got for being all too concerned with speed, for being frantic, for John's car door-slammed voice. And let's not discount this record's heaviness: I can't help but envisage that swords of truth like *Take Control*, *Run Silent Run Deep* and *Take It Away* must have influenced Mustaine in some covert or overt fashion in eventually finding *Symphony Of Destruction*, a song I feel was one of the most philosophically important in metal in the '90s, as distilled purity of power through simplicity, Kyuss-like in purpose but not Kyuss-like if you get my dune. Dig deeper, and **All For One** has four or five similarly leaden symphonies, resulting in an unbelievable rippling of brawn throughout all flanks of this record's dense hide. Man, the level of tragedy in all this just pops vessels in my head however when I think that after one fine live thrashing through the first three records, all creativity within Raven would vaporize with such finality. You'd do well to forget what came later from this band. Instead, please forthrightly revisit **All For One**. Let the plate in your head shift with the tectonic plates under your boots. Both gut-wrenching throbbing synchro-swells will inevitably become one as you witness the majesty of power chords at their most primordial.

Rating 10

Raven - Live At The Inferno
(Neat '84, 1020)

One full-length studio classic, one rip-roarin' EP, and now one dangerous live document, close out the second and last of two spectacular golden eras in the Raven saga. **Live At The Inferno** samples from all three studio albums to date, while also offering **All For One**-style technical updates on a few rarities, namely *Crazy World*, *Crash Bang Wallop*, and long-lost first single for the band *Let It Rip*. But really the metallic pleasure is in experiencing booming versions of early bashers like *Star War*, *Fire Power* and *Hell Patrol*. With Raven so obviously being naturals at the live act (at least technically), it's sad to see how

crappy the records would become. Still, this is one of the better live albums of all time, especially given the vehement statement denying any use of overdubs. Trivia note: these recordings were from a crucial show on tour with Anthrax and Metallica supporting, a show which resulted in all three bands getting their major deals.
Rating 8

Raw Deal – Out Of My Head
(White Witch '81, WIT701)
This Kent act were equally known for the slamming *Cut Above The Rest* on the **Kent Rocks** compilation as they were for this single. B-side for this record store-labeled single is called *In The Mood*, a heavy version of the Glenn Miller tune. A small number with picture sleeve, most without. And the a-side, you ask? Well, it's biker boogie metal filled up with snarl and sound and shuffle.
Rating 6

Raw Deal - Lone Wolf
(Neat '80, NEAT12)
Lone Wolf is by Leicestershire's Raw Deal; *Out Of My Head* (reviewed above) is by a band from Kent with the same name. The a-side is a warm, not very Anglo bit of southern rock boogie, reminiscent of Molly Hatchet or even BTO. B-side *Take The Sky* is similarly retro, but both funkier and heavier, similar to the meat and potatoes fare of any failed US major label signing circa 1974. Same grade, just to confuse you further. Nice, eh?
Rating 6

Red Alert - Break The Rules
(State '80, STAT101)
B-side is called *What Do You Do For Laughs*, a heavier number than the AOR-ish a-side, although that's belittling, because bloody *Break The Rules* sounds like Saga crossed with Squeeze and then razor-wired in guitars—just, like, totally strange and cool. Note: Red Alert opened '80's Reading Festival. Not to be confused with the band of the same name who recorded the odd, urgent, punky *Open Heart* on the seminal second **Metal For Muthas** comp., or for that matter, the band that had to change their name to Wildfire to be on **Mutha's Pride**, the follow-up EP to that compilation!
Rating 8

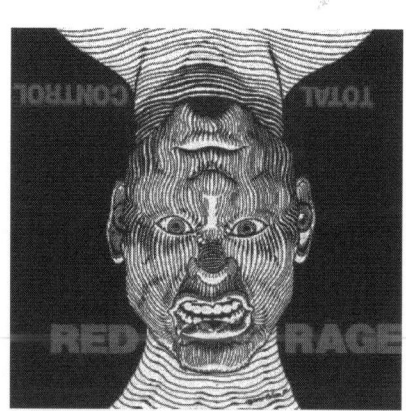

Red Rage – Total Control
(Flicknife '80, FLS203)
Weird one here, Red Rage sort of kicking ass with a high octane performance on something that could be the heaviest Jam song of all time kinda thing. B-side *I Give You This* is even more frantic although

less the stickler to the circuits. The picture sleeve cover art gives nothing away either, although one suspects Red Rage saw themselves at the heavy end of the mod revival well past The Chords. Part of the reason I loved doing this book: the rare as hen's teeth 45s that cross over or if they didn't, could instruct and inflame a NWOBHM punter to new possibilities, just like I saw at this widening juncture of my fall into the '80s. Deliberately left at a 7 to hide this gem from the appendix at the back.
Rating   7

Reincarnate - Take It Or Leave It
(Zipp '82, REIN001)
Here's one of those typical NWOBHM postures, taking a bit of biker boogie and raising the note density, Reincarnate then setting the whole thing spinning to a doomful melody not unlike Angel Witch's *White Witch*. B-side *Metal In Disguise* is even more like Angel Witch, trundling along with juiced guitars, sweet and innocent (and dangerous?) vocals and a palpable sense of English opacity. This quality non-picture sleever was produced by Les Hunt of Demon.
Rating   8

The Rejects - Quiet Storm
(Heavy Metal '84, HMRLP22)
Heavy Metal Records sorta skirted the metal the issue, signing acts from the logic-thwarting fringes, in this case, an ex-poverty punk band (Oi!, Sham) from as far back as '78 that obviously lacks any understanding of metal. **Quiet Storm** adopts flashy metal graphics, hiding a sorry case of mistaken identity, ultimately emerging as a record that offers nothing more than generic ruff rock, touching on non-committal reference points like The Stones, The Who... you get the picture. Plus the mix sucks, and the vocals sleep on the vine, betraying this project as a shameless leap to a bandwagon that will only reward those (well, the occasional poor sod anyways) who believed through the lean years. '82's **Wild Ones** is apparently their best. The band reformed in '90 and did an album for Neat called **Lethal**.
Rating   4

Renegade - Lonely Road
(White Witch '80, WIT1)
Raging, committed NWOBHM early in the grand game, this Kent act got it right and right away, grimly rocking a mid-speed working class hammer and tongs kind of sound until the skies darkened and we all thought wistfully of England. B-side to this surprise 12" presentation is *Last Thought* which considers nuclear destruction as we all spin and fire and fume why metal wasn't more popular... in Trail, BC and in Kent, apparently.
Rating   8

Requiem - Angel Of Sin
(Sacrificial '80, SAC-001)
6:12 b-side to this rocking, doomy, non-picture sleeve single from the equally rocking Midlands is called *Sacrificial Wanderer*, both tracks stretching to epic proportions. Drummer Karl Wilcox

would resurface in a later reincarnation of Diamond Head. Man, the 6:54 a-side though... that's a piece of strident power metal work egregiously depressed and depressive, so NWOBHM it's definitely not funny. The real deal, adding to the fun of putting this all in print because I can. I am becalmed... or something.
Rating 8

an odd arrangement, lots of bass playing and good thespian-projected vocals from Geoff Sewell. From West Midlands. B-side *Off The Rails* is more of the same, again shot through with enthusiasm, especially in the vocal department. And a party was had by all. Some in picture sleeve (goofy hand drawn band shot), some not.
Rating 6

Rhabstallion - Day To Day
(Rhabstallion '81, RHAB001)
One of the fallen, Rhabstallion released only this single plus the soggy, vaguely Trespass'ed track *Chain Reaction* on the **New Electric Warriors** comp. A-side *Day To Day* is a pretty laid back track with a sliver of star quality, sort of like Samson meets Praying Mantis. B-side *Breadline* goes similar raw but melodic places, all performances quite competent, pointing to a promising future that was not to be. Incredibly, Vinyl Tap released in '94, a CD called **Day To Day**, which included both single tracks, an improved version of *Chain Reaction*, material from '82 and '84 sessions, two BBC live tracks from '83 and a couple brand new reunion-type tracks. But back at the single... it arrived at yer shop with free badge.
Rating 7

Ricochet - Double B Side
(Heavy Rock '80, HER1)
This single is quite the interesting curio, the a-side *Midas Light* (subtitled *An Arty Pharty Look At The Weather*) being a fast, punky, urgent yet melodic and moderately majestic hard rocker with

Ritual - Widow
(Legend '83)
Long complicated story, but apparently this band goes all the way back to 1973 and was actual called Ritual all along, and yet when the lone incredibly indie album emerged, some just said **Widow** and some had Ritual and **Widow** on it, and then forever more, no one could figure out the name of the band. In any event, the album is one of those creepy, often mellow and acoustic affairs, haunting, dark, not particularly modern sounding for 1983, but a mood is achieved. Partly recorded in London on 16 track, partly in Surrey on 24 track, all analog, it's really quite scrappy stuff with wobbly vocals, trashcan drums, middling Maiden gallops, all told, comprised of a raft of songs the likes of which were all over indie 7 inchers in '81 and '82.
Rating 6

Roadster - Fantasy
(Mayhem '81, SRTS81/CUS 1171)
The Yorkshire-ground a-side adds to a large pile of slurred-words boogie rock

with oppressive drums—I guess France isn't the only ally that worshipped Krokus. B-side to this biker rocker was called *45 M.P.H* which out-Vards Vardis at their own goofed game. Rare in picture sleeve; most with enlarged hole for jukebox use.
Rating   7

Rock Goddess - Heavy Metal Rock 'n' Roll
(A&M '82, AMS8263)
Curious a-side to this cross between all of the Girlschools, *Heavy Metal Rock 'n' Roll* sounding like a punk version of a glammed up Abba or Queen disco track (!), stomped all over by muddy metal boots of course. *Satisfied Then Crucified* is a little more straight smearing, indicative of the debut album from which both tracks hail. Groovy gritty nasty raw sound to the thing, jes' like early Girlschool. 7" picture disc and regular black 12" as well (AMEP8263), 12" adding *One Hot Night*.
Rating   5

Rock Goddess - My Angel
(A&M '82, AMS8311)
A-side *My Angel* is a typical Motörheaded nutbar rocker from these worthy enough derivatives, crashing along to the band's rudimentary hookiness. B-side fuses a boogie structure with a couple of metal riffs inside a stomping glam rocker called *In The Heat Of The Night*. 12" (AMSX8311) adds *Our Love's Gone*.
Rating   5

Rock Goddess – Rock Goddess
(A&M '83, AMLH68554)
London's Rock Goddess were essentially the follow-up phenom to Girlschool, frightfully young sisters Julie and Jody Turner (dad managed them) coming up with a sound that is as much Runaways and Quiet Riot as Girlschool. Produced warmly and simply by Motörhead man Vic Maile, **Rock Goddess** contains a nice selection of not so obvious rockers, the band really drawing on the whole history of hard rocking girl bands for the album, as well as cannily soaking up a few NWOBHM influences, although not regurgitating that sound, nor that of Girlschool. If anything, there was a bit of new wave panache to this mildly likeable debut.
Rating   6

Rock Goddess - Hell Hath No Fury
(A&M '84, AMLX68560)
Rock Goddess' sophomore is quite the piffling annoyance, screechy, silly, limp and ineptly produced by Chris Tsangarides with too many overbearing '80s tones - basically garage metal mutton dressed up as lamb. Novelty has replaced charm, synthetic gang harmonies have replaced shouting and pointing, forced party rock has replaced raison d'etre. North American version has different cover art to the UK issue, as well as swapped and rearranged tracks. Sorry, review missing for third and last, **Young And Free** from '87.
Rating   3

Rock Goddess - I Didn't Know I Loved You ('Til I Saw You Rock & Roll)
(A&M '84, AMS185)
Both tracks, oddly, are non-LP back home yet on the **Hell Hath No Fury** album stateside. The a-side is a slavish shot at a Gary Glitter-type hit, big drums, big chorus, big bust, really. B-side *Hell Hath No Fury* is an anti-climactic and stiff mid-pacer with a botched attempt at yet another big gang bang chorus. Also released as a shaped picture disc (AMP185) and 12" (AMX185). Note: skipping '86 single *Love Has Passed Me By* on Just In Records
Rating   5

Rokka – Come Back
(Rock Trax '79, RT.01)

The biker-ish Rokka (from Yorkshire) was Glenn Marples' pre-Panza Division band, producing only this non-picture sleeve single, backed with *Touch And Go*. And hey, this is boogie rock done unpretentious and right, grooving like Foghat recorded with sizzle and slide. Although that's more so the b-side, with the a-side stepping it up a notch, through Quo, prescient into the Jacked indie rock of today. Brilliant, energetic and almost pioneering of boogie rock construct.
Rating 8

Rough Justice – Black Knight
(Croft '79)

This non-picture sleever (b-side, the droopy *White Dove*) hails from the Scottish islands of the Outer Hebrides.
Rating 5

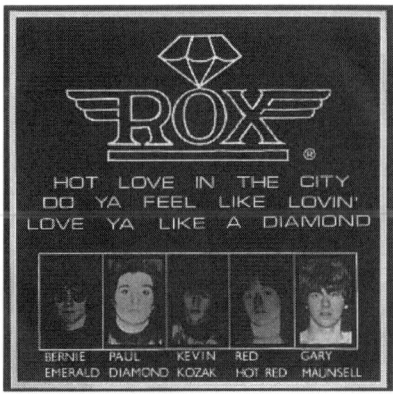

Rox – Hot Love In The City
(Teenteeze '82, ROX100)
This sourly glam-ish Manchester band is known mostly for their widely distributed **Violent Breed** album, released by Music For Nations in '83. Original name: Venom! B-sides are *Do Ya Feel Like Lovin'* and *Love Ya Like A Diamond*, the latter of which made it to the one and only LP, although in different version. This single was reissued as a 12" through Roadrunner in Europe.
Rating 6

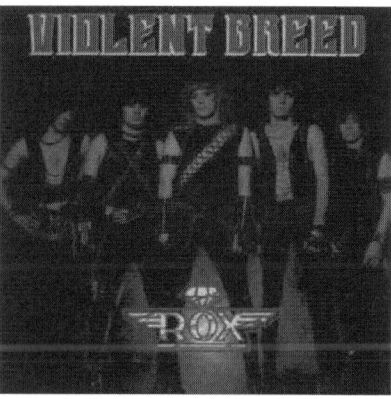

Rox – Violent Breed
(Music For Nations '83, MFN11)

Improbably beginning life as Venom, this Manchester band glammed up somewhat in look and sound, but kept things pretty rockin', like Crue and Ratt, even the lighter end of Priest… solid, really. In fact, the album was a fairly pronounced move away from the band's glam roots, most prevalent on the fairly buzzy **Krazy Kuts** EP. UK touring in support of Quiet Riot ensued, but the band called it quits shortly after. Still, the lone full-length left behind was of a guitar-charging sort that borrowed nicely from both German and American metal influences, the resultant sound being unique for a UK band, more the domain of something American signed to Metal Blade or Shrapnel.
Rating 6

S

Sabre - Miracle Man
(Neat '83, NEAT23)
Possessors of only one other recording (*Cry To The Wind* on cassette Neat comp. 60 **Minutes Plus**), Sabre were a noisy bunch of NWOBHMers, actually around since '80, but only coming up with three tracks total. Both *Miracle Man* and its b-side *On The Loose* are uptempo stormrunners with sizzling guitar tracks and undisciplined vocal flair, very much like the early sounds from the scene despite their release as late as '83. Bassist Geoff Gillespie onto Snowblind, with which he recorded one album, on Mausoleum, in '85. Cool indie look to this one, as seemed to be the case with most the Neat stuff, the coffers usually closing tight at a two colour print job.
Rating   8

Sacred Alien - Spiritual Planet
(Greenwood '81, GW1)
On the dark and proggy side of things, Sacred Alien backed this murky but intriguing speed rocker with something called *Energy*, also a tangled pile of brisk, electrocuted chords caught somewhere between Motörhead and Hawkwind, vocals recorded back behind the outhouse. Only other output was the track *Legends* on a gatefold split single with glamsters Virgin (SAD001Y), worth about $50 on the NWOBHM klepto-market. Admirable for its sci-fi lyrics and overall er, energy.
Rating   7

Salem - Reach To Eternity
(Hilton '82, FMR056)
Salem's a-side is a trashy little smudge of riff rock, good vocals, bashy recording, well-composed harmony solos (two bouts), biker metal all around. B-side *Cold As Steel* begins like a go-nowhere ballad and then fires up a galloping riff aimed squarely at NWOBHM underheroes like Trespass, indicative vocals,

great guitar tone all around, but weak on the percussion front. Note: drummer Paul Conyers was ex-Ethel The Frog. Some in wraparound picture sleeve, not non-ps.
Rating   7

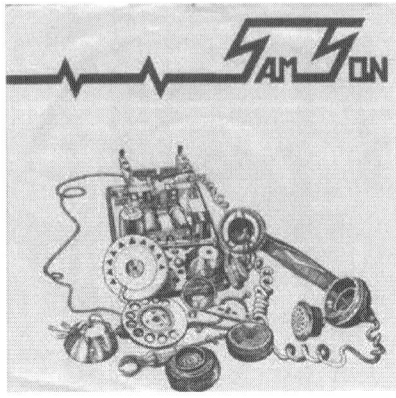

Samson - Telephone
(Lightning '78, GIL547)
This first missive for Samson is around a $50 item these days, neither track showing up on an LP. *Telephone* is an odd, energetic new wavey popster with a dash of commercial hard rock and a pinch of Quo. Oddly, it's more competent than most productions from the first two albums. The line-up here is a bare trio: Paul Samson on guitar and damn good vocals, Chris Aylmer on bass and Thunderstick on drums, with John McCoy producing and guest bass (*Telephone*). B-side *Leavin' You* is closer to metal but not by much, sounding like crackly Lynyrd Skynyrd as much as the product of what would become one of the best bands of the NWOBHM. Then there's the break which is a sort of eclectic new wave disco. Geez.
Rating   6

Samson - Mr. Rock 'n' Roll
(Lightning '78, GIL553)
Even though they sound like what would one day be Spider, Samson are at least copping to the NWOBHM thing, even if there's a bit of a pander to punk in all this. That's the a-side. The b-side is a much heavier, more complex item, *Drivin' Music* oscillating between the band's usual relaxed boogie and a chorus that flits around early Maiden. However, come break time, they still want to be Quo. Great 'n' green cover

graphic. Note: also a '79 Laser issue (LAS6; valued at about $20) with *Primrose Shuffle* (a hap-slappy enough heavy Quo-table) substituted for *Drivin' Music*.
Rating   7

Samson - Survivors
(Laser '79, LAP1)

And so it begins, one long exercise in futility, injustice and the hapless Spinal Tapped life of rock 'n' roll rogues. **Survivors** is Samson's squeaky, clanky NWOBHM-unsure debut, a pub rock affair with a little bit of hard-edged blues, some funky Gillan-style hard rock (Colin Towns and John McCoy are both featured here, neither as an official band member, although McCoy co-writes all but one tune on the record), and a couple of drip ballads. Most (and maybe all) the vocals are courtesy of Paul Samson, although Bruce Bruce is listed as an additional set of pipes. This happened because Bruce joined the band just as the record was coming out, Samson even re-recording it with Bruce in hopes of reissuing it, which never went down. Yet pay the musical chairs no mind, because the record ain't worth a dime, being badly mixed, written, played… pretty much nothing worth hooting over, save perhaps for rollicking lead track *It's Not As Easy As It Seems* and riff-mad Purple workout *Six Foot Under*. Fact is, Samson were simply nowhere ready to cut wax, even if they were entering the fray admirably early, at an opportune time for new metal. Reissued in '83 with black "ram's head" cover, then on CD in '91 by Grand Slamm with original white "band cartoon" cover, adding five of the mostly alternative and superior recordings of album tracks (more than half the album again) with Bruce singing. Sanctuary '00 reissue reverts back to the album's original state, making the Grand Slamm issue far more desirable.
Rating   6

Samson - Head On
(Gem '80, GEMLP108)

Proving themselves a band with both ideas and spark, Samson bounce back from their **Survivors** debut—surprisingly from '79—with a record that sadly wilts due to loose execution and junky mixing (nice drum sound, mates!), despite a robust performance from future star Bruce Dickinson and some hooky riffs and arrangements from one talented Paul Samson. At this point, Samson were still just a shoot 'em up, bash 'em out bunch of garage rockers that remind me more of co-underdogs Fist than anything worthy of rescuing from the underground. Preferential ditties: *Take It Like A Man* and *Hammerhead*, kicking in after an intro called *Thunderburst*, which is identical to Maiden's *The Ides Of March* (Who actually gets credit for it? Ask someone who cares.). Anyways, call this a record that if re-performed and remixed here in the '00s, would become a damn fine roots metal affair indeed.
Rating   6

Samson - Vice Versa
(Gem '80, GEMS34)

These are both album tracks from the under-rated **Head On** album, *Vice Versa* being a whole lot of things, a woe-is-woman tale set to dirty blues metal with a slightly jazzy touch, un-featuring a way-too-busy drum track from the masked marauder Thunderstick. Half way through however, there's a trashy metal break so we all remember we're supposed to be slumming it. B-side *Hammerhead* is similarly busy, buzzed and electric, distinguished by Thunderstick's, er, enthusiasm as he tries to keep pace with a career-aspiring Bruce Bruce. Both tracks are fairly magical if you read between the lines. Godawful die-laughing band shot on the back. NWOBH-wha?. Note: there's an EMI purple-sleeved demo version of this (EMI5061) valued at about $60.
Rating   7

Samson - Shock Tactics
(RCA '81, RCALP5031)

Tapping into a focused primal energy previously alien to the band, Samson hatch their classic, a record drunk with aggression, one on which everyone performs their duty with a life and death urgency. Stomping to centre stage with a kick-ass cover of Russ Ballard's *Riding With The Angels*, **Shock Tactics** proceeds to level the place with a grimy, street-level, full frontal attack. Sadly Bruce Bruce's swansong with the band, Dickinson makes **Shock Tactics** course with the stuff of life, the perfect complement to Paul Samson's blistering but traditional metal riffery. There's something so British and so pure about this record, the band turning in a compact, potent, screeching performance that's loud and proud without being flashy, delivering the goods without yapping about it, versatile, fully ready for glory and expecting carnage in its wake. And the flames are a' fryin', Samson smokin' ten-foot TNT on grey-scale pounders such as *Blood Lust* and *Earth Mother*, while revving it up for driving anthems like *Go To Hell*, *Bright Lights* and *Grime Crime*, where Bruce spits spit like nothing from Maiden, making this sonic resume for his hiring by that band, in actuality, the most blood-lustful performance of his long and distinguished career to come. I dunno, **Shock Tactics** just endures, year after year making my car deck with its perfect chemistry of trash and class, the band on a mission, unfortunately dealt the blow of the man at the mic leaving

Samson - Hard Times
(Gem '80, GEMS38)

One of the more substantial of Samson's many singles, this features a Tony Platt remix of **Head On**'s melodic and personable lead-off track *Hard Times*, which is more a rearrangement than a remix, no better no worse, just different ingredients. B-side *Angel With A Machine Gun* is a non-LPer that hasn't seen much re-release light at all. It's a bit of a *Radar Love* type thing, while also pointing to the direction of **Shock Tactics**. Bruce is downright sparkly too. Wotta cool band, really, driven by the twin weapons of Bruce and a guitarist who knows the world of sparse.
Rating   7

for greener pastures. Can't say he didn't give Samson 100% though, but that's business. Reissued in '91 by Grand Slamm and again in '00, neither adding any bonus tracks, the second set using some of my writings (basically an early version of this review), but do you think after repeated askings, I could even get a set? Dicks.
Rating 10

Samson - Riding With The Angels
(RCA '81, RCA67)
Riding With The Angels is of course the Russ Ballard classic, here delivered in its best version ever, Samson truly making this riff-rocker their own, previewing the traditional feel Bruce and Maiden would later capture with their own *2 Minutes To Midnight*. Killer song, and likely the best track on the band's best album, **Shock Tactics**, although this is a different version. B-side *Little Big Man* is also from the same Tony Platt sessions, and as usual, displays the crackly electrifying teamwork between a tasty Paul Samson and an infinitely projecting Bruce Dickinson. Quick, energetic, not too heavy, uniquely melodic chorus. Note: also available in 7" picture disc version, same cat. #, same value out there, or even a bit less, due to larger quantity than plain black version.
Rating 9

Samson - Before The Storm
(Polydor '82, POLS1077)
With Dickinson departed for more ghoulish, green and obscene stacks of cash, Samson pulls what I would consider a CLM (career-limiting move) in hiring Nicky Moore for lead mic duties. It's a sad commentary on the world, but looks unfortunately count for something in the world of rock 'n' roll—that's no surprise I'm sure—and this man, despite his soulful pipes, is a Tad wide of girth, especially for the central role of front man. You've heard my opinion, and I mean the man no ill will, 'cos I love the guy's voice and even the personality he has created with his words. In any event, after the shock, **Before The Storm** becomes a stirring record, taking full advantage of Moore's versatility, experience (with Tiger), depth and southern rock inflections, making exquisite hybrids of near origami beauty out of *Danger Zone, Life On The Run* and *Losing My Grip*, all richly recorded and harkening back to a large AC/DC groove, Samson making fresh new metal meat of tradition. The record's crowning moment however comes with *Test Of Time*, my fave Samson song with the mostest, Paul grinding out a killer chug riff with combustible authority and an urge to wreck large buildings. Overall, call this Samson's **Ready An' Willing**, a well-paced affair that isn't afraid of melody and a subtle assimilation of somewhat eccentric American traditions. It is an album of intelligent control and restraint, not to mention tasteful licks from a man not without a trace of Dave Lindley's work-is-pleasure ethic coursing through his nimble fingers.
Rating 9

Samson - Losing My Grip
(Polydor '82, POSP471)
Damn inspiring song, that *Losing My Grip*, a centerpiece of the **Before The Storm** album, a mix of UK magic, rustbelt rock AC/DC swagger and southern conviction. B-side is called *Pyramid To The Stars*, a non-LPer which is a pensive blues with enough full band fireworks and elegant Paul Samson texturing to keep it interesting. Comes in picture disc version (POSPP471) and 12" version (POSPX471), adding two live tracks, *Mr. Rock 'n' Roll* and *Tomorrow Or Yesterday*.
Rating 7

Samson - Life On The Run
(Polydor '82, POSP519)
The a-side is another of the band's proud, lusty, pushing and shoving traditional rockers made large through Nicky's barrel-chested roar. *Driving With ZZ* is, on the other hand, surprisingly pedestrian, a forced fast pop boogie thing, at least indicative of the band's southern rock chops, but all in all, a little er, plain and happy about it. Note: also available in double 7" gatefold (POSPG519), adding *Walking Out On You* and *Bright Lights*.
Rating   8

Samson - Red Skies
(Polydor '82, POSP554)
Red Skies is one of the dopiest tracks from **Before The Storm**, just a big boring stripper boogie thing with a pleasing enough southern rock "smooth it on over." Non-LP b-side *Living, Loving, Lying* is like *Red Skies* woken up and cantankerous, also sent through a southern grinder, but uptempo, mean like Waysted, and built around one of Paul Samson's simple and traditional yet brainy riffs. Note: also available as picture disc (POSPP554) and a 12" (POSPX554) which adds fierce non-LP track *Running Out Of Time*, maybe one of the coolest example's of the band's stellar direction with the two Nicky Moore albums. DJ promo edit version as well (PODJ554).
Rating   7

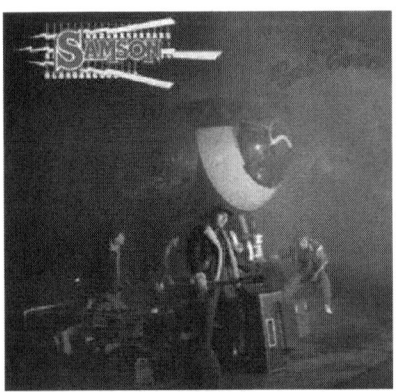

Samson - Don't Get Mad - Get Even
(Polydor '84, POLD5132)
Record II for the Nicky Moore configuration finds the band bulking up along with the big man for some of the most war-like and simultaneously hooky Paul Samson patterns of the band's dodgy career, hatching grand dive-bombers like *Love Hungry, Burning Up* and the headbanger simplicity of *Into The Valley*. **Don't Get Mad - Get Even** marks a sort of creative watershed for the band, matching stride-for-stride, and often exceeding, **Shock Tactics** for riffs, if a little downwind in terms of enthusiasm, with Moore's southern bite mellowing the tone compared to the infectious chair-throwing of Bruce Dickinson's OTT mania. But Paul Samson is as fluidly enjoyable as on any other release, riffing then embellishing with a self-esteem that points as much to street hardiness as the aristocratic echelons to which his playing belongs, the jean jacket at the black tie event as it were, exhibiting more manners, more depth and more human perspective than the egos crowding the snack tray. As a record, this one's more sure of itself than its predecessor, sporting a general consistency of volume and aggression and no ballads (basically **Animal Magnetism** smooth versus **Blackout** bumpy), both records near equals, this one better on the percentages, **Before The Storm** containing more tracks that will be putting a wistful, nostalgic smile on my face until I draw my last breath.
Rating   9

Samson - Are You Ready
(Polydor '84, POSP670)
Once more, Samson pick one of the more lethargic tracks from a great album to feature as a single, *Are You Ready* addressing well enough the band's AC/DC jones, just the sad-sack part of it. B-side *Front Page News* is also a track from **Don't Get Mad Get Even**, but it's a killer, built like a *Black Dog* gnawing on a classic, lengthy Paul Samson riff in duel with a hillbilly rap from the man with the mouth, blues monster Nicky Moore. A great time for the band, in retrospect possibly more everlasting than Bruce's late era and the resulting record **Shock Tactics**. 12" version (POSPX670) adds a

cover of ZZ Top's *La Grange*, presented as a "studio jam" with Les Femmes Fatales. Also issued as a picture disc 7".
Rating   8

Samson - The Fight Goes On
(Polydor '84, POSP680)
We'll forgive the band for pulling another turd from an otherwise hot-steppin' album, because the b-side to this is a metal-from-heaven remake of Russ Ballard's *Riding With The Angels*, first covered by the band with Bruce back on **Shock Tactics**. It was a highlight then and it is again, all swagger, spit and burning rubber, Nicky being as worthy as Bruce in bringing this classic riffster to life. 12" version (POSPX680) adds a droopy live version of *Vice Versa*. There's one more single after this, but we'll skip giving it an official entry, as it's merely a reissue of *Vice Versa* and *Losing My Grip* (CL395) from Capitol's **Head Tactics** compilation way up into 1986, also released as a 12" and a 12" picture disc.
Rating   7

Samson - Last Rites
(Thunderbolt '84, THBL015)
Simply a cash-in ploy on Bruce's good name, this is a compilation that takes in six of eight from **Survivors** while adding four non-LP'ers: *Mr. Rock & Roll* (punky speed), *Leavin' You* (punky boogie), *Telephone* (punky pop speed) and *Primrose Shuffle* (boogie, hold the punk), all of which expose the band's roots from way before the NWOBHM, like Saxon, like Lem.
Rating   4

Sam Thunder - Don't Take Forever
(Bullet '83, BOLT8)
Manchester's Sam Thunder debuted with this chummy enough poor man's Def Lep EP, capturing that NWOBHM atmosphere while party metalizing much like Heavy Pettin', Tokyo Blade or Pretty Maids. Three tracks, dead similar, but when they're this much of a groovy, almost Swedish-commercial blast, count me in for the duration.
Rating   7

Sam Thunder - Manoeuvres
(Bullet '84, n/a)
One lone full-length from these melodic rock unslottables, and only released as a picture disc, oddly enough. Alas, the magic of the EP is gone, as the guys look for fresh commercial rock, er, manoeuvres. The result is a bush-league melodic hard rock with out-of-tune vocals and keyboards that sounded like a well-equipped kitchen, basically Nightwing on a budget. Don't feel too bad about trashing this record, 'cause the band looks like they were still in high school when they assembled this personal artistic statement, which hopefully means they learned to play or perhaps moved on to day jobs.
Rating   3

Samurai - Sacred Blade
(Ebony '84, EBON24)
Samurai were a south Wales band that we all threw on the pile of very good

but not distinguished thus not entirely distinguishable Ebony bands that would have stood out like **Stand Up And Fight** in 1982, but by 1984, were sort of redundant, to little fault of their own, just literally redundant – a few dozen similarly rollicking modern metal records had gone before. Ergo, the sound was solid post-NWOBHM, with a touch of the German to it, hot clocking grooves at all speeds, a nod to the Americas, a nice plot start to finish.
Rating 7

Samurai - Fires Of Hell
(Ebony '84, EBON25)
B-side is non-LPer *Dreams Of The World*, while the a-side is from the excellent **Sacred Blade** album, one of two for the band, the second being '86's **Weapon Master**. Thrashing, trashing stuff, *Fires From Hell* pounding along to over-amped guitars and echoey, dramatic vocals, while *Dreams Of The World* finds the band's extreme production caving in on itself, burying the quick and dirty song deeper than Ebony head Darryl Johnston's reputation.
Rating 7

Sapphire - Jealousy
(Sapphire '82, SR001)
More of a poppy ploy for **Kerrang!** Journo Steve Gett, this one points to American metal lite sounds in search of cash but falls flat due to stiff deliveries and shoddy production. B-side *Let It Burn* picks up the pace capably, rollicking forth as a tidy little speed rocker, still wee and fey but snarling heavy for he time. Guitarist Rudy Riviere later hooked up with Terraplane.
Rating 5

Saracen - No More Lonely Nights
(Nucleus '82, SAR1)
Both the a and the b, *Rock Of Ages* are from the debut album **Heroes, Saints And Fools**. First copies included patch.
Rating 6

Saracen - Heroes, Saints And Fools
(Nucleus '82, MPRGR492)
Cloud-headed one chord wonders who worship to no avail at the ornate altar of finicky prog rock, Saracen were trying to be a guitar-directed Marillion or Pallas or IQ or GTR or Saga or sumthin', yet couldn't play their way out of a wet paper bag, the sum of the parts approximating quasi-cerebral Demon or Americanized and synthesized Witchfynde. All told, it aspires to music school but reaches only music class.
Rating 4

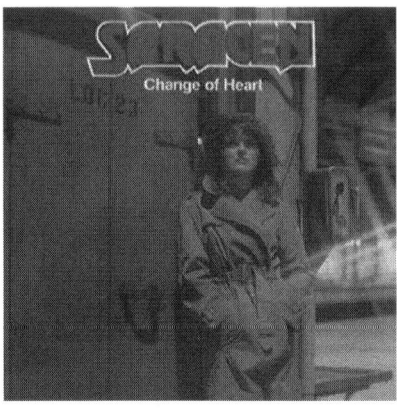

Saracen - Change Of Heart
(Neat '84, 1016)
Caught with their knickers around their ankles in that whole batch of bands the rockscrabble Neat brass had tried to make radio staples, Saracen go with a scruffy, ill-advised AOR sound that nonetheless works on the heavier tracks, save for those clarion keys. Actually, placed with someone with a bit more dosh than Keith Nichol, this batch of songs might have been worth US success somewhere between Axe and Autograph. Indeed CBS had circled, looking at the guys with the same eyes they had once seen Judas Priest, but it was not to be.
Rating 5

Saracen - We Have Arrived
(Neat '84, NEAT30)
Even though both of these can be found on '84's **Change Of Heart**, they're both cool songs, *We Have Arrived* being a Shiva-like hard popster and b-side *A Face In The Crowd* being a thick, dark power ballad with a vaguely medieval vibe. The usual cheap and simple Neat artwork

too: ominous black and red. Note: label (repeatedly) says '84, but by catalogue number, this would be an '83 issue.
Rating   7

Satan - Kiss Of Death
(Guardian '79, GRC145)
One of the grails of the NWOBHM singles, this is a $250 collectible due to the fact that neither track showed up on the band's lone LP at the time. As well, the label is well-regarded boutique imprint Guardian, and the music enclosed is true and grim NWOBHM, Satan (who became Blind Fury and eventually Pariah) rambling and rumbling like an underground version of Maiden. *Kiss Of Death* is a stinging, mysterious bleak rocker with all sorts of early NWOBHM window dressing, while *Heads Will Roll* is a thin speedster with eccentric lead texturing and a spooky mellow break that put the band at the prog fantasia end of the genre. Note: the band's other big collectible is the **Roxcalibur** compilation, which features two non-LP, very early, very obtuse and passionate Satan tracks, *Oppression* and *The Executioner*, both with original vocalist Trev Robinson.
Rating   9

Satan - Court In The Act
(Neat '83, 1012)
Before the metamorphosis into the much-improved Blind Fury in '84 (with new vocalist Lou Taylor, who was also Satan's original vocalist), Newcastle's Satan were an early and even influential gothic and sorrowful NWOBHM outfit, rife with ideas and British gloom, yet limited by the vocal range of the controversial Brian Ross and the sucked-dead production values characteristic of much early Neat product. As a result, **Court In The Act** fits the bill as admired, advanced for its era, but snuffed by its delivery, translating as a low-priced cross between Maiden and Angel Witch, buzzing and dour, underground and proud, cheap and distorted. Like I said, huge strides would be made as the band would trash its weak black metal premise and really let fry with **Out Of Reach**. Neat Metal reissue contains (uneventful) bonus tracks, but good graphics and info.
Rating   6

Satanic Rites - Live To Ride
(Heavy Metal '81, HEAVY8)
Later to be called Sacred Rites, Satanic Rites started with this intrinsic NWOBHM single, *Live To Ride* being a slightly new wavey benign mid-rocker with a very metal lyric. B-side *Hit And Run*, is also a mid-heavy, very melodic street rocker, browned out like indie NWOBHM but pretty competent all around, except for the cheesy new wave keyboards. Really a double a-side single. Odd punk paste-up cover art. Album in '85 called **Which Way The Wind Blows**, new line-up, new proggier sound, followed by **No Use Crying** in '87. This may, in fact, be a whole different band.
Rating   6

Savage - Ain't No Fit Place
(Ebony '82, EBON10)
Savage were simply the best, on the strength of one glorious album, boozing and buzzing the whole slightly tight NWOBHM world with a hot electrocuted riffs swarmed with sparks. The first and only seven inch from the band features two tracks from the seminal **Loose n' Lethal** album, but in rawer, wobblier form. Still, *Ain't No Fit Place* is a heaving metal classic, blessed with a riff for miles. *China Run* is edgier and a bit of a cliché gallop but still great, adding to the variety of speeds and styles and melodic shifts this band could manage with aplomb. Note I: *Ain't No Fit Place* showed up on the **Metal Fatigue**

compilation, in yet another version. Note II: there's a French single from '85 on Black Dragon of newer shelved material, an item the band themselves hasn't even seen.
Rating   10

Savage - Loose 'n Lethal
(Ebony '83, EBON12)

It was a wicked day in Metaldom, B.C., best bud Fiver and I returning from one of our vinyl expeditions in Spokane, snapping up Savatage's **Sirens** and Savage's **Loose 'n Lethal** at the same time. While **Sirens** scorched a mile-wide patch of lush B.C. forest as it ripped through the border crossing at Waneta, **Loose 'n Lethal** wasn't far behind, once home, leaping out of the Toops' Bose 901s with astonishing heat and power. **Loose 'n Lethal** is the perfect two-fisted descriptive for the charged grooves inside this molten mutha, a British debut that makes astounding use of a bristling Ebony mix, with vocals, riffs, percussive might and synergistic delivery that builds the most massive of metal walls from the roiling blood of bed-headed youth. For me, **Loose 'n Lethal** captured the core soul of metal, in crushing manner similar to Witchfinder General's **Death Penalty**, Diamond Head's **Lightning To The Nations**, Grim Reaper's **See You In Hell** and even Saxon's surprised and surprising **Power & The Glory**. In effect, Savage's concoction is a toxic blend of all four, the best of Britain at the turn of the decade, a war-torn sound more or less stumbled upon by the band and Ebony's Darryl Johnston by accident, basically in his living room. Once strapped under the phones, the record works best as one electrocuted smear, although particularly Valhalla-size riffs strafe *Cry Wolf*, *Ain't No Fit Place* and *On The Rocks*, riffs battered home by the vengeful cannons of power drummer Mark Brown, who can take large credit for this record's alcoholic sound and fury. What results is unadulterated heavy metal magic from the New Wave Of British Heavy Metal. Update: nicely reissued by Neat Metal in '96, including excellent insider essay by cover artist and metal book writer Garry Sharpe-Young (R.I.P.), also adding three crustified and ancient bonus tracks (Japanese issue offers the same three, plus two more, one being a '79 demo of this album's panoramic, tear-gassed opener *Let It Loose*).
Rating   10

Savage - We Got The Edge
(Zebra '84, 12RA4)

OK, this one ain't no fit record, this three track EP getting all tentative, unconfident and sloppy and stiff at the same time. Sort of a rushed, acrimonious thing, **We Got The Edge** finds Savage on the splits with Ebony who seemed to be concealing the band's very real success, which while quite significant, was being stunted in comparison to fellow Ebony acts Shy and Grim Reaper whose management was smart enough to take US distribution deals with RCA. Anyway, underneath the bad mix and/or performances on here, *Runnin' Scared*, *She Don't Need You* and *We Got The Edge* are actually fairly iconoclastic Savage tunes. But damned if you'd ever compare this to the resounding two-fisted brew pub wallop of **Loose 'n Lethal**. This was marketed as a taster for the new album, the title track showing up on **Hyperactive**, while the latter two tracks were live in the studio, perhaps accounting for their unfinished quality.
Rating   6

Saxon - Saxon
(Carrere '79, CAL110)

A pre-consciousness record from a foggy, leghorned ill-conceived band, **Saxon**, the wobbled debut, doesn't recognize the NWOBHM of which it will become such an integral part. Meekly recorded and timid in execution, this debut was to fade quickly into the woodwork once the take-no-prisoners crunch that was **Wheels Of Steel** revved up to stage central. Better left unheard, **Saxon** hearkens back to too many '70s styles, ones that barely fit together (say, boogie and prog), although *Stallions Of The Highway*, *Backs To The Wall* and *Militia Guard* do indeed sneak a peek at more uncompromising forms of metal around the corner. Still, without the benefit of knowing about the pile of records to come throughout the '80s and '90s and beyond, this sounds like the work of a wishy-washy band fronted by a vocalist (lanky white-suited suitor of many women Biff Byford) with a very strange, almost novelty-level voice.
Rating 6

Saxon - Big Teaser
(Carrere '79, CAR118)

Once Saxon gathered it together and sorted out a hasty allegiance to the NWOBHM, their first single was ready, pairing this sort of sour rocker with the much flashier *Stallions Of The Highway*, quite frankly a cracker of a track that demonstrated that these ill-looking roustabouts had talent. Non-picture sleeve. Note: also a version that pairs the a-side with the down-wound rote NWOBHM balladry of *Rainbow Theme/Frozen Rainbow*, as part of a singles series.
Rating 7

Saxon - Backs To The Wall
(Carrere '79, CAR129)

Pairing two polite tracks from the watery debut, this single would also later become part of the Heavy Metal series (HM6).
Rating 7

Saxon - Wheels Of Steel
(Carrere '80, CAL115)

If the band's self-titled '79 debut was a pre-consciousness record from a foggy, ill-conceived band, **Wheels Of Steel** was a qualified classic, putting Saxon on the map (it's their fault they later drove off it), cranking an early biker metal drone, a scuzzy jean-jacket-with-patches NWOBHM rock ride, one of really two or three of the movement's building bricks, which I just happened to acquire as an import along with another seminal wedge, Maiden's debut, the very same day. **Wheels Of Steel** was **Motörhead** with better riffs, better vocals—not great on either count; let's not get carried away—marginally cleaner mix, but an accomplished chugfest of distorted wattage nevertheless, a record on a mission, willing to take responsibility as spokesvinyl for legions of English punters with a thirst for regular metal, guys who are comfortable with and actually proud of their persecuted lot. So **Wheels Of Steel** motors along, riffs performing their toil over steady one note bass lines, most carnivorous displays being *Motorcycle Man*, *Freeway Mad* and early blueprint for speed metal *Machine Gun*, the record's "tour de force" if one must be named, although the title track is the "anthem," and, truth be told, quite stupidly insidious and effective. Zero ballads, which is another fairly new thing for an album. Anyways, raise one to Biff and the boys, will ya?
Rating 8

Saxon - Wheels Of Steel
(Carrere '80, CAR143)

Wheels Of Steel is of course one of the genre's top five or so classics, Saxon branding themselves with a hot tailpipe, riding a track that marries grim English grit with a forceful AC/DC vibe. B-side *Stand Up And Be Counted* is less of a winner, foreshadowing the third rate material that will surface on the band's next two albums. Note: French issue (49618 or CA141) has a textured cover and at least some (OK, this one) copies listing *Stand Up And Be Counted* as the b-side on both back sleeve

and label, while the 45 actually plays *Motorcycle Man*.
Rating   7

Saxon - 747 (Strangers In The Night)
(Carrere '80, CAR151)
No big deal here, Saxon offering two tracks from their seminal **Wheels Of Steel** spread, *747* being the relaxed melodic rocker with the *Louie Louie* riff, and b-side *See The Light Shining* being a slick marriage between fast boogie and the new biker metal Saxon would make famous. 12" version (CAR151T) adds *Stallions Of The Highway*.
Rating   7

Saxon - Suzie Hold On
(Carrere '80, CAR165)
Biff and the boys go for a bit of a hit with this embarrassing pre-hair band rocker from *Wheels Of Steel*, backing it with a live version of *Judgement Day* from the debut. Also a 12" version (CAR165T).
Rating   7

Saxon - Strong Arm Of The Law
(Carrere '80, CAR170)
The title track from Saxon's third album is a bit of a grower, sounding much better live with lager and ale than in original soggy mix. B-side is *Taking Your Chances*, also from the album, the track being a nice mix of sinister, aggressive riffing and angled melodics, set to one of the band's dependable one note bass lines. Also released as a 12" single (CART170).
Rating   7

Saxon - Strong Arm Of The Law
(Carrere '81, CAL120)
Proving my nagging personal theory that the aggression of **Wheels Of Steel** represented the band operating at the upper end of their potential, **Strong Arm Of The Law** and **Denim And Leather** prove to be an anemic two-step anti-climax indeed, quite featureless, starting with their slapdash cover arts. It's not so much that **Wheels** was such a monumental feat, or that **Strong Arm** is such a pooch, it's just that there's zero forward movement, **Strong Arm** sporting a car-sick share of nerdy riffs, as that within the childish and churlish title track, on *Sixth Form Girls* and especially *Taking Your Chances*. Still the gritty street nature of the sound is maintained, Saxon finding a stripped, basic and enthusiastic delivery of metal in an exciting new era, setting themselves up for derision but giving 'er once they've settled on settling. On the positive, *Dallas 1 PM* is a muscular and poignant Saxon landmark, harkening back to the AC/DC flat-line of *Wheels Of Steel*, but the rest, well... it sounds comfortable and nostalgic if never remarkable, built for the stage I guess, while definitely betraying Saxon's lack of ideas, evidenced perhaps most convincingly in the rehash quality of speedballs *Heavy Metal Thunder* and *20,000 Ft*. I like this record more now than I did at the time, believe it or not (Hell, I was even in the "Saxon Militia Guard"), 'cos I'm kinder towards my roots. But let's face it, creatively, Saxon was getting

left in the dust, both sounding and looking a bit like Slade.
Rating   7

Saxon - Denim And Leather
(Carrere '81, CAL128)
A curiously vacant, airhead sort of record from a band at the peak of their success, **Denim And Leather** highlights the band's progressively feeble song skills while gaining points for conviction, although this time with a strong, professional recording, Biff and (head)band leaving their grease chain sound at the side of the highway. On the whole, **Denim And Leather** is Saxon's stadium rock record, anthems well-recorded, the underground peering above and saying I'd like some of that please. Still, history (my version of it anyways) was on Saxon's side, as o'er the years, certain songs become personalities, with a few of these ones making a lasting impression (and then added to a few more, voila, there's a nice catalogue). Favourite tub-thumpers to myself and the Saxon faithful would have to include *And The Bands Played On* and *Princess Of The Night*, although the fraternal lyrics to *Play It Loud* and *Denim And Leather* also bring tears to my bloodshot, headbanged eyes. One final thought: this might just be Saxon's redneck record, **Denim And Leather** spiced with just a hint of Skynyrd, along with an uneasy number of songs about rockin'.
Rating   7

Saxon - And The Bands Played On
(Carrere '81, CAR180)
Here's the band's maudlin festival keepsake tune from **Denim And Leather** inexplicably backed with two tracks from the previous album, **Strong Arm Of The Law**, namely hard NWOBHM boogie tune *Hungry Years* and under-achieving OTT bore *Heavy Metal Thunder*. I guess when you are attempting to be bigshots, you don't want to give away rare material. And 20 years later, indeed, not much has surfaced (hence the filler all over their records?). Also a 12" version (CAR180T) and a picture disc version with a very similar front and back (CAR180P).
Rating   6

Saxon - Never Surrender
(Carrere '81, CAR204)
Never Surrender is one of the duller moments on **Denim And Leather**, ultimately a fairly eventful album, especially in Saxon's IQ range. But the message is buoyant enough, as are the performances. B-side *20,000 Ft* hails from **Strong Arm Of The Law** and is a Nigel Thomas remix, as if you'd notice. Note: also available in a gatefold double 7", which adds *Bap-Shoo-Ap!* live (an automatic and hideous crowd participation boogie), the **Wheels Of Steel** album version of *Street Fighting Man* (yawn), and in the gate, Saxon tour dates, autographs (printed) and album cover shots. This version carries the blanket cat # CAR204(F), which is also the cat # of the first single, the second being SAM134.
Rating   6

Saxon - Princess Of The Night
(Carrere '81, CAR208)
Once more, two album tracks, both *Princess Of The Night* and b-side *Fire In The Sky* hailing from **Denim And Leather**, a cleaner, more personable and hookier album than its predecessor. *Princess Of The Night* is a quick, disciplined anthem for the band, while *Fire In The Sky* was the record's heaviest track; score: one good riff for the chorus, one bad one for the verse. Damn heavy though. French version (49844 or CA161) sports textured cover and a cool pinkish platinum Carrere record label.
Rating   7

Saxon - The Eagle Has Landed
(Carrere '82, CAL137)

Recorded at the band's bloody 'ell British peak, **The Eagle Has Landed** found Saxon with a dear little franchise, punting it out with blue collar NWOBHM grit and determination, no sleep 'til Saltburn. The acceptable but rudimentary production values do indeed make you feel like you're right there in the crowd, even if most the time you wish you could be sitting at home having a pint. Anyhow, the record meekly but persistently makes the case that Biff et al. had strung together a modicum of good bangers and mash, *Wheels Of Steel* always shivering me timbers, even in this mud-caked state.

Rating 6

Saxon - Power & The Glory
(Carrere '83, CAL147)

Come on, admit it, none of us thought Saxon had it in them to crank a princely feast like this clang-banger, and really, in their previous configuration, maybe they didn't. But I would guess new ass-kickin' drummer Nigel Glocker and a new mad-eyed approach to production had conspired to push Saxon onto feverish plateaus, spawning one furious assault of caustic mayhem. **Power & The Glory** rages most heavily, and I couldn't be more pleased, each and every machinist in this clearly surprised consortium working a metal magic that is the embodiment of the NWOBHM's ideals now made real and right there. The Jeff Glixman production job is almost at Ebony standards—sizzling hot, buzzing, gutted guitars, piercing solos and violent brash percussion—while by some miracle, the band's songwriting is dead serious, eschewing their previously profuse paint-by-numbers riffs, generating power and then some glory, despite sophisticated mellow/heavy dynamics evident in *Nightmare*, *The Eagle Has Landed* and the stirring *Midas Touch*, the latter hard as nine inch nails yet still, essentially, a power ballad. But perhaps acting as metaphor to what makes this record great would be *Watching The Sky*, which would have been weak given **Strong Arm Of The Law** production and the expected cloistered delivery from this band. Burning white-hot right here it soars with aerodynamic displacement, large thanks to Glocker's raucous fills, but again, a surprise viciousness out of Glixman, who was hired somewhat to help Americanize the band's sounds and prospects. And there's the rub: despite everything being vastly improved, it really comes down to the crucible in which it's all fired, the frenzied chaos of the delivery. Elsewhere, blazing metal such as *Warrior* and the buzzsaw title track reinforce the disturbingly manic new side to the band, a band sparked to unbelievable heights, crystallized for me at a Spokane show where Saxon, sandwiched between Fastway and Maiden, kicked off their set with *Power & The Glory*, Biff entirely in white, fans blowin', belting it out in front of an awesome wall of guitars, loud and sonically accurate to this record's molten mix. Probably my most poignant live NWOBHM memory, of not many, having slaked all this geographically half a world away.

Rating 10

Saxon - Power And The Glory
(Carrere '83, SAXON1)

Ah yes, the magic OTT moment from the only blistering Saxon album, although the modern version of the band comes

surprisingly close to matching the vim and vigor of a Saxon propelled by drummer Nigel Glockler and Jeff Glixman as intense mixer. B-side is a live version of *See The Light Shining*, one of the band's odd marriages between metal, punk and boogie. Note: also released in picture disc form (SAXONP1) and 12" version (SAXONT1), which adds *Denim And Leather*.
Rating   7

Saxon - Nightmare
(Carrere '83, CAR284)
Released three months after the **Power And The Glory** single and four months after LP, this one pairs the elegant, melodic but brutish a-side with the driving, classic *Midas Touch*. Note: also a picture disc version CAR284P and a 12" version (CART284) that adds a live version of *747 (Strangers In The Night)*.
Rating   8

Saxon - Crusader
(Carrere '84, CAL200)
Maybe the boys were just as surprised as I was that their sweat and blood fireball **Power & The Glory** didn't break them big stateside (long story: it was more of a management slip-up, a truncating of touring in the US when it would most definitely have aided the assault). But for whatever reason, it's a second total paradigm shift this time around toward a kinder, gentler lo-cal metal stressing arrangement, open architecture and brains, that is to say a vigorous workout of what limited grey matter Biff and his '70s rejects could muster. Some call **Crusader** a failure, a bald-faced commercial maneuver, but I always found it refreshing if more than occasionally flawed. Sure the cavernous recording is downright distracting, but it's a well-conceived experiment, reaching peak with pleasurable lead single *Sailing To America*, the album's buoyancy being functionally life-affirming, even if it marked the death of Saxon as that thing on the cover of **Defenders Of The Faith**. So yeah, not altogether unenjoyable, despite a toothless wanker cover of Sweet's *Set Me Free*. Of note, same year, there came a comp. called **Strong Arm Metal** (no point 'aving a separate review), comprising tracks from the first four records, putting into high relief how Saxon was now twisting in the wind.
Rating   6

Saxon - Sailing To America
(Carrere '84, CAR301)
The great creaking collapse into an ill-fitting commercial direction began with the **Crusader** album, although single *Sailing To America* took advantage of the new spices with a buoyant, melodic, harmonizing chorus that stuck. B-side *A Little Bit Of What You Fancy* was the band's clueless attempt at trying to stay heavy. Histrionic, gay and harried, it's loud and raucous enough but ultimately a failure, shooting blanks, boasting an empty threat. Note: also released in 12" format (CART301), this was a severely hyped advance single, released one month before **Crusader**, even getting the obviously intended increased amounts of U.S. radio play.
Rating   6

Saxon - Do It All For You
(Carrere '84, CAR323)

The second single from Crusader pairs this irritating a-side with uninspired stripper rocker *Just Let Me Rock*. Also released in 12" format (CART323). Cut off point: getting late in game to be called NWOBHM and indeed, the band's next album wasn't out for over a year.
Rating   6

Scarab - Rock Night
(Inferno/Mews '81, Headbanger1)

Pretty scrappy-pants and likeable for it, *Rock Night* is a garage rocker that captures well the DIY attitude of the new metal. B-side *Wicked Woman* actually does a better job of stumbling over a NWOBHM riff, while Paul Britton does a poor man's Paul Mario Day. One of those true under-indie obscurities. Nice little exploding thermometer label graphic.
Rating   7

Scarab - Poltergeist
(Pharoah '84, PR001)

Different Scarab here, this one creating a midrangey mess of a recording, nevertheless somewhat gathering up songs that just might recall original Angel Witch crossed with Shrapnel rock over America. That's the a-side. B-side *Hell On Wheels* feels a bit like **Kill 'Em All**-era Metallica chilled by a bit too much NWOBHM, but is really *Under The Blade* casually rewritten, this West Midlands band certainly not creating music that is anything approaching 1984, certainly not bothering to scrape the old paint off their sound from three years back. Label sports a big pink fly or locust or something.
Rating   7

Scorched Earth - Tomorrow Never Comes
(Carrere '84, CART342)

A BBC session plus a four-track EP for Carrere, and yet, whither Scorched Earth? The sound was certainly grand, proggy, epic, and the performances spirited. I think I hear mellotron there, and certainly sincere acoustic guitar layering. In any even, the b-sides were *Questions*, *Where Do We Go From Here* and *So Long*, all good enough to get the thing reissued by Carrere in '85 and also to garner a Greek Philips issue that same year.
Rating   7

Scorpio - Taking England By Storm
(Quicksilver '81)

This Berkshire outfit rocked hard and chaotic with a mid-'70s punk edge if that can be said to even exist (straddle MC5 through Stooges and Christ Child (!) and you've got the idea), with b-side *Hawks* devolving further into the anarchic mire. Actually quite the performance, from the vocalist through to the futuro-keyboardist. I can understand why this might be collectible across boundaries.
Rating   7

Seducer - Call Your Name
(Sticky '83, SRR0017)

Seducer were a pretty cool band rendered that way by their rowdy vocalist Chris Hunt, whose biker-ish yowl tempered his band's Wolfsbane punk edge with a serious downspiral into Tank. The band had two albums, **Caught In The Act** and the

excellent and boozy '**Eads Down See You At The End**, plus an EP called **Indecent Exposure** and this single, the earliest and worst of the lot, but bloody' ell still a stiff shot. *Call Your Name* is a humorous attempt at mood, marauding along as Hunt tempers his echoey howl with creepy axe licks. *Survivor* moves at two incompatible speeds but is a cool attempt at something different, the sum total of the two combining glam and harsh biker rock like only Seducer could. Both tracks are on Mausoleum's **Metal Prisoners** compilation, *Call Your Name* also showing up on the debut LP. The albums proved that all these guys needed was a good studio and watch 'er rip (or get ripped).
Rating 7

Seventh Son - Man In The Street
(Rising Son '82, FMR067)
Still in operation as late as '97, Yorkshire band Seventh Son have no major connections to big bands to report, simply slogging on with four singles, a 12", a weird singles box set, a few sampler tracks and videos, and a cassette-only album in '87 notched to date. Brief a-side *Man In The Street* moves on a happily dated riff with a hint of boogie turning it into well-conceived Krokus, supercharged by a melodic guitar solo. B-side *Immortal Hours* is a solid mid-speedster with a light touch and a dynamic NWOBHM vocal. A mysterious track that gives this band a presence, and all in all, truly part of the genre despite their lingering haphazard presence.
Rating 6

Seventh Son - Metal To The Moon
(Rising Son '84, SRT4KS282)
Maybe 1984 is getting a bit late for our mandate, but geez, these guys were there in the beginning, and they're sounding more NWOBHM than ever, rocking down a dirty but dynamic path with this classic riff used by many a contemporary (see Handsome Beasts and Praying Mantis). B-side *Sound And Fury* digs further into the cozy naivety of the aging genre, those drum rolls, that watery guitar sound and the pint-liggin' vocals of Bri Shaugnessy. Note: new drummer and bassist since the last single. Next output would be the *Northern Boots* single in '87, way too late in the game to include here. Collectible like all their stuff, this one is a nifty gloss paper gatefold. Note:

front cover lists *Sound And Fury* first, but both the label and back make the case for *Metal To The Moon* as the a-side.
Rating 6

Severed Head - Heavy Metal
(Plastic Canvas '83, PC002)
B-side to this scrappy biker rocker was called *Killing The Kidz*, a quick, beat-up guitar slasher with infectious energy. Best thing about this one is its ghoulish cover art, although the a-side also gets you feeling pretty good about a life in heavy metal, singer Danny Morris helpfully informing us that he doesn't like country music, save for Dolly Parton, who he could play with all night.
Rating 7

Shader - Bad News Blues
(Piston Broke '81, REDASH1)
B-side to this amateurish basher is called *Banging Like A Shithouse Door*, proposed third track *The Pimp* dropped at the last minute.
Rating 5

Sheer Khan - Last Generation
(SRT '84, SRT4KS140)
The a-side is typical melodic crossover of the day, while the b-side is the heavier and moodier *Lady's Dance*. Issued in cheap picture sleeve.
Rating 6

Shiva - Rock Lives On
(Heavy Metal '81, HEAVY13)
A cool piece, given that neither track shows up on the band's lone LP **Firedance**. This is the band's first material, and their

confusion (or ours, depending how you look at it) shines through. Shiva were sort of a heavy Magnum or Demon, and *Rock Lives On* supports this premise, being a medium steeped power chord rocker with an annoying vocoder refrain. B-side *Sympathy For The Devil* is a ballad with fairly serious chords come chorus time. Stuffed recording, which is a big no-no for anything with prog pretensions, but good vocals from John Hall.

Rating   7

Shiva - Firedance
(Heavy Metal '82, HMRLP6)

One of the rarer pieces on the influential Paul Birch-run Heavy Metal label, **Firedance** is a confused (but better for it) hybrid caught wiggling between US commercial rock, the NWOBHM and modern UK prog, sorta like Demon or Nightwing or old Witchfynde but strangely more inviting. I dunno, maybe it's that eastern religious cover art, an image completely off-base for metal, one perhaps designed to take the band and label elsewhere, but I'm liking the raw but thoughtful riffery, the slightly off-tune vocals (John Hall sounds, considerably enticingly, like the Sortilege guy), the colourful lyrics and the inescapable clankery of the production values, which hint at a cleaner version of those strafing the Witchfinder General catalogue. Two singles and one compilation placement (plus of course this lone album) comprised the band's total output during their brief '80 to '82 lifespan.

Rating   8

Shiva - Angel Of Mons
(Heavy Metal '82, HEAVY16)

A-side *Angel Of Mons* is a great melodic hard rocker sporting a smart gallop, vaguely jazzy chords and a whole lot of hot-stamped lead guitar. It is about an apparition seen by British troops preceding their involvement in World War I's Battle Of Mons. B-side *Stranger Lands* is an equally cool track, more down their psychedelic prog pathway, basically a heavy power ballad with metalized surprises. Both would become album tracks.

Rating   7

Shock Treatment - The Mugger
(Skull '80, SKR2001)

Man, this one's got the attitude, rocking like dirty AC/DC but with an added jolt of Oi! and Warfare delivered in a big ball of aggression. B-side of this very heavy, very grim major rarity, *Nuclear Warfare*, is even more intense, the ruffians in the band settling on a half-speed groove until all listeners are spooked and break into a run, deafened by the whiskey-rough vocals and the even gnarlier guitar and drum scrape of the damn thing. Magic. Not exactly NWOBHM magic, but a sort of French/Spanish vibe going, going... where did it go?

Rating   9

Shy - Once Bitten... Twice Shy
(Ebony '83, EBON15)

Birmingham's Shy (previously Trojan) were a fish out of water on Ebony, but here they were following up a **Metal Warriors** compilation track with a set of melodic

rockers quixotically lacerated by a Darryl Johnston production job. The band's ace was vocalist Tony Mills whose flair for dramatic, thespian singing carried over to the visuals, Mills applying face makeup that made him look like an adolescent version of Marillion's Fish. But these songs were a welcome bit of fun amongst the doomy NWOBHM lot, especially *Give Me A Chance* and the Pete Way-ish *Tonight*.
Rating   5

Shywolf - Lucretia
(Shy Wolf '82, SW001)
Charmingly little and belittling sound to this Derbyshire band, especially come b-side *California Jam* which contains an infectious melody and performances that are, well, close and compressed. All in all it's a cool cusp phenom, the band caught in the headlights of being garagers rooted in the '70s and trying to figure out this new metal craziness. The lead guitarist, Phil Toone sings the a-side and the bassist Steve Littlewood sings the b. Both look like they should be in The Outlaws or Skynyrd circa '73.
Rating   5

Silverwing - Rock 'n' Roll Are Four Letter Words
(Mayhem '80, SILVER1)
This Macclesfield band were once called Venom, moving on after Silverwing to become Hanoi Rocks-type rockers Pet Hate, who bashed out two albums before Alistair Terry went on to a solo album before eventually moving to Toronto (he lived in the same building as me in the early '90s!). The a-side to this single is a hilarious, naïve bit of garage rock absolutely cut wide open by an absurd synthesizer solo (different than the version on the band's lone album **Alive And Kicking**). Barring that though, it's a minor anthem reminiscent of Weapon's *It's A Mad Mad World*. B-sides are called *High Class Woman* and non-LPer *Hot City Streets*. Note: the a-side also shows up on the crucial **New Electric Warriors** compilation.
Rating   5

Silverwing - Sittin' Pretty
(Mayhem '82, SILV002)
Silverwing (NWOBHMers by default more than anything) featured future Pet Hate vocalist Alistair Terry, and were good for this EP (also released as a 7") plus the live album. The sound was quite varied, with the title track being a stiff, disciplined party rocker, but *Teenage Love Affair* being an ambitious power ballad. The final two tracks are quite pedestrian pop metal with a punky bit of flair coming from Terry's less than precise vocal skills—to be fair, these tracks are demos from late 1980. The a-side is the title track to the most widely available Silverwing piece, the four track 12" EP (SILV2-12). The song is a mid-pace American-style party rocker with a weak "ol' college try" vocal over a thumping bass line and boxy riff. But as alluded to, b-side *Teenage Love Affair* is the real winner here, an elegant power ballad that sounds like a cross between Mott The Hoople and Boston, what with those big synthesizers. Melody compares nicely with UFO's *On With The Action*.
Rating   4

Silverwing - That's Entertainment
(Mayhem '82, SILV3)
This one's a bouncy, likeable enough track down a glammy yet punky pathway, featuring those barely in-tune vocals we all love. B-side *Flashbomb Fever* (both are album tracks) is an almost Warfare-level speed rocker replete with explosion sound effects, ripping leads and Eddie Van Halen-styled hammer-ons. Issued in poster sleeve.
Rating   6

Silverwing – Alive And Kicking
(Bullet '83, BULP1)
Not much more needs to be said about these guys except for the fact that the only time any metal band made waves with a full-length debut that was a live album was MC5. It didn't work for AIIZ and it wasn't going to work for Silverwing, underscored by the album cover sending out bootleg-style messaging. Throwing studio demos on were the last nail in the coffin. In any event, the band was already on its way out, shifting with the times and morphing into Pet Hate. Good riddance.
Rating 4

Sinner – Need Your Love
(Whitetower '79, AMC705)
Hard-hitting blues metal of a type that had the band persevered, they very likely would have adopted the NWOBHM stance. Gatefold indie-issued EP that features the *Baby Please Don't Go*-like title track, *Beggar* and *God's In His Heaven*. Recorded with the "binaural mic in the mix technique." Says so right on the back.
Rating 5

Skitzofrenik – U.S.A.
(Guardian '81, GRC120)
One of many obscure Guardian acts, Skitzofrenik actually placed two fairly fetching, well-sung tracks on the legendary **Roxcalibur** compilation, neither of which are this single's melodic a-side or b-side power ballad *Lonely Road*. Really, Skitofrenik are on the new wave side of town, *U.S.A.* stuttering along like alternative pop with a shouty vocal, while *Lonely Road* uses prominent electric piano against - granted - dark NWOBHM-styled power chord accompaniment and a gorgeous electricity-drenched and harmonized axe solo. Issued in very basic picture sleeve.
Rating 5

Sledgehammer – Sledgehammer
(Slammer '79, SRTS79CUS395)
NWOBHM slapdashers Sledgehammer independently released this first single (no picture sleeve) before having it picked up and reissued, with sleeve, by Valiant the following year, cat# ROUND2. The a-side is a rubbery, galloping retro-rocker somewhat in the rarified vein of Ethel The Frog. Its primary place of residence is on the first **Metal For Muthas** comp. B-side *Feel Good* is practically punk rock, or at least Hawkwind trying their hand at it. Both tracks can be found on the band's lone album **Blood On Their Hands**, in updated version.
Rating 6

Sledgehammer - Living In Dreams
(Slammer '80, CELL2)
This one is backed by *Fantasia*, which can also be found on the awesome **Brute Force** compilation from MCA. More singles exist, but past our cut off date of 1985. In any event, the a-side, a roiling post-Hawk rocker that is fast, circular and committed to the noble cause, is no match for the stomping biker charms of *Fantasia*, which one can almost envision as a DiAnno anthem track on the first Maiden album.
Rating 8

Sledgehammer - Blood On Their Hands
(Illuminated '84, JAMS32)
Argle bargle of the highest order, Sledgehammer were a ball of corny-coloured confusion on par with other no-names like Brocas Helm, Saracen, Dumpy's Rusty Nuts, Demon, Shiva, Ethel The Frog and yes, Witchfynde, even though this particular conundrum got to tour with both Motörhead and unfathomably, April Wine. Rumbling and rickety, nowhere to run, nowhere to hide, you get the picture, sorta

dense and unsure whether they're prog metal, biker metal, pothead metal, headcase metal or case of beer metal. One kind word that most definitely applies is imaginative, Sledgehammer charming you with a '70s-inspired creativity not unlike late '70s Hawkwind or Armageddon's self-titled from '75. Mausoleum's **Sledgehammer** (also '84) is the same record with a bonus 12". Highlight: the infectious Tanked-up dumbfoolery of lead track *Over The Top 1914*, although the whole thing is pretty damn amusing and yes, irresistible.
Rating   8

Slender Thread – I See The Light
(Rock/Ellie Jay '80, MHMS193/EJSP9342)
Recorded in the same place where Diamond Head did their *Diamond Lights* EP, *I See The Light* is an early, competent, squarely NWOBHM conceit clocking in at close to five minutes by a band that had been in operation a good 18 months. B-side is the 2:57 *Where Is The Beat?*. Solid stuff, with acoustic layering, multiple parts and thoughtful arrangements.
Rating   6

Slowtrain – Ronnie
(Spirit '80, SR1)
Ronnie is no more than a dark-ish, synthesizer-washed (slightly) power ballad, not without charm or tension-building drama, really. B-side to this major rarity is the heavier *Just One Way*, sort of a frantic and punky non-boogie Vardis or Ethel The Frog song, its significance being the complete about-face in arrangement and attack versus the anemic a-side. Cool Flying V picture sleeve.
Rating   6

Dick Smith Band – Way Of The World
(Hol-o-gram '80, HOL001)
A-side *The Way Of The World* is a curiously hooky pop metaller with a nice, somewhat new wavey chorus and a thick enough drop bass pound come verse time. Middle nerd vocals but technically fine. B-side *Giving The Game Away* is a solid meat and potatoes NWOBHMer, simple, to the point and Tygers-riffy with a classy break and pleasantly screechy guitar solo. Scary demon cover art.
Rating   7

Smokin' Roadie – Midnight
(Zone To Zone '83, ZON03)
Here's a funny tik-tok plodder old beyond its advanced '83 years, valiantly dynamic but pretty much hapless post-Kerrang! NWOBHM. Became Tempest and then reverted back to their previous name. 1988 saw the release of a Japan-only album as The Now. B-side *Rip Off* is actually a much better track, rollicking along firmly riff-metallic, drunken production values a plus.
Rating   7

Snakebite – Blow You Away
(Astor '83, ASTOR1)
B-side to this quality non-picture sleever is complex, slow-brewed NWOBHMer *Thin Ice*, a vaguely bluesy but riff-steeped track much more suitable for the times than the boogie-rocking a-side, although *Blow You Away* packs a rowdy, blustery punch indeed. High point: *Thin Ice*'s screeching, steel-on-steel fast break.
Rating   8

Snatch-Back – Eastern Lady
(CSS '79, CS002)
This Manchester band's only single was backed with *Cryin' To The Night*. Solid pre-NWOBHM for the early entrance.
Rating   7

Soldier - Sheralee
(Heavy Metal '81, HEAVY12)
Soldier's only other output besides this single was the track *Storm Of Steel* on the first Heavy Metal Records comp. **Heavy Metal Heroes**, plus a live cassette featuring songs from their shelved debut **Infantrycide**. At various times, the band included Mark MacKenzie from Gaskin and near the end, Phil Lewis from Girl and L.A. Guns. Both of these tracks (b-side being *Force*) showed major Trespass-magical promise, both finding an Americanized mid-metal sound with vocal hooks and an intriguing metal calm.
Rating   8

Sparta - Fast Lane
(Suspect '81, SUS1)
Yeesh, do these guys look like a grizzled lot, perched atop a tank, looking homeless or at least gigless. Anyway, for five cavemen, they don't make much of a noise, *Fast Lane* merrily banging along quite unjuiced and dare I say smooth, once more a case of a band quite amorous of their '70s roots, redeeming themselves somewhat with that rudimentary but musical guitar solo to jam it on out. B-side *Fighting To Be Free* combines the new note density with a *Louie Louie* riff and a few other lame but likeable postures, all set to a no hi-hat verse. A little upmarket from the a-side but still greaseburger rock.
Rating   6

Sparta - Tonight
(Suspect '81, SUS2)
Sparta's second and last single (there's also a track on the hallowed **Scene Of The Crime** comp., an unreleased single and a shelved album) is worse than the first, *Tonight* being almost trashy punk, while *Angel Of Death* attempts a bit of foreboding prog Maiden malevolence, once more, built on a punk riff, albeit one with doomier chords. With a bit of dressing up, it could have walked (there's a cool Angel Witch-y melodic change-up half way through), but as it stands, it's too ruff 'n' roll to matter. Comes in an awful fold-up poster sleeve.
Rating   6

Spartan Warrior - Steel n' Chains
(Guardian '83, GRC2164)
One speed, one chord stomach-churners from deep beneath the British pub circuit, Spartan Warrior sustained a machine-like and mediocre dragon-slayer drone throughout their stay, but offered nothing to

rescue said slab from the pooch-filled rock 'n' roll kennels. Still, it's a rare NWOBHM semi-indie, so if you cut it some slack, you'll find an amusing charm that pops the clutch somewhat biker-ish between Handsome Beasts, Vardis and Battleaxe.
Rating   6

Spartan Warrior - Spartan Warrior
(Roadrunner '84, RR9847)
Stealing and subsequently botching riffs from everywhere, Spartan Warrior and their whiny, off-tune lead singa walk us through another bang-by-numbers late-for-the-NWOBHM blunder that captures a trace of Euro-suicide à la Gravestone but still belongs on the scrap heap of one-time spinners, evoking thoughts of Battleaxe, Killer, Sinner, Grim Reaper and a bunch of French bands lofted into a sausage grinder (ha ha, hence it's not that low grade!). Of note, the debut is rare, but the second and last saw wide distro in North America, including through Attic Records in Canada. Rarer still is the Guardian **Pure Overkill** compilation on which the band offered two tracks.
Rating   6

Speed - Man In The Street
(Speed '80, EJSP9409)
A-side *Man In The Street* is a jumpy bit of unsuccessful rock experimentation, save for the fact that Bruce Dickinson guests on lead vocals (hence the price), making this quite the little jewel, despite that Hammond organ solo and annoying punk riff. Ultimately very much like early Samson, Speed capturing that band's lust for ahem, life. B-side *Down The Road* is an infectious cross between boogie, pop and metal. This feel-good track, with its inspiring wind-up and crunched axe solo, could easily have been a hit, given a dozen or so ducks lined up in a row.
Rating   7

Spider - Back To The Wall
(Pennine '77, PSS136)
This very rare first single for the band is backed with *Down & Out*. Hilarious picture sleeve featuring the band in matching costumes. Quite amusing to hear that the band's steadfast sound was cemented obstinately so early, *Back To The Wall* boogie-glamming like Slade, with *Down And Out* boogie-punking like The Vibrators or Eater.
Rating   7

Spider - Children Of The Street
(Alien '80, 14)
This one, like the debut, is backed with *Down & Out* as well, and features a more NWOBHM-worthy picture sleeve, a crude line drawing of the band cranking it live. Most copies are non-ps however, and those worth considerably less in the marketplace. But man, listen to *Children Of The Street* and a couple of haircuts, and Spider could have been some sort of post-punk pub rock revivalists.
Rating   7

Spider - College Luv
(Alien '80, 16)
Backed with *Born To Be Wild*, this one also features an early version of the ubiquitous Spider logo. Available in gatefold sleeve, but most copies are non-ps. The sound is beginning to gel however, or at least the band's one-track purpose. Wonder what the Teds thought of these hapless historians, if they happened to think of them at all.
Rating   6

Spider - All The Time
(City '80, NIK7)
The a-side is the typically Spider-boogied track from the **Rock 'n' Roll Gypsies** album, but here in an earlier version.

B-side, *Feel Like A Man*, in non-LP, almost six minutes long and pretty boldly heavy metal rocking, with myriad boogie bits, breaks and even a shot of punk turning it by land's end into one of the off-path gems of the Spider canon.
Rating   8

Spider – Talkin' 'Bout Rock 'n' Roll
(Creole '82, CR30)
The a-side is yet another rousing, quick-paced boogie song fully in the spirit of Status Quo (and perhaps Gary Glitter and Slade). B-side is a dark acoustic ballad called *'Til I'm Certain*, which picks up speed and of course, doesn't neglect to boogie a bit throughout its wiry and drowned slog to the finish.
Rating   7

Spider – Rock 'n' Roll Gypsies
(RCA '82, RCALP3101)
Lead track *A.W.O.L.* winds 'em up as a thoroughly detailed knock-off of Status Quo, a tag these liggin' Brits would never shake as if they would ever want to. And indeed, the boogie mechanix just roll right on through this small, ineffectual but amused dedication to late '70s Quo. On the upside, some of these matchbox rockers resemble filler from **On The Level** or **Hello!**, but mostly it's the sweet and sour and pale of lullabies like *Part Of The Legend* and *What You're Doin' To Me*. And not only is it all very much like second-string Quo compositionally, it's also anemic and under-charged to an extent Quo never

was until their stifled, parody-ironic latter years. Love the concept, but the execution is about as lackluster as could be proposed.
Rating   5

Spider – Rock 'n' Roll Forever Will Last
(RCA '82, 268)
Yes, yet again, Spider take us boogie rocking to the pubs, bouncing up and down to their latest anthem until the suds regurge. B-side *Did Ya Like It Baby* is a little different, pastiching all sorts of styles from '50s rock to boogie to punk, verse being sung over tribal toms, opening doing Gary Glitter and *New Orleans* at once. Note, first pressing included a second single with *Amazin' Grace Medley Parts 1 & 2* as bonus.
Rating   5

Spider – Talkin' 'Bout Rock 'n' Roll
(RCA '83, 294)
The second go 'round for this song now pairs it with old chestnut *Down & Out*. The fact that it's out at all underscores the UK's strange singles culture, no doubt inspired by the prevalence of the 7" in the last indie-fueled movement, namely punk.
Rating   4

Spider – Why D'ya Lie To Me
(RCA '83, 313)
Knees-up Slade-alike blues stomper whose enjoyment is enhanced by the accepting punter staring at the picture sleeve. B-side is called *Footloose And Fancy Free*. Best picture sleeve of a bad bunch to date. Patch included.
Rating   6

Spider - Rough Justice
(A&M '84, AMLX68563)

Rough Justice stays the course meekly carved on '82's **Rock 'n' Roll Gypsies**, with only ever so slight digressions into non-boogie mindspheres. Still, who cares, 'cos there's been zero progress in terms of chops or personal assertion, and the recording, despite production by the illustrious Chris Tsangarides, is still toneless and disinterested. Plus the boys persist in dressing like Spinal Tap or worse, Slade. The sorry verdict: look for endless permutations on featureless, numbskullian barroom boogie, with the odd side-romp such as *You Make Me Offers (I Can't Refuse)* demonstrating avenues worthy of consideration, although one should never overestimate a fanbase's capacity for change.
Rating 5

Spider - Here We Go Rock 'n' Roll
(A&M '84, AM180)

The a-side is a glammy boogie rocker again with a long but catchy slogan. Absolutely nothing new, except, subtly, the melodies. B-side *Death Row* begins with a long prison talk intro and then turns into a punky metal thing without boogie until the chorus (almost made it!). AMP180 is a web-shaped picture disc. AMX is the 12" version which adds a striper blues version of *I Just Wanna Make Love To You*.
Rating 6

Spider - Breakaway
(A&M '84, AM204)

The a-side, non-LP, is the sort of pop boogie we got out of early '70s glamsters like Mud (not pretty). B-side *The Morning After* is from the **Rough Justice** LP, residing more inside the band's working class wheelhouse. Skipping the band's last single, *Gimme Gimme It All*, as it hails from the decidedly non-Spider-friendly year of 1986.
Rating 4

Spitfire - So You Want To Be A Rock 'n' Roll Star
(Carrere '82, CAR253)

A rousing enough cover of the old classic, backed with the predictably bouncy and blueprinted *Spitfire Boogie*, the totality of this non-picture sleeve sounding suspiciously like a bit of a toss-off project.
Rating 5

Spitzbrook - Stranger
(Ace '81)

Hard to pin this particularly to the NWOBHM genre, as there's AOR and synths to Kent five-piece Sptizbrook, but also the creeps of Demon, Saracen, Legend and poppy Witchfynde. B-side to this nonetheless high quality prog metaller is called *Looking At You*. Limited number with picture sleeves.
Rating 7

Split Beaver - Savage
(Heavy Metal '81, HEAVY7)

Despite their joke name and expected homebase derision, Split Beaver rocked it pretty hard, sounding like Saxon crossed with labelmates Handsome Beasts, worthy biker grit strapped to hard-ass NWOBHM

riffing. *Savage* grooves mightily with a touch of boogie, but mostly black 'n' blue metal. B-side *Hounds Of Hell* conversely, is black 'n' blue all over. Incidentally, *Savage* is track one, side one on the LP, and *Hounds Of Hell* is track one, side two. Single up for review is on a cool black and green version of Heavy Metal's awesome Ozzy-lookalike label, although this was also issued with a silver label. A world of difference from their muffled, garagy *Running Wild* track on the first **Heavy Metal Heroes** compilation. Non-picture sleeve for the most part, although a few with sleeves exist.
Rating   8

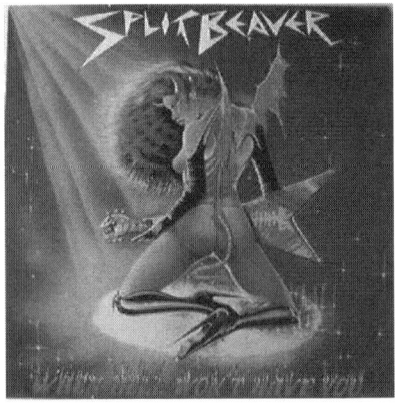

Split Beaver – When Hell Won't Have You
(Heavy Metal '82, HMRLP3)
Even though there weren't all that many NWOBHM albums to keep track of, this one's often forgotten. Then again, despite that horrid and horridly metal cover art, Split Beaver were as much a boogie and blues band than anything Maiden-goosed. Still, the band got up to rough 'n' tumble NWOBHM with tracks like *Savage*, *Levington Gardens*, *Likewise* and the signature speed metal of *Hounds Of Hell*. All told, what you got was a cheap, intimate, quite charming mix of old pub rock values mixed with valiant attempts at the new metal – roustabout UK biker rock basically. Nearly as renown for their *Running Wild* track on the seminal **Heavy Metal Heroes** comp as they are for this lone full-length.
Rating   6

Splitcrow – Rockstorm
(Guardian '84, GRC2167)
Interesting piece of arcana here, **Rockstorm** being a slab none too often seen. Music within: trashy, try harder boogie metal not unlike Spider or Vardis, but more so chained to '50s rock and blues. Brits of course, bewildered at the NWOBHM, but opportunistically signed to one of its minor (but years later, deemed influential) labels.
Rating   5

Squashed Pyrannah – Heartstop
(Rapp '82, 23457)
B-side to this retro-rocker is called *Dr. Jekyll*, which is the better track, a thoughtful light metaller with interesting parts and pervasively memorable melodies. Issued in picture sleeve featuring band name and a simple black and white illustration of an enraged lumberjack.
Rating   7

Stampede – Official Bootleg
(Polydor '82, ROCK1)
Strange that the band's debut would be a noisy, nasty live album, made to look like a boot as well, but there you go, Stampede (post-Lautrec) slamming their way through a bunch of tough commercial rockers at the Reading and Mildenhall rock festivals. Punchy, well played, spirited... this was obviously a studied band, arriving with songs that were simple enough to translate to the live stage with favourable results. Rueben Archer's got a bit of the Phil Mogg to him,

and his performance live beats the pants off the studio one from the follow-up. Fun, viable, bravely un-NWOBHM-ish stuff.
Rating   6

Stampede - Days Of Wine And Roses
(Polydor '82, POSP507)

Quite well-regarded, due to their two albums (one live, one studio), and the presence of Lizzy-like axeman Laurence Archer, Stampede had what the UK would deem a stadium rock sound, somewhere between early AOR, UFO and Lizzy, Archer actually joining UFO at one point, and playing with Phil Lynott in Grand Slam. Vocalist Rueben Archer was Laurence's stepfather, and had some acclaim with Lautrec before firing up this band. Anyway, the a-side shows all this promise, the guitars, the pop sensibility, the slight air of pomp. The live version can be found on the **Official Bootleg** debut, recorded live at Reading, looking very indie, but emerging on Polydor. B-side *Photographs* sounds increasingly UFO-like, albeit with a working class bent, which comes from Rueben's somewhat tortured tonsils. Still, there's a swagger, and I wish it translated into a long and illustrious raft of records. Note: there is a rarer, promotional non-ps version with *Photographs* as the a-side.
Rating   7

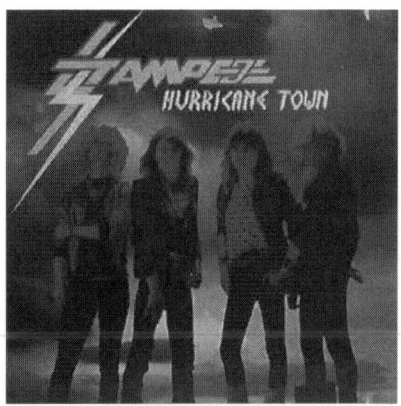

Stampede - Hurricane Town
(Polydor '83, POLS1083)

I somehow always wished more for these melodic, rhapsodic NWOBHMers, imagining wistfully hidden ambition beneath this crusty Def Leppard-wannabe record as well as the band's clankier **Official Bootleg** from the previous year. As background, Stampede's claim to fame was their hot young guitarist Laurence Archer, whose lovingly Moore-ish, Sykes-ish flourishes landed him a gig in Lynott's doomed Grand Slam project (Mark Stanway, keyboardist here, also got involved) and later as part of a low-years version of UFO. However, **Hurricane Town** coagulates and stalls more like a toneless Black Rose than a shaken and stirred Heavy Pettin' project, the band sounding rushed, as well as dragged downward by the vocals of Laurence's stepfather Rueben Archer. Long lost in time and long lost at the time anyways, it's sinful beauty nevertheless to hear Archer's archetypal fills and modern metallic Lizzy solos breathe some air into these frustrating songs. File with Wildfire as shaky, commercial, and oddly appealing.
Rating   6

Stampede - The Other Side
(Polydor '83, POSP592)

Both the a-side and b-side (*The Runner*) are tracks from the band's second and last album, *The Other Side* being a stumbling popster, again with UFO overtones, and *The Runner* being a quick melodic number with an expected lusty Archer solo or two closing off with a prophetic four notes that point to the man's Thin Lizzy aspirations and inclinations.
Rating   7

Starfighters - I'm Falling
(Motorcity Rhythm '80, MCR105)

B-side to this debut single is called *Heaven And Hell*. Neither track made it to any of this Birmingham band's (surprisingly major label) two LPs. Known for the fact that axeman Steve Young was a cousin to some more famous Youngs in a band called AC/DC, the band's sound going there as well.
Rating   6

Starfighters - Starfighters
(Arista '81, HOP200)

Alarmingly early for a band to be emulating AC/DC (well, I guess there's also Angel City), Starfighters' debut does a loose, new

wavier version of their blood relatives (see above), not on purpose but probably just from lack of funds, although Tony Platt is in producing. The result is something like middling Krokus although pub rockers from the Stiff camp also come to mind (and then quickly leave). So what? Well, it's reassuring in a fast world to have stuff like this collecting cobwebs in the ol' collection.
Rating   6

Starfighters - Alley Cat Blues
(Jive '81, JIVE003)
The a-side is a prime AC/DC-steeped track from the boys, with an exquisite rhythm guitar sound from Stevie Young. The UK issue of this is backed with the non-LP old rock barnstormer *Don't Touch Me*, while the German issue on Teldec is backed with *Power Crazy*, Stonesy Angel City fer miles. Also a French issue as JIV4001 with a different sleeve. UK 12" (JIVET003) adds *Rock 'Em Dead*, also non-LP. Good stuff, but all told, hobbled by vocals strangely lacking in personal magnetism.
Rating   7

Starfighters - Power Crazy
(Jive '81, JIVE6)
Power Crazy is a likeable enough anthem, sort of a cross between Spider and AC/DC, or AC/DC lite as it were, like something that might come from the band in the late '90s, or now, or next. The b-side to this debut LP track is the non-LP *I Want You*, quite bluesy for the band but yet again, an interesting permutation or proposal or twist on what AC/DC or Angel City might do. UK three track 12" version (JIVET6) adds the non-LP *Get Out While You Can*.
Rating   8

Starfighters - In-Flight Movie
(Jive '82, HOP205)
Starfighters' simple and unassuming second (and last) full-length circulated mightily throughout most of the dollar bins in North America, and fortunately one ended up in my hands given that, all in all, **In-Flight Movie** performs a warm and affable AC/DC-lite bar crawl, featuring a pubby Bon Scott/Rod Stewart-style throat at the helm. Overall, no surprise, the record sounds bigger and smarter and more arena-rocked and than the affable debut. But still, **In-Flight Movie** is held back by the band's adherence to the many rules of roots rock, adding a predilection for slow structures and build-ups long on payback, essentially emulating the most dull one-half of any given AC/DC record. O'er to the better tracks, it's tuneful, punchy, and fairly consistent given the band's modest chosen direction. And the main AC/DC connection? To reiterate, guitarist Stevie Young is a relative of Malcolm and Angus, who no doubt helped get their mixer bud Tony Platt on board to produce the record. AC/DC also pegged Starfighters for back-up slot on their UK tour in support of **Back In Black**.
Rating   6

Static - Voice On The Line
(Eeyo '82, EEYO1)
Promising sound here, Static recording these two songs and nothing else for a non-picture sleeve, hand-written label release. *Voice On The Line* is barely

NWOBHM, more happy pubby new wave crossed with AOR (!), featuring a peppy beat and a harmonized verse vocal. The guitar solo is vaguely Lizzy-ish and all go home optimistic at the end of the show. B-side *Stealin'* is much more NWOBHM, striking down a mid-metal path, riff-rocked, warm and combative. Extremely solid. Note I: became Snowblind, who did a record for Mausoleum. Note II: Eeyo stands for Extremely Excellent Yodelling Organization.
Rating   7

Steel - Steel
(Neat '81, NEAT14)
Quite the lost gem, this double 'A' side single features a Birmingham act managed by an ex-Judas Priest manager Dave Corke. Their sound was a bit unsure and loose on first track *Rock Out*, but the band is all guns blazing come *All Systems Go*, which is a confident swift piece of pure metal with good vocals from ex-Excalibur belter Paul Tunnecliffe, and a raucous live sound courtesy of ear-splitter Keith Nichol, who put this together at Neat's home studio.
Rating   8

Stormchild - Rockin' Steady
(Serpent '82, 001)
A-side *Rockin' Steady* is a little relaxed and lubricated to be considered full on NWOBHM. Plus there's that synth wash. But all told, it fits the lighter end of the sound, popping along with a nicely harmonized chorus, Archer-style axe solo, and half-time break. Guy can't hit the high notes though and then there's a ludicrous, preposterous synth solo that blows the track but good. B-side *Last Night* is an arch-NWOBHM power ballad, spooky, distinguished by a weird and chimey synth pattern which persists through the fast bit. Basic, but effective black and white picture sleeve.
Rating   7

Storm Queen - Come Silent The World
(Real Fire '82, RF001)
B-side to this quite heavy Welsh rarity is called *Raising The Roof*. Amusingly, a red label issue with the song misnomered *Come Silent The Night* was recalled and trashed.
Rating   7

Stormtrooper - Pride Before A Fall
(Heartbeat '80, BLAT1)
Here's a typical speed metal blaster, Paul Merrel (onto Jaguar after this) getting it right before most would take a stab at it, although that droning synth stuff sounds quite odd and Rush-like. B-side *Still Comin' Home* sounds like American hard rock, or worse, Canadian, even if it has a naive warmth which approximates a kindergarten version of the chord progression from Deep Purple's *Burn*. I dunno, the whole thing reminds me of looped San Franciscans Brocas Helm. Note: the fully crap Stormtrooper on **New Electric Warriors** is a different band.
Rating   7

Strategy - Technical Overflow
(Ebony '82, EBON7)
Technical Overflow and b-side *Astral Planes* are two instrumental tracks that sound like a convoluted and entangled

Maiden jam buzzed by prog, jazz and Rush. Adding to the caterwaul is piercing Ebony production values which sound like someone cracking walnuts next to your ear while your contractor is ripping plywood with a bandsaw. Dave Cook eventually went on to New England (U.K.).
Rating   5

Streetfighter – Crazy Dream
(JR '82, JR7049S)
Streetfighter's claim to fame is guitarist John Sykes, who went on to Tygers Of Pan Tang, Thin Lizzy, Whitesnake, Blue Murder and a prolific solo career. Their output consisted of this four tracker as well as *She's No Angel* from the **New Electric Warriors** comp. *Crazy Dream* shows just how suited Sykes would be for Lizzy, thumping along like a third rate Lizzy chord rocker with a tasty solo and even a vocal from Fenton that goes Phil. *Living On The Red Line* and *City Girls* both descend further into barwipe party rock, while *Streetfighter* tries valiantly and ultimately successfully to be metal, recalling the stout-swilling melodies of Trespass, further raising the game with a great bridge. Call it two out of four, with the two-years-earlier compilation track ironically being the tightest, most detailed of the band's five grizzle rockers.
Rating   8

Street Legal – Rolling On
(Weeird Brothers '84, SRT4KS052)
These guys were oddly more of a hard southern rock band, known for their ZZ Top and Skynyrd covers. However, this track is fairly dark and rocking, similar to mid-level Blackfoot, with great guitary uplift. The flipside, *Mississippi Moonshine* is a true southern toss-off. Worst picture sleeve in the business.
Rating   6

Stryder – Forcin' Thru'
(Quartz '80, 010)
Solid, melodic mid-intensity Irish metal, especially for 1980, *Forcin' Thru'* and b-side *Settle Down* both exhibit Thin Lizzy-like tendencies, through use of both pregnant pauses and twin leads. Plus that black and white, hand-drawn label art for "Quartz record" is classic.
Rating   6

Suspect – In The Night
(Ellie Jay '81)
Really borderline this one, with *In The Night* being perky Cars-styled pop crossed with commercial hard rock. B-side to this weak, out-of-tune picture sleeve is *Working It Out*, which is a bit darker, slightly impressive as a song, but again, near inconceivable as anything but a radio-friendly departure on a proper NWOBHM album.
Rating   3

Sweet Savage – Take No Prisoners
(Park '81, PKR1001)
Belfast's Sweet Savage was of course the breeding ground for Dio/Def Leppard guitarist Vivian Campbell, Jimmy Bain having recommended the crunchy shredder to Ronnie. The band's first single was this Chris Tsangarides-produced and Dublin-recorded bit o' flash. A-side *Take No Prisoners* is the inferior track

of the two, thumping along like a semi-committed Tygers-like barwipe. *Killing Time*, however, is a short sharp rocker (2:47!) featuring Viv doing a brisk take on the *Stand Up And Shout* vibe, less distinctive but every bit as fast, weakest link in the chain being vocalist Raymond Halter. Trivia note: Metallica included a cover of *Killing Time* as the flip to the single for *The Unforgiven*. Trivia note II: comes in two label colour variants.
Rating 8

were just another bunch of Mausoleum Brits with competence, no songs and a tin-ear producer, one who put too much of an uber-thud into the drums, chop-blocking Syar's songs before these rockers could get to the gate.
Rating 5

Sweet Savage - Straight Through The Heart
(Crashed '84, CAR48)
Straight Thru The Heart features one of the riffs plundered for Dio's **Holy Diver** debut (**The Last In Line** would contain no Sweet Savage vestiges). But although the title of the track would become *Straight Through The Heart*, the riff would become the backbone for *Caught In The Middle*, Sweet Savage cleaning up their sound by this point, better vocals, even taking a successful shot at harmonies, writing an American-style pop metaller all the rage with Kerrang! journos at that time. B-side *Teaser* looks at similar melodic riffery, coming off as bad Starz more than anything, exposing grave flaws in the band's rhythm section. Of course it rhymes teaser with pleaser. But you knew it would.
Rating 8

Syar - Death Before Dishonour
(Mausoleum '84, 8308)
Middle meat and potatoes metal that wasn't about to win any cooking awards, Syar

T

Tank - Don't Walk Away
(Kamaflage '81, KAM1)

A-side *Don't Walk Away* displays cogently Tank's ability to mix beer and melody in a way that put this band above their baby Motörhead status but quick, a tag encouraged by having Eddie Clarke produce them. It's a bracing kick-boogie anthem, driven by a great chorus and those gruff but wise vocals. Side two is just punk 'em up Tank, veering into warfare terrain, a disintegrating thrash that mixed, er, beer and vodka, perhaps, *Shellshock* being an early version of the LP intro track, and non-LPer *Hammer On* being a bit of a melodic stretch, sort of like hooligan punk. Released six months before the classic debut album, **Filth Hounds Of Hades**. Trivia note: also a cool Spanish DJM/Kamaflage/Chapa Discos issue (DJO638) with a rare cover band shot.
Rating   9

Tank - Don't Walk Away
(Kamaflage '81, KAMF1)

This is the non-ps free single with the album, a live version of the insanely catchy, melodic and perfectly boogie-graced a-side with modest, tacitly charming double-bass speedster *The Snake* as the b.
Rating   7

Tank - (He Fell In Love With A) Stormtrooper
(Kamaflage '81, KAP1)

Two of the gosh-darn greatest swilligan songs to ever burp forth from the NWOBHM, the a-side is the glorious album track, a critical mass of youth-fueled bravado, the lustiest song Motörhead never wrote. The b-side is a loud 'n' raw live version of the band's greatest tricky riffster *Blood, Guts And Beer*, driven by one of those violence-inspiring one note bass patterns, a rock bed of the cream of the scene. Picture disc only. Spanish issue uses a studio version for the b-side, and features different cover art.
Rating   10

Tank - Filth Hounds Of Hades
(Kamaflage '82, KAMLP1)

My beloved **Filth Hounds** was, and still is, a smokin', party-with-your-buds debut skid-mark from the British band often considered the poor man's Motörhead. And Motörhead elements abound, Eddie Clarke producing, Algy Ward's guttural croak resembling Lemmy's, and the patented distorto-bass buzz ringing loud, proud, front and centre. Comparing both grease chains however, Tank records have a higher percentage of classic and anthemic rockers due to more innovative riff-writing, more diddling, more bridging, more *trying*. So **Filth Hounds** is full of memorable pre-grunge rockers that range from all-out thrash (early '80s style) to mean-spirited mid-pace rockers with strong melodic choruses, all topped with lyrics that can

best be described as colourful. Don't let the odd use of melody fool you—Algy and the boys spew the most pleasantly putrid of chaos metal brews all the way, which unfortunately tended to reveal themselves as laughably fallible in the band's uniformly horrible live shows, which among UK punters earned the band no greater than joke status akin to that of Angel Witch. Back on **Hades**, the prime killers were *Blood, Guts And Beer*, *T.W.D.A.M.O.*, and *(He Fell In Love With A) Stormtrooper*, each brimming with alcoholic buzz, each blasting dangerously, each woefully and graphically showing hair metal peacocks how to be more bad-ass than anything from America could possibly handle.
Rating 8

Tank - Power Of The Hunter
(Kamaflage '82, KAMLP3)
Tank serves up another blast of biker metal classics, **Power Of The Hunter** clanging together the same dastardly elements as the first, but with a surprisingly welcome whiff of the regal. Enclosed, we get four or five speed rockers (which tend to be the weakest tracks), while the balance reveals such sweat ethic swillers as *Walking Barefoot Over Glass*, *Used Leather (Hanging Loose)*, and *Set Your Back On Fire*, all powered by inspired riffs, knee-slapping lyrics and relentless rhythms like a garbage truck driven by a drunk. And one of the better tunes (rendered heavy as hell of course), is *Crazy Horses* by those toothy Osmonds, Tank rassling the track to the ground and then going for a pint. Reflective on this night, I guess I've rated the first couple o' Tanks highly because although, really, I get into only about half of each record, the boys' knock 'em down attitude spreads o'er all of it, with each record's four or five best anthems turning out absolutely life-affirming to the extreme, kinda like early, out-of-control Megadeth on nothing more stimulating than warm beer, kinda like Motörhead as rabid buyers of NWOBHM singles, rather than Lemmy prattling on about Little Richard and the duckwalked like.
Rating 9

Tank - Turn Your Head Around
(Kamaflage '82, KAM3)
Not the greatest Tank track, the a-side is a bit awkward and panicked sounding. The b-side, however, is non-LPer *Steppin' On A Landmine*, and what an epic classic it is, trundling along to a dirty but thoughtful gallop, bloody and unbowed, the non-LP gem of the band's canon to be sure. Note: the same "filth hounds" cover art as the *Stormtrooper* picture disc.
Rating 8

Tank - Crazy Horses
(Kamaflage '82, KAM7)
Pouncing from the 7" vinyl, this nasty (non-LP) rendition of the Osmonds' classic captures the raw essence of English street metal like no other. Non-LP b-side

Filth Bitch Boogie does much the same, sounding much like its title, a slightly metalized take on a Tush-like boogie premise, bass-buzzed, gnarly and badly in need of a shower. Brilliant, as usual. Spanish issue as well, with different art.
Rating   9

Tank - This Means War
(Music For Nations '83, MFN3P)
Eschewing short punk metal attacks for more involved, more topographically-varied battlefields, **This Means War** rides an epic, panoramic war theme throughout, no doubt flesh-and-boned nicely by the addition of a fourth member, ex-White Spirit guitarist Mick Tucker. It's still edge-of-chaos, down 'n' dirty garage metal, but things are not the same in the bunker of mosh. On the upside, there's a higher proportion of tunes based around memorable classic metal riffs; on the downside, less toons that stand out as much as the life 'n' wife wreckers on the first couple 'o slime-buckets. Additionally, **This Means War**'s lyrics are more conventionally metal, lacking the eccentricity and humour afforded and latitude by the band's previous semi-joke status. Still, **This Means War** is a considerably rowdy album that actually becomes more impressive over time - this is the stuff beer bellies are made of. High Vaultage CD reissue contained thud metal bonus track *Whichcatchewedmycuckoo* which is more of a real song than you might think.
Rating   9

Tank - Echoes Of A Distant Battle
(Music For Nations '83, KUT101)
The very cool a-side is from the band's epic, serious and classic **This Means War** album, a record that solidified the band's war image, the song being the record's prime example of the band's hoary, beery battle cry. B-side is the non-LP *Man That Never Was*. Musically, the song would gallop perfectly onto the album, but the mumbled vocal is substandard, the source of the song's b-ness, as it were. Also released as a 12" maxi-single (12KUT101), adding *Whichcatchewedmycuckoo*.
Rating   7

Tank - Honour & Blood
(Music For Nations '84, MFN26)
Honour & Blood tries to emulate the critically-acclaimed **This Means War** with the same three-on-side-one, four-on-side-two format, alas, ending up with less monumental tracks than on either of the last three. But it's still a heroic effort, sending 'em to the mosh pits half-baked, untested but true, once more Tank lent battle-torn gravity through the workmanlike production of John Verity. *The War Drags Ever On* (lead cut) is a ringer for *Just Like Something From Hell* (lead cut, last album) which is fine by me, and the title track is somewhat of a new

modern style for the band, a band wracked by the departure of the Brabbs brothers, who come handily replaced by Cliff Evans (guitar) and another White Spirit bloke Graham Crallan (drums). But much of the rest lacks zip, perhaps reflecting a growing despondence for Algy at the band's continued lack of commercial success. Whatever the reason, there's an oppressive air of rehash. High Vaultage CD reissue adds perfectly serviceable Tank tattoo *The Man That Never Was* from the *Echoes Of A Distant Battle* 12". Note: next up was one of those nice but harmless Castle comps (a rite of passage), called **Armour Plated**, which was a gatefold double LP with 20 of your fave Tank brawls, including a handful of b-sides.
Rating   7

Terraplane - I Survive
(City '83, NIK8)
The a-side is this commercially viable band's most recognizable track, also the title of the 12" version (12NIK8). *I Survive*, alas, sounds completely Canadian, circa, let's say, '81, pomping along like a blue collar radio rocker, warm recording, melodic, innocuous but not offensive in any way. It is essentially what Neat had looked for but never achieved with their radio rock yearnings over ten or so faltering singles. As well, both the 7" and the 12" were reissued in '85 on major label epic, with alterations. B-side here is the non-LP *Gimme The Money*. Note: same label as Girlschool's first output, distributed by Cherry Red.
Rating   5

Terraplane - I Can't Live Without Your Love
(Epic '84, A4936)
The a-side is your standard perky pop metal number, solid stripey-pants vocals, old school synth percolations, dull but personable. B-side was called *Beginning Of The End*, a dark, proggy, ambitious, uptempo break-up ballad only available on the cassette issue of the band's held back album **Black And White**, which would only surface in '86. In fact, the cassette version would contain three extra tracks over the standard LP. Gatefold version as well, as GA4936. Many more singles, but they occurred from '85 to '88.
Rating   5

Thunderstick - Feel Like Rock 'n' Roll?
(Thunderbolt '83, THBE1002)
Like McCoy, masked drummer Thunderstick is a sort of solo break-off from Samson that regresses, unravels, proposes that the Samson of the first two albums was, well, good enough, cooked enough, half raw but that's fine. Nuh-uh. The title track is fast and melodic and simple, *Runaround* is punk, with the female vocals of Jodee Valentine (the band's second female vocalist) turning the thing into Girlschool searching for the pop charts, despite the song's intriguing guitar textures. *Alecia*, weirdly same kind of thing and with two of these, gosh-darn if I ain't starting to like it—it's them weird guitary breaks, I tell ya. Final track, *Buried Alive* is closer to metal, and again, oddly catchy, even if the whole thing is, at the end of the day, ruined by trashcan production. Initial copies came with free patch.
Rating   5

Thunderstick - Beauty And The Beasts
(Thunderbolt '84, THBL008)
Hard to believe these punk metal oddballs with female vocals worked their way up to a full-length but here it is. At times frantic, punky, poppy, completely AOR-ish, biker metal the next flash of th' blade... I gotta tell you, so many riffs and rhythms and yelps here are so bad they are good (see *Afraid Of The Dark*), Thunderstick most definitely building a shaggy band character

here that no one would dare try put out there, not even Girlschool. And then there's the production? Is that by choice? In any event, think very early Samson crossed with the Motley of the first two records, Wrathchild, Rogue Male and perhaps Gillan in an alcoholic haze. Strange, strange band indeed and half way through *Rich Girls (Don't Cry)* I had to ask myself if Thunderstick weren't laughing along with their perplexed but small fanbase.
Rating 6

Titan – East Wind, West Wind
(Wild Dog '80)
B-side to this lone single from the first recording band for Rock Shades of Wrathchild is called *Losing The Fight*. Non-picture sleeve and as a band, very short-lived. More sincerely NWOBHM than the flute 'n' folky other Titan we've banished from these pages as unworthy. A rollicking we-love-metal good time is the a-side, but it's *Losing The Fight* that snarls like Bruce-era Samson.
Rating 7

TNT - Back On The Road
(Neat '84, NEAT39)
Here's a fairly cranked piece of anonymous late NWOBHM, TNT certainly looking the part, and finding the loudest of guitar sounds to leap from the Neat environs. There's a whiff of both Y&T and Diamond Head about this one (OK, Tsunami and Wildfire), the a-side being quite poppy and the b-side (*Rockin' The Night*) more of a bruising blue collar rumblebucket. The vocalist is a bit restricted and flat, as is the drum sound, but there's a heroic forward thrust to the whole thing, a bit of a missionary zeal that overcomes the averageness of the band's talents.
Rating 8

Toad The Wet Sprocket - Pete's Punk Song
(Sprockets '79, BRS004)
Name nicked from a Monty Python sketch, a much more successful US pop band would inexplicably use the moniker yet again in the '90s. The a-side was more a slapdash bit of perky, new wavey generalist rock and the b-side *Feel It* wasn't even rock, more like botched, funky r+b, with a shot of Ian Dury. Would have left the band out, if not for a change of metal mind come next single. Fold-out sleeve.
Rating 2

Toad The Wet Sprocket - Reaching For The Sky
(Sprockets '80, BRS008)
This is more like it, Toad The Wet Sprocket living down their dumb name, jokey first single, and the crappy and loitered *Blues In A* from the first **Metal For Muthas** compilation with this pedestrian but heavy enough British pub metal nugget, rife with mischievous little change-ups and a carnal enough forward sturm. B-side *One Glass Of Whiskey* is a curious tune, almost like mid to high quality Foghat, odd arrangement, a few proggy breaks, heavy enough, and all told, a feather in a cap to a catalogue of wildly divergent styles.
Rating 6

Tobruk - Wild On The Run
(Neat '83, NEAT32)
With everybody gaga over Ratt, Twisted, Quiet Riot and Bon Jovi, a bunch of UK

bands tried the same thing, Midlands entry Tobruk as good as any, slathering up their hard AOR with keyboards and huge production values on this poppy but thick Nightwing-styled a-side. File with Shy and Chrome Molly. B-side *The Show Must Go On* is closer to true NWOBHM, unremarkable but squarely heavy. Following two singles found the band on up to Parlophone/EMI but alas are from '85 and out of our jurisdiction, as the band would be stylistically as well, along with every other UK act enamoured with MTV and the emerging hair metal phenom.
Rating 6

Tok-io Rose – Bad Girls
(Tok-io Rose '84)
Very heavy with a touch of early American hair metal (mostly Crue and Dokken and Metal Blade samplers), *Bad Girls* is the product of an accomplished Cardiff act that has soaked up all the tricks necessary to compete in '84, although it's clear from history they didn't. B-side to this quite aggressive late NWOBHM picture sleeve, *Desperate Situation*, is more of the same, thumping along with a bit of a Great White vibe. Solid stuff, anticipating quite well metal's quaking shift from England o'er to California, where metal would survive and celebrate for well on nigh the ensuing six or seven years.
Rating 7

Tokyo Blade – If Heaven Is Hell
(Blade '84)
This is the reissue and repack of the Ghengis Khan 7" under the band's new moniker. For a review, see that entry. Note I: there's also an interesting Spanish version (Victoria '84, 10418), which has *If Heaven Is Hell* as the a-side and *Liar* as the b, also from the first album (same photo session band shot as the back of *Power Game*). The UK reissue of this single occurs in two forms, one with *Highway Passion* as the b, and one with *Meanstreak* as the b.
Rating 8

Tokyo Blade – Power Game
(Powerstation '83, OHM2)
This is what it's all about, highly juiced guitars bulking up along a struggling percussion pattern. No question, Tokyo Blade had the power and the heft and the lunge, *Power Game* slotting these guys near the top of a certain accessible heaviness along with Pretty Maids. Non-LP b-side *Death On Main Street* does much the same scamper, excelling in the twin lead department and ear-splitting solos. As worthy a track as any on the debut. Note: there is also a French Bernett '84 issue of a *Midnight Rendez-vous* single backed with *If Heaven Is Hell*.
Rating 8

Tokyo Blade – Tokyo Blade
(Powerstation '84, AMP1)
A vital, spirited debut from these hopeful NWOBHM rockers, **Tokyo Blade** touches on many classic '70s and '80s styles from Priest and Maiden to Ozzy, while also making nod to motivational cock rock from America. Good headbangin' metal with enough licks, solos, inter-song variation, and roughness to make it interesting, but also just naive, cliché, and bush-league enough to keep it from really standing out. Could have used some selective editing, as tunes seem to drone on a shade longer than necessary. But give it an extra point for sincerity, ambition in the same vivacious frame of mind as Pretty Maids, which the follow-up lacks. Pushes 8 simply 'cos we really got into it back in the old days. Before record II, vocalist Alan Marsh would be replaced by Vic Wright, due to the former's case of stage nerves. Renamed **Midnight Rendezvous** for North American consumption.
Rating 7

Tokyo Blade - Night Of The Blade
(Powerstation '84, AMP4)

Less punky and insistent, leaning more towards an anthemic Def Leppard sickly meow (but much heavier), **Night Of The Blade** stands equally varied and interesting as the debut, yet not quite as inspired in the songwriting department. Slick, commercial production (complete with deep, wet snare) and melodramatic vocals from the new guy confound this ambitious yet oddly spontaneous effort, even if the sum total falls short on enthusiasm, the band sending signals that they are running out of cash and need to write some hits.

Rating   6

Tora Tora - Red Sun Setting
(Mancunian Metal '80, TT5000)

Surging, wall-of-sound guitars distinguish this kick-ass rocker, not quite to the point of Savage but at least past the likes of Soldier and even Holocaust. B-side to this heavy-on-electricity basher, *Highway (Shooting Like A Bullet)*, is more of the booze-swilling same, pounding drums and brat vocals (again like Savage but also Guy Speranza) helping with the youthful enthusiasm to the thing. Issued in picture sleeve.

Rating   8

Tora Tora - Don't Want To Let You Go
(Tora '83, TT5001)

Same root band as the promising one above, but quite the altered lineup. B-side to this much more commercial non-picture sleever (a cleaner sound than before) is called *Sorry I Broke Your Heart*.

Rating   6

Bernie Tormé - Turn Out The Lights
(Kamaflage '82, KAMLP2)

This hapless, bed-headed guitarist has toiled with a number of British bands, most notable being Gillan and very briefly, Ozzy. His solo albums have a post-punk wasted 'n' jaded mentality, but musically seem to wander through various well-traveled hard rock territories, resulting in only a handful of quality vignettes, best here being the wicked *Lies* and infectious popster *Possession*. Tormé sports a subtle sense of humour, sorta like Ray Davies meet Johnny Thunders, but the albums as a whole remain patchy, and the man ever so charmingly can't sing his way out of a wet paper bag.

Rating   4

Bernie Tormé - Electric Gypsies
(Zebra '83, ZEB1)

A punky, snarling delivery of variously spirited, variously tired hard rock; however, *Wild West* is a classic raver, one of the most intense fusions stuck quivering and dive-bombing between new wave and heavy metal ever penned. **Electric Gypsies** is adequately consistent stylistically, evoking an exotic, glam-hammed Hanoi Rocks, smearing forth with a squalid paid-my-dues feel, much more intense in comparison to the previous year's awkward **Turn Out The Lights**. Tormé's guitar work isn't exactly earth-shattering, but it does have a garagey sort of integrity, bending the man's delusions of grandeur toward gritty, economic and noisy riffing, the man doing an adequate job of smothering the rest of the band's watery performances in their tracks.
Rating 7

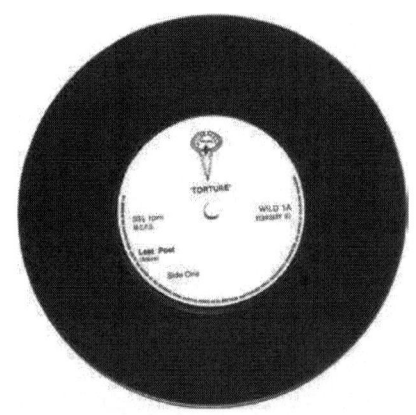

Torture - Last Post
(Widebeest '81, WILD1)

A-side *Last Post* is a stout AC/DC-style rocker with a borderline punk vocal performance from Ray Askew. It's a nasty little blast of carnal NWOBHM, more like mainland spoo from a bombed Krokus. B-sides are called *Lucky* and *Finding My Way Home*, both tracks also boogie/pub rocking like something from Switzerland or France, both handicapped by stiff drum beats but buoyed by the raucous vocals and molten guitar sound. No picture sleeve.
Rating 7

Touched - Back Alley Vices
(Ebony '84, EBON28)

The barreling nuclear boom box of Ebony's Darryl Johnston is cranked full bore on this far-gone mutation of the brilliant Savage, resulting in an album that kicks off inexplicably with a horrendously loud epic cum power ballad. The razor numbness of the production adds a wasted insistence to **Back Alley Vices** which, despite fairly traditional non-threatening structures, makes the difference between convincing and brain-dead (i.e. Mausoleum). And the presence of a shrieker along the fine line of Steve Grimmett or Chateaux's Krys Mason doesn't hurt either. Hopelessly Brit/Euro poverty metal with probably the most extreme of Ebony recordings, Touched kicks and destroys considerably, given their limited weaponry.
Rating 8

Touched – Dream Girl
(Ebony '84, EBON27)

Touched were formed from the ashes of Aragorn and Dragster, and were (un?) lucky enough to get two LPs out on Ebony, '84's **Back Alley Vices** and '86's **Death Row**. B-side to this raucous, commercial, likeable **Back Alley Vices** track was the non-LP *We'll Fight Back*. Quintessentially Ebony in every way, sizzled white hot with guitars, grim with grit like Chateaux and Grim Reaper, but with a paucity of good songs.
Rating 8

Tracer - Chanelled Aggression
(Mousehole '83)

This depressive EP from a rare band from Jersey contains four tracks: turgid, suicidal doom ballad *Memories Always Kill*, *Pain, Pain* (NWOBHM proper but horribly maimed by the production), *Neon Town* and *Don't Bless The Warrior*, a sorry bit of scrub rock, goofy vocals, silly creepy intro, and yeah... guitars that sound like an AM radio being strangled. Yes, that's how they spell it.
Rating 5

Track 4 – Mr. Charisma
(Track 4 '82, TR4001)
This stylistically diverse EP contains three tracks: *Chalk & Cheese*, *Freetime* and the title track, which lives between Thin Lizzy and power pop, or as they called it in the UK... mod revival! Very basic picture sleeve, some with lyric insert.
Rating   5

Trans Am – Crazy World
(Chub '83, SRTS83CUS1916)
Not surprisingly, *Crazy World* is well-recorded with super distorted guitars and some classy riffing at the pre-chorus and jammy bit (there is no chorus). B-side *Flash In The Pan* is a riffy brisk thing, again with thoughtful riffing with a bit of a post-punk vibe yet squarely metal. But alas, the band's female vocals... I dunno... I'd rather not, 'cos otherwise this is like a more accessible Chateaux. No picture sleeve, black ink on white label, very basic.
Rating   6

Trespass – One Of These Days
(Trial '80, CASE1)
One of the greatest NWOBHM bands that never made an album, Suffolk's Trespass caught our attention most cogently with this highly hummable track from the second **Metal For Muthas** comp. The single however, presents a much more laid-back version of the song, with vocals that are way up front and appropriately lackadaisical for its ancient '79 recording. B-side *Bloody Moon* is unfortunately what is essentially a bad re-write of *One Of These Days*, same tuneful chord pattern,

still quite likeable, just not a progression for the band. Yellow and black Trial label.
Rating   9

Trespass – Jealousy
(Trial '80, CASE2)
A-side *Jealousy* finds Trespass in more obvious NWOBHM terrain, cranking a somewhat wooden speedster with an interesting descending chorus break but a dull verse. Away from their forte, this one's a bit of a pooch. B-side *Live It Up* is also not one of the band's more personable tracks, straddling the leaden course of meat and potatoes metal and the band's effortless, exploitable knack for hooks. More of less solidly built, this one's just a bit on the dull side for a band this good, basically not taking its own advice.
Rating   7

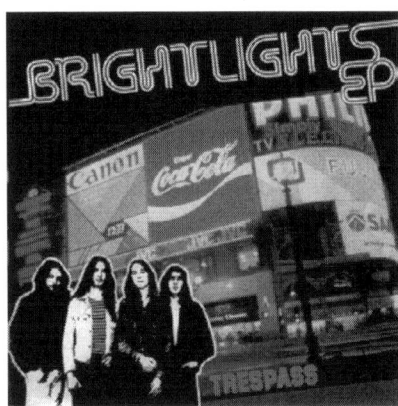

Trespass – Bright Lights
(Trial '82, CASE3)
This is more like it, *Bright Lights* rocking with authority but dealing lots of sweet

finesse, almost into a pop new wave direction, simply proving Trespass capable of the sturdiest and most memorable of songs, highlight being the vocal harmonies of the chorus. Nice job. First b-side *The Duel* is one of those Manowar-ish galloping metal things, quite effective given its dreary early English rainrot. Second b-side *Man And Machine* is more of a tight and tidy medium range rocker that shows the band's versatility into a straight immediate pub rock. Three good tracks with synergy. Blue and silver Trial label. Trivia note: the a-side is 45 rpm, the b, 33 rpm. Post-Trespass was an equally ignored band called Blue Bludd, who nevertheless managed two LPs. Note: the value of the Trespass singles have gone down over the years given the readily available CD reissues.
Rating   9

Triarchy - Save The Khan
(SRTS '79, CUS599)
Triarchy's first of two singles establishes the band's poppy prog take on the new metal. *Save The Khan* is a bit plain compositionally, but the recording is fine and the textures advanced. Plus it's got a nice cloud-breaking chorus, although I could do without the Stranglers-styled synth solo! B-side *Juliet's Tomb* is a brave bit of hard 'n' heavy balladry, proving the band's many futuristic dimensions. Cool band swirling around that Magnum/Nightwing zone and making it believable as well. Note: initial indie issue ran out quickly, being replaced by a non-ps issue in 1980 on Direct Records, as NEON1.
Rating   7

Triarchy - Metal Messiah
(Direct '80, NEON2)
Picture an Angel Witch/Rush hybrid and you'd be close to what this highly interesting Kent band provides. One is reminded of Hawkwind or those old Germans Jane with those buzzing synths and maniacal doom tones. First b-side *Sweet Alcohol* offers more of the same sinister underworld melodies, featuring a laid-back riff to a hypnotic drum beat that captures a sly and slippery cymbal-swinging groove that is quite the flavour indeed. Second b, Robert Johnson's *Hell Hound On My Trail*, becomes a similarly light-footed rocker that goes a little quicker, finding once again a slightly more note-dense riff placed on a sweet spot of percussive invitation. One of the better NWOBHM singles on a purely creative basis. No picture sleeve issue. Note: catch up with all of this material plus more old and new stuff on the Vinyl Tap full-length CD **Before Your Very Ears**.
Rating   9

Trident - Destiny
(Trident '84, TRI1/SRT4KS013)
A little late in the game, this one slides in 'cos it looks the part, and more importantly sounds it, scampering along like a cross between Tokyo Blade (loud guitars and that solo: youch!) and old Samson or poppy Angel Witch. Look for the double bass drum close that sounds more like someone banging the side of a plastic pail. B-side *Power Of The Trident* starts with one of those dreary slow builds and then turns into pedestrian and uptempo mid-metal rocker with an amiable enough melody. I'd rate this quite exciting for '80,

but merely average for '84. Recorded at Pink Studios, Liverpool.
Rating   7

Truffle - Round Tower
(Chestnut '81, NUT6)
Portsmouth's Truffle had a cassette album ('86's **Bacon Slicer Strikes Again**) on top of this single. Touring with the likes of Tank and Spider, these guys had a dark, hardscrabble edge to their sound, backing up the strident, over-reaching a-side with more of a doomy boogie rocker called *If You Really Want*. Again, another band who could have gone places with better production. Continued well into the late '80s.
Rating   7

Trux – Bad Luck
(indie '82, TRX01)
Solid, muscular biker metal with a hint of Paul Rodgers to vocalist Eddie Allen and heavy Bad Company at the music end. B-side *Movin' On* is even better, but bluesier, with harmonies vocals and a cool rootsy funky lope, bonus being the southern rock wind-up with tasteful lead licks. Apparently the height of fame for this Cambridgeshire act and their non-ps single was a favourable review in **Kerrang!**.
Rating   6

Turbo – 3 Track E.P.
(Cargo '81, CRS004)
Highlight here is *Running*, a high-octane riff rocker with modulation, spit, polish and drive, as well as a mid-track breather which explodes into a tidy NWOBHM solo. The other tracks are also squarely within the form, these being sophisticated a-side *Stallion* and second b *Take My Life*. Note: *Running* also showed up on the **New Electric Warriors** comp.
Rating   8

Turbo - Charged For.... Glory
(SRTS '82, CUS1261)
Not exactly charged, this mid-pacer bounces along, adding a bracing galloping section and a bombastic break that is all nuts, bolts and bike chains, pure poverty metal inspiration indeed. B-side of this non-picture sleeve is called *Race For The Dawn (Midnight Mover)* and alas, is an obtuse enough, modestly driving garage rocker not without ideas and eccentric charm.
Rating   8

Twisted Ace - Firebird
(Heavy Metal '81, HEAVY9)
A strange act this one, Twisted Ace fronted by a way thespian singer with ants actively rifling through his pants. Come chorus time they sound like Bread or Poco. A-side *Firebird* is buttressed by a raft of Thin Lizzy-like soloing, something which alas can't support the ancient Krokus boogie of the verses, nor the silk harmonies and cowbells of the chorus (spot the David Byron scream). B-side *I Won't Surrender* has the same vocal problems, roughing it like labelmates Handsome Beasts until the white bread chorus. Strange and well, bad. Navy and black Heavy Metal label. Note, a further track called *This Fire Inside* continued the band's quest for pop metal dominance, courting

keyboards and harmonies, chundled and chumbled by a sub-standard recording for such semi-hard AOR. It showed up on **Heavy Metal Heroes Volume II** and was scheduled to be released as a single but this never happened.
Rating   8

Tygers Of Pan Tang - Don't Touch Me There
(Neat '79, NEAT03)
Later in life, Tygers belter Jess Cox became operations point man at his long-time boutique gig Edgy Records, having sold off Neat Metal to Sanctuary. But in typical Neat fashion, his band had signed to the small indie and then left for higher ground with MCA almost immediately. The only Neat Tygers output was this debut single. *Don't Touch Me There* made the debut album, and is a smart, sassy rocker that demonstrates the band's star quality. *Burning Up* isn't as polished, while still demonstrating one of the band's strengths, their boogie fever, something which benefits in syncopation from Jess' biker throat. *Bad Times* sounds like a variation on *Don't Touch Me There*, and thus works in the new British metal manner. The single sold 7000 copies for Neat and was then reissued by MCA in 1980 (MCA582) with similarly successful results. Cheese graphics all around, with an extremely early band shot on the back.
Rating   7

Tygers Of Pan Tang - Rock N' Roll Man
(MCA '80, MCA612)
Non-LPer *Rock N' Roll Man* is one of those rich-of-history redneck rockers that could have really benefited by big production.

It's simple but highly infectious, a cool riff with an American feel. First b-side *Alright On The Night* (also non-LP) is a punky boogie with a Cox vocal mixed way too far back. Underachieving song, underachieving production. Second b-side *Wild Cats* is the album track. Comes with a "free patch offer." Pre-Japanese character logo.
Rating   7

Tygers Of Pan Tang - Wild Cat
(MCA '80, MCF3075)
Wild Cat is the raucous, street-treated debut from one of the NWOBHM originals, a band who never made the same record twice, slapping forth this charming little pre-Tank rust bucket, ricocheting like an errant bullet, punky, loud, loose-bolted, and heavy—fun for all and all for one. Of note, it's the lone Tygers album to feature Jess Cox on vocals. Granted the guy ain't no Dio or Halford, lacking a real singer's range, causing the boy to lapse often into a strained, conversational style, but I dig his Ace/Peter voice, his hearty metal growl that lends this album guts and grime. Scrappy, headbangin' metal at its most unloved and neglected, **Wild Cat** is a chaotic noisemaker steeped in the integrity of a Motörhead or Tank, but with better riffs than either; it's lusty, unpretentious rock 'n' roll, in creation of one of the early magic moments of the British invasion, and one of the very first releases we sought out after feverishly combing those bewitching issues of **Sounds** and **Melody Maker** from '79 and '80 trumpeting the new power surge-ables from all over jolly ol'. So yeah, mark this one as a stupendous drinking

record of long-haired biker metal, featuring enduring carnivores like *Euthanasia* and *Badger Badger*, amongst a general barrage that refuses to let up, give in or move over.
Rating   9

Tygers Of Pan Tang - Suzie Smiled
(MCA '80, MCA634)
Here's the band's almost glammy, dumbed-down shot at a hit single (not to be confused with Saxon's *Suzy Hold On!*), backed with a typically trashy but spirited run through ZZ Top's *Tush*, Jess also typically ignoring being in any sort of tune. Both tracks produced by Chris Tsangarides. A-side is a different version that that on the classic debut LP. Also in existence: a Yugoslavian issue on Beograddisk.
Rating   7

Tygers Of Pan Tang - Euthanasia
(MCA '80, MCA644)
Euthanasia is one of the band's killer compositions, great riff with that sublime and bluesy stop/start chorus break. It's one of the band's original four songs, *Straight As A Die* being another. This non-LPer is a bit of a belaboured quick mid-pacer with Jess mimicking his style from *Euthanasia*, until the whole thing collapses into that churlish and campy chorus line, which tends to undermine the narrator's humourous protests to an encounter with homosexual advances. The sleeve to this one is an out-of-character stark black with red writing, no band name, no credits (only other text being the catalogue #), I guess to evoke the bleakness of death or something.
Rating   8

Tygers Of Pan Tang - Spellbound
(MCA '81, MCF3014)
On their all-important sophomore, Tygers opts for a serious, upscale sound, adding a credible metal technician at the mic to wail forth standard tough guy metal lyrics, which are, alas and alack, too unsurprising to work, the band's songwriting reverting to bland formula metal lacking in the chaotic, torn and frayed blitz of the debut. And of course it wouldn't be a serious play for superstardom without the obligatory radio rockers, of which there are at least three. But neither the production nor the chops are up to serious contention for state-of-the-art metal, Tygers being a band that sounded best dirt-poor and under pressure, here their Judas Priest-y aspirations betraying the band as liggers

and punters before their prime. In time, maybe they could have pulled it off, but one more kick at the metal cat and they'd be hanging up those working man's riffs for a deep dive into confused AOR.
Rating   8

Tygers Of Pan Tang - Hellbound
(MCA '81, MCA672)
Enter rock god type Jon Deverill, for this restrained speedster from **Spellbound**, plus a non-LPer called *Don't Give A Damn*, a kind of mean mid-speed riffster that would have fit like a glove on the album. This was also released as a double 7" non-gatefold with 'The Audition Tapes': Jon Deverill taking a sizzling violent run at oldies *Bad Times* and *Don't Take Nothing*, both **Wild Cat**-type rockers built on fairly shoddy riffs. The second 7" features a plain white label with handwriting style text, and a catalogue # MSAM10.
Rating   8

Tygers Of Pan Tang - The Story So Far
(MCA '81, MCA692)
This one's two LP tracks, *The Story So Far*, different to album version, and *Silver And Gold*), plus the band's oddly appropriate cover of the Marriot/Lane classic *All Or Nothing*, which brings back the band's cogent penchant for a convincing boogie. Label sez "*All Or Nothing* recorded live one night (Know what I mean!)". Slightly textured cardboard sleeve.
Rating   7

Tygers Of Pan Tang - Don't Stop By
(MCA '81, MCA723)
This uncharacteristic **Spellbound** track was a welcome curio amongst the pugilistic fare on the record, perhaps setting a precedent for pop experiments from **The Cage**, specifically *Making Tracks* and *The Actor*. It's a masterful display of pacing and stadium rock dramatics and as I say, a welcome single for the band. B-side *Slave To Freedom* counters with one of the nasty kuts from the debut, while the 12" version adds a Live BBC Session version of *Raised On Rock*.
Rating   8

Tygers Of Pan Tang - Crazy Nights
(MCA '81, MCF3123)
Taking fiery cue from its album cover, **Crazy Nights** is the most confident, aggressive and heaviest Tygers of them all. The production makes your ears bleed. Loud, and oddly distorted, it's a perfect mix for the record's simplistic riff machines, which gather copious weight compared to the powerless speed rockers loitering the streets of **Spellbound**, or indeed even the punky flamethrowers of the debut. A good 80% of **Crazy Nights** is top-notch British arena fare, capturing the sparked, live mayhem of the debut while simultaneously making a convincing play for serious metal contention with a palpable renewed levity of purpose. And Jon Deverill sounds in complete control of the ship, growing into his role as prima donna and entertainer, vocalist of an elite class. Unfortunately it

didn't work at the bank, and next time out, the boys abandon heavy metal in search of some needed cash. Original pressing came with a second 12" single.
Rating   9

Tygers Of Pan Tang - Love Don't Stay
(MCA '81, MCA755)
Killer second track from **Crazy Nights**, simple, effective, true modern metal somewhat set up within a blues structure and a nice AOR chorus that offsets nicely the shark of a riff. Non-LP b-side *Paradise Drive* is a light-hearted boogie with nice twin guitar texturing and a characteristically solid vocal from Deverill.
Rating   8

Tygers Of Pan Tang - Do It Good
(MCA '82, 759)
No biggie here, just two album tracks (although b-side *Slip Away* is technically not an album track, being on the free 12" available with the initial UK pressing of **Crazy Nights**). Both rock it up good though, these sessions finding the band's largest guitar sound, something that kicked these simple tracks to a new level. No picture sleeve.
Rating   8

Tygers Of Pan Tang - The Cage
(MCA '82, MCF3150)
Tygers surprise wholesale on this shift to pop metal, engineered by neat freak Peter Collins who would one day encourage and enlarge Rush's weaknesses on **Hold Your Fire**. Clocking in at under 30 minutes, **The Cage** contains nary a single heavy rocker. However, despite its sell-out nature, I fell for the record in spades, feeding off its hope and energy and excitement at trying something new. Great hooks are everywhere, buttressed by a swagger straight outta David Lee Roth, delivered with a rich and unsure British twist, Deverill in full possession of the dramatic sense to pull it off. Highlights include a smokin' version of oldie *Love Potion No. 9* and the innovative, subdued atmospherics of both *Making Tracks* and *Tides*, odd bookender tunes which point to fresh vistas this band might have explored further. Ultimately, **The Cage** caused widespread revolt among Tygers' old guard and for all the clatter, it didn't pick up many fans from the AOR end of town. Nevertheless, **The Cage** was a refreshing, positive example of wimp metal, making no apologies for its romancing of style over substance.
Rating   9

Tygers Of Pan Tang - Love Potion No. 9
(MCA '82, 769)
One of many singles from **The Cage**, this one is the strongest er, potion, a fortified metalized cover with a great groove and recording, backed with album track *Lonely At The Top*, ushered out as the last potential single from **The Cage** a year and a half later. Also released as a picture disc (MCAP769). Note: awesome different sleeve on Japanese issue, as well as a Spanish issue as B104204 and a German issue as 104204100.
Rating   7

Tygers Of Pan Tang - Rendezvous
(MCA '82, MCA777)
The Cage was a shock to everybody, even more shocking when people decided that they liked Tygers as a pop band. *Rendezvous* was all that and more, but non-LPer *Life Of Crime* is straight **Spellbound** metal mania. Look for the Damned-like (*Burglar*) siren and effects break. Also released on white, red and blue vinyls and in a poster sleeve. German issue (104512) sports a different sleeve graphic.
Rating   7

Tygers Of Pan Tang - Paris By Air
(MCA '82, MCA790)
Another perfumed but impressionable track from **The Cage** backed with a non-LPer, *Love's A Lie* sounding like **The Cage** material performed recorded (and self-produced) down-budget to the standards of **Spellbound**. Fairly naff hair band sound, really, almost demo-level glam. Also released as a groovy picture disc with the Eiffel Tower on one side, band shot from the album on the other (MCAP790) and a German issue as 104686100. Some copies include Tygers earring.
Rating   8

Tygers Of Pan Tang - Making Tracks
(MCA '82, MCA798)
Here's the daring but ultimately successful album track (in different version), *Making Tracks* being an odd rhythmic piece of glam, backed with the band's highly emotive *What You Sayin'*, propelled by a sensuous hook and a flirtatious Deverill vocal performance, which lapses into a nice rap reminiscent of Freddie Mercury near the end. Should have been a hit. 12" version uses the extended remix version of the a-side.
Rating   8

Tygers Of Pan Tang - Lonely At The Top
(MCA '83, MCA841)
Again two album tracks, both *Lonely At The Top* and b-side *You Always See What You Want To See* being trademark hard AORists of this period for the band, stuffed with hook, melodrama, rock star aspersions.
Rating   7

Tygers Of Pan Tang - Tygers Of Pan Tang
(MCA/Victor Japan '82, VIM4083)
This is a Japanese comp which was quite important to own until the awesome Neat/Edgy CD reissues from '98 culled everything here except the two highly smoked live tracks *Slave To Freedom* (cool to hear Deverill give this a go) and *Raised On Rock*, both recorded like a magnificent train wreck, both fast, furious and filled to the brim with NWOBHM magic. Seven tracks total, marking Tygers' history as a band with solid, grounded working man's b-sides. Oh yeah, beware: it's made to look like a live album. Naughty, naughty.
Rating   8

Tyrant – Hold Back The Lightning
(SRT '83)
This well-regarded epic metal a-side is one of the lost classics of the age. Cirith Ungol-type vocals caw triumphantly to an intriguing

gallop of a riff, one that breaks down for quick single and twin leads here and there, the whole effect coming off like rarified Trouble (a bit of Eric Wagner in that mesmerizing voice) or perhaps Jag Panzer. Riveting rivethead stuff. B-side *Eyes Of A Stranger* is similarly magnetic, passionate, years ahead of its time, complicated, groovy, bombastic and exquisitely sung. Easily one of the top five bands in this book, with respect to acts that never released an album, indeed one single being all we ever heard from Tyrant.
Rating   10

(remember them?). Roughly recorded and executed, and generally badly written, but they try hard like Fist. Production by Cronos who curiously shortly thereafter slagged the band soundly. Deeply righteous NWOBpovertyM slammer: *Dog Soldiers*.
Rating   5

Tytan - Blind Men And Fools
(Kamaflage '82, KAM6)
Tytan featured Kevin Riddles and Dave Dufort from Angel Witch. This excellent a-side included *Ballad Of Edward Case* as its b, the two forming a base-rounding circuit that celebrates the cream of the exploding UK metal scene. *Blind Men And Fools* sounds like Angel Witch crossed with Tokyo Blade and Satan, many ideas, including commerciality, rolled into one ball of expert NWOBHM posturing. *Ballad Of Edward Case* is even better, a balls-out speed rocker with highly memorable riffing and an almost Metallica-level sense of confident helmsmanship. 12" issue (KAMA6) included *Sandman*.
Rating   10

Tysondog - Eat The Rich
(Neat '83, NEAT33)
Although likened to Judas Priest, Tysondog were closer to the scruffy likes of Jaguar. This debut piece from the band contains an early take on *Eat The Rich*, which would show up on their second and last album **Crimes Of Insanity** nearly three years later, plus an early version of the '84 debut's *Dead Meat*, live at Neat's own studio, Impulse. The sound is a medium type of thrash, dirty but behaved, the look of the single, gravely black and white and indie all over. Next and last single was '86's *School's Out* cover (Neat56) backed with *Don't Let The Bastards Grind You Down*.
Rating   9

Tysondog - Beware Of The Dog
(Neat '84, 1017)
Well, can't say they didn't warn us. Mangy mutt metal from Newcastle, shooting feebly but proudly at Priest, yet achieving a grimy din, sorta like Tank with less talent, or like the first hot mess from Jaguar

is truly light, although the riff is amusing and fresh, as is the damn title. Both, or either, in the right hands, possessed the personality to be hits.
Rating 7

Urchin – Black Leather Fantasy
(DJM '77, DJS10776)
This was Adrian Smith's band he formed at 16 before moving on to Iron Maiden. Not totally horrible, Urchin were a capable mid-rock NWOBHM outfit, good vocals from Dave Hall, decent production, but thin. B-side is the comparatively retro-rocking *Rock 'n' Roll Woman*, very specifically a heavy boogie, harmonica included. Modestly legit and very early in '77, this is one of the earliest NWOBHM pieces in existence. Most non-ps, but some promo copies included a perfunctory picture sleeve.
Rating 8

Urchin – She's A Roller
(DJM '78, DJS10850)
B-side to the second and last Urchin single is *Long Time No Woman*, both songs in demonstration of a commercial sound that was much more lightweight than the band was live. You can sort of hear this in the a-side, a song more or less sturdy, energetic, glammy hard rock in the spirit of early Sweet, yet thin in this version. *Long Time No Woman*, on the other hand,

the labels that dabbled (or shortly want to dabble) in this direction. Decent enough hard AOR, although as with most early UK knobbery, the keyboards stand out starky and distractedly. B-side, the Spinal Tap-ishly named *Trouble With You (Ain't Looking For Trouble)* is more of the same wobbly, ill-conceived pop metal faux finery as the title track.
Rating   5

Valhalla – Still In Love With You
(Neat '84, NEAT36)
Neat's third rate Bon Jovi begins '84 with a murky power ballad that is as uneventful as Thin Lizzy's crapster of the same name, and certainly no worse than Scorpions' similar long slog of hokum. B-side *Jack* pumps and pomps along like Nightwing, and indeed displays a penchant for logical songsmithing and arrangement. Production blows though, just like the debut single eons back in NWOBHM time.
Rating   4

Valhalla – Lightning In The Sky
(Asgard '81, ASG69151)
Valhalla is very much what the NWOBHM was all about, being inspired by the new metal movement and then putting yourself out there fast and furious with an indie single, all in the celebration that metal is defined and cool and vigourous and united for really the first time ever. *Lightning In The Sky* is all that and more clanging along at a spirited clip, strafed with Priest-mad riffery, pounded by a barrage of busy drums. B-side (or second a) to this truly worthy NWOBHM pounder is called *These Sunday Nights*, and it's a step back in aggression but blessed with a melodically complex and textured chorus. The drummer obviously fancies himself the second coming of Neil Peart, but that's OK, if his decisions aren't always the best, he nonetheless adds interest.
Rating   9

Valhalla – Coming Home
(Neat '82, NEAT22)
Here's an early entry into the AOR sweepstakes, Neat actually being one of

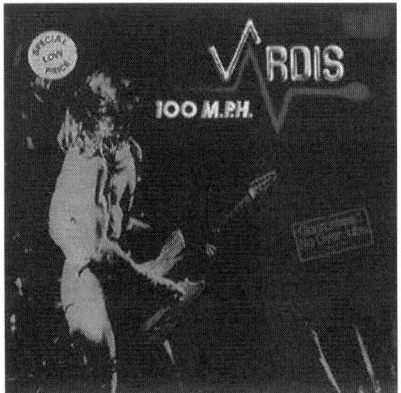

Vardis - 100 M.P.H.
(Redball '79, RB001)
A highly rare, highly collectible single, this first output for Zodiac and crew demonstrates the band's out-of-step variance. A-side *100 M.P.H.* delivers the core sound, a fast, tough biker boogie which is basically old Quo after a number of pints. *Destiny* lets up the throttle just a bit, but is also grim boogie. *Blue Rock* is the band's "you must be joking" number, while *The World's Insane* strikes once more at the friendlier end of the core sound.
Rating   8

Vardis - If I Were King
(Castle '80, QUEL2)

All metal, all the time. At least that's the impression you'd get from this single, the title track being the band's definitive anthem, a pulse-racing pantheon to simplicity, the band's *Overkill*. B-side *Out Of The Way* is also fairly heavy and struggling to let its riff be free. No boogie, although the bar rawk is definitely burped to the fore. Both would show up on 100 M.P.H. as the first and last tracks on the album, not to mention pretty much the first and last word.
Rating   9

Vardis - 100 M.P.H.
(Logo '80, MOGO4012)

This bumbling, out-of-sorts power trio was viewed as a ground-floor NWOBHM outfit, approximating a roughed-up, low-budget Motörhead from the '50s, or a heavier but not very talented version of Status Quo, a comparison Vardis would be proud to accept, having graciously called one of their albums **Quo Vardis**. **100M.P.H.** is actually live, "guaranteed no overdubs", and arguably, due to the play-to-survive intensity of the live experience, is one of their heaviest outings, mixing boogie woogie with metal the way Quo themselves managed so capably in days of old. Lead dude Steve Zodiac looks sorta like Edgar Winter. Too plain jane to rule the world, but parts of this rock smartly like a pedigreed Ramones. Entering the lower register of moshdom comfortably are *Situation Negative*, *Let's Go*, and most triumphantly *If I Were King*. First issue with poster.
Rating   7

Vardis - Let's Go
(Logo '80, VAR1)

Vardis were successful in turning their early singles into minor anthems, *Let's Go* being no exception, rounding the bases quickly with its punky Ramones metal feel and 'Let's Go' call to arms. B-side *Situation Negative* is a warmer boogie track with less metal and more pop, and was also a ditty that saw some positive exposure.

These are the studio versions of the tracks presented live on the seminal **100 M.P.H.** debut. Note: some copies came with an additional "free" 7" containing two live tracks, *100 M.P.H.* and *Out Of My Way* (VARFREE1). Note II: both Spanish and German Logo editions were issued, each with cover art unique to that issue (a Spanish-only *Power Under Foot* was also issued). Nice colour sleeve, a live shot of our man of white Steve Zodiac.
Rating   7

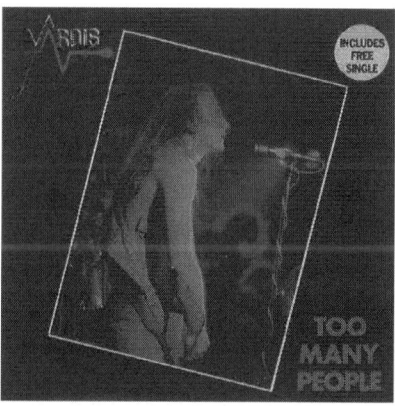

Vardis - Too Many People
(Logo '80, VAR2)

This double 7" gives you every move Vardis has in a tight and succinct four songs. A-side *Too Many People* is a catchy enough melodic pop boogie. B-side *The Lion's Share* is one of the band's heavier note-dense tracks and a live staple that keeps the band's hand in the NWOBHM. Over to the "free" 7" (VARFREE2), you've got oldie *Blue Rock (I Miss You)* previewing the band's maudlin cabaret rock with a swirling but sickening mixture of '50s rock and glam, while b-side *Dirty Money* is the mean medium average of all the traits in one song: a meat and potatoes boogie worth the quaffing of pints. Comes with cool bronze Logo label and a lime green separating merchandising. *Too Many People* never showed up on a Vardis LP in any form.
Rating   7

Vardis - Silver Machine
(Logo '81, VAR3)

Silver Machine slides in with the NWOBHM trend to try strike a hit with a cover, this time Vardis trash-boogie-ing Hawkwind's most famous and accessible song. B-side *Come On* is a non-LPer and is classic frantic Vardis confusion, fast, simple metal which collapses into a perplexed slow blues, acceptable I guess because there's some serious metal in there. Call this one a semi-non-ps, as it's a plain printed black sleeve with a die-cut whole for the appropriately silver label.
Rating 7

Vardis - This World's Insane
(Logo '81, LOGO1026)

This World's Insane is less the flat-out careening bar-room booger compared to the band's live debut, Vardis foolin' around with melodic variations of traditional r 'n' r, which would make it interesting, listenable and nostalgic if not for the surprisingly sickly-to-the-point-of-mistaken recording for this the band's first studio record. A likeable bunch of dented heads with no talent, it all flies out the window if the mix tanks as much as this does. Includes a spaceship ride on Hawkwind's *Silver Machine*.
Rating 5

Vardis - Quo Vardis
(Logo '81, LOGO1034)

All the more the hootenanny for its obvious disdain for the tenets of metal, **Quo Vardis** does a smooth boogie polyester hip-swivel, raising smiles all around the room, courting risk of ridicule at every corner, and coming off humble and fresh despite its ancient, low-budget placement in metal's shabby back books. Despite the confusing signals and the purportedly bad live gigs, Vardis assumes a semi-serious levity in the construction of decidedly flip song ideas. And despite your strong or weak opinions on the band's inconsequence (and many there are), the man can sing, and the man can wrap a bluesy solo around a bashful riff, Zodiac betraying his sense of folly and history at the same time. Maybe a wee chapter, but a chapter nevertheless, for there was nothing quite like Vardis and their slavish though low faculty focus on the love of Quo. Faves: the gushy and acoustic *To Be With You* and the no-ambitions *Where There's Mods There's Rockers*. Rock 'n' roll with heart but no money.
Rating 7

Vardis - All You Ever Need
(Logo '81, VAR4)

The a-side, a happy, humpy pop boogie number, is supported by *If I Were King* and (yawn) *Jumping Jack Flash* (live).
Rating 6

Vardis - Double 'A' Sided Single
(Logo '81, GO408)

This one pairs the guitar and dirty *Gary Glitter Part One* with *To Be With You*, a rare acoustic ballad for the boys, and a damn good one at that.
Rating 6

Vardis - The Lion's Share
(Razor '83, RAZ3)

A pointless mishmash of previously released studio and live material plus other questionable newies. I had a soft spot for this band because they were just so doomed from day one, so mercilessly panned by the critics, and so stung by the business side of life. But hey, nothing wrong with Steve Zodiac's smiling bleat and the spirit in which the moshable boogie histrionics blast forth in relentless succession.
Rating   5

Vardis - Standing In The Road
(Big Beat '84, NS103)

Searching for answers, Vardis keep down a path toward Sweet or worse, Slade (Vardis toured with them) with this flouncy pop cover. B-side *Freezing History (In Memoriam - Richard III)* harkens back to a clinical boogie sound like late-period Quo with a hint of pop and a smatter of Stones. Enjoyable chord changes and a timid but insistent groove. A true between-the-albums single, with neither track showing up on the album one year previous nor the album one year hence. Note: 12" version (NST103) adds *Who Loves Ya Baby*.
Rating   6

Various Artists - All Hell Let Loose (Compilation H.M.)
(Base/Neat '83, 102A/B)

This looks a lot older and mysterious than it is, but that doesn't stop the fact that these nuggets of NWOBHM wisdom are almost all rarities of various intensity. And Neat knew how to pick 'em, even bottom feeders like Steel, Crucifixion, Axis, Sabre, Warrior and Alien sounding no worse than Jaguar or Hellanbach or Raven or Venom, all bands included on this lather-wafting, almost boot-looking comp, assembled by Neat in conjunction with an Italian concern. Best rarities: Jaguar's *Dirty Tricks* and Hellanbach's *All The Way*, but like I say, most these acts are worth a frothy draft foisted above the pit. Note: this gathers up and vinylizes 12/16ths of a Neat cassette-only sampler.
Rating   8

Various Artists - Brute Force
(MCA '80, MCF3074)

Seminal NWOBHM compilation here, **Brute Force** trumpeting the fine taste of major label MCA in getting quick to the new metal bandwagon with the likes of Fist, Diamond Head, Quartz and White Spirit. Digging deeper into the obscure, there's the scrappy Prowler and May West, plus Colin Towns (keys) and Mick Underwood (drums) doing curious and divergent Gillan impressions. Closing out, you've got eccentrics Sledgehammer, plus rarities from Cryer and the excellent Xero. One of the top four early comps on a purely musical level, along with **New Electric Warriors** and the two **Metal For Muthas**.
Rating   8

Various Artists - The Friday Rock Show
(BBC '81, REH426)

Here's an under-rated, under-discussed compilation with respect to the history

of the NWOBHM, **The Friday Rock Show** gathering up some BBC studio performances, all of which are at least moderately obscure. Most famously you've got Spider, plus Diamond Head doing their mournful classic *Don't You Ever Leave Me* and Demon, their rousing party-'til-you-sacrifice anthem *One Hell Of A Night*. But Witchfynde chimes in with rarity *Belfast*, and then from there, things get weirder for a rare Sweet Savage recording, plus something from Last Flight, Black Axe and closing the record, Xero, with their catchy *Cuttin' Loose*. See also **Metal Explosion**.
Rating   8

Various Artists - Heavy Metal Heroes
(Heavy Metal '81, HMRLP1)
As the excellent liner notes to the '97 CD reissue (twinned with **Heavy Metal Heroes Volume II**) explain, this was the first release from Heavy Metal Records, making it, along with the **Metal For Muthas** albums and **New Electric Warriors**, one of the seminal sources (or more accurately, dirty well-waters) for the NWOBHM. At least six of these bands went on to make full-length albums, most collectible tracks of the lot being shaky pre-skill offerings from Grim Reaper, Jaguar and Witchfinder General (*Rabies*: yeah!). Most of the rest is well below any recorded standard of the day. But you get the idea... Buffalo, Expozer, Dragster, Twisted Ace, Soldier... I hope your lives improved.
Rating   6

Various Artists - Heavy Metal Heroes Volume II
(Heavy Metal '82, HMRLP7)
A considerable improvement, as metal acumen absolutely explodes since the first brave various artists spread offered by Heavy Metal's Paul Birch one year earlier. Still, shame on Jess Cox for *Devil's Triangle*. Best of the lot are saved for last, once more Witchfinder General powder-burning the competition with *Free Country*, while No Faith's thrashy cover of Fleetwood Mac's *Oh Well*, Persian Risk's poppy *Calling For You* and No Quarter's thoroughly groovy *Power And The Key* point to better days for metal. Ah, the days when we would pour over ever square inch of **Sounds** and **Melody Maker**, thrilled just to see a Budgie logo in some ad for a pub gig nine provinces and an ocean away. Note: As alluded to above, both **Heavy Metal Heroes** samplers were combined by British Steel in '97 on one CD.
Rating   7

Various Artists – Metal Explosion: From The Friday Rock Show
(BBC Records '80, REH397)
Not a holy grail of NWOBHM comps but one of the more valuable ones by substance, **Metal Explosion** gathers the best bands of the genre recording live for DJ Tommy Vance (deceased too young March 6, '05)—interestingly those bands tended to be the ones that got some fame but not too much. Kicking it off are Samson, with Bruce

rocking hard, proving himself worthy of the oncoming Maiden gig, bashing their way through *Take It Like A Man*. The Praying Mantis and Trespass tracks are disappointing, but unknowns Taurus turn in a happy, humpy Dark Star-ish galloper. Side two, you've got More grinding their way through the Sabbatherian *Soldier*, crap tracks from Money and Gillan (*If You Believe Me*, his snoozy slow blues), with Angel Witch's nasty, black metal-proud *Extermination Day* crumpling the whole thing up and hurling it across the room. Rating 7

Various Artists - Metal For Muthas
(EMI '80, EMC3318)

Pretty bad various album overall, but historically valid due to the inclusion of ground zero Iron Maiden renditions of *Sanctuary* and *Wrathchild* (un-featuring soon-gone axeman Tony Parsons) and prehistoric Angel Witch behemoth *Baphomet*, a bleak, careening mud-stomp through smoke-choked Hell, one of the band's roughest rides and a gem of inexorable doom when there was practically none to be had. Aside from these fossils and Ethel The Frog's nifty *Fight Back*, little else stands out, and indeed, some of it's got nothing to do with metal, betraying the fact that this release was so early, it actually pre-dates the concept of the coming British metal resurgence. Still, it is considered the bedrock album of said steely flood, not as bountiful as **New Electric Warriors** and not as exciting and fresh as **Metal For Muthas Volume II**, but nevertheless, a meekly offered calling card that mattered. Rating 7

Various Artists - Metal For Muthas Volume II
(EMI '80, EMC3337)

Big improvement over the disjointed and pre-understanding **Metal For Muthas**. Unfortunately none of these bands went anywhere, making this an unsuccessful attempt at garnering exposure for the wee acts enclosed. Coolest of the lot is Trespass, who offer forth the blistering *One Of These Days* and *Stormchild*. This band exemplifies the mystery and magic of early British gutter metal in the great tradition of Angel Witch, Savage and early Grim Reaper. Sadly missed. Other gems include Red Alert's punky *Open Heart* and Dark Star's melodic and gothic classic *Lady Of Mars*. Ergo, **Metal For Muthas Volume II** embodied the excitement of the NWOBHM in its formative years and stands as one compilation worth owning due to the obscurity and depth of the tunes enclosed. Both **Metal For Muthas** samplers were digitally remastered and reissued by Rod Smallwood's Sanctuary Records in 2000, neither adding any bonus tracks (uh, the **Mutha's Pride** EP might have worked, no?), nor much in the way of historical illumination other than short and shoddy original essay from scenester

Neal Kay on the first one, and a basically uncredited conversational and sketchy rundown for the second one. Damn, a bloody far cry from the magnificent—nay, unrivaled—Marillion reissues from the same label conglomeration.
Rating 8

Various Artists - Metallic Storm
(Ebony '82, EBON6)
Ebony was a wrenchingly rowdy metal label, and anything from house producer Darryl Johnston promises to, at minimum, melt the flesh from one's face. So **Metallic Storm** has got some stirring NWOBHM material sporting that trademark, messed-up Ebony crusty-tone sound courtesy of a surprising slew of no names. Contains an early take on Mercyful Fate's *Black Funeral* and a whole pile of bitchin' band names like Tarot Sutra, Wikkyd Vikker and Pentapus. God bless. Basically the second of a bunch, Ebony starting with nothing but these samplers from '82 to '83, and a bunch of 45s before exploding with all those great post-NWOBHM records in '84 and '85.
Rating 6

Various Artists - Muthas Pride
(EMI '80, 12EMI5074)
A curious extra bit of crumpet from the pioneering **Metal For Muthas** franchise (pretty commendable of a big ol' major like EMI, ain't it?), the **Muthas Pride** EP (much rarer than the two full-lengths and in fact, I've never see one!) comprises four tracks.

First up there's Wildfire with Wild Dogs, a strangely unsatisfying speedy rocker with pervasive synth line. Next is Quartz rarity *Back In The Band*, a grinding party rocker that shows off all of this band's many under-rated talents, from guitar sound to vocals to groovy drumming to effortlessly perfect songwriting. Geez. O'er to side 2 (two tracks each side), it's the UK's biggest Purple pompsters White Spirit with a taut and urgent track called *Red Skies*, the EP closing with Baby Jane's *Baby Jane*, a funky hard rocker that nonetheless contributes to this thing being a solid four out of four on the metal scale and the most consistent of the **Muthas** trifecta.
Rating 8

Various Artists - New Electric Warriors
(Logo '80, MOGO4011)
New Electric Warriors features a bevy of to-the-quick barroom metal highballs by an array of no-name entertainment combos from the first days of the illustrious NWOBHM, including easily five or six attention-grabbing scorchers. Totally worth owning for historical reasons, best of the pack include Turbo's *Running*, Tarot's *Feel The Power*, Jedediah Strut's *Working Nights* and absolute showstopper *Bedtime* by Race Against Time, the jewel of the record. The only bands of any commercial consequence were Vardis and Silverwing. CD reissue includes excellent historical essay plus thumbnail shots of ten other weird oldies reissues from the Metal Collectors series.
Rating 8

Various Artists - 100% Pure Metal Sampler
(Roadrunner '84, HEAVY002)

Roadrunner was the least discriminating of the small labels during the mid-'80s signing frenzy, and this low-priced compilation painfully highlights the label's ineptness. Although the Euro-tech Mad Max, the legendary Mercyful Fate, semi-moshers Jaguar (actually a Neat signing), and cement-heads Blackout somehow stumbled their way into the Roadrunner fold, the rest of this record displays some of the trop that would be forever doomed to obscurity, hogswallow such as Battleaxe, Dark Heart, Spartan Warrior and Samain making me chortle heartily at what metal used to be. Note: if you haven't gathered already, not all of this was strictly NWOBHM, given inclusing of bands from the continent.
Rating 4

Various Artists - One Take No Dubs: Live In The Studio
(Neat '82, NEAT25)

One of those weird releases, Neat assembling a four track EP right in the thick of the NWOBHM. All these jokers were minor sensations so here's the roll call, line 'em up! Alien - *Could Have Done Better*, Black Rose - *Knocked Out* (this one absolutely swings: potential untapped), Hellanbach - *All Systems Go*, and Avenger - *Hot 'n' Heavy Express*, this last track featuring one Brian Ross of Satan fame, in one of his super brief exo-band appearances.
Rating 5

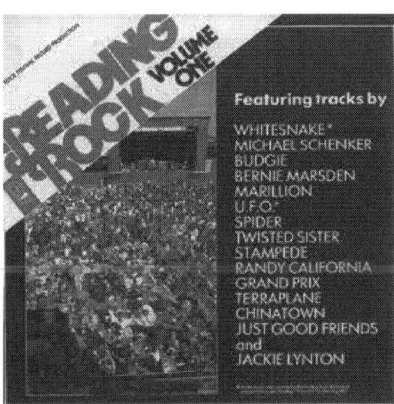

Various Artists - Reading Rock
(Mean '82, MNLP82)

Here's a momentous two LP memento of '82's Reading Rock festival in England. It ain't the greatest lineup they've had, and the recording is all midrangey and blocky. You wanna hear Marillion rawer than ever? Listen to *Three Boats Down From The Candy*. You want NWOBHM? Then there's Terraplane, Stampede and most surprisingly Chinatown, plus, to a lesser extent, Grand Prix and Spider. A bad Schenker performance is here as well, plus Budgie doing the butt-ugly *Superstar* and EP-only rarity *Panzer Division Destroyed*. Elsewhere, there's a surprisingly blustery *Hot And Ready* from UFO plus Twisted Sister and Whitesnake, both with rousing good choices. Quite the survey of Britain's has-been's, is's, might have been's and I doubt it's, all playing to the biggest crowd of their lives.
Rating 6

Various Artists - Roksnax
(Guardian '80, GRC80)

It don't get much earlier than this for metal samplers, kids, Guardian Records gathering up three bands, Saracen, Samurai and Hollow Ground for a rip roarin' NWOBHM bashfest, each band recorded like tin, but giving it their all in quest of a legitimately different metal than we would have been used to a couple years earlier. All the bands sound the same (thank Eddie!), each displaying a brisk diversity from heavy commercial metal like old Leps to the new gothic (Victorian?) sound first evident in Maiden, to the biker grime of Saxon. Gotta love those vocals too.
Rating 7

Various Artists - Roxcalibur
(Guardian '82, GRC130)

One of the more collectible metal samplers (but not up there with **Kent Rocks** or **It's Unheard Of**), **Roxcalibur** gives us two tracks each from Battleaxe, Black Rose, Brands Hatch, Marauder, Satan (this is the big selling point: two non-LP, pre-LP Satan ditties), Skitzofrenik and Unter Den Linden. Oddly, all of it sounds like the same bass-and-treble-less weak tea metal, extremely young, bashful and mired in the mindset of street-level NWOBHM. Obviously, it's inspiring for that reason also. Looks rare, is rare, sounds precious, sounds quaint, but not as uniformly entertaining as **Roksnax**. Both reissued on CD in '98.

Rating 6

Various Artists - Scene Of The Crime
(Suspect '81, SUS3)

Early and wildly heavy, **Scene Of The Crime** would have been the most buzzed-over of samplers (in our world it was the **Brute Force**, **New Electric Warriors** and the two **Muthas**), had it not been so indie and had the text font used been more metal—really the cover art of the first **Metal For Muthas** was the heaviest thing about it, indicative of an awareness that there was a defined movement to be addressed. Still, look closely, and the concept for the photo is pretty violently metal, a sort of precursor to MSG's **Built To Destroy**. Once past the wrap, we had two each from Panza Division, Manitou, Savage, Tyrant and one from Sparta. Tyrant is the weak link, Manitou is a stirring stir of the ol' Angel Witch pot, and Savage the hometeam favourites, but it's Panza Division's *Blitz* that makes ya wanna shotgun a beer.

Rating 9

Various Artists – Steel Crazy
(Abstract '82, AABT200)

One wonders how these compilations come together, but what we have here is a small French label grabbing ten tracks from all over the world. OK, Anvil, The Rods, Twisted Sister and Krokus are from elsewhere, and the rest is all UK rock, NWOBHM and NWOBwhatever (Starfighters, Geordie) sharing *Bedroom Games* with Lips. Wot the 'ell ever. Best thing about this is the headbanger-meets-Dali cover art.

Rating 4

Venom - In League With Satan
(Neat '81, NEAT08)
Here's a couple of soon-to-be album tracks comprising Venom's first single, Lant, Dunn and Bray joining forces to counter the softening of metal taking place around them, combining their punk roots and love of Kiss with Mantas' slavery to K.K. Downing. The a-side just sort of rumbles and marches and threatens but the b-side, *Live Like An Angel (Die Like A Devil)*, lets loose the scourge that will fill Neat's coffers for the next four years.
Rating 6

Venom - Welcome To Hell
(Neat '81, 1002)
The putrid initial burnt offering from the accounting firm of Lant, Dunn and Bray reeled 'em in by openly knock, knock, knockin' on Beelzebub's forked gate. Once inside, Venom invents a new phenomenon: the garage coven. Sloppy drumming, anti-Christ vocal mutterings, and horrid mixes to conceal said shortcomings are the order of the slobbery Sabbath. No denying that Venom, talentless as a wet bag of hammers that they were, had a prime part in the invention of both black metal and thrash, although thrash more in the sense of mental obliteration rather than speed. To messed-up limey earthdogs, Venom was the ultimate flag of anarchy and hate, the legendary live shows being the ultimate amorphous mass of confused rebellion on any given Friday night (well maybe not that often: the expense of the Venom presentation made gigs rare and legendary). To the English, Venom was their own sinister Kiss abortion gone very wrong, the annihilation of sound. And swear to God, many a leather-clad mutant claimed to like their music. Indeed, **Welcome To Hell**'s got a certain fabulously stupid forward impetus to it, despite the sub-bootleg-quality recording, and Cronos quickly establishes himself as the most annoying voice in rock. Not the band's most listenable product of on-purpose filth, yet a record of historical metal relevance on par with the Sex Pistols' lone album as it pertains to punk (well, not quite).
Rating 6

Venom - Bloodlust
(Neat '82, NEAT13)
Like any pin-up artist from the pop '60s, Venom have taken it upon themselves to crank out non-LP singles, *Bloodlust* being a standard though spirited mindchurn for the boys in black. B-side *In Nomine Satanas*

sounds like the same song slowed down, Cronos spewing his admonishments in another room until yer sufficiently creeped. Some came with a poster. Also available as a very rare purple vinyl 7" (NEATP13).
Rating   7

Venom - Black Metal

(Neat '82, 1005)

An album many a masochist consider the most quintessential Venom swillage, **Black Metal** is muddier and more lyrically Satanic than the debut, also somehow unleashing Mantas' axe genius, which rears its head infrequently and briefly throughout this awful but hilarious sonic hole. A few individual "compositions" climb from the muck, most notably stumble-frash anti-anthem *Leave Me In Hell, Don't Burn The Witch*, with its driving riffery, and one of Venom's most scorching and twisted marks on mankind, *Countess Bathory*, an enduring and anthemic classic of Baphomet vomit, its riff tune-void and tuneful at once. When you've given up on life, there's Venom and Venom alone, which is perhaps the only reason for this agonizing carcass of noise to exist, for it was widely believed in metal circles that Venom was your only friend once you'd downed that twentieth and damnation-deciding brew.
Rating   8

Venom - Die Hard

(Neat '83, NEAT27)

Both tracks, again, are non-LP, *Die Hard* pounding along real carnal-like despite the disadvantage of the badly punky backbeat. B-side *Acid Queen* begins like fast Motörhead before settling down to a brisk walk. Shudderingly and judderingly horrid recording, even by Venom's craptatious standards. First pressings included a poster. Also available in 7" picture disc format, 1000 of them produced for export to the US, and 12" version (NEAT2712), which adds *Bursting Out*. The UK edition of which we speak was also issued in France on Bernett.
Rating   7

Venom - Warhead

(NEAT '83, NEAT38)

The b-side to this almost psychedelic and truly elliptical track is *Lady Lust*, a standard "heads down, see you at the pub" OTTer. Neither track is from the LP six months before or six month after its February '84 release. Also available in scarce 7" coloured vinyl format (NEATP38), both blue and mauve, and 12" version (NEAT3812), which uses an extended version of *Warhead*, and adds *Seven Gates Of Hell*. There is also a blue vinyl 12" issue (NEATP3812). There are three different covers available with the 7" version, one each featuring the members of the band, something Motörhead also did.
Rating   8

Venom - Manitou
(Neat '84, NEAT43)
Those "Manitou" howls and solo troll vocals are pretty much the funniest thing in this very funny catalogue. B-side is *Woman*, a sub-par bit of violence with near indiscernible riffing. Released one month after launch of **Possessed**, but surprisingly, neither track is from the LP. Also available in picture disc format (NEATP43), devil-horned shaped picture disc format (officially NEATS43, although the item just says NEAT43), and 12" version (NEAT4312), which adds *Dead Of Night*. Also, white label test pressings exist. Next and last single is NEAT47 *Nightmare* from '85 (and hence no separate entry) backed with *Satanichist*. Also available in 7" shaped picture disc format (NEATS47) and 12" version (NEAT4712), which adds *F.O.A.D.* and is also available in picture disc format (NEATP4712). The first version of this was withdrawn because the illustration looked a bit too much like a demon raping a girl. Later issue of the 12" includes a live version of *Warhead*.
Rating 7

Venom - At War With Satan
(Neat '84, 1015)
Inna Godda Da Vidda for Satanists! At last the epic battle between good and evil is re-fought. The noise and stench is overpowering and guess what? Nobody wins. After the title track subterfuging the entire first side at a merciless 19:52, who could absorb any more mercury poisoning? Well, Venom oblige like rabid pharmacists, with six additional slabs of garbage dump filth, most horrific and pervertedly pleasurable of course being decipherable mid-pacers *Cry Wolf* and *Stand Up And Be Counted*. Actually, **At War With Satan** is one of the better Venom albums, if looking deep within the sewers of rock is your idea of party-time. The recording is almost tolerable in a filmy, hungover manner of speaking, and the choice of anti-songcraft, including the consistently sick and wonderful *At War With Satan*, is fairly high percentage. A loveable mess of sludge, this, Venom's third abortion, signs off with a neck-snapping slugfest aptly titled *AAAARGHHHH* which again presents our favourite lepers enjoying the last wheezing cackles as they fumble through your wallets.
Rating 7

Verity - Interrupted Journey
(PRT '84, LBP100)
Interrupted Journey is a warm, unassuming, hard-edged but unheavy rock 'n' roller which variously evokes images of Foghat, Foreigner, Russ Ballard, Derringer, even Mama's Boys at times. Ex-Argent dude John Verity and his wily band of veterans have come up with a soothing vibration that combines commercial American hard rock with wizened British defeat. It's the kind of stuff that sounds a bit too naive and retro to actually sell to the masses, but can still grab attention at a lower level, with its charming harmonies, hooky choruses, and punchy playing. The most convincing tunes are the heavy ones such as *Rescue Me, Are You Ready For This*, and *Chippin' Away At The Stone*, but it pretty well all works. Charming, rootsy and positioned rarely between survey of the '70s and the bluesy end of the hair metal explosion to come.
Rating 7

Vermilion - Angry Young Women
(Illegal '78, ILM0010)
OK, it's a real stretch calling this NWOBHM, Vermilion being more of a trashy hard X-Ray Spex-like punk act led by a biker-ish babe calling herself Vermilion. But punks didn't have

motorcycles, and this isn't far off of baby-steps Girlschool, and then there's that true metal warrior cover art, all hailing from early '78. Tracklisting is *Angry Young Women* and *Nymphomania* on the a-side (picture Lemmy leading the Buzzcocks), with a slower almost metal-riffed thing called *Wild Boys (Ride Their Bikes)* on the b. Produced by Dick Envy, bike built by Goat. A second single in '79 called *The Letter* (backed with *I Like Motorcycles*) under the guise of Vermilion And The Aces.
Rating   3

VHF - Heart Of Stone
(Lion '80, PAW1)
Quite the oddity, this one's got a thick '70s sound strapped to a motor of a NWOBHM riff; fine, until that high guest voice that sounds's like one of the guy's kids. Anyway, the main lead vocal is pretty good. B-side *Cheatin' Stealin'* is a slow grinder, quite amateurish but again, saved by the full-range recording. All in all, VHF sound suspiciously out of the loop, like they had come to this new metal stuff through the back door of pub rock or something. Non-picture sleeve.
Rating   4

Virgin Star - When The Reds
(Official '84, OFFICIAL1)
Like a raucous cross between Wrathchild and Bernie Torme, *When The Reds* and similar b-side *Shake The Towers* represent two tracks (among many demos) for a band that had more of a punk edge to them than most NWOBHMers, although there are more than enough hard rock/metal moves on the b-side to warrant entry here.
Rating   6

Voltz - Knight's Fall
(Airship '82, VLZ23420)
Killer NWOBHM artwork to this ultimate rarity of the scene, even if Voltz vault into our purloined view due to its mystical bent visually and lyrically versus the creepy, proggy, thoroughly engaging '70s hippie hard rock enclosed. Sure it's hapless and scrappy of production value, but that's this record's considerable charm, on top of the continual mellow-to-heavy dynamics, the oddball drumming, the chukka-chukka riffing and the stoner rock vocals. I mean, remember Dust, Captain Beyond, Bang, Sir Lord Baltimore, Pentagram? Well, put this in that smokehouse and smoke it, although yes, given that it's an indie on Airship out of Hampshire, UK, you'd have to chuck it into the pile of records any metalhead can appreciate. Thing is, anything that sounds like Rush crossed with **Raw Power**, count me in and beery-eyed.
Rating   8

Warfare - Noise, Filth & Fury
(Neat '84, NEAT41)

Warfare were always seen as the baby version of Venom, or perhaps the missing link between Venom and Tank, each of the trinity being leather-clad power trios of various dirt levels. The band's only independently issued single pairs the title album track, a catchy, grinding mid-pacer near as charming as *Countess Bathory*, with two non-LPers, *The New Age Of Total Warfare* (pure, stupid, very old school speed – no better than UK Subs) and *Burn The Kings Road*, kind of a crappy, punky, vaguely boogieing, mercifully short piece of piffle. The only other single that fits our timeframe parameters was the *This Machine Kills/Burn The King's Road* single (Neat '84) included as a freebie with some copies of the band's classic full-length debut **Pure Filth**. A final single in '87 was never released, although white label promo issues of it were manufactured. This featured *Addicted To Drugs* and a live version of *Hungry Dogs*.
Rating   7

Warfare - Pure Filth
(Banzai '84, 1021)

Venom contributes (but only on the UK version) and Tank's Algy Ward produces, but call it closer to Venom, these punk metal crossover disasters rumbling like a lower-end, alcoholic Cronos and crew (how snake-faced low can you get?), while Algy infects the sound with the loose bolts work non-ethic for which Tank was infamous. Sloppy, tepid, tuneless garage evilmetal with soccer match shout-and-bray, **Pure Filth** got press for a cover of Frankie Goes To Hollywood's *Two Tribes*, if you can believe it (Canadian pressing only, on additional 12"). Proud to have never heard the original but this sounds sorta like *Countess Bathory*. Overall, Warfare's almost seminally grungoid mayhem can handily amuse if you're easily amused, even as the band's tiring sound becomes paltry and unshocking with age, growing sonic desensitization to extremes. OK, here's this Canadian/UK thing in summary: The Canuck issue (on Banzai) contained 13 tracks over the LP and an included 12". The UK (Neat) issue contained 12 tracks (some swaps) over the LP and an included 45, the UK-only track being *Rose Petals Fall From Her Face*, which is the Venom collaboration, dropped from the Canadian, even though Venom's names were left on the printed credits. So... Canadians lose *Rose Petals*, but gain *Two Tribes* and *Hell Blown To Bits*, got it?
Rating   7

Warrior – Let Battle Commence
(Rainbow '80, RSL132)

Titled and packaged like prescient NWOBHM in our year one of 1980 (1979 being somewhat of a set-up anno), **Let Battle Commence** is in fact illustrative of how we got where we were going, combining a bit of acoustic pop circa mellow Rush or Wishbone Ash, a smattering of Groundhogs blues, but mostly cogent biker rock and whatever you wanna call what Samson was up to on the first two tooth-rattlers. Voltz and Saracen also come to mind, as do additional oldies acts like Stray and Rory Gallagher. Still,

taken as a multi-sense experience, drawing in the year of release and the music milieu in which it parachuted in, and what you've got is an important NWOBHM piece, that rare early full-length album that is also a woeful indie.
Rating   7

Warrior - Dead When It Comes To Love
(Neat '82, NEATLIVE20)
There were three Warriors participating in the NWOBHM, one from Chesterfield with an LP called **Let Battle Commence**, one from Essex with a 10" EP called **Don't Let It Show**, and this act from Newcastle with a track on Neat's **Lead Weight** compilation, an EP called **For Europe Only** and two singles. This one follows the '81 comp. track and is standard thrash-about NWOBHM somewhere between Fist, Jaguar, Tank, and due to the sonorous and confident vocals of Eddy Smith, Vardis. The a-side (different from the version on the 12") and first b *Stab In The Back* are quick, borderline punky, but squarely square-ish metal. *Kansas City* injects a little camp melody into the mix and slows it down, demonstrating that these blokes could write a hook when required. Still, quite amateurish, not helped by the fact that it was recorded live in the studio. Sleeve is just a plain cheapo white paper cutout with the credits and stuff stamped on it. Weird.
Rating   6

Warrior - For Europe Only
(Neon/Bullet '83, W001)
Five track 12" EP so obviously part of all of this and yet one is, alas, disappointed due to the heft-undermining scrappy playing and twee production to the thing. Think early Battleaxe crossed with Warfare and Dumpy's (and down the dustpipe we go toward Dark Heart and Tysondog and mainland acts on Mausoleum. Tracks are *Prisoner*, *Suicide*, *Kansas City*, *Warrior* and *Flying High*. Biker rock on them little Shriner tricycles.
Rating   6

Warrior - Breakout
(Warrior '84, W002)
Breakout (again with the Newcastle Warrior) rocks hard, smoky and chop-blocked, while on the b, *Take Your Chance* offers more of the same, if even more boisterous and drum-boomed. *Dragon Slayer* is a mess (the boozy recording not working here), the song being typical enough gallop metal. Recorded live in Neat's Impulse, this EP was withdrawn, partly due to the band's unhappiness with the production, the vocals in particular suffering the murks. A planned follow-up full-length LP never materialized. All told however, it ain't that bad, unless one takes into account its late vintage. I mean, in 1980, this would have been a golden nugget of sorts.
Rating   7

Waysted - Vices
(Chrysalis '83, CHR1438)
UFO's Pete Way puts his heart of ale on the line, fronting a crackling, dangerous band stuffed with sizzle, sleaze, and a brilliant grasp of the power shuffle. This strident, rumbling debut is chock-crammed with down 'n' dirty hard rock/

metal extraordinaire, plowed like a train with integrity and loose, apocalyptic professionalism. Way drags co-ex-UFOer Paul Raymond on this booze 'n' blooze, cokehead cruise along with the esteemed, bed-headed, Jack Daniels-schooled "Fin" on mic duties, one frontman way out on the edge of Desperado Town in terms of honest, biting, ragged hard rock hoariness. **Vices** somehow manages a vibe not unlike Aerosmith's **Draw The Line**, swelling with slurring, swirling fatman production, ideal for this a barroom brawl, pool cues a' swingin'. So 'ere we go... Pete, in one fell swoop manages to focus more bellyfire and spark onto his debut than UFO was ever capable of in 20 years of fine records, just not ones like this. Don't get me wrong, UFO is legendary hall of fame material, but **Vices** actually possesses more of a certain rock 'n' roll urgency than any single UFO disc cared to court, stumbling, shagging, shaking the apple tree while other bands were trying to clean up. Would have been pure top-to-bottom bliss if not for an unnecessary cover of Jefferson Airplane Starship Enterprise whatever's *Somebody To Love*, which is a useless song, no matter how renovated and enervated.
Rating   10

Waysted - Waysted
(Music For Nations '84)
Another rock-saving world-beater from Pete and the boys, Waysted's self-titled five track EP rocks with the same fighting intensity as **Vices**, while shifting to a tighter, stripped-down sound – Kiss chords this time as opposed to Aerosmith riffs. *Hurt So Good* steps to the fore, the band offering a warm melodic hard rocker, addressing a surprise area of songsmithing success for the band, Pete and posse penning a classic coursing with soul and ever-spiraling upward emotion, all within a song that would not be out of place on a Bryan Adams record. The remainder of **Waysted** consists of tidy, to-the-point '70s hard rockers; gritty street tales, that, in metropolitan total, comprise the perfect soundtrack for cleanin' out the carbons on the old car deck. And why an EP you ask? Waysted had been collared for a shortly ensuing Maiden tour, and wanted to have some product on the racks.
Rating   8

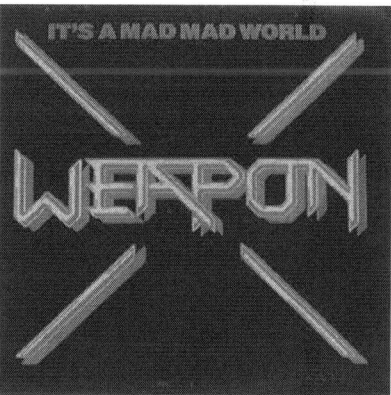

Weapon - It's A Mad Mad World
(Weapon '80)
This is an important NWOBHM piece, Weapon going barely one better than Holocaust with their dumb-stomped ligger anthem. The b-side is a less inspiring stab at early speed metal, still ruff 'n' tumble, good pint-faced vocals, but not as fun as the Tanked title track.
Rating   7

Weapon – It's A Mad Mad World
(Weapon '80, WEAPONE)
Weapon had a track here that was instantly catchy, that plain, square-jawed chorus, vocal and lyrical hook winning over the punters but good, the song's almost self-deprecatingly simple sound contrasting nicely with the much heavier, very, very

fast b-side *Set The Stage Alight*, quite an astonishing rocker given the year of issue. Also available on 12", with the same catalogue number. Jeff Summers and Bruce Bisland would move on to the excellent Wildfire.
Rating 8

Wendy & Lemmy - Stand By Your Man
(Bronze '82, BRO151)
Much like the Motörhead/Girlschool collaboration, this curio finds Lemmy snarling and screeching it up with the Plasmatics' Wendy O. Williams (now sadly deceased via suicide) on Tammy Wynette's *Stand By Your Man*. It's a hilarious, chaotic and scratchy punk version of the thing, a high watermark of metal and punk collusion, something which rarely happened between the two scenes. The b-side contains two tracks, a catty co-howl through Motörhead's *No Class*, and Lemmy turning the Plasmatics' *Masterplan* into a standard bike-clank 'headster. And a fun time was had by all, I'm sure.
Rating 6

White Heat – Soldier Of Fortune
(RSR '84, RSR007)
A-side *Soldier Of Fortune* sounds very much 1984, like similar serious fare from overseas all over Metal Blade or Shrapnel at the time. The riff is a little like Thin Lizzy's *Are You Ready*, but the tone is all metaller than thou. B-side is the comparatively lightweight *Lovemaker*. You can also tell how production values have improved over the years, even for poor blokes like this. Note: this band is led by JJ Cox, post-JJ's Powerhouse.
Rating 7

White Spirit - Back To The Grind
(Neat '80, NEAT05)
White Spirit were likely the most accomplished band to ever record at Neat's Impulse Studios, even if the band's first output, *Back To The Grind* is a little dull and uncommitted, sounding like heavy US AOR from the same era, punctuated by the band's requisite synth work. B-side *Cheetah* however, is one of the band's heaviest and fastest tracks (and er, it sounds like a cheetah), highly indebted to Ritchie Blackmore and Jon Lord, pointing, like all the band's material, to major potential beyond this pubby genre. Note: neither track is on the band's lone LP.
Rating 7

White Spirit - White Spirit
(MCA '80, MCF3079)
White Spirit was a commercially viable NWOBHM hopeful with a single admirable retro-keyboard metal album highly reminiscent of, in vibe and tonal alloy, Deep Purple's **Machine Head**, notable in

the guitar/keyboard interplay, and in the tightness and economy of songcraft, if not the quality of the songwriting. It's one of those serious long-lost British gems that in theory commands respect but in practice doesn't hit my table too often, I think due to the naivety of the songs and the ever so slight sub-par feel of the arrangements, although to be fair, this is what gives the band their nice antique-y feel more than 30 years on. Even though one can hear hints of *Highway Star, Never Before, Smoke On The Water, Smooth Dancer*, not to mention early Heep and Lizzy (through smatterings of subdued dual guitar harmonies), the main feel is Magnum or perhaps Nightwing. Trivia note: resident future rock star Janick Gers make this somewhat collectible. And on that note, **White Spirit** received a '92 Japanese reissue, which added three bonus tracks *Suffragettes, Back To The Grind* and *Cheetah*, only the latter scooting along metal-wise, all three kinda pomp rock dreary. Update years later: I'm quite digging this thing now, finding Bruce Ruff's vocals passionate yet not overbearing, and Janick similarly tasteful and composed (see *No Reprieve* and *Don't Be Fooled*). Plus *High Upon High* has turned into my favourite creepy pomp metal anthem. And with all those "metal" keyboards, it's no wonder why Gillan saw a match between White Spirit and his robust vision, the man snatching up Janick for a spell before Maiden got to him.
Rating   8

White Spirit - Midnight Chaser
(MCA '81, 638)
This single features one of the standout tracks from the lone full-length (in fact the first track, but different version here), *Midnight Chaser* demonstrating the band's canny mix of Purple, Heep, AOR and pomp, while b-side *Suffragette* is an emotional reading of the women's suffragette movement of the early 1900's (but it was probably just an attempt to pull the birds, nudge nudge wink wink). But seriously, it's kind of a cool, dark, melodic underground rocker with an eerie keyboard line.
Rating   8

White Spirit - High Upon High
(MCA '81, 652)
High Upon High is really White Spirit's most famous and well-regarded track, and it isn't even that heavy. Its mystique lies in its ability to cause the creeps like Witchfynde or Quartz or Nightwing while lounging only one step from heavy Styx or Magnum. All in all, it's a proud pomp with an addictive keyboard pattern and gloomy verse melody. Vocalist Bruce Ruff is as usual, restrained and technically perfect. Fetching NWOBHM outside the box, and also on the second **Metal For Muthas** comp. B-side *No Reprieve* is also an album track, but more of an authoritative Purple piece, hot-clocking it through fiery leads, key-and-guitar harmonies, and change-ups that befit its placement on the proggiest side of the lone album.
Rating   8

Wikkyd Vikker – Black Of The Night
(Boogie '83, FUR0235)
Black Of The Night is an acceptably solid mid-paced number with just enough sorrow in the main riff to give it levity, although the melodic, cowbell-clanged chorus (pre-chorus) is a really nice touch. B-side to this non-picture sleever is the comparatively weak *Release*.
Rating   7

Wildfire - Run To Ground
(Steel City '80, AJS7R)
The original name of the band was Red Alert, but this band is not to be confused with the one that recorded *Open Heart* for **Metal For Muthas Volume II** or, with their new name, with the excellent two LP band featuring More's Paul Mario Day. B-side is sweet and sour speed rocker *Wild Dogs*, which featured on the **Muthas Pride** EP.
Rating   7

Wildfire - Brute Force And Ignorance
(Mausoleum '83, 8307)

Wildfire were an ambitious, nearly post-NWOBHM band led by golden-throat Paul Mario Day, ex of More, a band which took a flying leap into the realms of major heftic brilliance upon his departure with **Blood & Thunder**. Wildfire's premiere gesture contains the odd example of excellent, hooky, complex metal such as *Another Daymare* and *Violator*, yet for the most part consists of fairly naive-sounding, loose bolts rock, kinda rough-shod, disjointed and powerless. Still the flash points of brilliance are hard to ignore, making **Brute Force And Ignorance** frustrating in its inconsistency, with hopes of what could have been. So look for some wily arrangements, innovative riffs and Thin Lizzy-ish soloing but also a fair bit of bar band songcraft. Shows thoughtful strategy not without promise, but nonetheless a lot of rust to lose in the process.
Rating   6

Wildfire - Nothing Lasts Forever
(Mausoleum '84, GUTS8403)

A-side *Nothing Lasts Forever* is one of the poppier tracks from the band's vibrant, underrated second album **Summer Lightning** (first album is the aforementioned **Brute Force And Ignorance**, both on Mausoleum), and sort of stumbles on the record's loose playing and recording, a characteristic that helps the album's rockers come alive. B-side *Blood Money* is also from the album, and is a true metal widdly-riffed speed metal highball reminiscent of prime Tygers Of Pan Tang. Second and last single is '85's non-LP a-side *Jerusalem* backed with *Fight Fire With Fire*, which is from 1984's **Summer Lightning**, cat. # of the quite rare single being GUTS8405.
Rating   8

Wildfire - Summer Lightning
(Mausoleum '84, SKULL8338)

Wildfire's second and last album continues with the classy, intricate but spontaneous riff rock of the debut, albeit with stronger, better-planned songs. **Summer Lightning** floats upon an eminently British mix of rich and rewarding traditional heavy metal, as evidenced by *The Key*, *Gun Runner*, and *Screaming In The Night*, but not so successful second-guessed melodic hard rock in *Nothing Lasts Forever* and *Fight Fire With Fire*. One general problem with this band is that despite the imagination and inherent hookability of their car deck anthems, the playing is fast and loose, the sound rough and lacking in bottom end, all of which is really no surprise for Mausoleum output, which is why the more virulent forms of metal on the label haul ass and the AOR material sounds like Dokken demos. Still, **Summer Lightning** emerges out the other end, positives and negatives balanced, as one of those star quality-type albums that can be home-spun start to finish without boredom, due to its unanticipated twists and turns, due to the brains of this band and the memorable hooks track to track. A promising potentially commercial force in the making, Wildfire's mandate unfortunately ran out when the money was all gone.
Rating   8

Wild Horses - Criminal Tendencies
(EMI '79, INT599)

Wild Horses were somewhat of a casual band of disgruntled and debauched drinking mates, some (Jimmy Bain) wanting to write more, some (Brian Robertson) just looking for a good time.

In any event, their first single was as wobbly as their two-LP output. *Criminal Tendencies*, from the debut called **The First Album**, is a poppy UFO-ish number without the polish or the hook. B-side *The Rapist* hails from neither LP, and leans more toward bottom-barrel Thin Lizzy. Oddly, it's the production of one Trevor Bain, soon to vault to stardom with Yes, that is a big cause of the band's coming up short.
Rating   6

Wild Horses - Wild Horses
(EMI '80, EMC3326)
With Thin Lizzy careening in drug an' drunken disarray, resident lunatic pugilist Brian Robertson piles on with equally difficult excuse for a human being Jimmy Bain for a little jamming outside the limelight. Along for the haphazard ride are Neil Carter and Clive Edwards, and what occurs is a simple pub rock record, fairly unflashy, strained and naive in just about every way. Only one co-write with Phil here, *Flyaway*, a decent ballad amongst a lot of Bain/Robertson exercises in humility, surprising, because at the time, the Lizzy org. was pooling their tunes, and picking them out as needed for whatever project was at hand. Strange though, that one of the band's biggest problems was the lack of convincing guitar, not to mention a bad drum sound, both somewhat the fault of producer Trevor Rabin, who would soon vault to fame with Yes. Hard rocky to the point of pop, jazzy to the point of Bolin, Wild Horses were fortunately put down after a couple of dozy kicks. Zoom Club CD reissue adds as bonus tracks the band's long and pointless live rendition of *Rocky Mountain Way* and another live in Japan track called *Saturday Night*, a horrid funk metal disaster that sounds like bottom-barrel Derringer.
Rating   5

Wild Horses - Face Down
(EMI '80, 5047)
Face Down finds this confused bunch of semi-stars trying to emulate the new wave of The Cars, albeit with a slightly elevated chug. Quite offensive really. B-side *Dealer* combines a lacing of Thin Lizzy harmonies with the thinnest of boogie premises, once again frustratingly substance-less. Both tracks are from the first of the band's two albums, the single being released a month before the full-length. Note: also issued in Japan with different art.
Rating   5

Wild Horses - Flyaway
(EMI '80, 5078)
For a guitar star band, Wild Horses were surprisingly weak, pretty Beatles-esque ballad *Flyaway* doing nothing to bolster the band's tough image. And once again, it's the crappy drum sound selected or captured by Rabin that distracts from potential warmth. A Bain/Robertson/Gorham composition. B-side *Blackmail* is a typical stumbled and compact rocker for the band, sounding like something the Eagles would come up with when walking on the wild side (ooh). Horrid but approachable and harmless. Both are from the first LP. Note: most of these are white vinyl with some demo/promo issues on black worth about double the below price. Also available in 12" white vinyl format (12EMI5078).
Rating   4

Wild Horses - Stand Your Ground
(EMI '81, EMC3368)
Thin Lizzy spawned a stable of fine, intelligent guitarists, Brian Robertson being perhaps the definitive contributor. Here

Robbo collaborates with veteran Jimmy Bain (who handles lead vocal chores as well as his trademark bass), plus assorted other old pros (John Lockton replaces Neil Carter on second banana guitar) in the pursuit of craftsmanship and a work ethic which fortunately always seems to be engrained in collusions between members of the British rock aristocracy. **Stand Your Ground**, the band's second and last, delivers much of what one could hope for, offering tight, highly strung melodic hard rockers amidst other much less metallic yet equally soulful vignettes in a fragile, third-rate Thin Lizzy vein, revealing taste and finesse without busy-ness or pretension or ahem, much song skill. Robertson and Lockton hold no reservations about smoothly dishing forth harmony axework, and lyrically, the proceedings are kept simple and human, hopeful and heartfelt. Although a good portion of this record rocks at a fair clip, absolutely nothing gets full-bodied or muscular, the band preferring nimble mobility, revealing links between the core hard rock sound and an appreciation of jazz, along with more conventional rock structures rather than leanings towards metal. Coolest cuts include riff rocker *The Axe*, smooth rider *Miami Justice* and the tricky *I'll Give You Love*. **Stand Your Ground** benefits from its project-like feel and its commitment to simple, emotional quality in preference to complication, offering forth a nice collection of Thin Lizzy-style rock, appropriately so, as Robertson was always one of the briskly beating hearts of that band's sound. Shortcomings: thin sound quality from Lizzy-turned-Cradle Of Filth producer Kit Woolven and occasional frailty in terms of vocal ability. Zoom Club CD reissue adds blue collar Lizzy-type *Louie Louie* thang *The Rapist* (b-side of the band's first single *Criminal Tendencies*), plus *The Kid*, a later b-side and one of the band's trickiest, heaviest riff rockers, this one, truly worthy of the Thin Lizzy tag (oh, to hear Lynott rip through this one).
Rating   7

Wild Horses - I'll Give You Love
(EMI '81, 5149)
Attempting to bulk up on the writing, Wild Horses find themselves chopped again by the production, this time at the bloody hands of Kit Woolven. Features new guitarist John Lockton who replaces Neil Carter. *I'll Give You Love* is the first track on the band's second album **Stand Your Ground** and is indeed a rocker, but unfortunately a dullish brown one. B-side is a 7:20 live version of Joe Walsh's uneventful heavy blues *Rocky Mountain Way*, also slept on by Triumph. Crap track, crap version. Some with free 7" (PSR45) featuring elegant straight-line metal rocker *The Kid*, one of the band's coolest tracks (worthy of Lizzy, really) and a camp, underachieving, Derringer/Bolin-like Robbo/Bain composition called *Saturday Night*, recorded live in Osaka, Japan.
Rating   5

Wild Horses - Everlasting Love
(EMI '81, 5199)
Features new drummer Dixie Lee from Lone Star. A-side is a cover of the Love Affair oldie. B-side *The Axe* is from the second album and is quite the shifty little rocker with a break that is almost reggae-ish. One of the more metallically pleasing tracks on the album, and one of the greasiest, given the record's general clunked deliveries.
Rating   6

Witchfinder General - Burning A Sinner
(Heavy Metal '81, HEAVY6)
Witchfinder General are widely considered the first doom band since Sabbath to get

it right. Or, if you figure Sabbath predates the concept of doom, then these unassuming roustabouts are the first doom band ever. In any event, slow, awkward Sabbath rocker *Burning A Sinner* is from the landmark debut (here in shaggier version), while b-side *Satan's Children* is deservedly non-LP due to its horrible demo quality, even if the composition itself is pure smoke-choked Sabbatherian metal madness somewhat along the lines of *Children Of The Grave*.
Rating   8

be. Adding to the venomous vibe, **Death Penalty** features one of the trademark naked chicks 'n' violence album covers preferred by Heavy Metal Records' owner Paul Birch.
Rating   9

Witchfinder General – Soviet Invasion
(Heavy Metal '82, 12HM17)
Soviet Invasion is a typically dirgey early Witchfinder sledge, humourous in its trudge and drag and fatigue, and also in its witty use of acoustic guitar, as hapless victim to blunt doomy chording recorded with remarkable tone. *Rabies* is more of the same top flight raw doom in no hurry to impress with flash. Best bonus to this black and blue cloud of smoke and smog is that neither track will show up on either of the band's seminal two LPs. Bonus is a version of *R.I.P.* said to be live but in fact recorded in a studio with crowd sounds at the behest of label head Paul Birch.
Rating   9

Witchfinder General - Death Penalty
(Heavy Metal '82, HMRLP8)
The pioneering debut from ultra-doom merchants Witchfinder General (from where else but the outer fringes of Birmingham) serves up a loose and inebriated display of dark psychotic black metal wholly lifted but brilliantly so, from Black Sabbath's earliest warfaring anthems. Although **Death Penalty** is raucously recorded and bluntly lacking in chops, the sledges within display a blood-soaked melancholy so downright sincere and unpleasant that one detects these guys may be kidding or at least contriving. *Death Penalty* and *Witchfinder General* rival the best of dirges from the more professional **Friends Of Hell** opus, while the rest is more so a shaggy hot mess. With a hint of the mighty Diamond Head in the delivery, this band is plagued by creaks and groans like no American kult kollective could ever

Witchfinder General - Friends Of Hell
(Heavy Metal '83, HMRLP13)
Same pioneering doom premise for this mysterious band's second and last (before reunion), but most Witch-watchers are in agreement that compared to the debut, **Friends Of Hell** demonstrates increased focus, precision of playing, punch to the production, all told, the band sounding a little boozy but not completely drunk off their asses like last loveable time. Bobbing bass, guttural guitar, soupy drums and

above the fray, the young Oz vocals of Zeeb Parkes, whose subsequent problems with the law, no one likes to talk about. And man, sure, you can be all Satanic, but *Love On Smack*?! That's a new level, as Pantera is wont to say, and as extra dagger to the soul, this happy, humpy opener is the album's catchiest track, rumbling like a Grim Reaper freight train until we get to *Last Chance*, *Shadowed Images*, the title track and smoke-choked closer *Quietus Reprise* where, collectively, a more familiar Witchfinder General world is at stigmata hand. Indeed outside of the sin-draped opener, acoustic wake *I Lost You* and a curious paean to music called *Music* (check out them juddering closing chords), the balance of **Friends Of Hell** is as framed above: a ship-shape, ready-for-duty re-proposal of the debut's shocking premise, the shock being that Witchfinder General unwittingly had established a new genre of music, namely doom metal. To be sure, it's so specifically a cop of Sabbath, but widen one's scope, and Witchfinder General are the first past the originals, bitter first shoot past the root, within a vibrant genre now made up of dozens upon dozens of bands.
Rating   10

Witchfinder General - Music
(Heavy Metal '83, HEAVY21)
Music seems to be a calculated departure for the band into everyman concerns, set to a thunking disco metal beat darkened by the band's turgid dungeon-dank doom chords. It works by not working immediately after construction. *Last Chance* on the other hand is quintessential Witchfinder General, the band letting that sin-soaked riff take over and run all good tidings out of town. Both tracks are from the second and last album. Also available in limited edition silver vinyl (HMPD21), although two sources call this item a picture disc. Released one month after the LP. Collectible because the band was so gosh-darn groovy, and in retrospect, ahead of its timeless time.
Rating   8

Witchfynde - Give 'Em Hell
(Rondelet '79, ROUND1)
This is one of the first NWOBHM singles I ever owned, and like Savatage's debut and Priest's **Sad Wings Of Destiny**, I was kind of creeped-out by the thing, this one by the evil cover art and the lack of a band photo. And *Give 'Em Hell* was a great track, killer metal riff, that odd vocal, a somewhat anthemic chorus, a great early NWOBHM anthem all 'round, sort of like a poor cousin to Quartz. B-side *Gettin' Heavy* demonstrated the band's left field poptastic grooves, slinking along to that high twisty guitar riff; a drinkable track, but Witchfynde already had us guessing (bonus: Steve Bridges' take on falsetto). The band's premiere output, after having formed in Mansfield, England three years earlier. Both were from the seminal first LP, launched two months later. Note: first issue is under label name Round Records, before the change to Rondelet, which issued the single a second time after the first er, round, sold out.
Rating   8

Witchfynde - Give 'Em Hell
(Rondelet '80, ABOUT1)

This unsolved mystery of a debut marks the beginning of a confusing and confused chapter in the NWOBHM sweepstakes, not to mention the first serious incarnation of black metal ever. Even though **Give 'Em Hell**'s cover is about as black metal as is demonically possible, lyrically, the band is only occasionally sat in Satan's lap, and never as approvers of his counsel. Musically, **Give 'Em Hell** approaches the warm and melodic (see *Gettin' Heavy* and *Leaving Nadir*), amidst other more traditional riff-maps of Lower Purgatory. Steve Bridges' vocal shriek represents a perfect fit, but the production slithers and slurs on the cheap and midrangey, causing an undermining of the band's periodically lofty goals. All of side one is pretty well eclectic and nifty, whereas side two, comprising only three cuts, is 50/50 at best, Manowar-like percentages of the album as a whole being the sorry result. **Give 'Em Hell** is definitely heavier than the strange and casual follow-up, and is quite uniformly standard '70s style hard rock or heavy metal, demonstrating that the boys have their heads roughly turned full twist to straight ahead, eyes on the future, even if they formed as a band as early as '76. Overall, possibly because of its obscurity and backwater oddity, this album carries a dark and uncommunicative sheen that establishes the Witchfynde mystique, if only momentarily. Highlight: the smart, modern NWOBHM riffery of the title track, which of course is as close as Witchfynde ever got to a tantalizing Quartz/Angel Witch hybrid they might have been able to own.
Rating 8

Witchfynde - In The Stars
(Rondelet '80, ROUND4)

After all the hype, Witchfynde's second album **Stagefright** was a bit of a poochy question mark. But the advance single was sweet and malevolent, *In The Stars* checking yer superstition quotient to a dark pop drive. B-side *Wake Up Screaming* is a barnstormer though, screeching into view on a negating bit of drum production, straight-lining it toward a finish featuring killer leads, a pounded mass of chaos, and that final foreboding explosion. Brilliant, mates! Both tracks hail from the second LP, this single launched one month prior to the release of sweet and sour album, and both, along with the title track, mark the highpoint of an oddly casual affair.
Rating 9

Witchfynde - Stagefright
(Rondelet '80, ABOUT2)

The sophomore blakwax from Derbyshire's favourite musical black arts practitioners graphically scares the pantaloons off the punter, but is, alas, an understated screwball of a release, fart-knocking the band's wee fanbase five steps backward. Talk about a confusing curio. The packaging is that of dead-serious early days black metal, but wrapped around songs that are schizo, cheap and chummy, including shamelessly embarrassing number like *Doing The Right Thing* and *Would Not Be Seen Dead In Heaven*. Then, jarringly conversely, Witchfynde serve up two manic, gloriously overblown metal scorchers in *Stage Fright* and *Wake Up Screaming*, songs that heave and creak with huge blasts of black wind, easily the band's most blatantly obvious symphonies of genius, the latter containing sabotaged drum production, emotion-building leads and a close that is like a rusty lock on your heartbeat. In between we get solid, European-styled, almost Angel Witch-y hard rock in *Moon Magic*

and *In The Stars*, plus a bouncy, harmless but warm little number, *Big Deal*, which is about being the lowliest of bar bands. Strange, endearing, bumbling, but when all is said and done, **Stagefright** somehow becomes the best Witchfynde album of all, due to a vibe that is humble and true, due to music that makes no attempt to hide the personalities behind props. Ultimately it is an enigmatic English oddity, a mistake that works, **The Who By Numbers** for NWOBHMers.
Rating 8

Witchfynde - I'd Rather Go Wild
(Expulsion '83, OUT3)
Both tracks here are from the third LP **Cloak & Dagger**, the single having been launched four months before the full-length. *I'd Rather Go Wild* is an acceptable though unremarkable bit of dark arts party fare, new vocalist Luther Beltz sounding like King Diamond at inspired spots. B-side *Cry Wolf* is a trashy OTTer which is ultimately just annoying, the band betraying their lack of ideas or indeed philosophical directive.
Rating 6

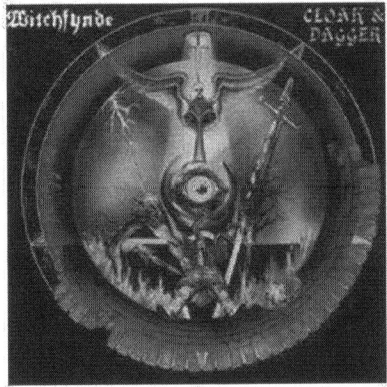

Witchfynde - Cloak & Dagger
(Expulsion '83, EXIT5)
This giant leap into the modern era finds the Witchfynde boys losing their quirks for a more uniform updated Halloweenie roast which comes off as less sincere but more metallic and rockin', although in terms of concept, the band was rumoured to have spent many hours in research of the black metal subject matter addressed, much to the detriment of their other musicianly responsibilities. Great cover art too, all witchy like a Ouija board that answers to the question: how many different Witchfyndes are there? Still, despite a fairly commercial raft of songs, the label offered zero financial support, dooming this hot mess of a covenly career in the process. **Cloak & Dagger** also saw release as a creepy picture disc. Highlight: the title track, which is sort of like Cathedral doing *Another One Bites The Dust*.
Rating 7

Witchfynde - Lords Of Sin
(Mausoleum '84, 8353)
Not that they could ever write consistently anyways, poor man's King Diamond, Luther Beltz and his conspirators come up with a sludgy, dark, British record of fairly standard hard rocking metal that hints at past exquisite blackness but usually just gets by with lazy, hanging chords and metal clichés. For the former, witness the Maiden-ish melody of quicky *Wall Of Death* and the slow but insistent *Conspiracy*. For annoying complacence, witness the tried and untrue riffery of *Scarlet Lady* and *Hall Of Mirrors*, the latter of which could be a heavy Angel City song without the black wrapping paper. Per usual, Witchfynde has no idea what kind of band they want to be, coming off here as both musical and lyrical moderates. All in all, call this one theoretically decent upon cerebral inspection but rarely played from the heart.

Note: The British Steel Metal Collectors series has issued a CD comp called **The Best Of Witchfynde**. Note II: the first 10,000 copies of **Lords Of Sin** came with a 12" live EP.
Rating   6

Witchfynde - Conspiracy
(Mausoleum '84, GUTS8404)
Both tracks are from the last and under-rated Witchfynde album **Lords Of Sin**. The a-side (different version) is an imposing, convincing Accept-styled mid-paced rocker with nice uplift to resolution come chorus time. B-side *Scarlet Lady* is a typical NWOBHM evil woman lyric set to a speed rock riff that is uncomfortably close to happy and vaguely boogie-steeped to boot—April Wine on steroids. Launched four months after the release of the album.
Rating   7

Wolf – See Them Running
(Gremlin '81, GREM72A)
This is a different Wolf from the post-Black Axe/Chrysalis deal one, these guys releasing the one single and that's it. Very cool a-side, *See Them Running* power-surging to a riff and rhythm combination that is hard to reconcile, the end result being a highly memorable wall-of-sound rocker. B-side *Creatures Of The Night* is pretty interesting, a stop/start power ballad type thing (well OK, it's got these fairly pointless mellow bits), co-produced by Colin Richardson, kinda proggy, very NWOBHM and pretty impressive on an emotional level, culminating in a nice wah-wah solo. No picture sleeve.
Rating   8

Wolf - Head Contact
(Chrysalis '82, CHS2592)
Wolf began life as Black Axe and ultimately became one of the prime examples of label mismanagement. First off, they shouldn't have been signed in the first place 'cos they sucked, and second, the label had them change their name, and then blew the timing on what became **Edge Of The World**, the band's rickety, unsure debut, which surfaced only after the band was dropped. This single however, was produced by Tom Allom, recorded two years previous to the album, with both tracks winding up on that doomed record. The a-side is fine for 1981, average for '82, but abysmally late fer dinner for 1984. Ultimately it is a mid-paced meat and potatoes rocker somewhere between Nutz-to-Rage with a bit of Wildfire polish, given that that band had little to spare. B-side *A Soul For The Devil* is a ponderous, dark, witchy ballad, somewhat effective in a Witchfynde way, but again, at this late juncture, a little laughable. Clear vinyl version as well (same cat. #); also available as a 12" with extended version of *A Soul For The Devil*. Some of the 7 inchers came with sticker.
Rating   6

Wolf - Edge Of The World
(Mausoleum '84, 8323)
Disposable jetsam from a flotsam raft of average-to-bad bands that found sanctuary on the grimy Mausoleum label, Wolf go

after an admirable traditional metal sound but fail due to substandard songcraft and what seems to be a lack of old-fashioned practice. Nevertheless **Edge Of The World** stood out from a pack getting faster and thrashier at this shifting time in metal. But its lack of polish applied to old tricks caused it to age badly in the competitive times just around the corner fueled and fired by the likes of Metallica and the first quite heavy hair metal albums crafted on the left coast of America. Handicapping the band further is the fact that most of the band's dowdy compositions were two or three years old by the time the record was haphazardly assembled.

Rating 3

Wrathchild - Do You Want My Love
(Bullet '83, BOLT5)

Wrathchild were a laughably over the top glam anomaly stuck in a country that just didn't stand for that stuff. This first single, released nine months before the debut album, is backed with *Twist Of The Knife*, both showing up eventually on semi-compilation album **Trash Queens**, out in '85. *Do You Want My Love* has a bit too much of a Gary Glitter gallop for my tastes, and those NWOBHM tom toms cause creaks and groans in my joints. *Twist Of The Knife* on the other hand is a trashy shot glass punk rocker with anti-production reminiscent of Crue's gutbucket debut. Note: also available in picture disc format (PBOL5) and 12" version (BOLT5) which adds *Cock! Rock!! Shock!!!*.

Rating 4

Wrathchild - Stakk Attakk
(Heavy Metal '84, HMRLP18)

Wrathchild proposed a sort of absurdist dirty glam welled up from Hanoi Rocks through Motley but the outcome is clunky, marred by awkward songwriting, a disorienting number of styles and production values that are hard on the ears, applied to music that should go down smooth. But these girlie-guys got a lot of hype in Britain, even if they were the laughing stock of their NWOBHM contemporaries and other industry insiders. Unfortunately Wrathchild didn't have the ideas to back-up the buzz they briefly inspired. Still though, they're heavier than they look, just like the Crue they emulated from that band's first and second.

Rating 5

Wrathchild - Alrite With The Boys
(FM Revolver '84, UHF3)

These two track, are featured on the screechingly harsh but sickly sweet debut album. The a-side is track #1 of that album and is a primary-colored kiddie rocker with the worst snare drum sound I've ever heard. B-side *Sweet Surrender* is similarly based somewhere in the fog of '50s and '60s worship that distinguished glam as retro in substance. Note: one more single in *Nukklear Rokket*, backed with a live take on *Trash Queen* (VHF50) in 1989, the 12" version adding *Pretty Vacant*.

Rating 5

XYZ

Xero - Oh Baby
(Brickyard '83, XERO1)

This one came out in both 7" and 12" formats, with one of the b-sides *Hold On* showing up on early and eventful NWOBHM comp. **Brute Force**. The band has a strange r+b bent (especially with Moon Williams' soulful Otis Redding vocals), *Oh Baby* barely being metal, *Hold On* toughening up a bit. Second b-side *Lone Wolf* was a scrappy recording which featured Bruce Dickinson on vocals, and the sleeve made sure to say so. In fact, it was a recording of Bruce fronting a band called Shots and not Xero at all! In any event, the Maiden camp was none to pleased, strong-arming the band into destroying all existing copies. Second pressings deleted the track and is actually said to be in shorter supply than the original, thus commanding an extra third or so in the marketplace. The reissue of the 12" added Van Halen-esque instrumental *Killer Frog*, in place of the tainted *Lone Wolf*, while the new 7" added nothing. All told, the band's best work remains *Cutting Loose* on the second (and more consistent) **Metal For Muthas** compilation.
Rating   7

Young Blood - First Blood
(Landslide '84, LANDT-1)

As one would expect late in the NWOBHM game, Young Blood are looking to the success of Def Leppard as well as what's starting to happen in LA for their sound, and lo and behold, they do a pretty good job of it, sounding like an amalgamation of Tokyo Blade, Pretty Maids, late-fer-dinner Tygers, Highway Chile and Heavy Pettin'. Tracks on this 12 incher are *Hold On To Love*, *Your Money Or Your Life*, *Dangerous Games* and *Good Time Tonight*, each and every one of them solid examples of rough 'n' ready enuff party metal capable of keeping your spirits up while you contemplate the impending hard stop demise of the New Wave Of British Heavy Metal that is to be complete by the end of the goddamn year.
Rating   7

Appendix 1: Blood & Thunder: LPs Ranked 8, 9 Or 10

Angel Witch - Angel Witch
Budgie - Power Supply
Budgie - Deliver Us From Evil
Chateaux - Chained And Desperate
Chateaux - Fire Power
Def Leppard - On Through The Night
Def Leppard – High 'n' Dry
Demon - The Unexpected Guest
Diamond Head - Lightning To The Nations
Diamond Head - Borrowed Time
EF Band - Deep Cut
Fastway - Fastway
Fist - Back With A Vengeance
Gillan – Gillan
Gillan - Mr. Universe
Gillan - Future Shock
Gillan - Double Trouble
Gillan - Magic
Grim Reaper - See You In Hell
Heavy Pettin' – Lettin' Loose
Holocaust - The Nightcomers
Iron Maiden - Iron Maiden
Iron Maiden - Killers
Iron Maiden - The Number Of The Beast
Iron Maiden - Piece Of Mind
Iron Maiden - Powerslave
Jaguar - Power Games
Money – First Investment
More - Blood & Thunder
Motörhead - Motörhead
Motörhead - Overkill
Motörhead - Bomber
Motörhead - Ace Of Spades
Motörhead - Iron Fist
Motörhead - Another Perfect Day
Motörhead - I Got Mine
Original Sin – The Shadow
Quartz - Stand Up And Fight
Quartz - Against All Odds

Raven - Rock Until You Drop
Raven - Wiped Out
Raven - All For One
Raven - Live At The Inferno
Samson - Shock Tactics
Samson - Before The Storm
Samson - Don't Get Mad - Get Even
Savage - Loose 'n Lethal
Saxon - Wheels Of Steel
Saxon - Power & The Glory
Shiva - Firedance
Sledgehammer - Blood On Their Hands
Tank - Filth Hounds Of Hades
Tank - Power Of The Hunter
Tank - This Means War
Touched - Back Alley Vices
Tygers Of Pan Tang - Wild Cat
Tygers Of Pan Tang - Spellbound
Tygers Of Pan Tang - Crazy Nights
Tygers Of Pan Tang - The Cage
Tygers Of Pan Tang - Tygers Of Pan Tang
Various Artists - All Hell Let Loose (Compilation H.M.)
Various Artists – Brute Force
Various Artists – The Friday Rock Show
Various Artists - Metal For Muthas Volume II
Various Artists - Muthas Pride
Various Artists - New Electric Warriors
Various Artists - Scene Of The Crime
Venom - Black Metal
Waysted - Vices
White Spirit - White Spirit
Wildfire - Summer Lightning
Witchfinder General - Death Penalty
Witchfinder General - Friends Of Hell
Witchfynde - Give 'Em Hell
Witchfynde - Stagefright
Voltz – Knight's Fall

Appendix 2: One Helluva Night: Singles & EPs Ranked 8, 9 Or 10

Angel Witch - Sweet Danger
Angel Witch - Angel Witch
Angel Witch - Loser
Aragorn - Black Ice
Arc - War Of The Ring
A-II-Z - No Fun After Midnight
Axis - Lady
Blitzkrieg - Buried Alive
Bronz – Send Down An Angel
Budgie - Bored With Russia
Chateaux - Young Blood
Chinatown - Short And Sweet
Cloven Hoof – The Opening Ritual
Crucifixion - Take It Or Leave It
Dark Star - Lady Of Mars
Dedringer - Hot Lady
Def Leppard - The Def Leppard E.P.
Def Leppard - Wasted
Def Leppard - Hello America
Def Leppard - Rock Brigade
Def Leppard - Let It Go
Demolition – Hooker Hater
Demon - One Helluva Night
Demon - The Plague
Demon Pact - Eaten Alive
Desolation Angels - Valhalla
Destroyer - Evil Place
Diamond Head - Waited Too Long
Diamond Head - Four Cuts
Dragonfly – E.P.
Dragonslayer - I Want Your Life
Dutchess – Your Love
EF Band – Self Made Suicide
Emerson - Something Special
Energy – Nowhere To Hide
Fastway - Easy Livin'
Fastway - We Become One
Fist - Forever Amber
Fugitive – Need My Freedom
Genghis Khan – Double Dealin
Gillan - Nightmare
Gillan - Restless

Girlschool - Emergency
Girlschool - Hit & Run
Girlschool - C'mon Let's Go
Glasgow - Stranded
Gypsy – We Came To Be Free
Heavy Pettin' - In And Out Of Love
Heavy Pettin' - Rock Me
Heavy Pettin' - Love Times Love
Hell - Save Us From Those Who Would Save Us
Heritage - Strange Place To Be
High Treason - Saturday Night Special
Hollow Ground - Don't Chase The Dragon
Holocaust - Heavy Metal Mania
Holocaust - Smokin' Valves
Influence – No Survivors
Iron Maiden - The Soundhouse Tapes
Iron Maiden - Running Free
Iron Maiden - Sanctuary
Iron Maiden - Women In Uniform
Iron Maiden - Twilight Zone
Iron Maiden - Purgatory
Iron Maiden - Maiden Japan
Iron Maiden - Flight Of Icarus
Iron Maiden - The Trooper
Iron Maiden - 2 Minutes To Midnight
Iron Maiden - Aces High
Jaguar - Axe Crazy
Jameson Raid - Seven Days Of Splendour
Jameson Raid - The Hypnotist
J.J.'s Powerhouse – Running For The Line
Alec Johnson Band - Busmans Holiday
Joker - Back On The Road
Karrier – I'm Back
Kraken – Fantasy Reality
Lady Jane – In Concert: The Sheer Power Of Live Rock
Lautrec – Mean Gasoline
Le Griffe - You're Killing Me
Le Griffe - Breaking Strain
Limelight - Ashes To Ashes
Lone Wolf – Cash For Candy
Marseille - Bring On The Dancin' Girls
Marz – Lady Of The Night
Megaton - Aluminum Lady
Money – EP.
Motörhead - Overkill

Motörhead - Bomber
Motörhead - 'The Golden Years' Live EP
Motörhead - Ace Of Spades
Motörheadgirlschool - St Valentines Day Massacre
Mythra - Death And Destiny
No Quarter - Survivors
Omen Searcher - Teacher Of Sin
Ore - Your Time Will Come
Original Sin – The Shadow
Paralex - White Lightning
Persian Risk - Ridin' High
Prowler - Forgotten Angel
Quartz - Sugar Rain
Quartz - Street Fighting Lady
Quartz - Nantucket Sleighride
Quartz - Satan's Serenade
Quartz - Stoking Up The Fires Of Hell
Quartz - Stand Up And Fight
Quartz - Tell Me Why
Radium - Through The Smoke
Rage - Out Of Control
Raven - Hard Ride
Raven - Crash, Bang, Wallop
Raven - Break The Chain (single)
Raven - Break The Chain (EP)
Raven - Born To Be Wild
Red Alert - Break The Rules
Reincarnate - Take It Or Leave It
Renegade – Lonely Road
Requiem – Angel Of Sin
Rokka – Come Back
Sabre - Miracle Man
Samson - Riding With The Angels
Samson - Life On The Run
Samson - Are You Ready
Satan - Kiss Of Death
Savage - Ain't No Fit Place
Saxon - Nightmare
Shock Treatment – The Mugger
Sledgehammer - Living In Dreams
Snakebite – Blow You Away
Soldier - Sheralee
Spider – All The Time
Split Beaver - Savage
Starfighters - Power Crazy

Steel - Steel
Streetfighter – Crazy Dream
Sweet Savage - Take No Prisoners
Sweet Savage - Straight Through The Heart
Tank - Don't Walk Away
Tank - (He Fell In Love With A) Stormtrooper
Tank - Turn Your Head Around
Tank - Crazy Horses
TNT - Back On The Road
Tokyo Blade - If Heaven Is Hell
Tokyo Blade - Power Game
Tora Tora - Red Sun Setting
Touched – Dream Girl
Trespass - One Of These Days
Trespass - Bright Lights
Triarchy - Metal Messiah
Turbo – 3 Track E.P.
Turbo - Charged For.... Glory
Twisted Ace - Firebird
Tygers Of Pan Tang - Euthanasia
Tygers Of Pan Tang - Hellbound
Tygers Of Pan Tang - Don't Stop By
Tygers Of Pan Tang - Love Don't Stay
Tygers Of Pan Tang - Do It Good
Tygers Of Pan Tang - Paris By Air
Tygers Of Pan Tang - Making Tracks
Tyrant – Hold Back The Lightning
Tysondog - Eat The Rich
Tytan - Blind Men And Fools
Urchin – Black Leather Fantasy
Valhalla – Lightning In The Sky
Vardis - 100 M.P.H.
Vardis - If I Were King
Venom - Warhead
Waysted - Waysted
Weapon – It's A Mad Mad World
White Spirit - Midnight Chaser
White Spirit - High Upon High
Wildfire - Nothing Lasts Forever
Witchfinder General - Burning A Sinner
Witchfinder General – Soviet Invasion
Witchfinder General - Music
Witchfynde - Give 'Em Hell
Witchfynde - In The Stars
Wolf – See Them Running

Design Credit

The visual splendidness of this book was created by one Eduardo Rodriguez, who can be reached at eduardobwbk@gmail.com.

About The Author

At approximately 7900 (with over 7000 appearing in his books), Martin has unofficially written more record reviews than anybody in the history of music writing across all genres. Additionally, Popoff has penned 45 books on hard rock, heavy metal, classic rock and record collecting. He was Editor In Chief of the now retired Brave Words & Bloody Knuckles, Canada's foremost metal publication for 14 years, and has also contributed to Revolver, CMJ, Live Wire, Guitar World, Goldmine, Record Collector, bravewords.com, lollipop.com and hardradio.com, with many record label band bios and liner notes to his credit as well. Additionally, Martin worked for two years as researcher on the award-wining documentary **Rush: Beyond The Lighted Stage** and on **Metal Evolution**, an 11 episode documentary series for VH1 Classic, and is the writer of the original metal genre chart used in **Metal: A Headbanger's Journey** and throughout the **Metal Evolution** episodes.

Born April 28, 1963 in Castlegar, British Columbia, Canada and raised in nearby Trail, Martin went on to complete an MBA, work for Xerox, then co-own a graphic design and print brokering firm, before becoming a full-time rock critic in 1998. Gillan, Max Webster, Deep Purple, ZZ Top and Black Sabbath are his favourite five bands of all time. An incurable collector, Martin's music archive consists of approximately 10,000 LPs, 18,000 CDs, 3,000 45s, 1200 backstage passes, 3100 personally obtained autographed items, and the tapes, digital files and hard copies of his approximately 1900 interviews conducted since 1994 (but he really wants to paint and maybe have his work appear on a ZZ Top album cover one day).

Martin currently resides in Toronto and can be reached through martinp@inforamp.net or www.martinpopoff.com. His website includes detailed descriptions and ordering information for the 30 or so books of his that are currently in print.

Ye Olde Metal "Discography"

- detailed examination of early hard rock and heavy metal albums
- each from brand new interviews with the artists, plus some archived material
- critical analysis and trivia as well
- 6" x 9" format
- most with rare, previously unpublished photos
- limited to 1000 individually hand-numbered copies
- personalized and signed by the author
- photography by Rich Galbraith
- more on the way, each examining a year at a time!

Ye Olde Metal: 1968 To 1972
Blue Cheer – Vincebus Eruptum, MC5 – Kick Out The Jams, Sir Lord Baltimore – Kingdom Come, Bloodrock – Bloodrock, Warpig – Warpig, Cactus – One Way… Or Another, Mountain – Nantucket Sleighride, Uriah Heep – Look At Yourself, Nitzinger – Nitzinger, Dust - Hard Attack, Humble Pie – Smokin', Buffalo – Dead Forever…, Captain Beyond – Captain Beyond, Trapeze – You Are The Music… We're Just The Band

Ye Olde Metal: 1973 To 1975
Status Quo – Piledriver, Alice Cooper – Billion Dollar Babies, New York Dolls – New York Dolls, Uriah Heep – Sweet Freedom, Nazareth – Loud 'N' Proud, Montrose – Montrose, Bachman Turner Overdrive – II, Deep Purple – Burn, Robin Trower – Bridge Of Sighs, Buffalo – Only Want You For Your Body, Bachman Turner Overdrive – Not Fragile, Alice Cooper – Welcome To My Nightmare, Nazareth – Hair Of The Dog, The Dictators – Go Girl Crazy!, ZZ Top – Fandango, Budgie – Bandolier, Foghat – Fool For The City, Deep Purple – Come Taste The Band

Ye Olde Metal: 1976
Max Webster – Max Webster, Scorpions – Virgin Killer, Point Blank – Point Blank, Angel – Helluva Band, Rex – Rex, Moxy – II, Teaze – Teaze, Lone Star – Lone Star, Starz – Starz, Ted Nugent – Free For All, Boston – Boston, Foghat – Nightshift, Kansas – Leftoverture

Ye Olde Metal: 1977
Derringer – Sweet Evil, Angel – On Earth As It Is In Heaven, Sweet – Off The Record, Moxy – Ridin' High, The Dictators – Manifest Destiny, Starz – Violation, Triumph – Rock & Roll Machine, Styx – Grand Illusion, Motörhead – Motörhead, Lone Star – Firing On All Six, Dirty Tricks – Hit & Run, Piper – Can't Wait, Goddo – Goddo, Ram Jam – Ram Jam, Rex – Where Do We Go From Here?, Point Blank – Second Season, Hydra – Rock The World, Legs Diamond – A Diamond Is A Hard Rock

Ye Olde Metal: 1978
The Hounds – Unleashed, Frank Marino & Mahogany Rush – Live, Starz – Attention Shoppers!, Yesterday And Today – Struck Down, Teaze – On The Loose, Ram Jam – Portrait Of The Artist As A Young Ram, The Dictators – Bloodbrothers, The Boyzz – Too Wild To Tame, Starz – Coliseum Rock, The Godz – The Godz, DMZ – DMZ, Styx – Pieces Of Eight, Pat Travers – Heat In The Street, Dead Boys – We Have Come For Your Children, Streetheart, Meanwhile Back In Paris…, Uriah Heep – Fallen Angel

Ye Olde Metal: 1979
New England – New England , Nazareth – No Mean City, Bad Company – Desolation Angels, Motörhead – Overkill, TKO – Let It Roll, Triumph – Just A Game, Legs Diamond – Fire Power, City Boy – The Day The Earth Caught Fire, Blackfoot – Strikes, Streetheart – Under Heaven Over Hell, Hounds – Puttin' On The Dog, Foreigner – Head Games, Riot – Narita, Whitesnake – Lovehunter, April Wine –

Harder... Faster, Teaze – One Night Stands

Price breaks available on multiple orders. Just email martinp@inforamp.net and tell me what you want and where I'm shipping to and I'll quote ya! See www.martinpopoff.com for ordering details on the first five of the Ye Olde Metal series plus approximately 25 other titles.